Dependency and Japanese Socialization

Dependency and Japanese Socialization

Psychoanalytic and Anthropological
Investigations into *Amae*

Frank A. Johnson

NEW YORK UNIVERSITY PRESS
New York and London

NEW YORK UNIVERSITY PRESS
New York and London

Library of Congress Cataloging-in-Publication Data
Johnson, Frank A., 1928–
Dependency and Japanese socialization : psychoanalytic and
anthropological investigations into amae / Frank A. Johnson.
p.   cm.
Includes bibliographical references and index.
ISBN 0-8147-4192-4
1. Dependency (Psychology)—Japan.   2. Dependency (Psychology)—
Cross-cultural studies.   3. Socialization—Cross-cultural studies.
I. Title.   II. Title: Amae.
BF575.D35J64   1992
155.8'4956—dc20   92-22540
                                     CIP

New York University Press books are printed on acid-free paper,
and their binding materials are chosen for strength and durability.

Manufactured in the United States of America

c 10 9 8 7 6 5 4 3 2 1

To the memory of a valued colleague and friend,
Professor Hiroshi Wagatsuma, whose understanding,
encouragement, and facilitation, are intimately
embedded in the composition of this manuscript.

Contents

viii / Contents

Foreword

I am very pleased that Frank Johnson has undertaken to write this book about theories of dependence, specifically examining cross-cultural perspectives concerning *amae*, a Japanese word indicating indulgent dependence. I became interested in *amae* behavior in the 1950s during my first sojourn in the United States when I was a fellow at the Menninger School of Psychiatry. Initially, the word *amae* occurred to me as a quite appropriate term to describe the Japanese type of dependence vis-à-vis the independent spirit of Americans. Then, as I was studying psychoanalysis, and particularly as I underwent psychoanalytic training, I became aware of the deeper significance of *amae* in its wider psychological relevance, beyond its applications in Japan. Soon I was rethinking psychoanalytic theories in terms of the concept of *amae*, and since that time I have written a good deal on the subject in both English and Japanese.

It is a very gratifying experience for me that my writings on *amae* have stimulated others to investigate and explain this need for human affection. Especially since the first English translation of my book *The Anatomy of Dependence* (1973a) appeared, interest in *amae* theory has flourished in both Japan and the United States. Initially the concern of a relatively small cadre of Japan specialists, *amae* now appears as a key concept in English writings about Japan in such diverse disciplines as anthropology, sociology, economics, business management, and linguistics. While scholars of various disciplines sometimes cite *amae* theory without true understanding, it has generated important discussion among scholars in linguistics and anthropology, but all too little discussion in American psychiatry. It is most appropriate that this book returns *amae* theory to the aegis of psychiatry and psychoanalysis.

I first corresponded with Frank Johnson in 1969 while he was preparing to investigate the presence of *amae*-related behavior in second *[nisei]* and third *[sansei]* generation Japanese-Americans living in Hawaii. I met him in Honolulu in 1970 and periodically corresponded with him thereafter. In 1983 he spent six months at the University of Tokyo as a visiting professor in the Department of Mental Health. During that time we met and discussed psychoanalysis, *amae*, and various aspects of Japanese and American cultures. Subsequently, we have had additional opportunities to meet at conferences and discuss topics of mutual interest. During the last seven years, while he was formulating and writing this book, Johnson and I have exchanged frequent correspondence. I have enjoyed observing his creative process and appreciate his rigorous, analytical approach, as well as his warm friendship.

In this book, he has undertaken the very difficult task of summarizing my own and others' work about *amae*. Drawing from these writings, he compares Japanese experiences and theories about *amae* with contemporary theories of dependence within Western psychology and psychoanalysis.

The first section of this book examines the theoretical and cultural backgrounds of dependence theory, assembling concepts of dependence, attachment, and interdependence, and the largely indirect ways in which psychoanalysis has addressed dependency. It also provides background on Japanese history and contemporary Japanese culture, emphasizing descriptions of normative childrearing, socialization, and education.

The second section contributes an analytical and multidimensional exploration of my writings about *amae*, examining them in the context of psychoanalytic theory about drives, psychosexual stages, separation/individuation, ego ideal/superego, and transference/countertransference. This section also extrapolates from a wider cross-cultural base some universal and holistic aspects of dependence behavior observed in cultures other than Japan and the United States. Synthesizing both critical and sympathetic writings about dependence, Johnson summarizes the body of knowledge related to *amae*. This section builds on some of my published work *(The Anatomy of Self,* 1986) and concludes with a psychocultural description of the Japanese "self."

The final section of the book relates psychoanalytic theory to

recent cross-cultural perspectives in psychoanalysis and anthropological studies, suggesting approaches to future research about human interdependence.

Most significantly, the book integrates *amae* theory with dependence issues in psychoanalytic theory. Dr. Johnson reviews a taxonomy of Japanese *amae*-related vocabulary, demonstrating aspects
of *amae* as they are manifested in daily life relationships, and analyzes these varieties of interdependence in terms of Japanese language and culture. The book examines the English- and Japanese-
language professional literature that treats *amae* theory, including
sociolinguistic and metalinguistic aspects of *amae*. The book also
suggests how *amae* may be manifested in other languages and cultures. Finally, it examines and suggests research methods germane
to the further study of *amae.*

This work is the result of a creative synthesis of complex areas
of theory into a thoroughly comprehensive framework of knowledge about human interdependence. A holistic and exhaustive review of salient theory, the book illustrates the connections between
theory and *amae* behavior. Readers will find the content to be
provocatively interdisciplinary and cross-cultural, and meaningful
to disciplines such as psychoanalysis, anthropology, child development, and other fields that seek to explain and analyze human
behavior.

TAKEO DOI

Preface

This book is a culmination of study and reflection about dependency theory that began in 1968. At that time I was a young academic psychiatrist at the State University of New York, Health Sciences Center in Syracuse. During my own postgraduate training in psychiatry I had been introduced to anthropology by Ernest Becker, through coursework covering material subsequently published as *The Birth and Death of Meaning* (Becker 1962) and *Revolution in Psychiatry* (Becker 1964). This introduction was followed by connections to the social sciences through Paul Meadows (Syracuse University) and Benjamin Nelson (the New School for Social Research). In the early 1970s, I devoted an investigational year to studying Japanese Americans residing in Hawaii. My research was designed to look into cognitive and experiential dimensions of dependency (called *amae* in Japanese) demonstrated in second- and third-generation *(nisei* and *sansei)* subjects living in Honolulu. My interest in Japanese manifestations of dependency was a direct result of reading the early publications of Takeo Doi, who had defined *amae* as "the need of an individual to be loved and cherished; the prerogative to presume and depend upon the benevolence of another." According to Doi's observations, the privilege of requesting and receiving special consideration from selected others was maintained in Japan throughout the lifespan. This was in contrast to many Western societies, where the acknowledgment and gratifications of dependency are consigned to early childhood, and subsequently become disguised and suppressed. Doi also concluded that the manifestations of dependency were of crucial, rather than incidental, significance in both cultures: in Japan where they remained conscious and acceptable prerogatives, and in the United States where needs for gratification were more conflictual and potentially regarded as negative.

Using a combination of open-ended questionnaires and informant interviews I attempted to find out the extent to which the experience and awareness of *amae* were present in the contemporary Japanese American subculture in Hawaii.

During the academic year 1970–71, I was a visiting professor at the University of Hawaii. I was also informally connected to the Social Science Research Institute, which provided contact with visiting Asian and American specialists. These connections gave me access to colleagues and students in the departments of psychology, sociology, and history on the Manoa campus.

During this investigational year I conducted an ethnographic examination of *enryo* (ritualized deference) with Colleen Johnson, and a survey of attitudes toward verbal behavior with Anthony Marsella. Extensive interviews with informants and participant observation into areas of dependency were carried out in a variety of private and public settings. Information about the communicative aspects of relationships with family, kin, friends, and workmates was accumulated through interviews with *nisei* and *sansei* contacts. Although the Japanese term *amae* was virtually never used, conversations and observations repeatedly documented the implicit patterning of a form of social and emotional relatedness parallel to the normative expectations for interdependency in Japan. These manifestations of *amae* in second- and third-generation descendants remained apparent despite an intervening forty to seventy years of disconnection from mainland Japanese culture.

As Doi might have predicted, I was unable at that time to carry these findings and interpretations to a conclusion that was satisfactory. This represented the recognition that dependency phenomena are unusually diffuse and complex. They are subject to variations according to position in the lifespan, the features of particular situations, and degree of subcultural identification. Also, as I extended my reading of the literature regarding dependency, complexities in Western psychological theory raised still other questions that required confrontation.

Following sabbatical, my study of *amae* proceeded to address these problems at both theoretical and experiential levels. Subsequent publications of Professor Doi's—particularly his *Anatomy of*

Dependence (1973a) and *Anatomy of Self* (1986)—were helpful in clarifying and extending his earlier work. As he describes it, the significance of *amae* became more obvious to him through noticing its attenuation and omission in American life, observed during extended periods while he trained and conducted research in the U.S. The American omission of allowable, overt adult dependency became even more evident to him after returning to Japan following living in Washington, D.C., Topeka, Kansas, and San Francisco. In a parallel manner, I found that the significance of allowable dependency found among some Japanese Americans began to arouse more questions following my return from field work and reimmersion into the culture of the northeastern United States. Subsequently, my efforts to embed the investigational findings into a broader context has taken three different directions: (1) a survey of dependency theory (including "attachment" and "interdependency") as it is variously modeled in developmental psychology and social science, (2) an attempt to describe systematically the ways in which psychoanalytic theory formulates dependency phenomena, and (3) a review of the effects of differential childrearing on both the forms and explanations of dependency among Japanese, Japanese Americans, and nonethnic North Americans.

Dealing with these three areas has postponed the synthesis of my reflections concerning *amae* until recently. The present volume addresses two of these areas. The first section on "Theoretical and Cultural Background" reviews the diversity of description and theory concerning the concepts of *dependency, attachment, and interdependency* as they appear in the recent Western psychological, psychoanalytic, and social science literature. Following this, literature on Japanese history, culture, childrearing, and education is reviewed, with a focus on the quality of interdependent relationships during early lifespan and adolescence.

The middle section of the book centers on a detailed presentation of *amae* through the works of Doi and others. A critical discussion of theories concerning *amae* leads to a synthesis regarding Japanese dependency, and a description of psychocultural aspects of the Japanese self.

An additional chapter reviews ethnographic commentary from other societies where interdependent affiliations are conspicuous, while a concluding section reflects on the viability of using concepts and constructs of dependency, attachment, and interdependency. Also, some conclusions about the significance of cross-cultural findings for contemporary psychoanalytic theories are suggested. Finally, some of the newer conceptual and methodological approaches in anthropological and psychoanalytic work are reviewed and discussed.

Overall, this book attempts to present both the substance and the criticisms of Takeo Doi's work (e.g., in Pelzel 1977; Lebra 1976; Kumagai 1981; Dale 1986; Taketomo 1986). This is facilitated through an examination of dependency and interdependency in their inherent psychological, psychoanalytic, and social-scientific dimensions. Although readers will arrive at their own verdicts, it is the author's conclusion that Doi's work (along with that of his critics and collaborators) succeeds in documenting a theory of indulgent dependency *(amae)* that contributes to a psychological theory of motive (i.e., "drive" or "desire"), an interactional theory of status relationships (based on an infant/mother paradigm), and a cultural theory of adaptation/maladaptation based on the differential child-rearing and interaction rules that foster a normative basis for interdependency, in Japan.

Acknowledgments

Since this project has occupied me for over fifteen years, my indebtedness to colleagues and other scholars is correspondingly extensive —particularly to the thinking and writings of Takeo Doi. Through continued contact with his own work and some of his students I have found the concept of *amae* to be a major intellectual preoccupation. During a sabbatical (1983–84) from the University of California I met directly with Professor Doi, and conducted a careful review of my early versions of chapters regarding his own work both on *amae* and on psychoanalytic theories applying to dependency. During my six-month visit to Japan Dr. Doi was generous in spirit and in making time available to discuss the cross-cultural implications of his theories on dependency.

Also, in many tangible ways I am indebted to colleagues who rendered advice, support, and collaboration during and following my original field work. Preceding and during my earlier investigations in Hawaii (1970–71), Bill Caudill was especially helpful and encouraging. Briefer meetings with George DeVos, Harry Kitano, and Gerald Meredith were also of assistance. Tom Maretzki and Bill Lebra facilitated my work with other faculty and informants both at the University of Hawaii and at the Social Science Research Institute. Professors George Yamamoto and George Akita were collegial in their accessibility and assistance. Numerous conversations with Takao Murase (at that time on leave from NIMH, Japan) were crucial in guiding my understanding of the subtle levels of interactional differences between Americans and Japanese that lie beyond the already well-publicized distinctions.

In helping me prepare for a second sabbatical, I owe special gratitude to Professor Hiroshi Wagatsuma, to whom this book is dedicated. His untimely death cannot erase my recollection of his encouragement and friendship. Takeo Doi's crucial assistance has already been mentioned. Nabuhiro Kumakura from the University of Tokyo School of Medicine also reviewed some of my chapters on *amae*. Following my return to San Francisco Calvin Settlage (San Francisco Psychoanalytic Institute) has been helpful in looking over chapters on childrearing and on psychoanalytic theories. Both while at the University of Tokyo and back in California, I benefited from the assistance of Regina Garrick. As a seven-year resident of Japan and former student of Doi's, she is very knowledgeable about the conceptual and behavioral meanings of *amae*. She also has translated a number of articles and selected portions of Japanese books for review and inclusion in this manuscript. Wherever possible, I have cited her contributions and critical commentary; however, this does not sufficiently attest to the extent of her collegial help and advice.

Also, Professor Doi has continued to lend his critical help at every juncture of the composition of this current work through frequent correspondence and occasional meetings. Selected chapters have been read by George DeVos, Harumi Befu, Christie Kiefer, Lillian Troll, Alicia Lieberman, Catherine Lewis, and Robert Wallerstein. Judicious recommendations were also made by Kitty Moore, former senior acquisitions editor at the New York University Press.

Finally, I wish to acknowledge those individuals whose administrative support has been sustaining. Don Oken, Richard Schmidt, and Bill Bleumle facilitated my sabbatical leave from SUNY Upstate Medical Center during 1970–71. The Research Foundation of the State University of New York and the New York Department of Mental Hygiene furnished grant support before and following my field work in Hawaii. Academic leave from the University of California during 1983–84 was facilitated by Bob Wallerstein through the academic vice chancellor, Dr. David Ramsay. Crucial academic and collegial connections in the School of Public Health at the University of Tokyo were provided by its chairman, Professor Takemitsu Hemmi. His cordiality in making me feel part of his department facilitated my work and elevated my spirit while I was in Japan. An award by the Mary Singleton Signourney Foundation provided specialized psychoanalytic consultation on my return to the United States.

Earlier versions of various chapters were typed by Nickie Dunne and Beverly Eschenberg. Revised chapters were transcribed by Shirley Pullan, Karen Wallack-Eisen, Evelyn Galenski, Peter Camarda, and Patrice Kleinberg. The high caliber of their work has been matched by their cheerfulness and perseverance in the face of many revisions and extensions.

Theoretical and Cultural Background

Introduction and Background

This book examines intersections among three areas of scholarship that address the issue of interdependency in human relationships. The first of these conceptual areas traces theories of dependency and attachment stemming from developmental psychology and social science. The second area reviews the largely indirect ways in which psychoanalysis has formulated concepts concerning dependent relationships. The third examines the prominent features of dependent relations in Japanese culture contrasted to conventions regarding affiliation in nonethnic American society. Some of this review also will involve a discussion of interconnections among psychoanalysis, social science, and developmental psychology regarding both methods and interpretation. A critical dimension of this review will focus on the dialectic between universalism and relativism, particularly as this tension is treated in the formulations emerging from both psychoanalysis and anthropology.

Psychoanalysis and Anthropology

Attempts to relate psychoanalytic theory to anthropology have a history as long as psychoanalysis itself. Freud was intrigued with accounts of exotic societies published during the late 1800s that described customs, ceremonies, and symbols observed in so-called primitive groups uninfluenced by contact with Western civilization (as reviewed in Edwin Wallace 1983). Along with the interpretation of myths, dreams, and dramatic literature, Freud used these descriptions to document metapsychological explanations of individual and group behaviors. In his interpretation, such texts and testimonials corroborated hypotheses concerning the presence of unconscious mechanisms whose manifestations were submerged in persons living in contemporary European societies. Paralleling Freud's interests, a series of productive connections between psychoanalysis and anthropology ensued. Some of the history and consequences of these connections have been critically summarized by Kluckhohn (1950), Boyer (1984), Gehrie (1978), and Edwin Wallace (1983).

Disputes arose between the two fields during the 1920s and '30s in regard to generalizations about universal formulations within psychoanalysis, which had been challenged on the basis of contradictory ethnographic evidence. A critical debate between Freud (1920) and Kroeber (1920, 1939) took place regarding the plausibility of the primal horde theory, and between Ernest Jones (1925) and Bronislaw Malinowski (1927) concerning the universality of the Oedipus complex. Appearing in the 1920s, these differences reflected a redirection in anthropological viewpoint crystallized at the turn of the century following the impact of Boas's (1938 [1896]) critique of the social-evolutionist tradition. As Edwin Wallace (1983) has argued, Freud's use of anthropological information was based on an evolutionary model that imposed an inexorable, progressive design onto the social development of human societies. Critical changes in the early 1900s that refuted "social Darwinism" went unnoticed in Freud's anthropological allusions and metapsychological speculations. Although this omission in Freud's understanding of cultural relativism is understandable, the effects of his evolutionist position have persisted in an institutionalized tendency to emphasize universal explanations of human behavior within psychoanalytic theory. This omission has not been distinctive to psychoanalysis, but has been shared with theorists in the disciplines of psychology and human development where, until recently, culture was not systematically or frequently employed as a variable.

These disputes earlier in the century were also symptomatic of the newness and institutional defensiveness of both anthropology and psychoanalysis. Moreover, they reflected genuine differences in the backgrounds, methods, and explanatory models used by the two fields. While a common interest in the study of so-called primitive behavior continued to encourage interchange, active collaboration was slight until a surge of studies regarding culture and personality appeared following the 1930s. In retrospect, the reasons for this earlier divergence are evident. In its efforts to become a respectable science of human behavior, psychoanalysis has traditionally sought to define basic factors and components of human personality that transcend the specifics of cultural diversity. Also, because of its origins, psychoanalysis has employed terms, processes, and metaphors borrowed from the physical and biological sciences, and from clinical medicine. Explanations have postulated functional principles based on observations and insights taken from clinical encounters, as well as inferred through the interpretation of ethnography, literature, and myth. Although some psychoanalytic scholarship has extended to the study of group behavior, biography, and literary commentary, its primary method of exploration has centered on the meticulous study of the discursive subjectivity of individual patients, directly witnessed in the clinical treatment situation. Through the use of the couch and free association, the subjective monologue of the patient has been epistemologically imputed to be a window through which the psychic structures and underlying dynamics of the analysand could be glimpsed and studied. The neutrality of the psychoanalyst was held to be an indispensable precondition permitting objective observations through which causal-motivational theories of human behavior might be postulated, tested, and refined. Thus, as another distinction from anthropology, psychoanalysis has always operated at once as a speculative (heuristic) enterprise and a practical (curative) discipline.

In contrast, anthropology until recently did not systematically deal with subjective factors related to the ethnographer, despite evidence that observer bias affected both the recording of events and their subsequent interpretation (Devereux 1969; Malinowski 1967; Crapanzano 1980, 1986). Moreover, although not ignoring universal human tendencies, anthropological methods have emphasized the manifest dissimilarities and variations within exotic and, more recently, postindustrial societies. Additionally, theories and methods in anthropology, except in physical anthropology and archaeology, did not arise in connection to the physical and biological sciences. Especially following the work of Boas, anthropological research centered on the production of detailed ethnographic studies of relatively small, exotic societies scrupulously judged in terms of their own internal coherence and meaning. In comparative studies examining cross-cultural differences, fastidious care was taken to avoid invidious ethnocentric judgments, and to use the distributive modes of analysis highlighting the diversity encountered in hundreds of recorded cultures (as accumulated in the Human Resources Area Files at Yale University). These methods and interpretive constraints methodologically resulted in emphasizing cultural relativism over universalism—quite opposite to the field of psychoanalysis.

As another distinction, most conceptual terms in anthropology (such as "culture," "norms," "kinship") pertain to collective, extrapsychic configurations while psychoanalytic constructions, especially prior to the 1940s, have emphasized individual intrapsychic structures and dynamisms. Significant differences in theory building are also evident. Reflecting its clinical orientation and the intangible nature of its structures, psychoanalysis has formulated metapsychological, motivational explanations of human performance, including taxonomies of pathological adaptations (as summarized in Fenichel 1945). It has also created a body of theory relating to the practical applications of psychoanalytic technique. Anthropology, in the opposite direction, has been reluctant to assemble its diverse findings into reductionistic generalizations applicable to all persons or all societies (as in Bidney 1967; Harris 1968). Also, although the possibility for what has been called "action anthropology" was tentatively raised during the 1980s, the field has generally avoided interventional strategies on the basis of contaminating the objectivity of the study or, in a more coercive direction, risking the imposition of foreign values (Angrosino 1976). Moreover, unlike psychoanalysis, anthropology has maintained a strong relativistic and culturological view of psychopathology and deviance (Kleinman 1980, 1988).

From the 1930s through the 1950s, cooperation between psychoanalysis and anthropology frequently used a coalition of investigators in the area of what was commonly termed psychological anthropology. These studies were influenced by psychoanalytic developmental hypotheses and speculated on the impact of differential childrearing on adult personality configurations. Such investigations frequently used projective techniques in addition to extensive interviewing of representative informants. Participant observation required a strenuous immersion into the society in order to elucidate both explicit and unconscious mechanisms explaining distinctive behavioral manifestations. Although some interest in psychological anthropology has survived, the mainstream has veered away from its relation to psychoanalysis and converted prior concentration on the "depth psychology" of culture bearers into investigational dimensions of *cognitive* and *symbolic* anthropology. While not directly hostile to psychoanalysis, investigators in these areas are committed to methodical explanations concerning the distinctive patterning of subjective awareness, and to the relationship between special symbolical features and the social organization of particular cultures.

Western Dependency Theories and *Amae*

The present book is specifically concerned with some of the intersections among contemporary social sciences, academic psychology, and psychoanalysis in regard to theories concerning what in the past has been defined as "dependency." This concept, also examined as *inter*dependency, will be reviewed from three separate perspectives: 1) academic and developmental psychology; 2) psychoanalytic theories of drive and object relations; and 3) ethnographic reports about Japan concerning dependency experience characterized by the Japanese word *amae* (pronounced "ah-my-eh").

Amae is a noun, defined as the need to be responded to, taken care of, cherished, and given special significance. The conspicuous forms of human dependency in Japan have been presented and interpreted in a series of publications by Takeo Doi, a Japanese academic psychiatrist and psychoanalyst. Written on the basis of his observations as a clinician and researcher with experience both in Japan and the U.S., Doi's work can be seen as both ethnographic and cross-cultural—what has been referred to as "an exposition of the cultural configurations that support personal interdependencies" (Pelzel 1977, 302). Doi's work has made a significant contribution to the postwar cultural commentary on Japan and has been influential in both Asian and Western circles.

Some excellent descriptions of Japanese culture were composed by early Western missionaries, government officials, merchants, and visiting scholars. However, modern ethnographic work did not achieve momentum until the 1930s. These studies were given additional impetus during World War II, exemplified by *The Chrysanthemum and the Sword*, written on the basis of historical research and interviews of immigrant Japanese residing in the United States (Benedict 1946). Following the war, investigation by foreign and indigenous scholars has produced a large body of published literature concerning diverse aspects of Japanese history, culture, and society. Within this body of scholarship, Doi's work has concentrated on *amae*, and has illuminated aspects of modal Japanese personality, psychiatric practice, and the social-psychological patterns of "ordinary behavior." In addition to his own formulations, other commentators have added to, challenged, and contradicted some of his findings and interpretations.

Although commending Doi's conceptual inventiveness and "enormous appeal," Pelzel (1977) has summarized some of the criticisms raised by both Japanese and foreign scholars concerning his work. One of these is that Doi's emphasis on *amae* has attempted to explain "too much of Japanese behavior," and detracted from a description of "competing drives and the traditional personality that was also idealized and reinforced by the culture" (Pelzel 1977, 302). He also felt that Doi had neglected social-institutional and cultural levels of dependency in favor of *personal* manifestations, and commented that Doi hinted at, but did not specify details about, the developmental aspects of *amae*. Additionally he noted that Doi did not methodically address factors regarding Japanese childrearing and socialization.

One of the specific objectives of this book is to respond to these criticisms through a comprehensive presentation both of Doi's work and of literature that emphasizes interdependency in social, historical, and cultural features concerning Japan. Another objective is to compare and contrast Japanese cultural phenomena connected to dependency with traditional psychoanalytic theory concerning drives, human development, and object relations.

In an earlier publication, Caudill (1962b) put his finger on a recurrent conflict between psychoanalysis and anthropology in regard to differential socialization. He framed this in the form of an "answer" to Heinz Hartmann's (1958) question on the relative impact of culture on development.

But the relation of the "psychological" and the "biological" is further complicated by their interplay with the endogenous and exogenous. Here the most important question is: are the exogenous factors the average expectable kind (family situation, mother-child relationship and others), or are they environmental conditions of a different sort? In other words, the question is whether, and to what extent, a certain course of development *can count on average expectable stimulations*. (Hartmann 1958, 35; italics original)

Caudill (1962b) then expanded the question:

A basic question for me, beyond Hartmann's discussion, is twofold and interrelated. As I see it, the average expectable environment is: 1) present generically as culture in the universal sense of a property of being human, and 2) present as a specific set of expectations in a particular culture. Thus, there are universal and relative ways of viewing the average expectable environment. (Caudill 1962b, 195)

In a different context, LeVine (1973b, 1987) has raised the same issue in what he has whimsically referred to as the "Japanese problem." This specifically addresses the serious issue of universalism present in much of psychoanalytic metapsychology (also mentioned in Tobin [1982]. His phrase has two overlapping meanings. In the first of these, the "Japanese problem" consists of the concrete ways in which studies of Japanese culture and descriptions of Japanese "personality" fail to coordinate with the principles of normative development and personality function as these are portrayed in Western psychoanalysis. This suggests that Japanese society illustrates a cultural diversity that conflicts with human development as portrayed in traditional psychoanalytic metapsychology.

The second meaning of the "Japanese problem" is metaphorical, and raises the general issue regarding the extent to which cultural forces affect deeper personality structures, thus challenging the very epistemology and deductive method through which such universal theories are posited in psychoanalysis.

The present book has been written to respond critically to questions raised by Pelzel (1977), LeVine (1973b, 1987), and others (Lebra 1976; Kumagai 1981; Taketomo 1986; Dale 1986) in an attempt to put Doi's published work into a broader psychoanalytic and social-anthropological context.

Objectives and Goals

Specifically, the book addresses the following issues and questions:

1. What is the current status of the concept of dependency in psychology, social science, and psychoanalysis?
2. What are the implications of Doi's work—along with other ethnographic commentary—for various traditional psychoanalytic theories?
3. Finally, how do theories dealing with *dependency* and the *self* (including Doi's) relate to new models of personality or self

coming from psychoanalysis, anthropology, and other disciplines?

Chapter 1 is a resume of the definitions of dependency from literature concerned with lifespan issues—primarily emphasizing theories of attachment and dependency developed during infancy and early childhood. A strong preference for the alternate use of the term "interdependency" is documented by investigators from ethology and human development. Sociological formulations of interdependency are also reviewed, along with interactional models introduced by gerontologists in their analysis of dependency experiences among the aged.

Chapter 2 explores the ways in which dependency phenomena have been dealt with historically in psychoanalytic theory and practice. Fundamentally, the term has not often been distinguished as a central, explanatory concept, although there are a number of crucial theoretical formulations where dependent and interdependent relationships are prominent. In what seems to be a Western cultural and psychiatric bias against using the term, dependency relationships are conceptualized using alternate definitions and technical terminologies. The most transparent of these is the area of "object relations," where the interdependency of two individuals is formulated in terms that emphasize *internal objects* (Kernberg 1976, 1980). In this explanation, internal objects are heuristically described as intrapsychic representations of "external objects"—including other persons, actual behaviors, and aspects of physical reality. Similarly, dependency is evident, although mostly implicit, in theories regarding early lifespan progressions—as in the psychosexual stages of development, or in the Ericksonian descriptions of the life cycle. Dependency phenomena are more explicit in Mahler's subphases of separation-individuation, which detail a sequence of qualitative changes in the infant-mother relationship during the first thirty-six months of life. Finally, three other areas of psychoanalytic theory emphasize interdependent human functioning: ego-ideal/superego formation, the oedipal resolution, and phenomena connected to transference and countertransference.

Chapter 3 presents a condensed historical and cultural view of Japanese society. This is laid down as a matrix upon which patterns of behavior in Japanese society may be examined for distinctive characteristics reflecting this specialized history. Cultural factors relating to interdependency are illustrated through a summary of

A P T E R I

pendency, Attachment, and
erdependency: Definitions from
chology and Social Science

nature of human affiliations has long attracted commentary in
rature, philosophy, and what eventually became the behavioral
nces. Among diverse human relationships, those involving the
st intimate and intense connectedness occurring within fami-
, close friendships, and relationships of fealty have been partic-
rly fascinating. Since the turn of the century the concept of
pendency has been used in psychology and social science to de-
e qualitative aspects of certain relationships based on its appear-
e in individual and specific role sets. At a more collective level,
pendency has been implicated in its varying cultural and ideolog-
l manifestations, which qualitatively affect how larger groups
th behave and "explain" their behaviors. In the past several de-
des the term "dependency" has been expanded to include "inter-
pendency" and contracted to focus on "attachment" and more
ecialized categories.[1]

ome General Definitions

Dependency" is defined by Webster as "the condition of receiving
sistance for the necessities of life . . . ; something necessarily
nsequent upon something or someone else . . . ; the quality or
ate of being influenced by, or subject to another" (Gove 1966,

4

older and recent ethnographic studies describing family organization, school and workplace adaptations, along with prominent social orientations readily observable in Japanese personal and group
behaviors. Part of this exposition is devoted to a description of
dependency manifestations in Japan. Along with these straightforward descriptions of Japanese culture, the tendency to exaggerate
Japanese characteristics or to portray them as unique and superior
will be discussed. The term *nihonjinron* (meaning Japanese cultural
chauvinism) is used to indicate a value-laden perspective about
Japanese life that voices an inflated, self-laudatory affirmation of
cultural features presumed as exclusive and outstanding in Japanese
society.

Chapter 4 examines the literature on Japanese childrearing and
growth during infancy and early childhood. Ethnographic, historical, and developmental literature surveys the characteristics of early
socialization processes. These are coordinated with manifestations
of dependency needs as sought from parents, siblings, kin, schoolmates, teachers, and certain instrumentalities in the society at large.
Chapter 5 then looks at normative Japanese child development
through a discussion of socialization processes during the years
spent in elementary, intermediate, and high school. Changes in the
forms of dependency seeking and gratification are examined in the
context of continued development within the family, and the evolution of school and peer relations accompanying psychosocial and
psychosexual maturation. Some contrasts between the quality of
the "average expectable development" among Japanese and conventional psychoanalytic models will be made.

Chapter 6 summarizes Doi's depiction of *amae*, first as a psychological construct used to explain individual behavior, second as an
interactional concept regulating statuses and roles, and third as a
cultural characteristic contributing to the quality of behavior in
small and large groups in Japan. The commentary of other authors
about *amae* is also listed and discussed. These will then be summarized in a multilevel survey of the term *amae* that places it in a
framework documenting the presence of motives for both the provision and attainment of dependency manifested during various
phases of the lifespan (F. Johnson 1984). Chapter 7 continues a
summary of the concept of *amae* based on a synthesis using Francis
Hsu's "psychosociogram."

Chapter 8 presents a psychocultural portrait of the Japanese self
through a summarization of descriptive characteristics noted in

social-scientific, psychologic, literary, philosophical, and psychiatric commentary.

The final chapters of the book are analytical in nature and are concerned with synthesizing materials from previous sections of the book. Chapter 9 applies empirical evidence and theorizations concerning dependency in Japan to conventional psychoanalytic theories involving psychosexual stages of development, ego-ideal/ superego formation, separation-individuation, and oedipal resolution. Although concentrating on evidence from Japanese culture, other ethnographic findings (from Indian, African, and Eskimo societies) are cited that conflict with Western psychoanalytic notions of dependency.

Chapter 10 reviews some concepts and methods connected to current anthropological theories, particularly in their implications for universal and relativistic perspectives. Also, some of the recent popularity of the *interpretist* position will be examined. The perspectives of universalism and relativism will be reviewed against the background of some new approaches in psychoanalysis, and will examine controversies concerning the interpretist position in psychoanalysis.

Inevitably, a survey of literature in these various areas of scholarship leads into a thicket of conflicting descriptions and commentary. However, behind this technical detail, certain base issues are elucidated through ordinary observation, intuition, and interest. The most fundamental of these issues concerns the manifestations and structures connected to dependent human affiliations. This book will provide a summary of explanations and hypotheses about how individuals form binding and continuing associations with one another, and how these qualitatively change according to maturational, cultural, and circumstantial factors. The application of a number of different theories that seek to explain dependency and interdependency will be critically examined for their capacity to account for these intricate and changing manifestations.

Central among these considered here is the critical presentation of Takeo Doi's work on Japanese dependency *(amae)*, which offers an emphatic contrast to Western conceptualizations of both dependency experience and dependency theory.

It is this author's position that the most practical considerations of dependency currently involve interactional formulations that study the nature and quality of interdependent connections. It also seems apparent that close attention must be devoted to develop-

older and recent ethnographic studies describing family organization, school and workplace adaptations, along with prominent social orientations readily observable in Japanese personal and group behaviors. Part of this exposition is devoted to a description of dependency manifestations in Japan. Along with these straightforward descriptions of Japanese culture, the tendency to exaggerate Japanese characteristics or to portray them as unique and superior will be discussed. The term *nihonjinron* (meaning Japanese cultural chauvinism) is used to indicate a value-laden perspective about Japanese life that voices an inflated, self-laudatory affirmation of cultural features presumed as exclusive and outstanding in Japanese society.

Chapter 4 examines the literature on Japanese childrearing and growth during infancy and early childhood. Ethnographic, historical, and developmental literature surveys the characteristics of early socialization processes. These are coordinated with manifestations of dependency needs as sought from parents, siblings, kin, schoolmates, teachers, and certain instrumentalities in the society at large. Chapter 5 then looks at normative Japanese child development through a discussion of socialization processes during the years spent in elementary, intermediate, and high school. Changes in the forms of dependency seeking and gratification are examined in the context of continued development within the family, and the evolution of school and peer relations accompanying psychosocial and psychosexual maturation. Some contrasts between the quality of the "average expectable development" among Japanese and conventional psychoanalytic models will be made.

Chapter 6 summarizes Doi's depiction of *amae*, first as a psychological construct used to explain individual behavior, second as an interactional concept regulating statuses and roles, and third as a cultural characteristic contributing to the quality of behavior in small and large groups in Japan. The commentary of other authors about *amae* is also listed and discussed. These will then be summarized in a multilevel survey of the term *amae* that places it in a framework documenting the presence of motives for both the provision and attainment of dependency manifested during various phases of the lifespan (F. Johnson 1984). Chapter 7 continues a summary of the concept of *amae* based on a synthesis using Francis Hsu's "psychosociogram."

Chapter 8 presents a psychocultural portrait of the Japanese self through a summarization of descriptive characteristics noted in social-scientific, psychologic, literary, philosophical, and psychiatric commentary.

The final chapters of the book are analytical in nature and are concerned with synthesizing materials from previous sections of the book. Chapter 9 applies empirical evidence and theorizations concerning dependency in Japan to conventional psychoanalytic theories involving psychosexual stages of development, ego-ideal/superego formation, separation-individuation, and oedipal resolution. Although concentrating on evidence from Japanese culture, other ethnographic findings (from Indian, African, and Eskimo societies) are cited that conflict with Western psychoanalytic notions of dependency.

Chapter 10 reviews some concepts and methods connected to current anthropological theories, particularly in their implications for universal and relativistic perspectives. Also, some of the recent popularity of the *interpretist* position will be examined. The perspectives of universalism and relativism will be reviewed against the background of some new approaches in psychoanalysis, and will examine controversies concerning the interpretist position in psychoanalysis.

Inevitably, a survey of literature in these various areas of scholarship leads into a thicket of conflicting descriptions and commentary. However, behind this technical detail, certain base issues are elucidated through ordinary observation, intuition, and interest. The most fundamental of these issues concerns the manifestations and structures connected to dependent human affiliations. This book will provide a summary of explanations and hypotheses about how individuals form binding and continuing associations with one another, and how these qualitatively change according to maturational, cultural, and circumstantial factors. The application of a number of different theories that seek to explain dependency and interdependency will be critically examined for their capacity to account for these intricate and changing manifestations.

Central among these considered here is the critical presentation of Takeo Doi's work on Japanese dependency *(amae)*, which offers an emphatic contrast to Western conceptualizations of both dependency experience and dependency theory.

It is this author's position that the most practical considerations of dependency currently involve interactional formulations that study the nature and quality of interdependent connections. It also seems apparent that close attention must be devoted to developmental variables that drastically alter the manifestations of reciprocal interdependent relationships throughout the lifespan. Finally, it is this author's belief that the profound impact of culture observed in the varying manifestations and theories concerning dependent relations furnishes a partial answer to Hartmann's (1958), Caudill's (1962b), and LeVine's (1987) questions concerning the significance of the "average expectable environment."

CHAPTER I

Dependency, Attachment, and Interdependency: Definitions from Psychology and Social Science

The nature of human affiliations has long attracted commentary in literature, philosophy, and what eventually became the behavioral sciences. Among diverse human relationships, those involving the most intimate and intense connectedness occurring within families, close friendships, and relationships of fealty have been particularly fascinating. Since the turn of the century the concept of *dependency* has been used in psychology and social science to define qualitative aspects of certain relationships based on its appearance in individual and specific role sets. At a more collective level, dependency has been implicated in its varying cultural and ideological manifestations, which qualitatively affect how larger groups both behave and "explain" their behaviors. In the past several decades the term "dependency" has been expanded to include "interdependency" and contracted to focus on "attachment" and more specialized categories.[1]

Some General Definitions

"Dependency" is defined by Webster as "the condition of receiving assistance for the necessities of life ... ; something necessarily consequent upon something or someone else ... ; the quality or state of being influenced by, or subject to another" (Gove 1966,

604). Gurian (1984) expands the definition to include "the seeking of identity, support, security and/or permission outside the self." In his explanation, dependency is reciprocal: the dependent partner seeks and anticipates receiving a response, while a gratifying partner expects to give. Such transactions are also obligatory: dependents are expected to seek support and return favors. "Failure to participate in this circle of obligation may result in a range of responses from verbal disapproval to ostracism" (Gurian 1984, 353). Bonner (1964) reviewed the use of the term "dependency" in political science to denote the "subjugation of a country, a province or minority group to the control of a dominant host nation." Citing G. C. Lewis (1891) the term was held to be one of three fundamental factors describing the relations of dominant powers to their trust territories and colonies literally, in the past, called "dependencies." In a broader meaning, Bonner (1964) applied the term "dependency" to social psychology, where it denotes universal affiliative needs observable in all individuals "to relate to, rely upon, and find gratification in another person" (Bonner 1964, 189). He also observed the common distinction raised between the biological basis of dependent helplessness (for example, certain "instinctual" needs for connection and physical survival) versus the social basis of dependencies, established through a series of interpersonal relations with parents and caretakers during a long process of socialization. Gurian (1984) discussed the term "*inter*dependence," which has emerged as a more phenomenologically accurate description of the interactional processes through which "separate entities reciprocally seek identity, support, security and/or permission from one another" (Gurian 1984, 353). In contrast, the word *independency* is defined in Webster as "not being subject to control by others . . . not affiliated with or integrated into a larger controlling unit . . . [and] not requiring or relying on something else" (Gove 1966, 1148).

In their use in social-philosophic and political contexts, "dependency" and "independency" are commonly polarized as antithetical extremes, often presented in an idealized and rhetorical sense. Also, in legal contexts "dependency" is defined using specific age criteria, rather than operational qualifications of individuals to be functionally independent. Aside from legal or technical definitions, the cultural significance of being independent is generally regarded as being inflated and overvalued in Western societies—particularly in the U.S. Conversely, being dependent is held to be undesirable, disadvantageous, and potentially humiliating. Addressing this bias, Neki

(1976a, 1976b) has speculated that the strong pejorative connotations of "dependency" in Western societies have both linguistic and sociohistorical origins. Linguistically, the word is derived from Latin and has the lexical meaning of "being suspended" or "hanging down," both suggesting a state of encumbrance or inconvenience regarding others. (The negative connotations of "down" have also been stressed by Lakoff and Johnson 1980). In contrast, the Hindi-Sanskrit equivalent of "dependency" derives from a stem word that has the nonderogatory meaning of "resting on," "taking shelter," and "seeking security" (Neki 1976a, 3). Neki also makes the interesting observation that although "dependency" and "independency" are opposite terms in regard to political sovereignty, they are not *logically* antonymic in human developmental perspective, except through conventional usage and interpretation.

Definitions from Developmental Psychology

By all accounts "dependency" is a most generic term whose definitions, applications, and reputation have undergone considerable change during the past fifty years. Bandura and Walters (1963) defined "dependency" as "a class of responses capable of eliciting positive attending and ministering responses from others." Reflecting its high level of generalization, "dependency" has been used both as a theoretical construct in psychological research, and as a colloquial expression signifying states of human relatedness experienced in both natural and clinical encounters. Although not elevating the word to the status of a systematically applied concept, Freud used the term *anlehnung* (literally meaning "leaning on") to describe the infant/mother relationship in his essay *On Narcissism* (1914). Within developmental psychology the term originally referred to crucial aspects of the infant-parent relationship during an early period of human development (birth to thirty-six months). This reference has been based on the imputed presence of urgent drives that facilitate an intimate connection between the infant and mother. Such neonatal patterns of intense infant/parent connection are conspicuous in many species, but are especially complex and protracted in humans. The biological helplessness of the human infant and the extended period required for childrearing involves a combination of biological, social, and psychological connectedness not present in other species.

The timing and manner in which these dependency relationships undergo qualitative changes during childhood and adolescence has generally been held (but not conclusively proven) to influence patterns of adult behavior. This may be expressed in terms of *personality*, which can be seen as a set of predictable responses to the demands of here-and-now situations, or in terms of *character* as a patterning of traits and general modes of self-presentation consistent over long periods of time. These features may be seen either in individuals—where specific parents impart their versions of acceptable dependency—or in cultures, where groups transmit normative standards stipulating acceptable dependency relations at various stages of development and involution. Although dependency relationships undergo complex changes throughout the lifespan, certain phases are especially critical and connected with potentially dramatic shifts in dependency status. These include weaning from breast or bottle, the independent control of excretion, subsequent birth of younger siblings, and alterations in relationship to the same- and opposite-sex parents encountered during what in psychoanalysis is termed the oedipal transition. Other dramatic shifts occur at puberty, with the acquisition of early adult status, and during social transformations accompanying courtship, marriage, childbirth, and childrearing. Additionally, critical incidents throughout the lifespan are acknowledged to transform existent patterns of dependency, such as severe illness or handicap, physical separations, natural catastrophes, divorce, death of parents, widowhood, and other forms of sudden loss or separation. Changes in dependency also routinely occur during middle age and later years accompanying the exiting of children, retirement, normal physiological decline, and generational shifts in power, responsibility, and status.[2]

Most commonly, the term "dependency" stands as a generalized concept defining the relationship between two individuals. Less frequently, it is used to define an individual's relations to small and large groups, to institutions, and even toward "causes" or ideologies. In its commonest usage, "dependency" defines asymmetric, unbalanced relationships where one partner is more needful than the other. This condition of imbalance is established on the basis of one partner's possessing higher status, superior resources, greater skills, or more options than the second, or inferior, partner. Another asymmetrical quality should be mentioned—namely, that the dependency relationship is additionally unbalanced by the stronger partner's superior perspective and understanding of the dependency relationship itself. This asset invests that partner with a heightened sense of strategy concerning outcomes of interdependent activity.

In both developmental psychology and psychoanalysis the infant-mother dyad has been the paradigmatic model of dependency. In much of the earlier literature, dependency was minimally conceptualized in terms of an "intrinsic needs system" existing within the dependent partner. Accordingly, psychological and psychoanalytic observations were centered on instinct-based, object-seeking dependency, described mainly in terms of "forces" activating the dependent member, while ignoring or minimizing the significance of the gratifying partner (as in Freud 1914). Later versions in academic psychology took into account the complementary fit between the need to be nurtured and both the need and the capacity to provide nurturance.[3]

Dependency and Dyadic Interaction

Murray, et al.'s (1938) formulation of adult "personology" described dependency as a "secondary needs system" arising out of a fusion of two underlying primary systems that he termed "n-affiliation" and "n-succorance." Looking for more specificity, later theoreticians divided dependency behaviors into two general components: *instrumental*, which was concerned with physical and practical requirements, and *emotional*, which was concerned with affections, moods, and feelings. Systematic studies in developmental psychology subsequently focused on measurable factors in experimentally controlled situations designed to identify processes connected primarily to instrumental aspects of dependency. As noted repeatedly, research conducted by behaviorally oriented investigators has generally emphasized quantifiable stimulus cues and responses rather than qualitative, affective factors. As within psychoanalysis, but for quite different reasons, this emphasis on measurable responses in the dependent infant methodologically excluded consideration of the mother's motives, secondary responses, or feelings. Many of the earlier studies based on social learning theory relegated the dependency-satisfying mother to a "stimulus object," and studied the infant-mother relationship in terms of the effects of reinforcements observable in controlled experimental situations. Despite this, other factors were acknowledged to influence the experimental results, producing certain differences that reflected cultural or familial variations.

In contrast to studies done by social learning and developmental specialists, ethological studies involving primates or other mammals have routinely concentrated on the interaction of the infant/ mother pair, examining variables in a system of shared behavior observed in both experimental and naturalistic settings (e.g., in Rheingold 1961; and Rheingold and Eckermann, 1970). Emerging from this tradition Harlow (1966) attempted to reduce the vagueness of "dependency" by characterizing it in a series of qualitatively varying structural partnerships. In a definitive review of the subject, Maccoby and Masters (1970) summarized the published work of various investigators and operationalized dependency as a cluster of behaviors consisting of 1) "seeking physical contact," 2) "seeking to be near," 3) "seeking attention," 4) "seeking praise and approval," and 5) "resisting separation." They later added "seeking help" and "asking questions" (in Maccoby and Masters 1970). In their comprehensive summary of behavioral, psychoanalytic, ethological, and cognitive theories, they discussed the accumulated commentary that criticized an earlier, more generalistic concept of dependency, and the trend among theorists since the mid-1960s to differentiate between "attachment" and "dependency."

Dependency and Attachment

Bowlby (1958) has been credited with introducing the term "attachment" in an attempt to claim a distinction for the infant/maternal connection, and to avoid some of the vagueness of the term "dependency." In his classification, "attachment" described activity directed at seeking to be near, or to have physical contact with, specific, targeted persons—ordinarily the mother. The term "dependency" was reserved for more ambiguously directed expressions of physical and emotional needs that were relatively undifferentiated in regard to target. In contrast to nonspecific dependency needs, attachment behaviors were seen as relating to proximal physical associations, and as demonstrating an urgency and heightened emotion closer to Freud's (1914) and Spitz's (1965) descriptions of "libidinal" or "object cathexis." While influenced by developmental theories in psychoanalysis, Bowlby's speculations were indebted to ethological studies of infant/parent relations in other species (e.g., in Hinde 1956). As Ainsworth (1976) comments, Bowlby also gave attachment the status of a primary rather than a secondary drive, reflecting its hypothetical basis as part of a structuralized, "instinctive" biological system. In a series of publications (1969, 1972, 1979, 1980) Bowlby has argued that separation experience in early life constitutes a paradigm for subsequent adaptations. Although not always discussed explicitly, unanticipated changes in dependency status were seen as crucial in the development of subsequent clinical disturbance (Bowlby 1988).

Ainsworth (1976) has contrasted attachment and dependency according to eight points of differentiation. In terms of specificity, she defines attachment as "an affectional tie or bond that one individual ... forms between himself and another specific individual. ... [while] dependency is a generalized or nonfocussed response" (1976, 100). In terms of duration, attachments are seen as highly durable over time, in contrast to dependencies, which may be transitory and yielding to substitution. In terms of maturity, Ainsworth suggests that attachments of varying intensities are observable throughout the lifespan, but that "it is popularly held that dependence should give way gradually to a substantial degree of independence" (1976, 101). Considering affective implications, attachments are described as strong and urgent, in contrast to the weaker and less passionate dependency relationships. In terms of proximity-seeking and contact-maintaining behaviors, both attachment and dependency are seen as similar, except that attachment behaviors selectively seek specific, high-valence connections (e.g., a parent or lover). In terms of learning, Ainsworth accepts the opinion that both attachment and dependency are influenced by learning, through a series of coordinated actions with a sequence of partners. She also acknowledges the subsequent generalizability of dependency behaviors learned in infancy and early childhood. This is in contrast to the more questionable generalizability of attachment behaviors, which are not so readily transferred. In terms of biological functioning, the need for the infant to establish a fierce primary attachment is regarded as instinctively regulated. This need is coordinated with reciprocal maternal behavior focusing on providing protection, feeding, comfort, and nurturance.

Although preferring his own term of "focused relationship," Yarrow (1976) describes attachment as an interactional concept that is multidirectional in its processes and consequences—rather than merely an innate "drive." It involves age-regulated attempts at forming persistent and crucial relationships, first within the immediate family, but later within a wider circle of social objects in relationships characterized by "strong interdependence and affective components."

An ethologist, Cairns (1976a, 1976b) sees attachment as referring to "an emotionally intense relationship that has special motivational properties, whereas 'dependency' refers to instrumental, interpersonal behaviors" (1976a, 32). From a psychobiological standpoint, Cairns describes attachment as connected to endogenous, inborn structures where environmental influences "play only a permissive role in [guiding] the development of the structure" (Cairns 1976a, 38). Looking at a number of species, he sees attachment as typified by behavioral continuity over time and space, but still permitting flexibility in accommodating to situational social occurrences and maturational changes. In most species, early attachment is fundamentally concerned with facilitating close physical proximity between mother and infant, including nutrition, cosleeping, cooperative foraging, and parental defense of the young. The timing and extent of these shared activities vary according to the species and the age of the animal. Consulting comparative studies he concludes that "the primary features of human infant 'attachment behavior' are observed in part or in total in several other species from rodents to primates" (1976a, 39).

Conceptual Inconsistencies Connected to "Attachment"

Troll and Smith (1976) examined the concept of attachment through the qualities of dyadic bonds expressed in adult linkages within extended families. Although concentrating on later periods in the lifespan, these authors raised a number of critical questions concerning both the qualitative and quantitative aspects of relationships defined as attachments (that is, two-person, intense, reciprocal relationships) and dependencies (relationships involving potentially interchangeable partners). They commented on the relatively higher durability of attachments observed in women compared to men, and noted the persisting significance of the parent-child relationship throughout the life cycle.

In addition to the qualitative changes, Troll and Smith (1976) suggested that some differences might be related to quantitative factors, where the "tight psychological space" of a two-person system reflected the inordinate amount of time and intensity manifested in intimate partnerships encountered during childhood, courtship, early marriage, and preschool parenting. These authors also presented a critical discussion of attempts to measure "strength of attachment" according to residential propinquity, frequency of interaction, and amount of material aid. They suggested that simple numerical counts of such behaviors may impart a misleading quantitative significance that belies the actual intensity of these relationships. They also pointed out that measures of "strength of affect" often ignore the importance of strongly *negative* emotions, which may be equally or even more binding than positive emotions. All in all they find "that *affect* was more important than proximity," suggesting that the actual emotionality or valence of the relationship may be more significant than geographical closeness, frequency of encounter, or the magnitude of material aid. They end by endorsing the conclusion that "family bonds, both in dyadic affect and in family integration, override separation and distance" (1976, 168).

Problems Evaluating Proximity Seeking

In their criticism concerning the complexity of proximity-seeking behaviors, Weintraub, Brooks, and Lewis (1977) point out that proximity seeking should be conceptualized in its psychologic as well as physical specifications. The prototypical need for physical nearness is of great consequence in early attachment behavior, and conceivably may generalize to subsequent states of attachment established later in life. Proximity seeking is a readily observable event among infants and younger children. However, such contact for older children, adolescents, and adults may be supplanted by diverse physical and symbolical activities: talking together, gazing at one another, or even corresponding or telephoning while geographically separated. Subjectively, contact may also be established through merely thinking or fantasizing about another person. Such diffusion of proximity behaviors makes quantitative study difficult to carry out systematically. Moreover, these authors discuss how proximity seeking is confounded by factors of psychological state, situational changes, passage of time, and, of course, culture.

Even in children, the analysis of proximity seeking is elusive. As Ainsworth (1982) comments, attachment itself is only one of a number of behavioral systems including exploration, food seeking, and general affiliation. Behaviors that resemble attachment may implicate a number of other motives contributing to the seeking of affiliation. Also, as Rheingold (1961) commented, the human infant's need to cling and seek cutaneous contact diminishes after three months, whereafter visual contact becomes more significant in sociability and in satisfying needs for close proximity.

Weintraub, Brooks, and Lewis (1977) have addressed the problem of the uniqueness of attachment relationships. For example, a child may demonstrate close attachments to a number of different people, but such a plurality of special, intense relationships dissipates the idea of uniqueness. Also, some problems regarding whether attachment is an "all or none" phenomenon were raised. This pivots on the limitations of studying manifest, resultant behaviors and not accounting for the unobservable subjective reactions which accompany experimental or naturalistic conditions. This problem is also reflected in the tendency to study positive—that is overt and forthcoming—as opposed to negative attachment behaviors, such as silence, withdrawal, or immobility. For example, some youngsters in the second year of life, when forcibly separated from mothers, display diffidence, remoteness, or even shunning upon reunion. Also it is common for closely attached partners of any age to show aloofness, retreat from interaction, and silence following an argument or disruptive event. However, in both of these examples, it is misleading to regard the sheer lack of "positive attachment behavior" at these moments as suggesting an absence of significant connection. Additionally, looking at attachment as a tie or bond involves making inferences concerning hypothetical structures and processes that these authors find difficult to study systematically.

The Measurement of Early Attachment

One of the methods used in both experimental and clinical assessment of infantile attachment is the "Strange Situation" procedure (Ainsworth and Wittig 1969). This test is devised to measure the capacity of infants to display their use of an adult as a "secure base," and to measure their reactions to separation and reunion through a graded series of "challenge episodes" used to develop increasing distress. Infants are classified into groups and subgroups according to the qualities of their responses to separation and reunion. Lamb, et al. (1984) have contributed an exhaustive review and critique of the reported literature and concluded that there is little reliable evidence about the specific dimensions of parental behavior that affect Strange Situation behavior. . . . Temporal stability in security attachment is high only when there is a stability in family and caretaking circumstances. (Lamb, et al. 1984, 127)

The clinical utility of this test to discriminate qualitative features of the ongoing attachment between mother and infant is generally acknowledged. However, the capacity of the Strange Situation to predict future reactions to separation has been harder to establish conclusively. Also, the extent to which this test substantiates a putative sociobiologic "drive" for attachment—with implications for evolutionary survival—is considered moot.

Clinical popularizations of attachment (inexactly called "bonding") have also led to an intensified focus on the early maternal/infant relationship. This has included both a cultist and scientific concern with early neonatal and even prenatal aspects of "maternal-infant bonding." As Chess and Thomas (1982) have critically observed, this absorption in the crucial nature of neonatal connectedness occurred following sixty years of clinical beliefs concerning the high significance of early developmental behaviors for future adaptation (Freud 1910; Watson 1928; Bowlby 1958). From the perspective of both psychoanalysis and academic psychology, the quality of the mother/infant relationship has been regarded as pivotal for subsequent psychological adaptation. A cultist exaggeration of the significance of attachment *immediately* following birth has also infiltrated some obstetrical practices. Attributing a high significance to early postnatal attachments has undoubtedly helped to humanize obstetrical procedures and encouraged practices of responsible mothering and fathering. Regrettably, it has also tended to reinforce the myth that consequent maladaptive behavior reflected inadequate bonding (Svejda, et al. 1980). In the opinion of Chess and Thomas (1982), subsequent research has not sustained these speculations.

Attachment to Groups

Weintraub, Brooks, and Lewis (1977) have broadened the concept of attachment through a series of propositions that imply an innately social-interactional basis of behavior. They assert that infants and children distributively attach to a variety of human objects available within a social network. These authors propose that the structural aspects of the social network can be analyzed both as "interactions" and "relationships." However, at any given time, the quality of interactions and the significance of these relationships may not directly correspond. They suggest that interactions are specifiable behaviors accessible to observation and measurement, while relationships must be abstracted from a series of interactions, and require the imposition of meaning through a process of inference and interpretation.

In a developmental context, Knudson (1976) has examined attachment in terms of various sequences of the lifespan. She concludes that the number of potential interacting variables dictates a systems approach, utilizing multilevel structural analyses. She also notes the tendency of researchers to ignore the differences in social as compared to nonsocial object relations and calls attention to transitional objects where nonsocial "things" are socially used by young children in ways that are substitutional for actual human contacts. She also discusses self-produced feedback ("self-attachment") as a significant element in the social-learning experience during early childhood, and emphasizes the significance of "self-talk" through which transitions to new lifespan attachments are partly accomplished on the basis of internally rehearsed feedback.

From Dependency to Interdependency

As described in the previous section, the term "dependency" has undergone revision, specification, and redefinition under the influence of diverse investigators and theorists—especially following the introduction of the competitive term "attachment." Recently the term "interdependency" has been used to depict an interactional, reciprocal, and social-symbolical characterization of dependency. In discussing some clinical features of interpersonal relationships, Stierlin (1958) used the term "interdependence" as analogous to the biological term "symbiosis." As such "interdependence" was capable of being divided into "commensalism," "mutualism," and "parasitism." Among these "mutualism" was seen as having application to close, interdependent human affiliations.

In advocating the substitution of "interdependency" for "dependency," Van den Heuvel (1979) summarized earlier classifications of dependency, including Clark's (1966) taxonomy, which was composed to distinguish between cultural meanings and behavioral dynamics. Although devised to analyze dependency in later life, Clark's approach is generic and includes 1) socioeconomic dependency, 2) developmental dependency, 3) dependency of crisis, 4) dependency of nonreciprocal roles, 5) neurotic dependency, and, finally, 6) dependency as a culturally conditioned character trait. Van den Heuvel has attempted to avoid idealized and culturally biased definitions of both dependency and independency. He states that "most relationships are interdependent; the limits of interdependency are set by generally accepted norms" (1979, 162). George Bernard Shaw (in *Pygmalion*, 1983 [1887]) came to the same conclusion in suggesting that "independence is a middle class prejudice, for we are all dependent on each other." Cohler and Geyer (1970) similarly state that "although autonomy and independence are held up as ideal adult values, interdependence is more characteristic of real relationships within actual families or working groups." Munnichs (1976) also sees sharp dependent/independent polarities as deductive idealizations leading to interpretations that do not reflect reality. Beattie (1975) commented that "there has been too much stress in the gerontological literature on independence as a goal for later years. I would like to suggest that interdependence may be a more appropriate goal. It is also more related to man's identity as a social animal" (Beattie 1975, 40).

Colleen Johnson (1974, 1977) applied the term "interdependence" to describe the close-knit network of relationships among Japanese-Americans. The instrumental and emotional characteristics of these relations were seen to be manifested through a complex system of gift giving requiring the scrupulous observance of weddings, funerals, birthdays, holidays, and other significant events. These served as occasions for formalized gestures of remembrance and generosity that actualized the underlying interdependency.

Although not specifying the term "interdependency," Knudson (1976) suggested the use of research strategies employing dyadic relational terms, the analysis of bidirectional effects, and a systems approach examining a combination of affectional and instrumental effects. Cohler and Geyer (1970) have argued for using the term "interdependence" as a central concept when using the family as a psychosocial unit of study. They see lifespan issues pivoting on qualitative changes in interdependency during various stages of family relationship throughout the lifespan. They distinguish between the development and maintenance of intrapsychic autonomy versus interpersonal autonomy. Citing the clinical studies of Boszormenyi-Nagy and Spark (1973), Cohler and Geyer examine the conflict and shame that accompany the exhibition of dependency among adults. They suggest that either expressing or demonstrating a desire to remain dependent upon others causes conspicuous discomfort within nonethnic North American families. Summing up, Cohler and Geyer state that

> much of the tension that exists between culturally shared assumptions about the importance of independence and autonomy in contemporary society, and the reality of interdependence within the family of adulthood is reflected in contemporary theories of personality and socialization. . . . What has been viewed as an incomplete resolution of the issue of separation-individuation, . . . may be better understood as the preservation of psychological interdependence among persons who care very much for each other, and who maintain satisfying mutual ties of caring and sharing across adulthood. (Cohler and Geyer 1970, 221)

In concluding, they point to the necessity of attaining a degree of personal autonomy and individuation, but at the same time holding onto a balanced interdependency, simultaneously permitting personal satisfaction and continued development within a modified extended, multigenerational family.

More conflicted versions of interdependency are constituted in the colloquially used terms "counterdependency" and "codependency." Counterdependency suggests that an assertion of dependency needs by one partner may justify counterassertion by another partner as a defensive maneuver. This involves a type of aggressive but balanced reciprocity, using techniques to deflect, neutralize, or defeat demands for dependent connection. When discussed in clinical or psychotherapeutic contexts, "counterdependency" is a strategy used to contain, equalize, or neutralize attempts that patients make to establish a dependent connection with the therapist. "Codependency," on the other hand, is a term popularized in the drug and alcohol treatment community. It stands for the pathological, dependency-gratifying involvements that marital partners or other individuals may be coerced into by persons who are addicted to alcohol or other substances. Although unsubstantiated by research (Gomberg 1989), the explanation is formulated that highly dependent persons (alcoholics or addicts) either induce a codependency on persons around them, or attract individuals who because of their own needs are seeking an asymmetrical, destructive relationship.

Social-Scientific Formulations
of Dependency

Sociological and social-psychological formulations have dealt with questions concerning various forms of dependency, interdependency, and independency—however, mostly through using other terminologies and formulations. Gouldner (1960) specified distinctions between the concepts of "complementarity" and "reciprocity," defining "reciprocity" as a pattern of mutually contingent exchange of gratifications, whose normative regulations operate in the maintenance of stable social systems. "Complementarity" was defined as standing for a balancing of disparate roles occurring in "complementary role sets," as in husband/wife, teacher/student, minister/parishioner statuses. Issues concerned with dependency/interdependency were also addressed using the concept of *power* (as in Baldwin 1974). In a formulation that has become quite popular, Emerson (1962) introduced "exchange theory" as a dynamic approach to examine the interconnections according to the factors of "power," "authority," and "legitimacy." He conceptualized power as vested in the *relationship* rather than in the separate individuals, and described "balancing operations" that characterized the functions of exchange. One of these balancing operations centered on maintaining an equilibrium or assuring that each partner remained free "to grant or deny, facilitate or hinder, the other's gratification" (Emerson 1962, 32). He also addressed the question of inequality and instability of power within dyadic relationships, seeing a *cohesion* form through a succession of balancing operations.

Building on the concept of reciprocity, Takie Lebra (1969, 1976) synthesized a definitive reappraisal of the Japanese concept of asymmetrical obligation called *on* (pronounced "own"). In contrast to reciprocal and symmetrical relationships, the Japanese concept of *on* is a culturally defined system of permanently unbalanced, asymmetric relationships, kept in equilibrium by a series of control mechanisms. In her analysis, Lebra concludes that both symmetrical and asymmetrical exchanges are involved in the complexity of the noneconomic aspects of reciprocity—manifested as prestige, honor, or affection. She suggests that each culture is concerned with the provision of mechanisms that regulate what she describes as "the tension generated in the mutual constraint between symmetry and asymmetry" (Lebra 1969, 130).

Lebra (1976) has also addressed the issues of *affiliation* ("belong-ingness") and dependency, again using illustrations from Japanese patterns of behavior. She divides dependency into four categories: dependency of *obligation*, dependency of *patronage*, dependency of *indulgence*, and dependency of *pity*. These categories, operating alone or in combination, may be used to characterize the nature of diverse human associations and role sets.[4]

In an early work looking at "gregariousness" and motives for affiliation, Schachter (1959) deductively examined the range of hu-man experience relating to strategies for making and retaining con-nections to other persons. Gurian and Gurian (1983) also developed a categorization of dependency built on an interplay between social-psychological attitudes and actual, situational networks of partner-ship. Using a normative design they describe "negative" and "posi-tive" dependency relationships for diverse experiences of closeness and affiliation. Each dimension of dependency experience is poten-tially accompanied by what these authors define as "negative states" consisting of either reduced or excessive dependency—both of which represent the possibility of unhealthy or destructive experiences.

In a social-psychological description of emotion theory, de Rivera (1977) implicates *belongingness* as generic to the establishment of "object relations" (i.e., affiliation).

Our first postulate, that we may meaningfully contrast two basic forms of both positive and negative movement, implies that there is another funda-mental distinction. . . . This is related to whether emotional movement is oriented to moving an other toward or away from the self (whose position remains constant) or moving the self toward or away from the other. (de Rivera 1977, 42)

Thus, de Rivera sees a basic element of "belongingness" underlying a series of structured emotional transformations involving move-ments away and toward the self and others. Depending on age, gender, and status qualifications, these transformations can reflect varying and different states of obligation, love, and interdepen-dency.

In other social-psychological analyses, dependency and indepen-dency have long been applied to situations relating to normal aging, to physical infirmity, mental or psychological disability, indentured and unindentured servitude, legal or capricious incarceration, or political oppressions of various sorts. Most pertinent to this chapter are the recurrent ways in which Western descriptions of illness and disability are connected to states of relative helplessness, forced dependency, reduced status, and role constriction. Particularly in societies stressing meritocracy and where independency and individualism are idealized, the prospects of becoming economically invalid, physically decrepit, or emotionally disabled are especially awesome. As Neugarten (1979) states, "Dependency and deterioration, not death itself, are the specters of old age" (1979, 890).

Social-Philosophic and Psychiatric Applications

In the Western world, the word "independence" carries the connotation of having *escaped* from dependency through intrigue or rebellion, rather than being granted autonomy through a course of ordinary events or gradual development. Thus, political, legal, or personal independence is not necessarily given, but must be taken from others, or maintained against the possibility of loss. In real-life situations among ordinary persons, states of "pure" dependency or independency are improbable. Most commentators feel that independency and dependency function as falsely idealized poles on a continuum of actual experience. Relationships are always structurally bilateral (or multilateral) and characterized by various kinds of reciprocal, interdependent exchanges that fluctuate over time, and accommodate to situational changes. Despite this realistic perspective, attitudes and rhetoric toward "independency," "individualism," "self-determination," "self-actualization," and "self-reliance" are normatively extolled as a constellation of traits idealized within Western communities. In a cross-cultural comparison, Wagatsuma and Rosett (1983) comment that "Western insistence on the rights of the weak against the powerful is based on the illusion of individual autonomy and choice. . . . The Japanese live by the illusion of harmony, while the Americans live by the illusion of autonomy and self-sufficiency" (1983, 95–96).[5]

In American social science and psychiatry, dependency is also connected to a spectrum of normatively *negative* performances involved with undesirable states of heightened needs, frequently defined as "maladaptive," "maladjustive," "age-inappropriate," or "deviant." Talcott Parsons (1951) described the early internalization of independency and self-sufficiency among Americans as operating to negativize experiences of helplessness or ineptitude, which might be associated with increased needs for dependency. As he states it,

The American must therefore go farther in the process of socialization for two sets of reasons: first, because he must reach higher levels of affective neutrality and universalism, and second, because he has a more strongly developed set of dependency needs from which he must become emancipated. This seems to be one of the focal points of strain in American society. (T. Parsons 1951, 269)

Postulated on a socialization that stresses independency, the experience of illness potentially places the patient into what Parsons calls a "passive-alienative category"—or, more colloquially, "the sick role." Illness thus becomes a form of deviance constituting a withdrawal into a dependent, helpless position, signaling the requirement for some kind of assistance and care giving. In a resume of contemporary trends in American life, Lasch (1977) has reexamined Parson's "sick role" in the perspective of what he sees as a sequence of professionalized appropriations of functions that were previously supplied by parental, familial, or pastoral sources. He traces the emergence of institutionalized disciplines that gradually supplanted the family in addressing various kinds of dependencies —including some of the natural dependencies of childhood and adolescence. Lasch (1977) reviews the development of various helping professions developed during the early 1900s in response to a series of "needs" and social pathologies. These provided programmatic responses for deficiencies in caring for young, sick, elderly, inept, and deviant populations. He reviews the circumstances under which educators, psychiatrists, social workers, and criminologists were authenticated as "doctors to a sick society [who] . . . demanded the broadest possible delegation of medical authority in order to heal it" (1977, 15). In discussing the "ethics of helplessness," Szasz (1961) also reflects on the conflictual norms that regulate disability and illness, and diametrically oppose the Western values of self-conscious rationality and independent direction of life and livelihood.

Both the young and the old are prominently at risk of being defined as helpless, "sick," or dependent. With younger persons this reflects the realistic needs for protection, nurturance, education, and training required to attain psychosocial competence. With the elderly, however, pat assumptions concerning increased dependency may reflect biased cultural attitudes toward older persons. Clark and Anderson (1967), in an anthropological study of the aged, have discussed factors that when added to problems in health and declining income, may lead to stereotyping the elderly as a dependent and disabled population.

Dependency in Western Clinical Psychiatry

Within Western systems of psychiatric nomenclature, "abnormal" conditions of dependency are represented in terms of *adjustment disorders, developmental disorders,* and *personality disorders.* Diagnostic terms define certain states of excessive (meaning age- or situation-inappropriate) dependencies as being abnormal and pathological. Interestingly, there are no classifications relating to excessively *in*dependent states, although Birchnell (1984) has alluded to "detachment" as a potentially maladaptive condition of exaggerated independence. However, the diagnosis of "avoidant personality disorder" does not indicate diminished dependency, per se, but rather a categorical aversion to interpersonal connections. Within child psychiatry, disabilities concerning dependency center on versions of "separation anxiety disorder" (American Psychiatric Association 1987). Criteria for this condition include excessive anxiousness in children who anticipate physical separation from a primary attachment figure—ordinarily their mothers. This may include unrealistic brooding about the safety of parents, fantasies about becoming lost, maimed, or kidnapped, a reluctance to sleep alone, refusal to attend school, and nightmares centering on separation themes.

With adult patients, both the revised *Diagnostic and Statistical Manual* (American Psychiatric Association 1987) and the *International Classification of Diseases* (World Health Organization 1979) define a diagnostic category of "dependent personality disorder." This is defined as being manifested by a lack of self-confidence, low self-esteem, and a conspicuous handicap in making decisions or assuming responsibility. Usually there is an inflated need to depend on spouse, parents, siblings, friends, or superiors, which forces others to supervise and regulate behavior. Also a declared lack of self-confidence may be manipulated to avoid responsibility or subvert the expectations of others for performance. Additionally, some dependent individuals may openly cling to others, and through their helplessness induce their superiors to "take over." Such persons formerly were diagnosed as "passive dependent personality" (American Psychiatric Association 1968). This classification was balanced by a category of "passive aggressive personality," where heightened dependency needs were concealed beneath superficial bravado and pseudoaggressive behavior designed to hide personal incompetence, and at the same time fend off any expectation of responsibility. Such protestations and bombast also generated an indirect appeal

for care and attention, which could not be asked for in a straighfor-
ward manner.

Heightened states of dependency may be encountered in both
clinical and naturalistic situations that fulfill the diagnostic criteria
for either adult or pediatric disorders. As in all personality disorders,
it is not a question of whether these conditions "exist"—that is,
can empirically be "found" or diagnosed—but rather of examining
the social-interactional and contextual factors that account for their
development and persistence. In the case of purportedly excessive
dependency, the prevailing cultural and socialization processes must
be examined for the ways in which they stimulate, reward, and
punish according to expectations for mature functioning in particular societies.

Despite its common use in clinical descriptions, "dependency"
is rarely advanced as a central dynamic concept in the explanation
of overall personality functioning in the Western psychiatric literature—except in the context of exaggerated or age-inappropriate states
or disorders. However, some exceptions to this should be mentioned. Goldfarb's (1965) descriptions of the psychological dynamics
in a three-generational family placed the concept of dependency at
the center of his formulations of transference and countertransference, and in illuminating the affiliative relationships in which both
children and adults were enmeshed. Another therapeutic use of the
concept has already been noted in Boszormenyi-Nagy and Spark
(1973), where transgenerational aspects of interdependency are regarded as pivotal in explaining both positive and negative adaptations of persons within families. Snyder (1963) also directly approached the issue of dependency as a central ingredient in certain
psychotherapeutic work. Defining dependent behavior as "involving
the need for more help than the average person requires in meeting
problem situations," Snyder used a number of indicators to identify
dependency in a content analysis of statements taken directly from
transcripts of recorded psychotherapy. He also analyzed the quality
of the psychotherapist's responses, which were devised to enhance
patients' esteem, change their attitudes about resolving problems,
and coach them in handling conflictual situations—all explained
as ways of overcoming excessive, age-inappropriate dependency.[6]

Birchnell (1984) has examined "dependence" in its relationship
to clinical depression. He sees three possible components in dependence: "affectional," "ontological," and "deferential." "Affectional"
dependence corresponds to "anxious attachment" (Bowlby 1969),

while "deferential dependence" is similar to Beck's (1976) conception of the "depression-prone" individual. Both of these predilections may be associated with a tendency to fall into clinical depression in the face of separations, stresses, or alterations in personal status. In contrast, the state of "ontological" dependence is based on a more schizoidal position of unrelatedness or alienation from others, and may be associated with an existential state of objectless despair.

Another recent dimension of depicting dependency status cuts across medical, social, and psychiatric contexts, using the concept of social support or "social network." Applied in both clinical and investigational work, these terms are used to examine the quality of interdependent relationships available to individuals in the midst of stressful life circumstances and comprise a way of estimating the availability of external resources that may be mobilized in the process of stabilization, coping, and recovery.

Summary

This chapter has assembled a chronology of the various observations, definitions, and applications of the term "dependency," primarily in the Western psychological, social-scientific, and clinical literature. Although qualitatively varying in its applications, the term has been used to describe ubiquitous aspects of human affiliations and associations in both intimate and nonintimate contexts throughout the lifespan. As a word semantically defining the act of "leaning on" or "receiving assistance from" other persons, the term "dependency" had its earliest meanings defined according to the model of the asymmetrical infant-parent relationship, primarily in terms of the putative "need systems" of the infantile partner. The term was later expanded and refined in developmental work centering on infancy and childhood—eventually becoming summarized as a cluster of behaviors seeking physical contact, proximity, attention, praise, and approval. It was also associated with behavior concerned with resisting separation, seeking help, and asking questions.

Cresting in the late 1960s, this omnibus term underwent critical examination and was significantly redirected by Bowlby's definition of "attachment" as a fierce, highly valent, exclusive connection that was specifically concerned with making proximate attachments, primarily during childhood but also later in life. "Attachment" has thereafter been distinguished from dependency, which is currently reserved for facultative interpersonal connections, more readily transferable and accompanied by less energy and intensity.

The term "dependency" has undergone another important modification—in being expanded to "interdependency." This word emphasizes the interactional nature of reciprocal behaviors emerging out of affiliative relationships in which partners need and use each other in various ways. Although not eliminating dependency as an internal trait, the concepts and methodologies connected to interactional formulations have made it possible to visualize the complex ways in which persons actually lean on each other and provide support throughout the lifespan. Other qualitative distinctions have been useful in specifying the qualities of interdependent relations, as in Lebra's (1976) examination of dependencies of obligation, patronage, indulgence, and pity. In that she writes from the Japanese perspective, her classification has particular utility for this book, which is interested in qualitative differences in the description and formulation of terms concerning dependency in Japan and the United States.

The Western cultural biases concerning adult dependency as a negative experience is both implicit and explicit in much social-scientific, social-philosophic, and clinical literature. Explicitly, the values concerned with autonomy, independence, independency, self-actualization, and individuality are ceaselessly promoted in aphorisms, actions, and statements concerning expected, age-appropriate behaviors. Just as explicitly, the negative consequences attached to inflated states of dependency are articulated in psychiatric and social-philosophical literature. The more implicit consequences of this Western focus on individuality and the avoidance of dependency are also conceptually apparent in the formulations popularized in Western psychology. These are consistently concerned with examining the concept of either "self" or "personality" in terms of traits, dispositions, temperaments, and thoughts heuristically seen as residing *within* specific persons. The contrast with Eastern psychosocial formulations will be addressed later in the book and is apparent in the cross-cultural differences in characterization of "self." Some of the ways in which psychoanalytic theories have also dealt with these implicit presuppositions will be addressed in the next chapter. Contrasting modes of defining and explaining personality —pivoting on the central issues of dependency and interdependency—will be the subject of subsequent chapters concerning Japanese culture and childrearing, including Professor Doi's work regarding *amae*.

Notes

1. The words "dependence" and "dependency" represent two versions of spelling for the "the state of something leaning on or hanging from something else." However, in North American usage, the word "dependen*ce*" tends to be selected for certain obligate relations between people and *things*, as in "She has a problem of drug dependence." The word "dependen*cy*" is more likely to be used in defining human relations or specifying personality traits, as in "For her age she shows entirely too much dependency." These connotational distinctions are not uniform, and the words remain technically interchangeable. British authors (e.g., Ronald Fairbairn and Donald Winnicott) prefer the word "dependence," as does Takeo Doi. In this volume, the more popular American term "dependency" will ordinarily be used.

2. In all societies, the scheduled reduction of infantile dependency is achieved through cultural and familial prescriptions that dictate increasing responsibility for dressing, cleansing, and feeding, for independent play, and for toleration of relatively unsupervised activity. Degrees of increasing self-sufficiency are inculcated through reduction of direct supervision from caregivers who promote the capacity for emotional self-control and accommodation to public situations. Throughout this progression, there is a tension between the desire to remain dependent and the challenge of accepting more sublimated rewards that accompany the attainment of more mature levels of performance and competence. At the other end of the lifespan, the imposition of lowered capacity for independency is often experienced as a reluctant loss of prior competence, sometimes evoking feelings of helplessness and even shame.

3. The literary use of the word "instinct" as a "basic drive" or "intrinsic need system" continues to appear as a generalistic expression long after it has been scientifically discarded in zoology. The term loosely implies sets of biologically inherited "fixed action patterns" that are more or less automatically activated by both internal and environmental stimuli, and that produce specific and relatively unmodifiable behavioral patterns. Although having some application to certain behaviors in lower species, application of this to human behavior is generally regarded as invalid.

4. Although the dependent qualities of "obligation," "patronage," "indulgence," and "pity" emerge in many relationships, some of these are most clearly encountered in relatively closed institutions (religious orders, military organizations, jails, hospitals). These also are clearest in fixed,

obligate relations such as between master and servant. In these latter situations, interdependent obligations are established on the basis of overt hierarchical status in the context of stipulated duties, responsibilities, and rewards. Most naturalistic dependency relations in the real world are not so clear cut, tending to fluctuate over time and to be continually modified by circumstantial factors.

5. Within the rhetoric of Western social-philosophic descriptions characterizing "independency" among adults, a gender bias is persistently unexamined. As in virtually all societies, adolescent and adult women characteristically perform most domestic services and childrearing. They also are held responsible for the emotional tone of the household. This operationally creates a system wherein children and husbands (and sometimes other kin) are *dependent* on the adult female, who sustains these individuals and provides nurturance and comfort. She may or may not receive complementary dependency (on the basis of protection and financial support) but rarely has prerogatives for reciprocal need satisfaction involved with domestic or household duties.

6. The psychotherapeutic treatment of "excessive" dependency requires addressing the revision of the patient's instrumental task orientations, along with the underlying feelings about relinquishing the rewards of helplessness. Successful treatment involves transferring dependency and helplessness from real-life transactions into the therapeutic relationship, where prior relationships and feelings may be productively examined for factors that induce indecisiveness and the need for others to control. This still leaves the requirement of having to resolve the transitional dependency on the therapist, which is ideally done through the interpretation of the transference. This may be difficult to achieve in expressive psychotherapies where the therapist actually has provided overt support and dependency during the treatment—as contrasted to psychoanalysis, where such requests for support are almost always interpreted rather than fulfilled.

CHAPTER 2

Psychoanalytic Formulations Connected to Dependency

This chapter will examine how the concepts of dependency, interdependency, and attachment are addressed in traditional psychoanalytic theory. Perhaps the most interesting fact is that dependency has not attained the status of a central explanatory concept in metapsychological writings, nor has it become tightly formulated in a direct way that relates to other concepts and explanations. One might ask how such a ubiquitous and significant characteristic of human relatedness became overlooked amid the comprehensive formulations generated by Freud and subsequent psychoanalytic authors. The answer is that dependency (and interdependency) has been diffused and appears as an underlying component in a number of theories addressing psychological development, function, disability, and rehabilitation. As various aspects of psychoanalytic theory are carefully examined, dependency emerges as it were in bas relief: implicitly present but rarely stipulated, and moreover subordinated to other technical, metapsychological explanations.

Background

Parens and Saul (1971) are responsible for belatedly but comprehensively confronting both the psychic and behavioral manifestations of dependency in psychoanalytic formulations about psychological structure and function. They carefully examined Freud's writings, where the term was explicitly used in a descriptive, qualitative manner—notably in relation to the infant/mother relationship and the manifest helplessness of early human development. They describe dependency as having two separable but interrelated coordinates. The first of these is concerned with *dependency on an object*; that is, on a person or persons for the gratifications of needs. This coordinate is defined as "nonautoerotic," and described as urgently focused on eliciting nutrition, tactile contact, comfort, warmth, and security. It putatively is driven by the "ego instincts." The second coordinate seeks dependency for the more complex satisfaction of what have traditionally been defined as "libidinal needs," earliest divided between sensual and affectional, but later acquiring more refined expression as ego-developmental needs "wherein the child turns to the object for training, . . . motor coordination, in communication, general skills and for education" (Parens and Saul 1971, 143).

These authors carefully trace the characteristics of psychological dependency from infancy through old age. They illustrate the changing need satisfactions over the life course, examined according to categories of physiological, libidinal, and ego-developmental needs. (Libidinal needs are subdivided into "sensual" and "affectional.") These needs evolve by way of a biologically and socially regulated progression from the obligate dependency of earliest infancy, through an intermediate state of emotional self-reliance, eventually reaching a reciprocal interdependency attained in adult object relationships. Picking up on some of their own earlier work, they describe the psychological dimension of this progression in terms of achieving libidinal "inner sustainment" (Saul 1970; Parens 1970).

The satisfaction of these needs, and the processes through which they proceed, are portrayed as unconscious in two ways. First, they are manifestly unconscious in neonates, infants, and young children, who are oblivious of these processes. Second, these needs are unconscious in the sense of constituting a group of structural components that function largely out of awareness regardless of age.

Although Freud did not use "dependency" as a major conceptual or constructional term, there nevertheless are 383 references to the word (or a compounded expression) cited in the *Concordance to the Standard Edition* (Guttman 1984). In many of these, the word is used to define a functional relativity between two or more people involved in some form of affiliative, interdependent association.

Less frequently, it is used to indicate a dependent relation between a person and either "things" or "ideas."

In the German language, the word *anlehnung* semantically means "leaning on," and is close to the English etymological definition of dependency as "to hang from or lean on." Both definitions portray a connectedness between something *inferior* (weaker or lower), which either "hangs down from" or "leans up against" something that is *superior* (i.e., higher or stronger). Freud's use of *anlehnung* frequently referred to dependent connections between infant and mother, infant and parents, sons and fathers, children with older siblings, and the relationships between patients and their physicians or psychoanalysts. In his initial discussion of dependency, Freud (1914) introduced the term "libidinized object" to describe an internal structure that connected with or "depended" upon an outside, human object.[1] Albeit in a discursive rather than tightly formulated sense, Freud also described dependency as existing between individuals in their connections to ideologies, beliefs, gods, or myths.

The important 1914 essay *On Narcissism* contains Freud's earliest formulations that by inference are connected to dependency. Written when Freud was beleaguered by the intellectual defections of both Jung and Adler, this exposition was composed to explain the process of human relatedness using the freshly introduced concept of "libidinal object." In response to Adler's radical social formulations, Freud's explanation of the nature of human relatedness included a differentiation—for the first time—between "ego libido" and "object libido." This induced him to define the concept of narcissism as an intermediate stage occurring between a putative period of neonatal autofixation, and the later period characterized by investment in the external world through the gradual development of object love. Freud also attempted to build on his original drive hypothesis through specifying the "sexual instincts" and "ego instincts," speculating that the first autoerotic satisfactions were experienced in conjunction with vital functions serving self-preservation.

Because of this . . . the sexual instincts were at the outset attached to the satisfaction of the ego instincts; only later did they become independent of these, and even then, we have an indication of that original attachment in the fact that the persons who are connected with the child's feeding, care, and protection become his earliest sexual objects: that is to say, in the first instance his mother or a substitute for her. (Freud 1914, 87)

He called this relationship and source of object choice *anaclytic* or "attachment type" *(anlehnungstypus)*.[2]

Freud recurrently but indirectly addressed the issue of infantile dependency in references to the protracted period of childhood helplessness mentioned incidentally in numerous articles. Freud also related the exorbitant anxiety underlying some psychoneurotic conditions to protracted infantile helplessness, specifically to the threatened disconnection from the earliest security object (Freud 1931). The psychoanalytic formulations for this process postulated a behaviorally induced event (involving helplessness), becoming an affective mental event (the experience of anxiety concerning helplessness), which was then constructed into a psychic representation —symbolically characterized by dependency.

In reviewing the applications of dependency to psychoanalytic theory, Parens and Saul (1971) faced the dilemma of trying to give form to a concept that was only indirectly formulated by Freud as his corpus of theory emerged over a long career of scholarship and commentary. Some of the internal inconsistencies, notably between "id-psychological" and "ego-psychological" versions of metapsychology are particularly problematic for psychoanalytic theorists (Settlage 1980). The problem is that the significance of biological and social dependency was noted by Freud, but explained in a nonrigorous manner as being connected to the poorly defined and nonpsychologized "ego instincts." Freud's more serious treatment of this powerful trend was deferred until 1923, in dealing with the concept of psychic structure *(The Ego and the Id)*; in 1926 in its relation to anxiety as loss of cathected object ("Fear of Loss of the Object"), and in the primordial roots of religious belief in 1927 and 1930 (in *The Future of an Illusion* and *Civilization and Its Discontents*). In all of these accounts, the original drive theory was preserved, which identified the origins and nature of dependency as a strong but *derived* motive, developed secondarily through experiences of the frustration of libidinal drive.

In Freud's writings, then, we find the thesis that the life-preservative function of dependence on the object is universal in man . . . the recurrence of need forges the cathexis of the object and dependence upon it and secures the formation of persisting object relations. . . . Thus helplessness leading to anxiety and, in turn, to dependence on the object—and then on the object's love—is a principal adaptive sequence of earliest childhood. The child early *learns* to seek shelter from mounting anxiety by turning to the object. With this seeking, passive dependence becomes active dependence.

With the introduction of anxiety between helplessness and dependence on the object, the dependence becomes libidinized. (Parens and Saul 1971, 22; italics mine)

In this restatement of Freud's position, these authors identify an original "passive drive" (or "object hunger") in the ego-instinctual, infant/mother relationship. This dependent connection is then seen as becoming converted through learning into an "active dependence," which at that point becomes libidinized. This hypothesized progression makes the critical distinction that "active dependency" occurs at a symbolical level and comes into being as a product of anxiety. Moreover, it suggests that "active dependency" is learned through experiencing frustration of libidinal drive. Although internally consistent, this formulation seems inconclusive, and not in keeping with present-day theories of infantile development that posit observable active systems at and even before the moment of birth. These systems are automatically engaged to secure "attachment," and to instigate nurturance from the maternal object (as formulated in Emde 1980; Stern 1985).

According to Parens and Saul (1971), dependency is conceptualized in psychoanalytic theory as a "learned" resultant derived from a primary libidinal drive, operating differentially throughout various stages of development and particularly conspicuous during infancy and early childhood. Within psychoanalytic writings, the use of "dependency" as a fundamental constructional term is relatively rare. When mentioned, it is connected with ego-instinctual, pregenital activities (being fed, cared for, held, groomed, cleaned, kept warm and protected). It is not ordinarily associated with genital awareness or behaviors, which are seen as directly driven by the sexual instincts and ordinarily identified as lust or "love." A distinction—really a polarity—is thus made between tenderness and sexuality (or sensuality) in categorically separating pregenital from genital drive expressions, and their accompanying modes of human relationship.

Both within and outside psychoanalysis, dependency is generally defined in the context of a nonsexualized intimacy—although it may simultaneously be present as a component in the relationship between partners who are incidentally involved sexually. As in developmental psychology, dependency relationships in psychoanalysis are encountered in a broad number of contexts and embedded in a variety of hypothetical formulations. Dependency relationships are intrinsic within instinct theory, in the psychosexual phases of development and in superego and ego-ideal formation. They are even more explicit in descriptions of object relations and separation/individuation. They also are integral in transference phenomena and in explanations of some clinical conditions.

Dependency and the Drive/Structure Model

Beginning with Freud's (1914) theorizations concerning the differentiation between the ego and sexual instincts, dependency phenomena were described as manifestations of patterned, intrapsychic energy (i.e., drives) explained as striving for satiation and tension relief. Seen first as fused, the sexual and ego instincts were described as becoming differentiated during the first year of life—the ego instincts remaining mainly connected to self-preservative survival, while the sexual instincts underwent a progressive series of object cathexes coordinated with the child's psychic assimilation of an increasingly complex social and physical reality. Teleologically, Freud connected the sexual instincts to a biological drive for species preservation, and the ego instincts to individual survival.

Currently, drive or "instinct" theory is critically regarded as unsatisfactory by a number of psychoanalytic theoreticians (as in Gedo 1979; Eagle 1987). Greenberg and Mitchell (1983) have made an historical and conceptual review of the topic using a drive/structure model to trace the evolution of explanations accounting for patterns of energy that underlie and activate human behavior.

Theories of *action* (or "behavior") in the disciplines of philosophy, psychology, psychoanalysis, and social science usually posit the presence of some organized internal forces that engage and direct human behavior. These theories often employ terms for putative psychic structures that are seen as having effects on somatic functions ("body"), on symbolical representations ("mind"), and, ultimately, on actual social relations ("behavior"). Seeking structuralist explanations, Freud attempted to embed his drive theory in biologically determined structures (not topically or physiologically specified) that mechanistically sought goals related to individual survival, pleasure, growth, and development. Thus, biologically based structural explanations were persistently retained despite Freud's acknowledged inability to establish a "scientific metapsychology" at the turn of the century (Freud 1895).

Greenberg and Mitchell (1983) address one of the fundamental conflicts concerning the rift between innate, *structural* explanations of psychic drives and the learned, *interpretive* explanations of the relationship between drives and their objects. The problem resides in trying to accommodate to psychoanalysis as a metapsychological science of symbols and meanings, and to psychoanalysis as a biological science of drives and single-minded motives. These authors ecumenically conclude that a biology of motives and a psychology of intentions can produce independent and separate explanations that are not so much incompatible as parallel.

We suggest . . . that the distinction between psychoanalysis as a natural science and as an interpretive discipline is spurious. The very principles Freud thought explanatory in the mechanistic sense also provide an interpretive thrust; his theory of mechanism is a theory of meaning. Seen this way, the drives are not only the *mechanisms* of the mind, they are also its *contents*. (Greenberg and Mitchell 1983, 23; italics original)

However, the controversy continues partly because of the reductionistic and overly simplified nature of the original drive/structure model. In one of Freud's early dual instinct theories (Freud 1915), all behaviors were reducible to governance by sexual and self-preservative instincts. In a crucial extension of drive theory, Freud added the "aggressive instinct" (1923, 1930), seen as coexisting with sexual instincts and operating in their ultimate (biological) goal as a "death instinct"—that is, one that seeks obliteration or psychic entropy. Freud's attempt to balance the primary instincts through addition of aggression ("destrudo") has since its introduction met with criticism and only qualified acceptance. As Greenberg and Mitchell point out, aggressive instincts were not given a developmental significance by Freud comparable to that of libido; nor were they as rigorously applied to theories of neurosis, with the exception of repetition compulsion and obsessional conditions. They also discuss the problems with Freud's turn-of-the-century views on the constancy principle, which held that the ultimate aim of innate biological drives was to achieve a state of lowered tension—ideally a condition of "zero stimulation." This principle is metaphorically analogous to sexual (orgasmic) physiology, but grossly inapplicable to the ego instincts (e.g., breathing). Moreover, it is incompatible with later neurophysiological and neuropsychological explanations of central nervous system activity.

Nevertheless, some contemporary clinicians and drive theorists still conceptualize human behavior as psychologically reducible to the dual instincts of aggression and libido, operating singly or in combination as basic activators of motivation. In this view, social and communicative aspects of interaction, such as love, empathy, dependency, or altruism, are conceptualized as combinations of the object cathexes of the drive systems of ontologically separate creatures. Social ties and affiliations, regardless of their urgency (as in the neonate), would still be formulated as secondary drives representing libidinal, intrapsychic object cathexes that are derivatively converted, sublimated, or channeled into social behaviors.

Dependency and the Psychosexual Stages of Development

The psychosexual stages represent the earliest formulation of a consolidated psychoanalytic theory of development. This theory flowed out of Freud's descriptions of infantile sexuality, later more concisely chronologized by Abraham (1927) and summarized by Fenichel (1945). The psychosexual stages became not only a metapsychological theory explaining the developmental sequencing of behavior during infancy and early childhood, but also constituted formulations for subsequent periods of growth and development in latency and puberty. Equally important, these stages became the basis for a theory of conflict, using the concept of *fixation* to explain psychological regression on the one hand, and character inclination on the other (Reich 1949 [1933]). Initially the various stages were formulated in intrapsychic terms as a libidinous drive evolving through a succession of erogenous zones. Later, the concomitant extrapsychic features of these stages received attention. In response to some of Freud's early work in ego psychology, social dimensions were formulated in object-relations terms that parallel the physiological foci of the psychosexual stages. Erikson's (1950, 1959) formulations were particularly illuminating in characterizing processes of ego development in both childhood and adolescence.

These stages are deceptively simple and are concisely summarized in Fenichel (1945). Freud's *Three Essays on Sexuality* (1905) characterized an initial period of unfocused ("polymorphous perverse") sexuality containing elements of what later would be technically considered "partial instincts." These were organized from birth to about age two around an *oral stage* directly coordinated with nutritional needs, but extending beyond this to constitute a general incorporative mode, metaphorically "sucking in" the environment. Later, this was theorized to include an ambivalent chewing or spitting out of objects experienced as undesirable. Relationally, the oral substages have been regarded as constituting the highwater mark of human dependency, reflecting a universally normative infantile helplessness for that period of life.

An *anal stage* was described as ascendant in its influence from the second through the fourth year of life, characterized by a libidinal focus on elimination, manifested by a hostile expulsive phase, followed by an ambivalent, retentive substage. The adaptive and relational atmosphere of this period has been characterized as concerned with issues of control—psychoanalytically concentrating on excretion, but importantly connected to muscular coordination, control of emotionality, and, finally, a degree of control over the social and physical environment. The characteristics of dependency during this period involve an increasing awareness of psychological, physical, and social *in*dependency, not intrinsically addressed in the original theory.

The *phallic stage* is described as predominating from ages four to six and consists of a concentration of sexual pleasure in a heightened awareness of the genital region. It was postulated that boys, stimulated by awareness of this potential pleasure, experienced castration anxiety accompanying the expectation of punishment through their competition with father in the triadic relationship of mother, son, and father. In girls this same awakening of genital awareness has traditionally been explained as evoking "penis envy," purportedly as a reaction to fantasied disfigurement and inferiority.

The phallic phase is succeeded by a *genital stage* began at around five or six years of age. This stage follows the completion of shifts in libidinal cathexes toward both parents, reorganized to permit the eventual attainment of "genital primacy"—although in no sense always or uniformly accomplished. In both sexes—although in different ways and with different consequences—oedipal resolutions involve the renunciation of mother as a genital sexual object. For boys, the renunciation is achieved through repression and ideally is accompanied by a conversion of anxious competition with father to an identification with him. Girls also renounce mother as a potential sexual object and repress their sexual desires for father pending the redirection of their drives later in life. Such a reorganization of drive objects for both boys and girls is ordinarily a requirement for the initiation of *latency*. Latency occupies a period approximately between six and twelve, during which overt sexuality is relatively repressed and suppressed—although there are both individual and cultural variations to this pattern. The relational shifts during the oedipal transition have been regarded as highly significant for subsequent maturity, gender identity, and social competence. This includes the beginning consolidation of sexual identification, and a significant change in the exclusive attachments and degrees of dependency on both mother and father. Other versions of these relational consequences will be discussed in subsequent chapters from both psychoanalytic and cross-cultural perspectives.

The psychosexual stages represent a deductive rather than an experimentally derived scheme. The manifest behaviors typical for each stage are expected to vary according to specific maternal, environmental, cultural, and situational factors. Sequential stages overlap with each other, and the residual effects of each stage continue to be influential throughout the life course.

The consequences for changes in dependency status during these successive stages are not highlighted in either the original or subsequent theories. Broadly speaking, dependency is highest in the earliest stages and gradually diminishes due to the interacting factors of growth, development, and the socializing impact of "the average expectable environment" (Hartmann 1958). Paradoxically, as psychological omnipotence becomes attenuated through maturation and normative socialization, the child's awareness of dependent needs on powerful family figures increases. Such awareness becomes particularly prominent during the oedipal period, as the nature of these primary attachments undergoes potentially conflictual reorganization.

Dependency and the Development of Ego Ideal and Superego

Dependency phenomena are also implicit in theorizations connected with ego-ideal and superego formation. Freud (1914) identified the ego ideal as a residue of and replacement for the lost narcissism of earliest childhood, "in which the child was his own ideal." He also identified the incipient development of conscience reflecting the critical influence of parents, "conveyed to the child through the medium of vocal admonitions as well as other injunctions." These were observed to accompany socialization, which in all cultures acts to abridge infantile demandingness, and gradually implant internal constraints. Furer, in Goodman (1969), also cites Freud's *Group Psychology and the Analysis of the Ego* (1921) as extending ego-ideal formation beyond the parental demands to the general extrapsychic environment of social requirements and cultural restrictions embedded as part of the "reality principle."

Hartmann and Loewenstein (1968), in a review article on superego formation, also see this structure emerging as an attempt to retain the omnipotence and entitlement of the earlier state of primary narcissism. This is perpetuated through the projection of strength and power onto the now partially internalized parental images—particularly that of mother. The residues of these early projections operate in both positive and negative ways during subsequent development. Positively, they function as elements of "ego ideal" in stimulating strivings for perfection, achievement, and mastery. Negatively, they function as a critical superego providing prohibitory sanctions against potentially conflictual drive representations. Although acknowledging that preoedipal ingredients were significant in the timing and shaping of ego ideal and superego, these authors suggest that the oedipal resolution is most ascendant in the first phasic completion of superego formation. Looking at the superego holistically, they state, "Something of both the loving and the aggressive relations to the parents is preserved in this agency. In particular, this agency offers one of the main avenues for dealing with one's own aggression, namely by turning it against oneself" (Hartmann and Loewenstein 1968, 69). The implications of aggression toward self will be discussed later in terms of the proclivity for abasement among Japanese.

Hammerman (1965) cites both Lampl-DeGroot (1962) and Spitz (1958), who, "note the ego ideal as pregenital in origin, and as a wish-fulfillment agency which provides the child with a basis for self-esteem derived from narcissistic gratifications and identifications with the gratifying mother" (1965, 328). He concludes that the affect of shame arises in reaction to a threatened regression to a state of infantile helplessness. Conflicts reflecting inflated ego ideal during both adolescence and adulthood are seen as releasing embarrassment, shame, and disgust in regard to the self-consciousness concerning the emergence of exhibitionistic, pregenital drives. Using a psychosocial analysis, Erikson (1950) postulated that losing or failing to achieve "competence" in terms of psychosocial and psychosexual maturity mobilized shame originating from latent conflicts around regression to infantile helplessness. Here, again, the contrasting manner in which Japanese handle both shame and dependency is most conspicuous and will be addressed later.

Although not organized around dependency per se, ego ideal and superego are presented as being shaped and refined through a socialization process in the context of intimate, obligate relationships with parents, other family members, and ultimately the outside world. Moreover, these internalized regulatory forces are explained as periodically recurring in conflicts between drives and their internalized drive objects. Such intrapsychic explanations underplay the contributions of social and cultural determinants of embarrassment and guilt, and lead to presumptions of a universal structural and chronological basis for developmental progression. However, crediting the crucial effects of social reality on superego formation has been explicit since its original formulation (Freud 1921, 1923). Nevertheless, until the refinement of more recent object-relations theories, explanations for the impact of society on the individual were tilted toward the operations of intrapsychic processes, where society merely stimulated an innately determined superego structure operating to constrain libidinal and aggressive impulses within a tripartite personality system. Given this emphasis, the dependent consequences of the actual social interconnectedness have remained relatively unarticulated.[3]

Dependency, Interdependency, and Object-Relations Theory

Freud (1923) is responsible for the introduction of object-relations theory through the formulation of a tripartite structural model of human personality comprised of id, ego, and superego. This formulation introduced the necessity for progressive definitions of the psychological mechanisms regulating the relations between internal drives and external reality. Even at its onset, this addition to theory had consequences that were not compatible with the previous id-psychological explanations. With this advent of ego psychology, conflict theory was refocused onto a consideration of intrapsychic tensions between and among three structural "compartments": ego, id, and superego. Although simplified explanations of these compartments are seriously questioned now, the *ego* was formulated as arising developmentally out of an undifferentiated id, with which it subsequently was in conflict. Similarly, the ego was seen as colliding with and being shaped by the reality-oriented superego, which operated both unconsciously, in directly opposing libidinous and aggressive drives, and consciously, in channeling the ego's expression of otherwise threatening impulses.

Following 1923, extensions of ego psychology were made in detailing the patterns developed by ego structures in the process of character formation (Reich 1949 [1933]), and as a compendium of unconscious defense mechanisms that operated to filter, divert, o refine unregulated drives (Anna Freud 1946). Hartmann (1958 [1939]) significantly expanded the functional territory of the ego by establishing the legitimacy of executive (action-oriented) and adaptive (socially integrative) functions alongside the earlier defensive functions. This expansion succeeded in upgrading the significance of ego operations as part of a more comprehensive personality system including conscious adaptations and social connections. However, this system still retained the topological and dynamic features of traditional drive and structural theories within an integrated body of metapsychology (Rappaport 1960).

A number of theorists have subsequently contributed to a more detailed definition of "internal objects," which are conceptualized as fusions of intrapsychic drives in their combination with psychic representations of both "self objects" and "external objects." These are described as being unconsciously (and automatically) formed through processes of incorporation and internalization, later being aggregated into clusters of unconscious and conscious identifications. Melanie Klein (1946) is credited with recognizing the splitting of internal objects in regard to their status as partial, distorted incorporations of threatening external objects and situations. Following Klein, Fairbairn (1954) radically placed object relations at the epicenter of his theory of personality, replacing libidinal drive as a prime mover with a drive for "infantile dependence." He conceptualized the need to connect to external objects as a primary, directly socializing force, rather than as a secondary drive. Although not the first revisionist to promote the importance of social or interpersonal connections, Fairbairn was distinctive in proposing a systematic, although adumbrated, psychoanalytic theory of development, drives, and psychopathology, subsequently clarified and extended by Guntrip (1961).

Other clinician/theorists have been associated with the development of object-relations theory (well summarized in Kernberg 1980;

Greenberg and Mitchell 1983; and Buckley 1986). Some of these have focused on the developmental deficiencies clinically accentuated in adult borderline and narcissistic character disorders. In a more radical version, Kohut (1971) posited *narcissism* as a central intrapsychic component whose expression is directed toward both external objects and self-objects. Kohut's description of both the development and psychoanalytic treatment of narcissistic conditions has emphasized relational connections, and used the concept of "selfobject" in a manner that is difficult to integrate with traditional drive/structural, psychoanalytic theories. The ramifications of Kohut's restructuring of theory have occasioned strong counter-reactions (Kernberg 1972, 1974; Wallerstein 1983; Greene 1984).

Kohut's formulations on self give an unmistakable interpersonal and intersubjective tilt to psychoanalytic theory. In this sense he is the most recent and prominent in a succession of schismatic writers (Jung, Adler, Horney, Sullivan, Fromm, Winnicott, Fairbairn) who have shifted, revised, or discarded traditional drive and structural theories in favor of more psychosocial explanations of human personality. Each of these theorists has met with a stiff rejection from mainstream psychoanalysis. The persistent omission of dependency as a central factor in metapsychological explanations of personality probably is partly due to defensive refutation of the schismatic theorists.

The fact that the socially dependent characteristics of human relations have been most conspicuously addressed by revisionist elements in the field may partly account for their continuing to be only indirectly acknowledged in conventionally accepted psychoanalytic explanations. However, of equal significance is the difficulty involved in formulating a system that can plausibly speculate about the complex connections between intrapsychic and extrapsychic structures. Kernberg's comments capture this complexity:

In broadest terms, psychoanalytic object-relations theory represents the psychoanalytic study of the nature and origin of interpersonal relations, and of the nature and origin of intrapsychic structures deriving from, fixating, modifying, and reactivating past internalized relations with others in the context of present interpersonal relations. Psychoanalytic object-relations theory focuses upon the internalization of interpersonal relations, their contribution to the normal and pathological ego and superego developments, and the mutual influences of intrapsychic and interpersonal object relations. (Kernberg 1976, 56)[4]

Dependency, Interdependency, and Separation/Individuation

Mahler's description of the four substages of separation/individuation has deepened psychoanalytic understanding of the early years of human development. Although formulated in a manner following the traditional patterns of psychosexual progression, Mahler's view of maturation is coordinated with changes in the nature of the *relationship* between the infant, the mother, and ultimately to the child's interaction with the extrapsychic world.

Mahler and Gosliner (1955) metaphorically designated the psychological quality of the infant/mother relationship during the first few months of life as "a normal phase of human symbiosis." Two phases were described as traversed during the first few months of life: the normal autistic and the symbolic. During this early period, a fusion of identity with the maternal object was hypothesized, while the psychological atmosphere of the infant's consciousness was characterized as one of omnipotence (Ferenczi 1950). This "phase of normal autism" was depicted as gradually relinquished through a relational process of "growing-away" (Mahler 1972).

Growing away is described as

a lifelong separation-individuation . . . since inherent in every step of independent functioning is a minimal threat of object loss. Consciousness of self and absorption without awareness of self are the two polarities through which we move with varying ease and with varying degrees of alternation or simultaneity. (Mahler 1972, 335)

The first substage of *differentiation* takes place between the second and eighth month and is associated with increasing discrimination of visual, auditory, and spatial orientations. With increasing perceptual discrimination, cognitive and operational differentiation of the social and physical environment becomes progressively apparent. This includes the appearance of the social smile, recognition of favored objects, cooing, and cooperative playing. At about seven months, stranger anxiety is noted by developmental investigators observing infants in a number of different countries and cultures. Also, after about six months a strong exploratory hunger emerges, manifested by curiosity about the texture, shape, taste, and size of objects. Psychoanalytically, this curiosity is regarded as representing ego drives displaying both adaptive and executive expression.

Differentiation is followed by a *practicing* substage, beginning at seven months and lasting until about sixteen months. The first part of this is characterized by the infant's capacity to move away from the mother by crawling, climbing up things, and righting itself. The second part of the substage is manifested by acquiring the ability to stand upright and begin independent walking. Concomitant psychological development permits brief expeditions away from security contacts and the progressive expansion of ego drives connected to curiosity and exploration.[5] The manner in which children are encouraged to remain in close physical contact to adults or siblings follows cultural preferences that influence the frequency, duration, and extent of practicing behavior. The implications of closer and more protracted contact with caregivers in Japanese settings will be subsequently highlighted in terms of increased encouragement and tolerance for dependency.

As a third subphase of separation-individuation *rapprochement* is evident between sixteen and twenty-five months, extending toward what Mahler terms *progression toward object constancy*. Rapprochement begins at the time of complete mastery of upright locomotion when the child no longer devotes conscious attention to walking, and thus is free to experience more independent exploration and social engagement. An important psychological component of rapprochement is the paradoxical development of increased anxiety about the lack of mother's presence. Previously this had not been prominent in the self-contained smugness of the practicing substage. As Mahler puts it,

There is a noticeable waning of his previous imperviousness to frustration, as well as of his relative obliviousness to the mother's presence . . . it has already begun to dawn on the junior toddler that the world is *not* his oyster; that he must cope with it more or less "on his own," very often as a relatively helpless, small, and separate individual. (Mahler 1972, 336)

Accompanying the awareness of separation from mother, this substage is concerned with the mastery of a partial independency from her as an object of security. This is accomplished through tolerating physical separations and enjoying solo play and activity away from mother. This mastery is facilitated through the refinement of oral communication, and consolidation of an internal mental life capable of experiencing coherent thought and fantasy. This consolidation of mental life is accompanied by the capacity to recollect the past, and to predict future events, permitting the child to conduct increasingly purposeful and strategic object relations.

Progression toward Object Constancy

The acquisition of *object constancy* takes place between twenty-five and thirty-six months of juvenile life. Object constancy is based on the stabilization of internal representations of experience with the primary love objects. It is defined as "denoting the individual's capacity to differentiate between objects, and to maintain a relationship to one specific object regardless of whether needs are being satisfied or not" (Edgcumbe and Burgner 1972, 283). Directly pertinent to dependency and interdependency, these authors listed the following criteria connected with object constancy:

the capacity for neutralization and fusion of drives directed to a specific object, the capacity to maintain a positive (loving) emotional attachment to a particular object regardless of frustration or satisfaction of needs, drive pressures, and wishes; the capacity to tolerate ambivalent feelings toward the same object; the capacity to value the object for qualities not connected with its ability to satisfy needs and provide drive satisfaction. (Edgcumbe and Burgner 1972, 284)

In terms of dependency, the progression toward object constancy involves a gradual reduction of obligate helplessness as the child tolerates visual and physical separations, accepts periods of frustration, and renounces demands for immediate gratification or solace. As part of this progression, Winnicott's (1953) focus on *transitional objects* has concentrated attention on aspects of development where physical objects and motor behaviors are employed as substitutional "maternal objects" in smoothing over the separation experience and moving on toward object constancy. Following his lead, a number of psychoanalytic researchers have interpreted the use of various objects (dolls, thumbs, blankets, pacifiers) as well as behaviors (rocking, sucking objects, vocalizing) as representations that nostalgically recreate the security of earlier periods of dependency. A parallel but more complex substitution is exemplified in the companionship provided by imaginary playmates.[6]

By definition, object constancy permits the clearer differentiation of internal objects from their external referents, and is accompanied by the capacity to make accurate predictions concerning navigation within social and physical environments. Object constancy also permits the critical differentiation of *self-object*, composed of a series of internalizations clustering around the individual's own characteristics, temperament, abilities, and orientations toward action. The initial consolidation of earliest object constancy is followed by a process of continuous modification as the child encounters experiences that alter and add to previous internalizations both of self and external objects.

Some Criticisms of Mahler's Theories

Mahler's contributions to psychoanalytic developmental theory have generally met with acceptance—particularly in their clinical applications. Possibly the most attractive feature in separation-individuation is the chronology that identifies discontinuities (i.e., substages) in the reciprocal and bilateral object relationship between infant and mother. Although explicitly concerned with object relations, Mahler's formulations are only mildly interactional. In fact, another way of accounting for the popular acceptance of her model is that much of her descriptive terminology superficially fits into traditional developmental explanations in terms of drive theory and psychosexual stages. However, as pointed out by Milton Kline (1981), Mahler's attempt to straddle id- and ego-psychological explanations carries along some anachronistic conceptions of the psychology of early life postulated in earlier theories. Summarizing contradictory evidence from current research on infancy, Kline (1981) undercuts Mahler's formulations concerning a putative period of "natural autism" by citing reports that reflect patterned physiological reactivity present from the moment of birth. He also cites Emde and Robinson (1979), whose survey of recent research disputes the probability of early infantile "passivity," "undifferentiation," and "tendency toward drive reduction."[7]

Kline (1981) also challenges the literal meaning of "symbiosis" as a true psychological *fusion* that necessarily precedes separation and (ultimate) individuation. Peterfreund (1978) has also focused criticism on Mahler's use of the traditional conceptions of "primary narcissism," "omnipotence," and "absence of boundaries." Another anachronism has been the persistent attribution of "hallucinatory experiences" to the infant, partly based on the clearly disproven notion of a "stimulus barrier," which supposedly prohibited or retarded ordinary sensory intake and perception during early neonatal life. He sums up his general arguments by saying,

This frame of reference naturally leads to the idea that the psychological birth of the individual does not coincide with the biological birth, an idea inconsistent with everything now understood about evolutionary theory, the genetic code, and everything learned from sophisticated studies of infants. (Peterfreund 1978, 438)

Neither Kline (1981) nor Peterfreund (1978) mention another general criticism of Mahler—namely that her interpretations are largely based on observation of selected subjects in Boston and Great Britain—leaving open the question about variability according to cultural and social class factors. Pavenstedt's (1965) descriptions of Japanese mothers and infants offer some striking contrasts to both the quality and timing of Mahler's substages. These contrasts will be addressed in several subsequent chapters.

Dependency/Interdependency; Transference/Countertransference

Until recently the manifestations of dependency have been largely implicit in psychoanalytic descriptions of transference and countertransference. Orr (1954) critically summarized transference as having three dimensions: first, as a universal capacity to relate symbolically to other persons; second, as an exaggerated symbolical relationship developed by patients during psychoanalytic treatment; and third, as a "transference neurosis" consisting of patients' misidentifications of their analyst, who is psychologically experienced by them as exaggerated replicas of reactions to early significant persons.

Countertransference was initially defined only as the analyst's distortions, which were sympathetically drawn out in reaction to the transference distortions of the patient. Countertransference was earliest seen only as an error in technique, but later definitions have paralleled Orr's (1954) descriptions of transference, seeing it first as a general symbolical orientation of the analyst, second as a way of relating to the patient in the psychotherapeutic situation, and finally as occasionally present in distorted fantasies stirred either by the patient's transferences, or by the biases or inclinations of the analyst's own prior or contemporaneous experiences.

Interactive aspects of dependency have become more acknowledged as ego-psychological and object-relations descriptions have been applied to transference and countertransference. A number of authors have identified "realistic" (i.e., relational) aspects in the environmental and interpersonal factors operating in psychoanalytic treatment. Zetzel (1956) used the term "therapeutic alliance" to justify realistically constructive and collaborative features of the therapeutic relationship. Greenson (1965) popularized a plausible, "reality/nonreality" distinction through the concept of a "working alliance." Szasz (1963) constructed a micropolitical analysis of transference and concluded that the definitions of reality/nonreality pivoted on evaluative judgments shared (or not shared) between the psychoanalyst and the analysand. However, even with some of these changes in the formulation of transference and countertransference, the conspicuous dependency of the patient on the analyst has been consistently underrecognized. In the opposite direction, the dependency gratifications of the analyst on his or her patients have tended to be muted or disguised through platitudes or idealizations (see Greenacre 1963).

The procedural rules of the psychoanalytic situation are defined in such a way as to enforce a highly asymmetric relationship in regard to the statuses and activities of the participants (summarized recently in F. Johnson 1988a). Because of this structuring, the therapeutic situation inherently operates toward placing the patient in a dependent relationship, although this is usually not examined as such. The patient's use of the couch, the frequency of encounters, the asymmetric exposure of self, and the fact that one of the parties is exceedingly needful while the other is optionally available all constitute power vectors that implicitly reinforce an atmosphere of dependency, and work towards creating an "optimal frustration." Positively, these procedural rules facilitate free association and foster an interaction in which past and present thoughts of the patient may be productively reviewed and analyzed. However, more problematically, the psychoanalytic procedure creates a highly asymmetric, dependent relationship that because of its implicitness may be difficult to analyze.[8]

Dependency and Clinical Conceptions of "Normal" and "Abnormal"

Since its inception, psychoanalysis has presented a nonmoralistic and cautiously nonjudgmental acceptance of human behavior in all of its ordinary and outlandish manifestations. Because of this, questions involving gradations of psychopathology tend to be posed on a linear continuum between "normal" and "abnormal." Clinically verifiable conditions are defined according to behavioral manifestations, but are traditionally explained according to conflict theory and "fixation." In explaining significant characterologic deviation, the life-historical failures of normal development are sought to facilitate a structural and behavioral reorganization of anachronistic adaptation. Within this model, excessive dependency is heuristically related to *oral fixations*, including a number of clinical conditions that exhibit excessive appetites or habituation to intoxicating substances. With or without the presence of actual habituation, the psychoanalytic category of "oral character" describes persons who lack the genuine capacity for sustained psychosexual functioning at a mature level. This is clinically manifested by uninterest in sexuality, poor control over impulses, and lack of purposeful planning. In object-relations terms, overly dependent individuals are observed to have problems relating to age contemporaries, and to have a strong tendency toward indecisiveness and a preference for getting into subordinate positions vis-à-vis others, preferably in functional activities that involve little risk, originality, or responsibility.

A more subtle pathology in dependency relations may be exhibited in narcissistic character, where individuals are considered to be arrested in their early emotional and social development, particularly concerning their incapacity to empathize and "feel" the sympathies of others. Depending upon the degree of impairment, this deficiency can be associated with problems regarding authentic presentation of a social self, accompanied by serious and chronic miscalculations of other persons' intentions and moods.

In chapter 1, a number of childhood and adult psychiatric conditions were listed where disturbed relations in dependency were incidentally or primarily present. It was also stressed that Western societies in general support an ethos that inflates the value of independency to the point of denying or obscuring the ubiquitous dependent characteristics inherent in many adult relationships. As a primarily Western institution, psychoanalysis has been influenced by this same ethos, both in regard to ideological values implicitly embedded in its metapsychology, and in the practical explanations of objectives for clinical improvement in specific instances of treatment. In metapsychological concepts of personality, the high priority on individualism is fundamental to explanations of both structure and function, which monolithically stress egocentric architecture and intrapsychic process over social-interactional frameworks. In a parallel way one of the principal goals for psychoanalytic treatment is a focus on the fostering or restoration of *independency*, pursued through mastering anachronistic conflicts induced during juvenile development. This high investment in independency, implicit and explicit in theory and practice, will subsequently be examined against Japanese models of dependency/interdependency.

Summary

This chapter has been concerned with documenting the ways in which dependency and interdependency are represented in basic formulations within psychoanalytic theory and practice. The point has been made that dependency is present, but mostly implicit rather than directly formulated in pschoanalytic metapsychology. Moreover, when aspects of dependency are acknowledged, they are regarded as the product of secondary rather than primary drives, even in the clear and comprehensive treatment of the subject by Parens and Saul (1971).

Looking at this historically and conceptually, the concepts of dependency, attachment, and interdependency have been crowded out by the preeminence of traditional drive theory, stages of psychosexual development, and the oedipal resolution. This is evident in the ambiguous and nonpsychological way in which the "ego instincts" were postulated by Freud and his successors, and the exclusiveness of the later versions of the dual instinct theory (of sexual and aggressive drives), which continue to ignore metapsychological explanations for ego drives.

Another deterrent has been the sentimental adherence to the "constancy principle." Although incongruent with neuropsychological evidence, older conceptions about the organism seeking zero stimulation directly oppose any support for the existence of a primary "drive" that seeks contact, warmth, companionship, and other forms of human stimulation and association. Similarly, Freud's formulation of the aggressive instincts as ultimately seeking a kind of psychic entropy discredits any primary drive seeking to make contacts that create and sustain social relationships. Also, earlier formulations of the "reality principle" depicted the social environment as basically hostile and antagonisitc both to the individual and to the (putative) "pleasure principle." Taken together all of these suppositions combine to discourage the elevation of dependency-satisfying, "object hungry" drives to more than secondary interest and significance.

In addition to historical and conceptual problems, certain terms and theories concerning interdependency have suffered from political backlash. The history of psychoanalysis as an institution and intellectual movement has included a series of attempts to introduce social-interactional explanations, either as competitors or additions to mainstream, metapsychological theory. Alfred Adler's work (in Way 1962) advanced social-interactional terms and explanations ("will to power," "inferiority complex") that directly challenged psychoanalytic theory (Becker 1963). Freud regarded these and later attempts to "psychosocialize" psychoanalytic theory as premature and dangerous. Later revisions formulated by other traditionally trained persons (Horney 1945; Fromm 1944) or other theorists (Sullivan 1962, 1964) also attempted to emphasize interpersonal and social perspectives. Even more radically, Fairbairn (1954) placed "dependency" at the epicenter of his personality system; and Bowlby (1960) used "attachment" and "separation" as core concepts for a revised formulation of personality. Most recently, Kohut (1971, 1977) has suggested a revision of theory by positing the parallel development of narcissistic instincts operating alongside aggressive, libidinal, and ego instincts.

One could view these attempts as recurrent reactions occurring within a kind of vacuum in psychoanalytic theory regarding the issue of nonlibidinous attachment. These various revisions have arisen to confront the conceptual weakness of an oversimplified and archaic drive theory: specifically one that omits the significance of earliest object relations. These periodic attempts at revision also represent the recurrent problems in balancing id-psychological and ego-psychological theories of personality within psychoanalysis, as discussed in Greenberg and Mitchell (1983) and Settlage (1980).

One final comment may be raised to explain some of the confusion regarding the status of dependency in theories concerning human development and personality. Specifically, the application of cross-cultural studies to modify psychoanalytic theory has not been systematically employed, although there have been some exceptions. In later chapters evidence will be assembled to study the impact that cross-cultural studies lend both in support and in criticism of traditional theory—particularly in terms of dependency and interdependency.

Notes

1. The term "cathexis" was originally used by Freud to denote the investment of libido into specific persons, ideas, activities, or material objects. Later, "cathexis" became a more metaphorical term, but still suggested an emotional quality of special investment and signification that rises above ordinary attachments to persons or objects.

2. Freud's (1914) allusion to "attachment" is a fascinating but undeveloped presaging of Bowlby's extensive use of this as a major structural factor in his writings from 1960 on. Freud's early amendment of drive-structure theory represents only one phase in a succession of confusing revisions extending over the long period of his creative scholarship. One of these developments was the neglect of ego instincts. More critical summaries have been documented by Greenberg and Mitchell (1983) and Eagle (1987).

3. As reported by Goodman (1969), the structural, psychoanalytic configuration of the superego (Freud 1923) was preceded by a number of descriptions qualitatively outlining aspects of its conscious and unconscious dimensions, respectively reflecting external and internal connections. Ego ideal was originally considered as partly coterminous with superego, although clear distinctions have accumulated in subsequent writings. Both are considered to have negative (prohibitive) and positive (rewarding) components and to operate on conscious, preconscious, and unconscious levels. Both are based on putative internal structuralization that is activated by early socialization experiences in positive and negative directions. Both involve the mostly unconscious incorporation of parents' feelings, moods, intentions, prejudices, ideologies, and, of course, reflect the culture wherein such socialization proceeds.

However, in terms of contrast, superego tends to be associated with the incorporation of authoritarian, rigid standards associated with the affects of anxiety and terror connected with potentially breaking rules, or failing to comply with internal standards. Typically, the contents of superego conflicts are ambiguous and less accessible to consciousness. Responses occur instantaneously and are associated with a penitential feeling of intense and incommensurate guilt or self loathing. Ego ideal is more consciously associated with wish fulfillment and expectations of meeting high (external) standards for performance and competence. Conspicuous failure to achieve these is experienced as severe embarrassment and shame, which are unambiguously connected to some kind of definite social audience.

4. From a conceptual standpoint *internalization* is central to the process of forming object relations. As Behrends and Blatt (1985) comment, "From our view . . . internalization is the primary vehicle whereby psychological growth is accomplished" (1985, 12). Kernberg (1976) has suggested that introjections, identifications, and ego identity constitute three different

levels of a process that contribute to the internalization of objects and object relations into the intrapsychic apparatus. He refers to all three of these as *identification systems* (Kernberg 1976, 26).

5. Such exploratory behavior has also been studied among primate infant/mother pairs in naturalistic and experimental settings, demonstrating parallels to "practicing" behavior in human infants (Rheingold and Eckermann 1970). As in the human situation, the behavior of juvenile primates varies with age, maternal responsiveness, the social organization of the troop, and, of course, the situation. Unlike the social regulations within primate groups, human childrearing involves considerably more variability in the extent of human practicing experience, especially in terms of its timing and the amount of "ranging." Such practicing is also influenced by realistically dangerous or uncomfortable climatological conditions that modify the frequency and extent of being away from mother (Whiting 1964, 1971).

6. As reviewed by Baumbacher (1983), "transitional objects" and "transitional phenomena" are represented by the youngster's fierce attachments to stuffed animals, blankets, or other objects in a clearly substitutional manner. Hong (1978) demonstrated that the majority of children in what he called "Anglo-Saxon cultures" display this tendency, in contrast to children from cultures where cosleeping is present. This was shown in contrasts examining Korean children (Hong 1978) as well as Italian youngsters (Gaddini and Gaddini 1975). Imaginary playmates (J. L. Singer 1973) also exemplify the substituted creation of an artificial "partner" projected by the child to fulfill a variety of relational and psychological needs.

7. Daniel Stern (1985) has put together a topography of the "interpersonal world of the infant" based on a synthesis of his own and others' research and clinical observations. Although not conceding a "fused" system between infant and mother, Stern makes a strong case for "shared affectivity" and "shared intentionality" (although in no sense requiring cognition) occurring in the context of "intersubjectivity."

8. Although described earlier by Freud (1914, 49), the power issues involving the manifest asymmetry of the psychoanalytic relationship tend to be downplayed. Partly this is due to the tendency to ignore the unequivalent statuses and privileges in the analytic situation in Western societies that cherish egalitarianism. Also, there has been a trend to idealize the purposes of the analyst, and to obscure other legitimate needs for gratification that reflect monetary issues, status enhancement, or mastery (Greenacre 1963). When not borne in mind, the pleasure of being a status superior and "authority" may make the analyst unaware of both the authoritarian *and* dependent ingredients of the analytic situation. (Also see Doi 1989a.)

CHAPTER 3

Cultural and Historical Background of *Amae:* Dependency Experience in Japan

As defined earlier, *amae* is a commonly used Japanese word denoting "the ability and prerogative of an individual to presume or depend upon the benevolence of another" (Doi 1956, 1962a). This mandate for special and continued leaning on selected others is embedded into Japanese life in ubiquitous and complicated ways. Although previously intuited by many observers of Japan, the psychological and cultural consequences of *amae* were not explicitly formulated until Takeo Doi furnished an interpretation of their significance. As a psychoanalytically oriented academic psychiatrist with clinical and cultural experiences in the U.S. and Japan, Doi expanded his original insights about *amae* through a series of illuminating publications. Although initially focusing on psychological versions of dependency in terms of an intrapsychic motive, he has related his work to personality theory itself, and to psychoanalytic metapsychology. He also has specifically applied the concept of *amae* to speculations about cross-cultural differences between Japanese and Western societies. Additionally, he has comparatively related dependency to features of the psychotherapeutic process in Japan.

His formulations about the significance of *amae* were organized during the mid-1950s following clinical experience and study in the United States. A synthesis of his observations led to conference presentations followed by a succession of writings on *amae*, culminating in *The Anatomy of Dependence*, published in 1971 in Japan, and in English translation in 1973. The originality of his observations, combined with his applications to theory and practice, have aroused interest, acclaim, and criticism, both from Japan and from the international scholarly community.

The present chapter will only briefly note Doi's contributions regarding dependency. Two subsequent chapters will depict a multilevel exposition of the concept along with additional work and commentary by Doi's supporters and critics. Before examining the cultural meanings of *amae*, some exposition of Japanese history and culture is obligatory. Although dependency and interdependency are universal features of human behavior, their manifestations are orchestrated through distinctive cultural traditions and specialized language in Japan. Beyond these behavioral specializations, certain ideological and social-historical differences must be exposed to understand factors that purport to explain Japanese culture. Doi's explanation of *amae* will be placed in this context by sketching salient aspects of Japanese history and culture. Before doing this, a precaution is necessary relating to the translation of the term *amae*. Although *amae* can be roughly translated as "dependency," it in no way stands for all forms of dependent relationships, but rather is confined to the dependency based on the desire and craving for closeness, security, and cherishment—called "indulgent dependency" by Lebra (1976). This is exemplified by the infant/mother relationship but not restricted to this particularly intense, asymmetric connection. Such close relationships appear throughout the lifespan, in relations with other family members, closest friends, and specified superiors, such as teachers or supervisors (Weiss 1982).

Historical Summary

Geography and Early History

Japan consists of four large and numerous smaller islands. Their distance from the Asian continent (about one hundred miles) fostered an unusually homogeneous ethnic and linguistic continuity. The historical development of Japan did not involve significant foreign invasion or military domination, although there are suggestions of prehistoric migration by populations from China and the Korean peninsula. Selective migration began in the fourth and fifth centuries and brought a cadre of mainlanders who introduced new technology and commerce. Gradual absorption of Chinese culture, social organization, and literature reached a peak during the sixth century. Following the introduction of Buddhism, priests and scholars imported elements of Chinese philosophy and the arts. Practical forms of government, politics, and military organization were also developed on mainland models. The written Chinese language was used for official documents, and gained a status similar to Latin in medieval Western European countries. Chinese ideographs were adopted to represent Japanese cognates—completely ignoring the fact that these two spoken languages are linguistically unrelated.

The loose sovereignty of early Japan was threatened by two unsuccessful Mongolian invasions in the late thirteenth century. Unlike the Norman Conquest of England in 1077, the Mongols were repelled by a combination of ingenious defenses and a propitious typhoon *(kamikaze,* or "divine wind"). Resistant to outside domination, Japan developed its few mineral resources and manufacturing. The arrival of Portuguese traders in the 1540s established commercial connections with Europe, along with the introduction of Western medicine and advanced technology. This commerce opened the country to Jesuits and Spanish Franciscans who converted some regional nobility and peasants to Roman Catholicism. Rivalries with Buddhism and political meddling led to the expulsion of missionaries and the rigid suppression of foreign religion in the early 1600s. In a sweeping move against outside influence, trading opportunities were restricted to a group of Dutch Protestant merchants confined to a small enclave in the port of Nagasaki. These events were part of a centralization of authority undertaken by the Tokugawa Shogunate, whose political consolidation by 1630 ended a long period of sporadic civil wars and destabilizing power shifts. A strict closure of the country to outside influence was instituted to forestall European colonialization such as had occurred elsewhere in Asia. This stringent policy grew into a reactionary xenophobia that defined the Japanese as racially unique, and superior to other peoples. Non-Japanese were categorized as impure and dangerous barbarians who were best ignored or rebuffed.

1650–1852

To reinforce its legitimacy, the Tokugawa Shogunate inflated the significance of the Imperial family and publicized the mythic origins of the Emperor and the Japanese people. In breaking with the past, the Shogunate relocated the government from Kyoto to Edo, where an imposing military and administrative complex was built to signify the centralized power of the new regime. This consolidation was achieved at the cost of considerable regimentation and rigidification of social behavior. Also, the radical separation of Japan from the rest of the world eliminated both the incentive and the opportunity for development in industrial and technical areas. Japan maintained this closed-door policy for nearly 250 years, solidifying as a feudal society with institutionalized divisions among five major social classes: the nobility, the military (or *samurai*), the peasants, the merchants, and the "untouchables" *(eta)*, who lived in ghettos adjacent to large population centers.

The long-established indigenous practices associated with Shinto had evolved into an eclectic system of beliefs operating alongside the accepted Tokugawa versions of Buddhism. An explicit system of rules and customs regulating political and social life were authorized through a series of edicts regarding a "Divine Way of Order" written in the form of "patterns for correct behavior." Although this code was primarily established for the aristocracy and *samurai*, it was influential through imitation among the merchant class, and to some extent among ordinary people.

In the early part of the nineteenth century, attempts by Russia, the United States, and England to introduce trade, establish diplomatic relations, or arrange for refueling in Japanese ports were uniformly rejected.

1852–1900

The arrival of Commodore Perry's American naval squadron to Edo Harbor (later Tokyo) in 1853 reawakened the feudal government to the aggressiveness and technological superiority of the world outside Japan. The threat raised by this superiority persuaded the government to recognize the inevitability of relating to foreign nations. Traditional factions that still opposed diplomatic concessions attempted to topple the Shogunate. In a dramatic conciliatory move, the newly installed Shogun turned over his secular rule to the then fifteen-year-old Emperor, whose reign was given the name "Meiji." Realizing the impossibility of resisting the Westerners, a coalition of younger bureaucrats, former *samurai*, and merchants acquiesced to the outside demands. Imperial ratification of foreign treaties was completed in 1865, confirming these new relationships.

This action reversed nearly three hundred years of self-imposed isolation. Beginning in 1868 the Meiji Restoration swiftly implemented social and economic policies that sought diplomatic, commercial, educational, and technological connections to Western nations. Delegations were sent to acquire experience and techniques concerning all areas of national development. In the opposite direction, scholars, engineers, and military specialists were brought to Japan to consult within the areas of education, manufacturing, military development, and technology.

The signing of a constitution in 1899 integrated the nation internally, and achieved legal parity with sovereign states in Europe and the Americas. Following the Meiji Restoration, compulsory education for both sexes was made mandatory for four years in 1872, extended to six years in 1907. National and prefectural universities were established during the late 1900s to prepare qualified male students for positions in government, industry, finance, humanities, and education itself. The former class structure was officially abolished in 1869. Although this did not create an egalitarian society, it removed previous demarcations that had strictly regulated social mobility. Subsequently, meritorious performance was more likely to be rewarded with increased status and reward. Even more significantly, the erasure of fixed social classes conferred the behavioral norms and explicit expectations of the former aristocracy onto other social classes. Ordinary citizens thereafter were normatively influenced by standards that previously had been reserved for the gentry, *samurai*, and wealthy merchants (Hasegawa 1966).[1]

Because of the long tradition of centralized, feudal control, a relative cultural homogeneity was present within Japan at the time of the Restoration. Universal education intensified an already latent cultural homogeneity through standardized curricula and rigorous ethical training. Military conscription added to this through recruiting eligible males from all sections of the country and bringing them together for periods of national service. Ethical training *(shūshin)* in elementary education was taken very seriously and inculcated precise and standardized forms of public behavior. Although ideologically based on Confucianism, *shūshin* also endorsed mythic beliefs about the specialized racial ancestry of all Japanese. An historical continuity with the Sun Goddess, Amaterasu-omikami, was alleged through a succession of emperors constituting an uninterrupted lineage from the moment of "racial creation." The Emperor was revered as the divine personification of this special national origin and destiny. Power from this living deity flowed downward through the institutions of government, bureaucracy, military, schools, neighborhood, and, ultimately, the *ie*, or patrilineal, collective household.

Although Japan was no longer a feudal society with rigid social stratification, rules regarding status emphasized a strong neo-Confucian model of superior-inferior hierarchy. The enduring significance of patriarchal family authority, with subordination of women's status and emphasis on filial piety, was given added normative weight through analogy to the imperial household. Choices concerning occupation became possible, and opportunities for higher education were available through competitive examinations. The alternate use of Western clothing was promoted. Newspapers and periodicals flourished, helping to educate a growing literate public. Architecture based on Western factories, office complexes, and multilevel buildings appeared. Cultural importations included translated literature, and even some exotic customs, such as ballroom dancing—originally regarded as ridiculous and too intimate for public display, but grudgingly adopted as "modern." In fact, from the 1870s until after World War I, there was a strong tendency to regard many aspects of traditional Japanese culture as "old fashioned," while adulating modern, European innovation.

As documented by Shishido (1980), the development of Japanese industry, science, and technology was fostered through carefully coordinated cooperation among national government, capital resources, universities, and various agencies concerned with accumulating information and technical processes from abroad. These came together in the form of both ad hoc and permanent institutes, which focused on specific areas of industrial and technological development—a pattern still prominent in the commercial achievements of Japan.

Military Activity

The success of programs for industrialization and military development culminated in Japan's conquests on the Chinese mainland in 1894, and subsequent control over Formosa and Korea. These expansionist successes were followed by the decisive defeat of Russian forces in 1905, ensuring Japanese control over the Liaotung Peninsula and the Manchurian railway. These military achievements also conferred the status of a world power onto this developing nation (Reischauer 1964). Given new areas of influence, Japan expanded its control in Korea, formally annexing it in 1910. Reinforcing its position as an international power, Japan participated in World War I and, following the conflict, was awarded Pacific territories formerly under imperial German control. While attending the 1919 Paris Peace Conference, the Japanese delegation proposed two articles for the Covenant of the League of Nations: one explicitly rejecting economic imperialism, and a second abolishing discrimination against orientals by whites. Neither of these measures was incorporated, and the Japanese returned from the conference with considerable cynicism toward the idealism of the Western democracies (Murakami 1982).

External racial discrimination continued to be a humiliating and thorny issue. In 1913 an Alien Land Law was passed in California, prohibiting Japanese from owning real estate and allowing only limited options for renting property. In 1924, the Oriental Exclusion Act was passed by the U.S. federal government, unconditionally barring immigration of Japanese to the U.S. except for families of émigrés already relocated. This was preceded in 1921 by an international conference regulating Japanese naval strength at a formula not to exceed three-fifths of the fleet size of either the U.S. or Great Britain. Moreover, an attempt by the Japanese to establish a mutual defense treaty with England was successfully opposed by the U.S. Taken together, these events produced a strong trend of anti-Americanism, and led into plans for unilateral expansion in Asia.

As Reischauer (1964) has discussed, the 1920s saw the rise of a new generation of politicians, bureaucrats, military personnel, and industrialists, many of whom had risen through the meritocratic process to positions of influence. In sheer numbers, they created a complex political process, which was compounded by extending suffrage in 1919 and 1925 to franchise additional numbers of male Japanese.

Mercantile Development in the 1920s and 1930s

During World War I, importation of technology and manufactured goods from Europe dwindled to a fraction of prewar levels. This compelled Japan to assume its own technological upgrading, while responding to Asian markets that had opened up because of the decline in European exports. Japan was thus prepared for a postwar leap forward in manufacturing and trading, first concentrating on textiles and manufactured goods. Despite high protective tariffs that followed the worldwide depression of 1929, Japan was able to gain a competitive edge in a number of markets in Asia, Africa, and North and South America.

Gibney (1979) has quoted portions of a 1937 *Fortune* magazine article on Japan that summarized the Japanese commercial accomplishments at that time.

There is no sinister explanation.... The great competitive superiority of the Japanese is not a superiority of natural resources, of which they have few, nor in sources of capital, which are limited, nor in mechanical genius, which is still rare, but in a homogeneous, highly integrated, and beautifully adapted social organization permitting a unification of national effort not possible in any other country. (Gibney 1979, 45)

During the 1930s, senior military officers in coalition with reactionary politicians extended their control over ministerial policies. Liberal and egalitarian trends of the early 1920s declined, partly because of their association with the distrusted and "decadent" Western democracies. The powers of both the conventional and secret police were expanded, ostensibly in response to the threats of subversion by communists and radicals. A series of violent acts and assassinations by ultranationalistic groups and dissident military evoked fear and deterred countermeasures by moderate members of the Diet, the press, or liberal intelligentsia.

Control of the government was insidiously commandeered by the military. Following the unauthorized takeover of Manchuria in 1931, Japan began to execute plans for overseas conquest and expansion. Declaration of war against China in 1937 was followed by Japan's assault on and conquest of Nanking and Canton. The invasion of Indochina in mid-1941 led to a direct confrontation with the U.S. and Great Britain over the issue of critically needed petroleum. This in turn led to the onset of the "Pacific War" in December 1941, and involved the neutralization of the American fleet at Pearl Harbor, followed by the invasion of Singapore, the Philippines, and New Guinea. Japan's military strategy was to create a hegemony of Dutch, British, and U.S. protectorates that, when added to conquests in China and Korea, would constitute an expanded imperial Japan with sources of energy, raw materials, and markets for products. After initial success, the new empire retracted as Allied sea and land forces converged toward the home islands. In 1945, the invasion and occupation of Okinawa, together with the methodical destruction of larger cities on the principal islands, presaged Japan's defeat. Despite some fanatical opposition, Japan agreed to unconditional surrender following the atomic bombing of Hiroshima and Nagasaki in August 1945.

American Occupation, 1945–1952

By the end of World War II Japan lay devastated and the people demoralized. The American military government's administration of Japan provided structure and direction, but few resources for recovery. Significant changes in the civil code were made that instituted land reforms, removed primogeniture, and dissolved many prewar industrial coalitions. Changes also established civil rights for women, including suffrage. Under the guidance of the occupation authorities, a new constitution was developed that renounced war and only permitted maintenance of a self-defense force. In constitutional law, the Emperor was redefined as a secular, heredity leader whose lineage symbolically personified the Japanese nation (as in Great Britain), but not through any "divine" connection. Education was reformed by prohibiting "moral training" *(shūshin)* and attempting to decentralize the control of curriculum. In 1956 moral education was resumed using inspirational texts that did not refer to Shinto or ultranationalistic ideologies.

The recapitalization of Japanese industries was mobilized through some grants from the American government and corporations, but mostly involved reinvestment of concealed residual assets into government subsidized developments. At the brink of severe economic recession in 1950, the beginning of the Korean Conflict massively restimulated Japanese manufacturing and service sectors as the country became one "vast repair and supply base" for the United Nation's Far Eastern military forces (Murakami 1982, 230). Although the Korean War was the occasion for the sudden rehabilitation of the Japanese economy, the structural explanations for recovery and development are connected to the Ministry of International Trade and Industry (MITI). This organization is the bureaucratic descendant of several centralized agencies for policy that, since the 1880s, were responsible for coordinating development of agriculture, industry, banking, and commerce. As described by Chalmers Johnson (1982, 1983), MITI has exercised extensive control over industrial investments, the quality and quantity of imports, the types and amounts of exported materials, and the pricing of domestic goods—all with the objective of achieving controlled economic growth. As Johnson states it,

MITI's overall policy was to transform Japan from a light-industry, Asia-oriented economy to a heavy-industry, globally-oriented economy. It also erected formidable barriers to protect the Japanese economy from international competition. (C. Johnson 1983, 190–91)

Subsequent Postwar Development

The recent, spectacular growth of Japan's economy can partly be attributed to centralized, coordinated national planning. Such control involves a balancing of the needs of political constituencies, industries, banks, and trading companies in a consolidated effort to expand markets and fulfill domestic improvement—as summarized in Livingston, Moore, and Oldfather (1973), Vogel (1979), Gibney (1979), Prestowitz (1988), and van Wolferen (1989).

A number of factors supporting this growth are listed by observers commenting on the postwar economic development of Japan. Central coordination is focused on the development of objectives through long-range planning involving capitalization, product development, manufacturing, and marketing. This central planning has directed the disciplined allocation of funds and responsibilities among potentially competing factions. Because its basic industries were obliterated by the war, Japan rebuilt its manufacturing base employing the most modern technological improvements. Eventually this put them at a competitive advantage over producers in other countries. A high investment in technology from abroad (detailed by Shishido 1980) conserved indigenous research costs and reduced start-up time. Also, a high capital accumulation through the proverbial thrift of ordinary Japanese citizens permitted investment into new factories, inventories, and commercial ventures.

Despite recurrent denials, protectionism has always been prominent in Japanese international trading and takes many forms. The least contrived of these is a pride that Japanese have in buying their own products. Another is the generally high quality of Japanese products and customer service. On the other hand, direct deterrents toward outside products include legal restrictions, informal quotas, and complicated regulations designed to suppress levels of imports from abroad. Imports also have been discouraged by a complex process of distribution, where interlocking groups of Japanese middlemen operate to channel goods and commodities through a series of wholesalers before they reach the actual marketplace.

Prestowitz (1988) has documented other intentionally exclusionary activities in the Japanese exploitation of joint venture situations, licensing agreements, or encroachment of patented technology. Each case has involved the acquisition of foreign research and development to produce and export comparable but less expensive equipment while essentially excluding American and other foreign manufacturers from Japan. The consequences for this in the microchip and electronics industry have been most sobering.[2]

The presence of a disciplined, educated, and highly motivated work force is prominent in comparison to comparable industrialized countries. Also, the relative congeniality between labor and management removes obstacles that otherwise might lead to strikes and increased production costs. Certain cultural traits (to be reviewed subsequently) promote efficiency, corporate loyalty, and the sense of collective achievement that are generally acknowledged to give a competitive edge to Japanese productivity.

Working toward long-range marketing objectives is accompanied by renouncing short-term rewards both for individuals and companies. Salaries and bonuses of major executives are low in comparison to those of U.S. managers, and neither stockholders nor trustees are involved in manipulating sales or transferring assets to achieve short-range profits through "buyouts." Marketing development customarily involves entering new countries with artificially low-cost goods in order to secure a favorable sales and service position. Domestic Japanese consumption of goods has been regulated through both artificial price controls and the relative unpopularity of installment buying. When necessary, voluntary quotas are used overseas as a fall-back position in reacting to complaints about underpricing or unfair domination of a foreign market. A final but important factor contributing to Japan's success in international competition is the relatively small percentage of gross national product has been allocated to military self-defense, although this has changed since 1991. Also, unlike the U.S., research and development investment in Japan has primarily been concentrated on nonmilitary projects.

All of these factors have combined to produce an exuberant and enterprising Japanese economy with distinction in exporting electronics, automotive products, steel, and capital resources to other countries—notably the U.S. and portions of Europe. Japan is now concerned with research and development leading away from imitative production and trade orientation toward becoming a technology-producing country, exporting sophisticated devices in the areas of third-generation computers, automation, and robotics (Shishido 1980; Schodt 1986).

Since the 1970s (Vogel 1979) the increasingly dominant position of Japan in manufacturing, trading, and marketing has received public attention but until recently little counterreaction. Prestowitz (1988) has provided some case histories demonstrating the transfer of ascendancy in several important marketing areas. Van Wolferen (1989) has contributed a more intrinsic, structural explanation of Japanese planning, capitalization, research, manufacturing, market sharing, and foreign trading. In his analysis, Japan does not operate as a modern democratic state, nor do the various participants in the society function as they do elsewhere. Instead of being consolidated in government, policy is controlled by a *system* composed of participants whose power is vested in various manufacturers, businesses, unions, trading groups, and banks. As in Japanese interpersonal relationships, no one of these constituencies predominates. Decisions are made through compromise or payback that take into account the needs and sensitivities of other groups.[3]

As compared to the U.S., in Japan there is a great deal of cooperation (even collusion) in planning and power sharing among various interest blocs. For example, the Japanese press corps is socially integrated through membership in press clubs (called *kisha-kurabu*) with the very people they are supposed to write about objectively (bureaucrats, executives, Diet members). Organized criminal groups (called *yakusa*) are informally cooperative with the police in containing the amount of "amateur" crime and also maintain ties with the political "far right." A revolving door openly operates between various ministries and private industry. Numerous public officials retire (at age fifty-five) to assume positions in the private sector, often in roles directly related to their former positions. Employment of entry-level executives is on an "old boy/old school chum" basis, where new graduates of elite schools are selected to join coalitions of older alumni in corporations, banks, and government. Loyalties mimicking the reciprocal relationships within families (*oyabun-kobun*) proliferate throughout business. Longevity of employment in most corporations and businesses generates unflinching loyalty within a coalition of corporate relationsips. Diet members have close and enduring contacts with corporations and ministries in a way that would strain Western norms concerning conflict of interest.

Changes in Popular Culture

Following the Meiji Restoration, the selective assimilation of European and American culture included the translation of literature and the importation of art, sports, films, and Western music—classical and popular. Assimilation initiated the adoption of hundreds of loan words—particularly from English—including both technical terms and popular expressions. In all areas of importation, these ingredients were "Japanized"—that is, converted and contextualized into the landscape of Japanese life, thereafter becoming a hybrid of outside and inside culture. In addition to imparting a strong indigenous stamp to imported culture, the Japanese have characteristically demonstrated a capacity to adopt innovation—even fad—while still maintaining traditional values and culture.

Cultural Background

The remarkable technological and commercial success of Japan has been a matter of general knowledge since the 1970s. Almost as well publicized is the degree of cultural homogeneity and retention of common tradition preserved by the Japanese throughout various periods of growth and change between 1887 and the late twentieth century. There has been a cascade of information in technical journals, fiction, motion pictures, and the public media concerning aspects of Japanese culture. Some of these have attempted to account for Japan's economic success by extolling their methods of corporate decision making, efficiency in manufacturing, high quality control, and the industriousness of average workers. Other commentary has transmitted information about general cultural traits, aesthetics, and the exportation of "soft culture," such as sushi bars, futon-style bedding, Zen Buddhism, and sake. Intentional or not, much of this information is itself positively stereotyped, and serves to create a monolithic and exaggerated picture of contemporary Japan (Peter Dale 1986).

Before the war, the Japanese family was formally constituted around a patrilineal "household" *(ie)* consisting of main and branch families of the male line, whose authority and descent were regulated by primogeniture. Reflecting Buddhist traditions, families were biologically and socially connected to the past through their lineage to near and remote ancestors. As repeatedly noted, Nakane (1970) has characterized Japanese society as determined by a vertical, hierarchical system of statuses. Practically speaking, this means there is an emphasis on superior/inferior, superordinate/subordinate gradations rather than on egalitarian social relationships. Within this, individuals are structurally positioned through the collective organization of their immediate and extended family. The individual person's position is established according to a hierarchy based on birth order, gender, and, to a certain extent, personal achievement. For the average person, concepts of personal existence have not stressed the Judeo-Christian or Muslim notion of individual *soul* in the Western sense of a specialized ontology that transcends biological creation.

In respect to dependency in Japan, this appreciation of genealogy has focused consciousness on individual existence in terms of a continuity through ancestors, patrilineal family, parents, and even, more abstractly, nationality. Within this consciousness, personal satisfactions and individual enhancement are subordinated to one's obligations toward others. Responsibilities are carefully prescribed toward parents and relatives (although not always observed), with the injunction to be accountable to expectations, requirements, and duties regarding others in a highly stipulated fashion—particularly toward status superiors.

Such a conception contrasts with the Western ideas concerning personalized individuality and a close relationship with a remote, monotheistic god represented in Hebraic, Christian, and Muslim theology. Instead, in Japan there is a conception of self as a particle within a collective social and "racial" identity, which locates primary ethical responsibilities and obligations toward specific persons, rather than as connected to a meddling, monotheistic god (Plath 1964).

Accompanying this nonegocentric conception of self is the tendency to avoid sharp categorical differentiations between subject and object—differentiations that are more strenuously made in Western theology, philosophy, and psychology (Nakamura 1964; F. Johnson 1985). Reflecting the philosophies of Buddhism and Confucianism, as well as the more pantheistic Shinto, Japanese impute an implicit connectedness and mutuality among humans, other living things, the spirits of deceased family, and even inanimate objects.

The strong connectedness between family members is conceptualized as immutable and unextinguishable—even in instances where separation is de facto, or where conflict may be prominent.

Some of the Japanese tendency toward guilt-induced suicide is associated with the inability to separate personal failures from collective dishonor, brought upon a whole family or even one's company or nation as a result of individual transgression. From a Western standpoint this collective, sociocentric orientation is readily misunderstood (Kitaoji 1971). For example, the emphasis on group norms and "positional" rather than "individual" identity is sometimes regarded as a radical loss of subjectivity or "self." On closer inspection there would seem to be more of a difference in how subjective experience is communicated and socialized, and how individuality is expressed, rather than a wholesale difference in self (Murase and Johnson 1974; Doi 1986; Reynolds and Kiefer 1977; Befu 1986).

At a more interpersonal and ethical level, the relative lack of sharp distinctions between subject and object is accompanied by a lower sense of differentiation between polar or categorical opposites. Reflecting Eastern philosophical concepts, temperaments are seen as interplays among various, even opposite, dispositions that are conceptualized as integrally interconnected. Subjects and objects are seen as partially merged or flowing together (as described by Veith 1974; and Nakamura 1964). At the level of personal relatedness there is a higher toleration, or at least an acceptance, of apparent inconsistencies in human nature and personality (Pelzel 1977; Wagatsuma 1984). Paradox and contradiction are thus philosophically anticipated as inevitable, and regarded as natural dimensions of human experience. The implications for dependency in this acceptance is that there is a higher cultural mandate to continue relating to others, despite the appearance of irregularities or inconsistencies in behavior or experience. Various Western authors have neutrally described this as "a logic of situations" (Benedict 1946), "case-to-case variation in reality" (Pelzel 1977), or simply as "naturalistic" (Reynolds 1976). Other interpretations define this as a kind of "radical situationalism" (Lebra 1976) or point to the potential for inconsistency or even amorality inherent in a situationally based system of ethical behavior.

Contrasted to Japanese and some other Asian cultures, Western norms for behavior accentuate categories that establish idealized standards for judging gradations between polar extremes of logically incompatible opposites, for example good/bad, beautiful/ugly, "right"/"wrong" (F. Johnson 1973, 1985). Correct behavior is established by measuring compliance to essential principles held to be "hierarchically opposite, which are applied in an evaluation holding situational or contextual factors as less significant" (Doi 1986, 11). Although real-life behaviors in Western situations may be modified by circumstantial or extenuating factors, these factors do not usually alter underlying imperative and categorical moral principles.

Norms Concerning Japanese Behavior

Considering the manifold changes in Japanese national life during the past 120 years, there has been considerable constancy in traditional behavioral norms concerned with regulating social behavior (see Caron and Shouten 1935 [1636]; Hearn 1971 [1901]; Inouye 1985 [1910]; Cooper 1981; Pelzel 1970). Behavioral norms regarding deference, respect, and obligations toward elders and superiors have been consistently reinforced within the family, school, workplace, and general society—both in the past and presently.[4] Virtually without qualification, individuals are influenced through aphorisms, direct instruction, and tacit example to defer to parents (particularly the father), older male siblings (especially the first son), teachers, employers, civil and military authorities, persons with superior education or station in life, and, at a symbolical level, the Emperor and his household. Similarly, there is an unequivocal portrayal of male superiority wherein fathers, male heads of family, and men in general are granted both titular and real authority. In contrast, women are explicitly subordinated to their parents, husbands, bosses, older siblings, and in-laws. They are enjoined to be deferent in their public behavior and demure in their conversation. In certain functional areas, women are allowed to be more directive: notably with their children, adult sons, daughters-in-law, or—if the woman is the wife of the head of the family—sometimes toward subordinates within the extended family. Also, despite explicit differences in gender roles, some women are psychologically dominant in the marital relationship, although even there, tact requires that they suppress contradiction or dominance toward their husbands in public situations. Moreover, some daughters may achieve sentimental preference over sons based on their winsomeness or talents. Still other women, through their social position or achievement, may be publicly granted deference. However, this is usually justified on the basis that their position (physician, university professor, concert violinist) is itself *manly*. Such treatment (as males), however, only applies to their work role, and not to their function within the family. Nor does it modify their need to observe the usual feminine deference in conduct toward men. Also, such women often find their opportunity for marriage lowered because of their superior education and social role—which traditional Japanese men may find offensive and intimidating.

One of the few natural opportunities for informal and close functioning with men is the special status granted to women who are hostesses or bar girls *(hosutesu)* in the so-called water trades *(mizushōbai)*. Here the sentimental, flirtatious, and playful qualities of male-female relations are permitted, along with the relaxation of the customary restraint and propriety. Such women, however, are marginal in their social reputation and usually have gravitated to such work through divorce, unmarriageability, or some form of misadventure. Frequently, such women are from lower-class families who seek such employment as either a desperate choice or an entrepreneurial opportunity.

Among Japanese, propriety in public transactions is distinctly patterned and carefully monitored. When contrasted to encounters in analogous North American situations, politeness, discipline, formality, and control of emotion are conspicuous. Proper deportment requires concentration on both verbal and nonverbal aspects of communication. The use of language itself compels the selection of correct polite forms *(keigo)* entailing honorific prefixes and suffixes for nouns and specialized verb forms in keeping with the social-positional features of the conversational partners. In addition to using correct honorific speech, persons must cultivate the proper modulation of voice, control of facial expression, and calibrated significations of gesture (Miller 1967; Morsbach 1973).

Of course, relationship, gender, and situationally dependent speech differences are observable in Western life—but not so prominently. Although less consciously monitored by the participants, variations in diction and degree of assertion and deference fluctuate according to the differences in status, context, and purposes of the conversation. For example, Americans intuit the observance of these differences and are semiconsciously aware of the nuances required in speaking to persons of different statuses under varying conditions or circumstances. However, such nuances are more readily recognized in the breach of status and linguistic norms—such as their exaggeration in situation comedy, where flagrant incongruities are manufactured for the purpose of amusement.

However, there is a striking difference between average adult Americans and Japanese in terms of their awareness concerning the regulation of speech that observes gender and status distinctions. Japanese interaction rules regarding positional status hierarchy are taught explicitly and repetitiously during early childhood, and moreover are a ubiquitous element in both written and spoken language. These rules continue to be reinforced during later socialization in schools and the community. The status norms that accord respect to parents, older siblings, and others are also tacitly communicated through the example of others. In contrast, American children are taught to display respect toward status superiors, and to defer to "important people" in the social environment (grandparents, patrons, older persons, neighbors). However, this is conveyed more by way of *not showing disrespect* rather than being inculcated with perfunctory forms of overt deference to status alone.

In some American families children may even be encouraged to call their parents by their given names—something that would be absolutely unthinkable in Japan. The use of first names even among equals is comparatively avoided in Japan, although it does occur. Persons who are superior in age or status may elect to use the first name of a subordinate, but subordinates cannot reciprocate. Within families the generic status terms of "older brother," "little sister," "grandma" are used in preference to given names. The failure to conform to these status markers elicits swift negative sanction and potential embarrassment. However, such formality in no way extinguishes the direct and subtle communication of feelings, intentions, or desires; nor does it preclude spontaneity per se. These speech and interaction rules (Goffman 1959, 1967), although prominent, are only part of the heightened social-psychological sensitivity among Japanese. Nakamura (1964) has described such concentrated attention on communicative features of small group behavior as a "focus on a close interpersonal nexus." The energy and concentration for such circumspect use of language is difficult to intuit for average Americans. Appreciation for this kind of awareness is only gained through immersion in the culture and in the grueling attempt to master proper use of colloquial Japanese speech.

Norms Regarding Obligation and Feeling:
On, Giri, and Ninjō

Although a number of norms operate around the priority for observing and accommodating to status, the most compelling of these is connected to the Japanese concept of *on* (pronounced "own"). Deriving from Confucian moral precepts commanding unlimited filial respect, *on* requires a special sense of obligation, gratitude, and dedication toward certain superiors who are pictured as having bestowed benevolent care and favors toward their status subordinates. *On* was described methodically in the Western literature by Benedict (1946), based on her remarkable analysis of interviews with Japanese informants in the U.S. and her synthesis of readings about Japanese culture. Since then, a series of commentators has illuminated the nature of dependency arising from this overt and intense form of obligation. In a definitive analysis of the concept, Takie Lebra (1969) emphasized the basically asymmetric and unbalanced dependency created by *on*, which imparts a relatively unlimited sense of emotional debt and obligation toward a superior. Bellah (1957) characterized this feeling of undischargeable debt as psychologically analogous to the latent anxieties connected to original sin in Judeo-Christian theology. In order to minimize the potential indebtedness of *on*, Japanese strive to reduce obligation by rebalancing indebtedness through "returning the *on*" or reducing the obligatedness through a calibrated payoff of prior indebtedness (Lebra 1969).

Contrasted to the unlimited indebtedness of *on*, the term *giri* (meaning "social obligations") is used to categorize more restricted, but still potentially onerous, obligations, which require a reciprocal, calibrated equalization. Although there are some exceptions (as mentioned by Doi 1967), these *giri* obligations ordinarily pertain to relations with persons outside the family, and involve what Lebra (1976) defines as "a social order consisting of a set of social norms that assign every status holder a certain role to be carried out" (Lebra 1976, 93). Paraphrasing her definition, such relations are long in duration, comprehensive in their mutual involvement, and constitute a potential license for the imposition of demands for reciprocity. Such *giri* relations may involve peers or friends and be conducted in an egalitarian and reciprocal manner. However, since Japanese society is so hierarchically arranged (Nakane 1970), *giri* is more often concerned with indebtedness toward persons of varying and different statuses, involving relations that are outside the immediate family or close friendships.

The emotional concomitants of human relations are called *ninjō* (meaning "human feelings"). These are not so much sought through *giri* relations as intrinsic to them. The actual amount of feeling *(ninjō)* varies according to many factors, including the statuses of the participants, their respective ages, and the duration of the relationship. Positive recognition of feelings of acceptance and worth may alternate with suspense over having done enough for the other person, or fear of one's own inferiority and unworthiness vis-à-vis the other partner. Interestingly, Doi (1967) terms some of the human feelings that accompany giri relations as "pseudo-Ninjō," to make the point that the most authentic feelings of acceptance are reserved for the intimacy of close family ties or for very special friendships, where cherishment is expected without the need to estimate worthiness, or to worry about calculated repayment.

One system through which the limited indebtedness of giri is negotiated is called kōsai or, more commonly, tsukiai. These involve ceremonial gift giving designed to balance prior debts and obligations among kin, friends, fellow workers, or employers (Befu 1968; Colleen Johnson 1974; Kinoshita 1985). Fundamentally, tsukiai is a neutral term and refers to one's social network. By extension, it implies an awareness regarding the potential for reciprocal acknowledgments and, often, the exchanges of gifts, which occur within the perimeter of specified relationships. Such awareness includes obligations that have arisen in the past, as well as those that may be anticipated or required in the future. Such observances may involve the punctilious exchange of gifts or money. Obligations are discharged through presenting communications or gifts at holidays or weddings, upon beginning a business, leaving or returning from trips, or moving, and, especially, at the time of funerals. Such emotional debts are felt both individually and collectively— for example, as a family or a business. In family situations, the "social debts" of deceased parents are posthumously assumed by the surviving family, ordinarily through the transfer of responsibility to the new family head.

The implications of these reciprocal interchanges for dependency are manifold. For one thing, the apprehension about incurring indebtedness operates to restrict the extent of relationships outside the family or workplace. This form of ritual interchange also distinguishes the limited obligations of giri from the more compelling and undischargeable on relationships. In the opposite direction these ritualized remembrances distinguish between the limited obligation of reciprocal involvements from the nongiri but friendly involvement with persons outside of this network of obligation that lack the specified interdependencies of giri. Most important, however, these reciprocal obligations promote a continuity of interdependent relationships at varying levels of intensity, which are concretely manifested in the exchange of gifts and remembrances.

Two Other Norms: Enryo and Amae

Before discussing *amae*, an additional, major norm should be defined. The celebrated and pervasive Japanese emphasis on humility, self-effacement, and understatement is incorporated in the term *enryo*, defined as "ritualized hesitation or deference." *Enryo* consists of a systematic modesty and self-denial expressed through behavioral rules and customs that may be misunderstood outside the culture (Johnson and Johnson 1975). It involves the ritualized renunciation of self-importance and operates to deny one's intrinsic worth, as well as to minimize and disavow self-serving motives (Doi 1973a; Lebra 1976). Such ritualized effacement—at times bordering on self-abasement—may be mistakenly taken at face value or appear contrived and pretentious to outsiders. However, within the culture, such denial of individual pride operates indirectly to enhance the potential recognition of worth and esteem from others. For example, the ritualized denial of one's achievement ("My recent promotion is really nothing") often elicits a compensatory affirmation of worth from others ("Surely you forget how much you have done for the company!"). Also, a balanced use of *enryo* promotes respect from others in a way that sincere modesty impresses people in many cultures. Excessive protestations of *enryo* may even be used sarcastically, or as an inverted and disguised declaration of inflated worth. Exaggerated *enryo* may also function as an indirect request for compensatory affirmation of self by others.

North Americans, in quite the opposite direction, are allowed and even encouraged to make announcements of self-worth or achievement both at home and in other situations. Unless excessive, such reports will usually be accepted and reinforced by others. On the other hand, declarations of self-abasement are less tolerable, and may in fact promote feelings of embarrassment, and even animosity or contempt by others. In the opposite direction, excessive or unrealistic boasting may prompt skeptical replies, denial, or confrontation by others. But even this is less offensive than exaggerated abasement, which is clumsy and more difficult to refute smoothly in American situations (Johnson and Johnson 1975).

As a prominent characteristic of self-presentation in Japan, *enryo* behaviors constitute a distinctive set of social-psychological techniques affecting communication. When added to the abundant use of nonverbal signals, the tactical significance of silence, and the attention to honorific status markers, the differences in communication among average Japanese and Americans are conspicuous (Morsbach 1973; Kondo 1987). The developmental aspects of these differences will be discussed in a subsequent chapter in terms of childrearing and its effects on adult personality—notably in terms of channeling aggression.

Another important dimension of ritual self-abasement in *enryo* has implications for the quality of superego. By inflicting one's own punishment (through denial of worth or need), individual Japanese may sociolinguistically avert external criticism at the price of repetitious self-criticism. The Japanese sensitivities about losing face, being ridiculed, or failing in public situations are well known. Although *enryo* can be seen as warding off external accusations leading to shame or guilt, the habitual display of a ritualized, lowered self-esteem may create a propensity toward actual self-punishment and poor self-image. In its automatic and partly unconscious operation, *enryo* might be classified as a culturally reinforced reaction formation against narcissistic, egoistic expression.

Amae

Integrally interconnected with these other norms, *amae* is concerned with patterns of affiliation and interdependency that regulate the nature of intimate relationships. As mentioned previously, *amae* is a noun, defining the condition of being able to depend and presume upon another's benevolence, basically "to be catered to or waited on" (Doi 1956). A Japanese-English dictionary lists the vernacular equivalents of "to be babied, to act like a spoiled child, to coax, to be coquettish, to request favor, to avail oneself of another's kindness" (Masuda 1959). Other English equivalents include the "desire to be pampered" (Lebra 1976), "to seek the goodwill of others . . . flirt with, take advantage of, or 'butter up' " (Pelzel 1977). Doi (1973a) himself suggests the word "wheedle" as an homologous English expression for manifesting the desire to *amaeru*. He speculates about the etymology of *amae* as related to the adjective *amai* ("sweet"), which has the connotations of pleasantness, optimism, and oral satisfaction. *Amai* also has negative connotations when it is ironically used to suggest "sweetness" as a lack of decisiveness, seeing the world through "rose-colored glasses," or a kind of "sweet innocence" bordering on naiveté or ignorance.

The term *amae* may be examined in both its intrapsychic and its behavioral dimensions. Intrapsychically, it is present as a motive, drive, or "desire" (Doi 1973a) that becomes expressed as a yearning and expectation to be held, fed, bathed, made safe, kept warm, comforted emotionally, and given special cherishment—what Bowlby (1979) would term a drive toward "primary love" or attachment. Interactionally, *amae* is manifested through the transactions of such yearnings in numerous culturally acceptable situations where such drives are allowed to seek objective satisfaction. The paradigm for these internal cravings and their external objectifications is in the infant-mother relationship, notably during the preoedipal stages of development. As discussed in the previous chapter, the hypothetically fused sexual and ego instincts were described as separating during the first three months of life. However, in traditional psychoanalytic theory, the sexual instincts are regarded as psychologically preeminent in their function as basic, unconscious determinants of behavior. Classically, the sexual instincts are described as progressing through a series of phasic changes predetermined by the migration of libidinal cathexis from oral, anal, phallic, and genital foci. Within this metapsychological description, *amae* would not qualify as a primary drive (or "instinct"), but rather would represent a secondary, derived drive consisting of sublimated or repressed libidinal motives.

A prominent characteristic of *amae* in Doi's writing is that it constitutes a combined verbal *and* nonverbal request for cherishment and security in a *passive* yearning for support and love. Another crucial characteristic of *amae* is that it is not consigned to early childhood in Japan—as it is in many Western cultures—but is allowed to remain manifest in attenuated, but overt, forms throughout the lifespan.

Psychocultural Characteristics

The previous section has been concerned with the description of norms identified by Japanese and outside scholars as prominent in the governance of interpersonal behavior. This section will list additional behaviors that are associated with patterns of normative regulation readily observable in Japanese life. Some of the psychological concomitants associated with these will also be noted—hence justifying the term "psychocultural." Other social-psychological and psychocultural features relating to indulgent dependency will be discussed in chapters 6, 7, and 8.

Harmony, Conflict, and Aggression

In both public and private behavior, the preservation of social harmony *(wa)* is a major objective in Japanese life. This means that disagreements, conflicts, antagonisms, and cross-purposes are handled in ways that minimize overt contention and avoid direct assertion, argument, or aggression. The high awareness of vertical social hierarchy (Nakane 1970) also works to conceal open disagreement through automatically enforcing deference toward status superiors. Also, the polite hesitation of ritualized *enryo* operates in persons of various statuses to minimize needs, disguise purposes, and avert disagreements with others. Additionally, the Japanese preoccupation with achieving consensus in group decision making operates to conceal opinions that might lead to open disagreement. Achieving consensus is more taxing and time-consuming than reaching agreement through a democratic process, where a simple majority opinion is sought to direct the course of action, and there is no need to conceal differences.

In Japan, mechanisms to govern conflict abound and are regulated by the nature of the social relationship and the context in which the potential disharmony may arise. A number of strategies and processes designed to preserve the sense of agreement have been identified. As described in Krauss, Rohlen, and Steinhoff (1984), these are first concerned with reducing escalation of conflict in an attempt to confine or divert dissension. A second series of maneuvers is concerned with the management of conflict using psychological mechanisms (repression, denial) as well as social-psychological strategies (avoidance, diversion, resolution). Ishida (1984) describes conflict management occurring with close in-group members, where even the appearance of conflict, if possible, should not be expressed in public. Resolutions proceed through indirect means, compromise, or change of opinion—ideally without overtly acknowledging the problem. Conflict in less intimate connnections also strives to avoid direct expression whenever possible, and the use of explicit, negotiated resolutions to achieve compromise are favored. In both situations, negotiations are conducted in a manner that avoids loss of face to the participants. The protection of face is at the core of all modes of conflict management, since public humiliation is difficult if not impossible to forgive or forget, and serves in the future as a reminder of animosity toward the person who caused the other to lose face.

Lebra (1984b) has made a succinct resume of strategies for conflict management among Japanese, beginning with anticipatory modes of prevention, which review possible future problems and deal with them preventively. She describes the use of third parties to buffer otherwise threatening encounters. Third parties may also be used to approach a delicate problem obliquely, by separately conversing with individuals about difficulties, and staving off conversations between the antagonists themselves. (This same use of a third person is documented by Valignano in the late 1500s, as recorded in Cooper 1981). Lebra (1984b) also notes various forms of self-aggression that function as modes of conflict management, whereby an injured partner exposes the unfairness of an antagonist's position through appearing to comply with an obviously unfair and distasteful resolution.

In concentrating on the avoidance of conflict, Japanese neglect becoming directly socialized in techniques of displaying or reacting to overt aggression. Except for persons whose instrumental roles are potentially connected to violence (e.g., the police, the military, and some athletes), the average adult Japanese is ill prepared to deal with unmitigated, overt aggression. Since personal aggression is disavowed and regarded as ego-dystonic, when it does appear it may become unregulated and lead to overreaction. Also, Japanese are not methodically socialized to intervene definitively with physical aggression that may develop in their midst, except by way of making indirect and mostly verbal attempts to admonish the contestants. Thus, they do not learn ways of physically containing, reducing, or stopping violence once it gets started.[5]

Parallel to the issue of conflict resolution, the general maintenance of order in Japanese society has been addressed by Rohlen (1989). He highlights three factors in accounting for the manner in which large groups of people follow orderly procedures. The first of these relates to the prominence of mutuality and reciprocity in relationships of every description—called "attachments" by Rohlen. The second factor is the ubiquitous expectation for compliance to hierarchical authority in basically unquestioning ways. The third factor concerns the inculcation of *routines*, which are rehearsed and ritualized in socialization procedures in the family, school, workplace, and general society.

The monitoring of behavior control through the realization of being observed in public interaction is defined by the term *seken*, which translates as "society or the public" but actually refers to a critical evaluation by others. As discussed by White and LeVine (1986),

Seken is not something to which you belong, like a family or a school or a workplace; it is a watchful normative presence, the equivalent of "what will the neighbors say?" All valued qualities, either personal or social, are important to *seken*, not just those that explicitly help to bond relationships. Ultimately, all valued qualities are relevant to one's place in the social nexus. (White and LeVine 1986, 57)

In the past this normative atmosphere was institutionalized through the surveillance of both appointed neighborhood leaders and the local police. This surveillance achieved several purposes. Dividing villages and municipalities into neighborhood units created a social membership involving groups of families united in the common purposes of fire prevention, cleaning streets, superintending property, and solving disputes involving dissension or minor unlawfulness. Traditionally, police have been distributed in a decentralized manner and assigned to particular neighborhoods. They have the responsibility of annually visiting each household to check on current occupancy, inspect for illicit or suspicious activity, and look for the presence of illegal inhabitants. Positively, such surveillance provides security, discourages criminal activity, and creates an atmosphere of public safety and order. Negatively, such surveillance—either by neighbors or the police—may induce an inhibiting and oppressive conformity, particularly evident during the 1930s and 1940s. Since the American Occupation, neighborhood organizations, especially in large cities, have less significance and the police, although still responsible for specific neighborhoods and households, are seen as more benign (Bayley 1976; Ames 1981). Although they are polite in their demeanor, this tight surveillance by neighborhood police permits a close observation of foreigners, potential criminals, visitors, and certain ethnic groups (e.g., Koreans) who are required to register and be fingerprinted every five years even after living in Japan all their lives (Wetherall and DeVos 1975).

Endurance and Suffering

Among Japanese there are a cluster of idealized characteristics that center on the attributes of fortitude, determination, and a capacity to endure difficult situations *(gaman)*. The desirability of these virtues is inflated in folklore, drama, and aphorisms, and frequently mentioned in everyday conversation. Perseverance includes the ability to suppress complaints, conceal discomfort, and demonstrate a tolerance for adverse circumstances. Beyond mere tolerance, hardship is seen as an opportunity to display courage, resourcefulness, and personal stamina. The cultural message behind this is that if one endures long enough, opposing forces may recede —almost as if endurance itself can produce such effects. Fortitude is also associated with the Japanese sense of fatalism and the predictable anticipation of adversity, historically witnessed in disasters such as earthquakes, typhoons, droughts, civil wars, and famines. Fatalism is also associated with the expectation of adversity in human affairs, where tense and potentially ignominious situations develop that can only be faced with endurance rather than direct resolution or counteraggression.

In their most dramatic rendition these virtues were associated with the code of *Bushidō*, which was the ceremonially reinforced courage of the *samurai* warrior (Nitobe 1969). *Samurai* were expected to endure and sacrifice on behalf of their lords, and were trained to ignore pain in performing obligatory duties. In less vainglorious versions, this endurance is looked on as a national characteristic, an integral part of the "Japanese spirit" *(Yamato damashii)*. In everyday forms *gaman* is idealized, as in the capacity of the Japanese mother to endure discomfort and deprivation in order to provide emotional and physical sustenance to her family (DeVos 1960, 1978). It is also seen even in young children, who are expected to study in unheated rooms in order to strengthen their endurance. (One commonly sees lightly clad, red-cheeked boys and girls playing outside during quite cold weather, cheerfully accepting the cold.)

The need to display a long-suffering attitude is not theologically justified as it is in the Western, Judeo-Christian world, where pain, infirmity, and adversity have been seen as opportunities to experience penance and gain redemption. Instead, these virtues are looked on as tapping inner resources that reflect a special capacity, based on *Japaneseness*, to endure hardship and eventually succeed. As Smith (1983) has commented, the expression of these values was prominent in the Showa Emperor's radio broadcast of August 15, 1945, which announced the conclusion of hostilities in the following way:

According to the dictates of time and fate . . . we have resolved to pave the way for a grand peace for all generations to come by enduring the unendurable and suffering what is insufferable. (Smith 1983, 115)

Reserve, Understatement, and Simplicity

Japanese have an investment in displaying simplicity, naturalness, and understatement, although these are counterbalanced by subtle exhibitionistic trends. Traditionally, they avoid forms of personal exhibition, ostentatiousness, or overt vanity. Behaviorally, this includes cultivating an economy of bodily movements, brevity of speech, and control of emotion, and a tendency to favor unobtrusiveness and avoidance of appearing conspicuous.

Such economy of expression and simplicity also influences styles of architecture, modes of dress, graphic art, and classical theater. The word *shibumi* (connoting "astringent") stands for a subdued elegance that is expressed in diverse ways. *Shibumi* has the additional connotations of uncluttered simplicity and naturalness along with a disdain for anything gaudy or spectacular. This economy of expressiveness is held to mimic the inherent unobtrusiveness of nature, where beauty is portrayed quietly and without fanfare. *Shibumi* implies the notion of reserve, simplicity, and restraint, but also the presence of an underlying latent power, whose strength is implicit in its very containment.

This Japanese sense of reserve also resonates with the proverbial habits of thrift and frugality, where the conservation of resources is regarded as virtuous. In those instances where individuals intentionally exhibit their wealth or possessions, the importance of these are discounted or severely rationalized, suggesting that they have not forgotten the ethos of reserve and simplicity. In a similar manner, emotions are conserved with the underlying idea that beneath the surface of controlled interaction, more powerful feelings are present.

Pollution and Purity: The Perimeter of
Cleanness and Uncleanness

Following a psychoanalytic model, some anthropologists in the 1940s (LaBarre 1945; Gorer 1943) interpreted the conspicuous Japanese characteristics of thrift, formality, orderliness, and ritualistic behaviors as due to juvenile conflicts surrounding toilet training. Subsequent studies uniformly reversed this speculation through documentaries that indicated a general permissiveness and relaxation concerning excretion. These demonstrated that control of soiling did not become a central preoccupation, nor did it ordinarily constitute a power struggle between child and mother. Instead, toilet training took place gradually, amid a number of other socialization procedures designed to produce cooperative control of infantile and childish behaviors.

There is, however, a prominent concern among Japanese concerning the generic issue of pollution and purification, which has an influence on world view, body image, social-psychological discriminations, and internalized dispositions. As reviewed by some commentators (Lock 1980; Ohnuki-Tierney 1984; Lebra 1976; Namahira 1987), the Japanese awareness concerning pollution and purification is extensive, and constitutes a dimension affecting subjective experience and interpersonal behavior.

In a conceptual and cognitive manner, Ohnuki-Tierney (1984) has analyzed purity and pollution according to a symbolical map of dichotomizations of "above/below," "inside/outside," "living/dead." Traditions substantiating the conceptual dimensions of pollution have been summarized by Namahira (1987), citing Japanese historians, theologians, and philosophers. Such commentary topographically connects pollution to two regions: an "underworld" inhabited by spirits, gods, and rambunctious natural forces, and an "outside world" incorporating foreign things, strangers, and even ideas that are exotic or culturally dystonic. Pollution is also prominently associated with death, particularly in its direct manifestations of corpses and totemic spirits, but additionally associated with organic decay and a series of unpleasant body products.

Philosophically these distinctions are related to both Shinto and Buddhist traditions, although in different ways. Buddhism characteristically maintains notions of the complementary balance existing between opposites versus the more compulsive and absolutist Shinto beliefs, which regard opposites as categorically separate and divided. Although both systems contribute to beliefs about pollution, Shinto traditions are concerned with a more phobic dread of filth, and distinguish an absolute boundary between dirty and clean. Contrastingly, Buddhism takes into account transitional gradations between apparent opposites, as manifested in the purification rituals chronologically connected to funeral observances, and in the ambivalent veneration and appeasement of deceased ancestors.

Paralleling ideas concerning pollution and illness, concerns about disfigurement or physical anomaly through birth defect, accident, or injury are high in Japan (Yokoyama 1984). In the past, birth defects were explained as spiritual punishments or the negative effects of prior incarnations. Physical deformities have always strongly decreased opportunities for a desirable marriage. Recently, a greater acceptance of physical infirmity seems to have been promoted through compassionate publicity about the effects of industrial accidents and injuries.

Topographical concerns about pollution and purity are integrally connected to the body image, and to cultural beliefs about the symbolic aspects of anatomy and physiology. Within the cultural topography of the body, the region below the navel is prone to contamination because it is in the general locale of excretion. Feet are also regarded as highly prone to pollution because of their contact with the "outside world" and "below world" of soil, streets, pavement, and excreta. Hands are vulnerable since they are engaged in social transactions involving touching other people and various objects that are potentially contaminated. In addition to urine and feces (which are rankly polluting), blood, sweat, vomitus, mucus, and even tears are potentially dangerous. Menstrual blood and vaginal secretions are regarded as strongly polluting. Skin lesions and exudates (pus) are contaminating, potentially transmitting illnesses. Other objects and places are culturally held to transmit pollution—particularly money (contaminated with germs), hospitals (where sick people reside), and even books (because they are touched by other persons). Secondhand articles of all kinds are disdained in Japan on the basis that their contamination is unknowable, and the objects may be unpurifiable.[6]

The Impurity of Objects

The rituals connected to purifying or neutralizing "dirty" objects and the situations where these may be encountered are publicly observable in Japan. Hands should be washed before eating, and after coming into the house from outside. Food should not be touched except by those who process or prepare it. Clean, white gloves are mandatory for elevator operators, drivers of public transportation, ticket punchers, ushers, and some store clerks. Underwear is supposed to be washed separately from other clothing. The futon, which is a combination mattress and quilt, is methodically aired and beaten each morning to discharge any accumulation of sweat or dust. Wearing special indoor footgear—socks or slippers—within the house is absolutely mandatory. Outside footgear is regarded as particularly contaminating. Special clogs are provided in toilets to restrict the transfer of "people dirt" from the toilet to other areas of the home or business establishment. Traditionally, areas for bathing are separated from the water closet or latrine. Many public and some private toilets avoid the Western-style toilet seat because of possible contamination from others. As mentioned by Ohnuki-Tierney (1984), domestic pets constitute a problem since they readily transmit "outside dirt" indoors, calling for the scrupulous cleaning of paws. Plath (in Ohnuki-Tierney 1984) privately communicated that some of his Japanese friends have "inside" and "outside" dogs to take care of the contamination problem.

The profession of nursing is still considered potentially contaminating since personnel have to handle other people's "dirt" and, moreover, are in contact with diseased persons. Doctors and dentists share this exposure; however, because of their more restricted physical contact with patient's bodies, they are considered less vulnerable to contamination. As emphasized by Namahira (1987), women are particularly prone to pollution—both physiologically and in their housekeeping functions. Menstruation is still regarded as personally and socially polluting. Women are encouraged not to bathe or wash their hair during the time of their period, and by law are allowed two days leave from work per month. (This prerogative is not universally offered or taken.) Women are seen as potentially polluted in their normal sexual and reproductive activities. Moreover, their house cleaning, having direct contact with raw food, and being responsible for cleansing other people's bodies and clothing implicate them as more vulnerable to pollution than are men, boys, or nonmenstruating girls.

Social Interaction and Impurity

As analyzed by Ohnuki-Tierney (1984) and Namahira (1987), the interactional and social-psychological connections between pollution and purity are multiform and distributed along an inside/outside dimension. In these terms, the inside of the body is seen as pure but prone to outside pollution, penetration, and infection.

"Inside" analogically also involves the relative purity of one's own household or rooms, contrasted to the dirtiness and potential contamination in the outside community. In social-interactional terms, "inside" versus "outside" has a parallel in defining the most intimate relationships as pure, unsullied, and natural, while peripheral attachments are potentially more polluting, dangerous, or even "dirty."

Medically, these inside/outside dimensions hold that the interior of the body—including one's spirit or "interior self"—is pure, but may be subject to invasion by germs, spirits, and penetrations by the unclean outside world. These possibilities for contamination call for propitiatory rituals involving avoidance of strong elements such as severe cold, heat, wind, and rain, which can reduce the resistance of persons. In the opposite direction, regular bathing and purification in a hot tub tends to sweat out accumulated pollutions and to prevent illness and disability.

The Pollution of Social Class

Pollution has also been associated with the older, historical class structure. This stratification was partly predicated on the avoidance of contamination, as in Indian society (Dumont 1970). In earlier periods, persons below the nobility and *samurai* were involved in occupations that were at least potentially polluting. Merchants, for example, faced contamination because they had contact with money, and also because ideological notions defined mercenary matters as demeaning and spiritually impoverishing. Entertainers, artisans, and folk healers were even more impure, since the nature of their employment and impermanent residence consigned them to positions of lower social approval. Historically, this disapproval applied to criminals, beggars, derelicts, and orphans, who were considered "nonhumans" *(hinin)*, either because of their social deviance or merely through their disconnection from families and enduring community relationships. At the very bottom of the list, however, were those occupations filled by persons who were in direct contact with objects related to extreme pollution. These included butchers, tanners, shoemakers, undertakers, makers of *tatami*, executioners, and workers connected to collecting garbage and "night soil" (human excrement).

Legislative changes beginning during the Meiji Restoration and continuing in the postwar period have removed the legal definition

of outcasts, and attempted to ameliorate the long-standing prejudice toward these individuals—estimated to be perhaps three million people. Despite this, most persons and families from this socially marginal group remain visible through their consignment to
undesirable occupational statuses and places of residence, and their
difficulty in "passing" into an upwardly mobile life through education, marriage, or personal achievement.

Behavioral "Impurity"

Finally, behavior itself may be submitted to a qualitative pure/
impure evaluation, as discussed by Lebra (1976), Lock (1980), and
Namahira (1987). Within colloquial and emic classifications, Lebra
(1976) sees the "pure self" as morally demonstrated through altruism, selflessness, sincerity, and the absence of overt personal vanity. As mentioned by Lock (1980), the concept of *hara* is partly
equivalent to the Western notions of "guts" or inner strength, and
constitutes the presence of an authentic, inner (i.e., "pure") direction of behavior. This is also expressed in terms of the pure *kokoro*
("heart"), demonstrated by a nonegotistical composure reflected in
kind and gracious interactions. Diametrically opposed to these are
behaviors connected to deviance, crime, and misbehavior, regarding
which Namahira (1987) stated that "acts that disturbed social solidarity and persons who had committed social crimes or disrupted
the social order were shunned as impure" (69). In this sense, behavioral disorderliness, untoward aggression, assertion, or other antisocial exhibitions may be regarded symbolically as constituting
forms of impurity. As discussed by other authors (Doi 1973a; Rohlen 1974a), the presence of manifestly deviant behavior itself suggests an impairment or imbalance of internal regulation.[7]

Japanese Cultural Chauvinism
and *Nihonjinron*

This chapter has furnished a historical and cultural resume concerning Japanese society. It is fitting to conclude by examining a
controversial area of recent criticism surrounding Japanese studies
under the rubric of *nihonjinron*. *Nihonjinron* literally means "theory of being Japanese," but also can be translated as "discussions of
the Japanese" (Dale 1986), "treatises on Japaneseness" (Kelly 1988),

or "analysis of Japanese identity." Other definitions are "cultural nationalism" (Befu 1988) or "philosophy concerning the Japanese spirit." Looked at collectively, the literature on *nihonjinron* is strongly—even lavishly—*emic.*[8] It strictly uses indigenous explanations and interpretations of Japanese history, family life, national destiny, spirit, and personality. What is implied by this term, however, is an uncritical and culturally chauvinistic description that inflates the significance of Japanese culture and ethos, and uses self-serving explanations of national identity. Such descriptions of Japanese life either implicitly or directly suggest superiority and "uniqueness" in comparison to other societies and cultures.

Peter Dale (1986) sees three implicit assumptions in writings that center on *nihonjinron.* In contrast to the conclusions of objective and empirical research, these assert 1) that Japanese are culturally and socially homogeneous—despite historical evidence to the contrary, 2) that Japan differs radically from all other societies—ignoring commonalities and continuities with other societies, and 3) that Japanese writings are conspicuously self-serving and boastful—overlooking comparisons and analysis, which might be more dispassionate and objective.

In a less incriminating sense, *nihonjinron* may be seen as a species of the tendency of all cultural groups to define their own specialized ethos and identity in terms of superiority to other groups, and to manufacture stereotypes validating their own solidarity, strength, purity, and racial destiny. As DeVos and Romanucci-Ross (1975) have discussed, ethnonationalistic solidarity pivots on ethnicity operating simultaneously as a "vessel of internal meaning" and an "emblem of contrast." What is distinctive about *nihonjinron,* however, is not only that this term captures the ubiquitous tendency of groups to flaunt their inflated identity, but also that the scholarly attributions concerning Japanese history, culture, personality, and national character have also exaggerated these characteristics into reified systems of hyperbole. Thus, in actual practice, *nihonjinron,* as a term, potentially includes both the social-scientific descriptions of Japanese life *and* the folk documentaries about Japanese "uniqueness."

Within the last ten years a number of critics have described the tendency to confuse folk testimony with scientific information. This has been illuminated in a series of counterreactions from commentators who have pointed to exaggeration and reification in some scholarly writings concerning Japanese life. These critics assert that such exaggerations have led to a monolithic and inaccurate portrayal of Japanese personality, social relations, and identity. Counterreactions to *nihonjinron* have taken a variety of forms in their criticisms of both indigenous and foreign commentators. In their most strident versions, counterreactions to *nihonjinron* have been called "Japanology bashing" by Kelly (1988). He reviewed critiques that focused on exaggerated descriptions of Japanese sensibility (Peter Dale 1986), psychocultural characteristics (Mouer and Sugimoto 1981), and the Japanese language itself (Miller 1982, 1986). He also notes reports concerning the "uniqueness" attributed to Japanese soil, animal life, the psychology of indigenous monkeys, and even the behavioral characteristics of bees (as criticized in Peter Dale 1986).

Mouer and Sugimoto (1981) are relatively moderate in their treatment of the alleged speciality imputed to Japanese in regard to their group affiliations, consensual decision making, vertical relationships, and maintenance of social obligations through *on* and *giri*. In the book they edit, a number of arguments are devoted to softening these generalizations through citing alternate information showing trends for individualism, evidence of contractual relationships, and the existence of social stratification. Taken together these seriously qualify some of the generalities publicized about Japanese culture.

Emphatic criticisms concerning the alleged uniqueness of the Japanese language have also been made. Miller (1986) is particularly forceful in his criticism of what he considers to be a mythologizing of the Japanese language by a series of indigenous language specialists. Unger (1987) exposes these same tendencies, which venerate the language as ineffable and ultimately unknowable to non-Japanese. He also points out the absurdity of the nearly mystical significance given to Japanese ideographic representations *(kanji)* by proponents of *nihonjinron*.

Sweeping his sights across the whole spectrum of *nihonjinron*, Peter Dale (1986) has organized a methodical critique of what he considers extremism in the psychological and social-scientific literature concerning Japanese culture, personality, politics, language, and history. Analyzing what he calls "the dialectics of difference," he has systematically tabulated a series of polarizations supposedly existing between Western and Japanese versions of cosmology, racial origin, sociocultural patterns, social-psychological functioning, intellectual styles, language use, and national character. Several of Dale's categories cut across typifications of Japanese personality in both self-presentational and subjective characteristics.

He states his purpose in the following manner:

This book is an attempt to write out the ground rules which govern the production of this kind of nationalistic idea through successive layers of thought: from linguistics through to family structure theory, sociological concepts and psychoanalytical notions to philosophical constructs, in order to show that this established way of interpreting Japan is formally invalid. (Dale 1986, iii)

Some of the ways in which Dale has attempted to undercut generalizations about *amae* will be addressed in chapter 6. He explains what he calls the "logic" of *nihonjinron* as arising from "a severe defensive, combative endeavor to overcome a diffuse sense of inferiority to the West" (Dale 1986, 188). In contrast, Wagatsuma (1973) has examined Japanese identity historically and cross-sectionally, and called attention to a century-old *ambivalence* toward Westernization rather than inferiority per se. He speculates that particularly in the postwar era, this ambivalence became both more conflicted and visible, appearing as feelings of rivalry mixed with admiration. Other authors have traced elements of ambivalence concerning outsiders during earlier centuries when the consciousness of foreigners' technical or numerical superiority simultaneously aroused awareness of both their dangerousness and attractiveness (Pelzel 1970).

As reviewed by Williams (1988), some of the deeper issues underlying the conflicts between Japanologists and critics of *nihonjinron* converge on the issue of cultural relativism. Williams cites Aoki (1988), who called attention to a fifty-year history of uncritical, emically oriented, and highly relativistic interpretations of Japanese society. He sees this as producing a noncritical anthropology that "has disguised and softened the otherwise hard contours of intercultural relations between nations for half a century" (in Williams 1988, 2).

In looking at both sides of this argument, one might conclude that fifty years of cumulative scholarship concerning Japanese studies have inevitably drifted toward some instances of caricature, exaggeration, and monolithic description in a way that calls for reexamination. It is equally evident that the Japanese themselves have intensified their claims for uniqueness, superiority, and exclusiveness following a series of outstanding economic and commercial achievements—particularly when contrasted to the relative decline of the U.S. during the past decade.

In an insightful book, van Wolferen (1989) has added to the discussion on *nihonjinrin* from several perspectives. Although he sees the "political management of reality" as part of the normal operations conducted by most nation-states, he feels that the Japanese stand out in this endeavor. This is because of the discrepancy tolerated between "truth" and "the appearance of truth," and the cultural acceptability of both duplicity and outright disinformation. His conclusions about Japanese political management are based on a comprehensive examination of the complex institutional interrelationships among the press, various organs of government, corporate leadership, capital resources, and trading institutions. The ability to say one thing and at the same time conceal the truth is related by van Wolferen to the commonly understood *tatemae* ("public" or superficial explanation) versus *honne* ("inner feelings" and true motives). He sees the *tatemae/honne* distinction as an ethically neutral "given" among Japanese, and views it as providing a frame of reference in which deceit may be socially sanctioned. Individuals and corporations may pretend to be honest while actually being dishonest, as evaluated in Western terms. He also looks at the tendency to make tautological excuses that use cultural justifications to argue for specialness or "uniqueness." Such excuses rationalize inconsistencies or idiosyncracy (including injustice or unfairness) on the basis that "that is the way we are."

Van Wolferen lists a number of categorical "specialities" of the Japanese reflecting the ideological use of culture as an inflated and unique ethos. Similar to Dale (1986), he finds these descriptions exaggerated. Unlike Dale, however, he sees these self-serving descriptions (of being irrational, of not following logic, of being moved by emotion, and of desiring to be dependent) not merely as propagandistic, but also as reflective of how most Japanese "believe they believe." Reflections on *nihonjinron* and its critics will be resumed in subsequent chapters.

Psychoanalytic Observations on History and Culture

In concluding this chapter, some generalizations about the psychological and psychoanalytic aspects of Japanese history and culture should be mentioned.

Probably most prominent is the long-standing cultural chauvinism and xenophobia in an insular nation that has historically felt itself vulnerable to invasion or domination from outsiders who possessed superior military capability, technology, and other resources. These fears, justified on a number of occasions, have coexisted with an inflated sense of superior racial identity and national destiny that resisted contamination by outsiders. Fears concerning excessive dependency on foreigners have been associated with realistic worries about Japan's lack of petroleum, natural resources, agricultural products, and even sufficient population to serve both as a base for production and as consumers to promote marketing. The combination of fear of outsiders and dependency on outsiders clearly has been one of Japan's persistent conflicts. Also, the desire to "identify with the aggressors" (Europeans and Westerners) has been accompanied by overcompensatory defenses of cultural, racial, and moral superiority to these same groups. In terms of superego, the government from the Tokugawa period to the end of the Pacific War was coterminous with the divinity of the Imperial system. This linkup of secular government and divinity was furthermore reinforced by the nationalistic practices of state-sponsored Shinto. Government itself was centralized in the mid–seventeenth century and promulgated standardized protocols for behavior, educational curricula, and control of neighborhoods and municipalities. This standardization created a high degree of national uniformity concerning acceptable norms, customs, and interaction rules. Although individual reactions to failure to meet normative standards varied, the uniformity of these proscriptions, along with their public visibility, favored their internalization as superego contents in both children and adults. Similarly, norms concerning the fine distinctions in hierarchical statuses have been ingrained throughout Japanese society along with conventions regarding the consequences of gender, age, occupational, and social role. Failure to observe accepted norms in regard to status have also been accompanied by mixtures of embarrassment, fear, and guilt.

At an ego-defensive level, various reaction formations have operated to convert *narcissism* (including inflated demands for entitlement and selfishness) into ritualized self-effacement, reserve, understatement, and denial of worth *(enryo)*. Individual narcissism is also transformed (sublimated and projected) into group narcissism. Reaction formations against *aggression* are also prominent and are inculcated with the objective of producing harmony, social cooperation, and orderly public behavior. Achievement (DeVos and Wagatsuma 1973) and perseverance, which Pelzel (1977) sees as "linchpins" of Japanese identity, are prominent and can be analyzed as evoking several adaptive unconscious ego mechanisms. Severe discomfort is tolerated, even emulated, on the basis of identification with long-suffering parents, teachers, fictional characters, and exemplary historical figures who endure and persevere through adversity *(gaman)*. Achievement also involves the sublimation of baser drives for aggression or domination into culturally accepted modes of accomplishment and socially approved success.

A strong trend for cultural chauvinism *(nihonjinron)* and "uniqueness" has been analyzed partly as a reaction formation converting a long-standing sense of inferiority (to China, Europe, and the United States) into an overcompensatory sense of superiority. Projection might also be used to explain the channeling of self-contempt and hate onto other persons or nationalities. Both Maloney (1968) and DeVos (1985) have separately emphasized this latter possibility.

From a Western psychoanalytic standpoint, the Japanese would be seen to impose excessive *repression* on the sexual overtones of juvenile development (to be discussed in chapters 8 and 9). Similarly, if Western schedules of development are used as standards of comparison, the Japanese might be considered "deviant" in their emphasis on life-long inclinations toward dependency and seeking a continuation of pregenital gratifications. This might be interpreted as *repressing* the sexual significance of oedipal cravings and seeking regressive, libidinal satisfactions at a lower level of development. However, just the reverse might be alleged. Perhaps it is the case that Westerners systematically repress and disguise a primary, nonsexualized drive for affiliation and indulgence. Also, it may be the case that the application of sexual formulations to the early instincts is itself an artifact of a Judeo-Christian tradition that inflates the significance of sexuality and transposes oedipal guilt onto the pregenital strivings for closeness, security, warmth, and cherishment.

This might partly explain the degree of embarrassment, shame, and even revulsion connected to dependency cravings in adult Western life, contrasted to Japanese society, where the idea of being dependent on other persons, institutions, and groups is completely acceptable. This could also be associated with what van Wolferen (1989) has noted as a conspicuous response to authority in Japanese life. DeVos (1989, private communication) has linked these two together—specifically the cultural acceptance of respecting authority, and the belief (or hope) that one can *depend* on authority. This will be returned to in a later chapter on the Japanese self.

Notes

1. A number of basic social transformations occurred as a result of the legal elimination of fixed, hereditary class positions. Household designations *(ie)*, with all their consequences for patrilineal descent, primogeniture, and stratification within families, were extended to the kinship organization of ordinary citizens. Surnames were established for all persons, while social designations regarding dress codes and hair styles were gradually abandoned.

2. These extraordinary achievements in production and marketing have been favored by the internationalization of investments, manufacturing, and trading, which has flourished since the early 1970s. In the American market, the Japanese success has involved avid (if at times naive) cooperation of federal and state governments, along with the collaboration of U.S. investors, industry, and distribution sectors. Successful Japanese trading techniques have exploited the American ideological dedication to "open markets" and laissez faire capitalism in gaining unreciprocal commercial advantages. Coalitions with lobbyists and exploitation of the complexities of American legislative and judicial systems have retarded counterreaction to severely unbalanced exporting opportunities in Japan. Prestowitz (1988) has written an evenhanded but critical documentary of Japanese gains and American losses in the steel, electronics, automotive, and microchip industries. Fallows (1989a, 1989b) has addressed more general aspects of Japan's one-sided trading processes. Choate (1990) has organized a documentary detailing the manner in which American lobbyists, attorneys, ex–public officials, politicians, and political advisors are employed by Japanese companies in helping to capture strong marketing positions in various exports to the United States.

3. Van Wolferen's (1989) critical book has stirred both support and criticism. Wysocki comments on van Wolferen's provocative argument, which suggests that despite postwar constitutional changes, Japanese still favor hierarchical and closed systems operating on informal traditions and reciprocity rather than fixed standards and rule of law. Tanaka is more critical of the overall "logic" used in van Wolferen's argumentation, and of his tendency to denounce all Japanese intellectuals as producing propaganda for the "system."

4. The usually observed distinction between *norms* and actual *behavior* should be noted here. What individual culture bearers either say they do (or say they *ought to do*) is generally understood to be different than what they actually do in their behavioral performances in the real world. This difference is present in Japanese society as it is among any group.

5. In the uninhibited atmosphere of elementary school playgrounds, children are exposed to considerable potential hazing and mild physical aggression—particularly among boys. The author has witnessed a number

of episodes of moderate physical aggression in public areas. One of these involved two twelve-year-old boys returning from school in midafternoon accompanied by three friends. One boy, who was slightly larger than his opponent, was rhythmically striking his companion around the lower head, shoulders, and upper arms. The victim did not retaliate but only moved his head and elevated his shoulders to avoid being struck, all the while continuing to walk along the sidewalk. The three noncombatant friends trailed along, but neither spoke nor directly intervened. When the victim stopped next to a light pole, two of the noncombatants stepped close to, but not quite between, the combatants. Although intrusive with their bodies, they directed their gaze elsewhere, and also did not speak to the two who were fighting. What was most distinctive, however, was how this one-sided contest went on and on. The pummeling continued as the boys slowly walked about half a block. It finally stopped when the antagonist seemed to tire of what he was doing. All five boys then rapidly rearranged their positions and walked off together in a spirited manner—as if nothing had happened.

The author also recalls a protracted physical attack observed in a metropolitan train station where a man in his early forties was repeatedly striking another man (who looked around fifty) about the head and shoulders. A railway guard was more or less in the middle of this pummeling, saying virtually nothing but attempting to insert his body between the two (like a boxing referee). However, he did not use his own hands and arms to restrain the antagonist or shield the victim. A man and a woman who seemed to know the person being struck circled around this group, calling out for the antagonist to stop. The fifty-year-old man only passively resisted by putting his hands up to protect his head. What was most interesting however, was that the aggression continued because no one (including the antagonist) seemed to know how to stop it. It became like a macabre dance, with the security guard interposing himself, the injured party pulling away, the couple chattering at the assailant, and the assailant running around the protective trio to find his target and resume pummeling him.

In both the case of the twelve-year-old-boy and the forty-year-old man, several things seem unusual to a Western observer. First, in each instance the pummeling was unilateral; the victim mainly attempted to fend off blows, but did not retaliate. Second, in both situations, the intermediaries attempted to interrupt the fighting in a quite passive manner—largely by trying to place themselves *between* the contestants or by distracting the aggressor. Finally, it seemed remarkable how extended both of these encounters were—as if no one knew how to bring them to a conclusion.

6. Even while visiting or living in Japan for short periods, one's awareness is drawn to the potential contamination from the ground. This subjective feeling is reinforced by observing the scrupulous avoidance of touching the ground or pavement. For example, it is not unusual to see travelers spread newspapers underneath their suitcases on a station platform. Home-

less men may be seen outside railway stations sleeping in large cardboard boxes with their footware carefully placed outside. It is most common to see cab drivers feather-dusting their spotless cars while waiting for their next fare. Possibly the most frequent reminder is inculcated through repetitiously taking off one's shoes when entering a home, certain eating areas, temples, or bathhouses.

In contrast to some of these fastidious observances, Japanese show generally less repugnance to urine and vomitus in outdoor situations. It is common to see children and adult men relieve themselves when facilities are not nearby. Jolly or not-so-jolly drunks may vomit in public places without stirring much commotion. Finally, Japanese males do a great deal of spitting on sidewalks and streets in a manner that is surprising and somewhat revolting to Westerners.

7. Intepreting the extent and significance of Japanese preoccupations with impurity in comparison to other societies is problematic. Virtually all cultures have concerns about contamination and pollution regarding bodily products, soil, garbage, refuse, and so forth. Similarly, there are concerns about contagion, avoidance of contact with dirt, and rituals concerned with hygiene and cleanliness. What seems distinctive to Japanese is the manner in which these beliefs and rituals are publicly conspicuous, and have a strong normative impact on a large proportion of the society regardless of age, social status, or situation. However, ethnographic reports may unintentionally exaggerate the significance placed on purification rituals, simply because they seem to be unduly prominent to the outside observer—as satirized in Horace Miner's (1956) spoof on American purification rituals.

DeVos (1975) has raised another caution about the tendency of a methodological focus (as in Douglas 1966) that concentrates on collective symbolism while ignoring complementary or alternate explanations based on internally structuralized formulations—either biological or psychological.

8. Distinctions between "emic" and "etic" modes of observation and analysis have become established conventions in anthropology (Pike 1954; Harris 1968). "Emic" is a contraction of "phon*eme*" and refers to the description and explanation of cultures in the specific terms and formulations of the culture itself (i.e., from the "natives' point of view"). "Etic," contracted from "phon*etic*," refers to descriptions and explanations of culture based on higher-level abstractions relating to more universal conjectures about categorizations of observed behaviors and customs. Also, *emic* statements refer to causal explanations and descriptions of general cultural phenomena as depicted by representative members of that society. *Etic* statements are those explanations and descriptions that conform to standards of scientific observation and categorization. These distinctions offer a useful segregation of ethnographic data and their organization/interpretation. However, there are many ways in which such distinctions are *not* easily made—as discussed in Harris (1968).

CHAPTER 4

Japanese Childrearing and Early Socialization: Implications for *Amae*

In all cultures, the period of early childhood is a high-water mark for dependency, when caregivers are responsible for providing security, physical nurturance, and emotional comfort. Qualitative and quantitative differences in childrearing have been studied cross-culturally, partly with the objective of illuminating processes connected to distinctive adult adaptations. There is a large literature of cultural descriptions, ethnographic studies, and popular information concerning childhood socialization in Japan. These contain descriptions of actual practices as well as social-scientific and folk explanations that justify and rationalize these practices. These can be examined to address Pelzel's (1977) question about the relationships between childrearing and the prominence of *amae*.

Some cautionary statements are in order. Cultural descriptions of childrearing and socialization seek generalizations that may suggest a monolithic standardization or even "uniqueness" (Peter Dale 1986). Unfortunately, this tendency is inherent in descriptions composed by both indigenous and outside observers. The reader should realize that generalizations about childhood socialization procedures in no way void the diversity exhibited within these normative guidelines. Regardless of cultural specificity, childrearing styles reflect the personalities and communicative patterns of particular parents, and vary according to education, economic status, and residential location. Stratification in social class is itself coordinated with differential awareness and compliance concerning the normative order in Japan as it is elsewhere (DeVos and Wagatsuma 1973, 391).

Another problem in reviewing generalizations about cultural practices is that some behaviors and attitudes undergo change over a number of decades, reflecting differences in historical era. During the past forty-five years Japanese society has moved toward increased urbanization, diversification in education and occupation, higher consumerism, changes in women's roles, and reactions to contacts with outside cultures. Taken together, these have fostered modifications both in practice and in explanations of practice and belief. Despite these changes, certain normative and behavioral characteristics have been comparatively uniform over a long period of time in Japan. Prominent among these, marriage and childrearing have retained certain conservative tendencies even in the face of postwar changes in legislation, politics, income, and roles for both mothers and fathers (Smith and Schooler 1978).

Marriage and Childrearing

In the letters and journals of some of the earliest visitors to Japan, reports concerning social practices recorded that differences in expectation regarding gender were inculcated early in life, conspicuously reinforcing the status superiority of males (Caron and Shouten 1935 [1636], 48; Hearn 1971 [1901], 55–79, 421–23; Chamberlain 1971 [1904], 165–66). Then as now, the polite and decorous behavior of little children was commended by missionaries and members of trading companies, who related these virtues to compassionate but firm parental discipline (Valignano 1954 [1583], as reported in Cooper 1981, 4; von Siebold 1973 [1841], 125). More recently, systematic studies have focused on childrearing practices in greater depth and precision, often examining these in the context of courtship, marriage, and relations to extended family.

Courtship, Marriage, Pregnancy, and Childbirth

As Long (1987) has commented, marriage remains an ascendant institution in Japan. Marriage is centrally concerned with the continuation of family lineage through procreation. This concern is accompanied by a stress on proper childrearing in order to create adaptive, disciplined, and happy youngsters capable of meeting the challenges of later development and maturity. Single status not only deprives an individual of a primary adult role, but presents the risk of social isolation and insecurity in a childless old age (Lebra 1984a). Fumie Kumagai (1984) reported that by age forty, 95 percent of contemporary Japanese men and women have been married. Not being married is thought of as socially peculiar—more so for women than men (Tanazaki 1957).

Traditionally, courtship and marriage have been regarded as too important to pivot on the vagaries of romantic love. Although there have been significant postwar changes in courtship, formal negotiations are still preferred. Arrangements (called *miai*) are carried out through friendly or professional intermediaries *(nakōdo)* who broker the process of making introductions and initiating meetings between the families. The backgrounds of both partners are usually investigated to confirm the absence of genetic, health, socioeconomic, and other factors that might affect eligibility. If arrangements proceed smoothly, the ceremony often seeks a strong patron to add further endorsement to the union. Actual romantic attachment or prior informal association may or may not be connected to these negotiations (Hendry 1981). The presence of love is desirable, but ideally is thought to develop after rather than before marriage.

As summarized by Long (1987), qualitative and quantitative changes in courtship have affected the methods of proper introduction and the duration of engagement. Recently, the ratio of "arranged marriages" *(miai kekkon)* to "love marriages" *(ren'ai)* is now estimated to be about half and half. Particularly in cities, individuals are likely to have met each other at school or work, and to have been the primary participants in their decisions about marrying, length of their engagement, and nature of the wedding ceremony.[1]

Romantic love has traditionally been treated as exhilarating but dangerous. Ambivalence concerning passionate love is common in Japanese literature and drama, where romance is portrayed as potentially destructive toward both families and individuals. Melodramatic stories of double suicide illustrate both the allure and the precariousness of passionate associations (See DeVos 1960).

In urban environments before the 1950s, relatively little opportunity existed for social contact with the opposite sex prior to marriage.[2] Postwar coeducation has changed this, although Japanese secondary students still remain relatively shy with the opposite sex (Rohlen 1983). Work associations now serve as a preparation for premarital interaction. However, after-work socializing still divides men into their employment and friendship groups, while women return to their homes to perform domestic duties.

Communication patterns between the sexes in Japan are based on sharp socialization differences where modes of expression, degrees of assertiveness, and choice of subject matter are more gender-specific than in many Western cultures (Miller 1967; Shibamoto 1985). Since the socialization process producing male and female roles is highly differentiated in Japan, the relationship between husband and wife reflects this, although the degree varies with generation, age, and social status. Women typically do not discuss politics with men, although their participation in lobbying and voting is notable, particularly regarding domestic, environmental, and consumer issues. Women also tend to avoid topics concerning sports or business affairs with their husbands. Husbands ordinarily do not discuss the workplace, nor do their wives inquire about this, except in elliptical ways. Contrasted to American couples, Japanese wives do not socialize with the husband's associates, nor with their wives. Husbands and wives may go out together to shop, visit relatives, and perhaps sight-see with the children, but generally not for dinner, theater, or concerts.

In comparison to Americans, adult Japanese avoid touching others during conversation (Barnlund 1975). This also pertains to married couples, who strictly avoid physical contact, let alone caressing either in public or in front of the children at home. Also, affection is not ordinarily expressed verbally, and the expectation for protracted conversation is not present among average Japanese couples. Except on playgrounds, in bars, at parties, or among groups of young people, conversation among Japanese is relatively subdued and abbreviated. Conversational partners are accustomed to interpreting subtle meanings from verbal expression and to reading between the lines. At the same time, they pay close attention to nonverbal indicators regarding mood or intentions. Although descriptions of this nonverbal communication can be exaggerated (as noted in Peter Dale 1986, 100), wives and husbands commonly use intuition to guess at the moods and thoughts of their partners.[3]

Culturally, there are sharp demarcations between behaviors at work and home, and between men's and women's roles. This sustains a complementary marital relationship that, on the surface, appears formal and noncompanionate in comparison to American and European marriages. However, as Blood (1967), Long (1987), and Lebra (1984a) point out, the actual power structure and decision making follows carefully assigned roles where wives exercise control over family finances, childrearing, home management, and education of the children. Wives inform and consult with husbands about major decisions, but husbands usually occupy a position of titular rather than operational authority. Wagatsuma (1977) has discussed the declining authority of fathers, due to the absence of Confucian moral training in the schools and the rapid increase in nuclear families living in congested, urban apartments.

Recent Trends in Marriage and Home Life

Recent changes in Japanese family life have been summarized by Long (1987) in a survey of both the Japanese and English-language literature. Two retrospective studies (Norbeck 1978; Smith 1978) have involved the reexamination of rural villages after a twenty-five-year interval. Results of both studies paralleled statistical reports of national changes demonstrating a decrease in mean family size, fewer three-generation households, and a rise in the proportion of nuclear families (Yuzawa 1977). More geographic relocation following marriage was represented, along with fewer instances of economic ties to extended kin. Household size shrunk from a mean of around five (from 1920–55) to a level of three persons (Long 1987). The average number of children born in the 1920s was nearly five per family, shrinking to four in the next two decades, but dwindling to two since 1952. Accompanying the trends for women to work during marriage, and the acceptance of smaller families, the current childrearing strategy is to have fewer children, to have them early in marriage, and to provide educational and other enrichment to make their futures smooth and successful (F. Kumagai 1984). Countering this, the government has promoted greater reproductivity through posters, billboards, and commercials exhorting families to have three children—called "the happy family" (Garrick 1991, personal communication).

Long (1987) also reported that the length of the conjugal period has doubled from twenty-two years in 1940 to forty-four in 1972, reflecting the shorter period of childrearing (fewer children), increased longevity, and a decline in the three-generation household. Although traditional gender-role differentiation has continued, there are qualitative modifications in many middle-class marriages. This is attributed to the economic contributions of wives, but also the effect of normative trends that encourage husbands' participation in some domestic affairs. Long (1987) cites Kokichi Matsuda (1981), who concludes that these changes combine the effects of postwar coeducation, more educational and work opportunities for women, the increase in love marriages, decreased age differential between spouses, and the tendency toward a greater degree of companionate and shared activity among younger couples.

As in all marriages, the arrival of the first child alters the relationship of the new parents, and imposes significant changes. The cultural expectations for maternal and paternal roles are clearly prescribed, and transmitted to successive generations with consistency. Children learn these through imitation as well as direct instruction. Some trends since the 1950s have recommended earlier weaning, crib sleeping, and supplementary bottle feeding. While some young working couples may adopt these innovations, traditional practices still remain favored and idealized. Dr. Michio Matsuda, Japan's Dr. Spock, has authored a number of popular books on childrearing; his advice uniformly reinforces traditional customs (M. Matsuda 1967, 1973).

Early Socialization: Nutrition and Sleeping

The Japanese infant is born into an architectural setting smaller and less private than among young marrieds of similar backgrounds in the U.S. Although currently not common, young Japanese couples used to move into or near the home of the husband's parents, where the husband's mother was closely connected to supervising the daughter-in-law in child care—sometimes actually displacing her. Now that many newlyweds reside at a distance, the potentially harsh effects of the mother-in-law are attenuated, and her influence over both son and grandchildren may be more symbolic than actual (Frager 1971; Lebra 1984a). Young mothers are also influenced by the peer pressure of friends and coworkers who affirm conservative traditions concerning pregnancy, delivery, and childrearing (Carter and Dilatush 1976). Motherhood is generally accepted as the most important female role in Japan. The sobering responsibilities of childrearing are elevated above those of working, or duties toward her husband and natal family.

By Western standards, Japanese living space is confined. The average single room in Japan is roughly nine by twelve feet (Dore 1958), and apartment size is commonly eighteen by thirty feet overall. Room separations are created by interior walls or sliding doors (called *shōji* and *fusuma*) made of wooden lattice covered by paper or translucent plastic. Rooms are diversified and serve multiple purposes during the day, evening, or nighttime. Bedding and quilts (futon) are spread directly onto straw floor mats *(tatami)*. Japanese have a tradition of sleeping adjacent to one another in various configurations, discussed in detail by Caudill and Plath (1966).

A small futon is prepared for infants and located directly next to the mother. Toward the end of the first year, the baby may begin to sleep in the same futon as its mother. In a way that seems unusual —even peculiar—to Westerners, children may cosleep with their mothers and fathers for an extended period—often until they are five or six, and sometimes longer. Following this, they may sleep next to grandparents or adjacent to same- or opposite-sex siblings. Often a child is displaced from cosleeping next to mother following the birth of a younger sibling. If this occurs before age five, the child is often given the compensatory privilege of sleeping next to father. Sleeping adjacent to parents early in life is a normative pattern (Vogel and Vogel 1961). Moreover, sleeping adjacent to others is a lifelong expectation, appearing in a variety of arrangements. Same-sex cosleeping adjacent to siblings is standard, but is always the case after puberty. Older adolescents may end up sleeping alone, because of their study habits or because older siblings have left home. Late adolescence and early adulthood are mentioned as the rare times of life when individuals have to sleep alone. In general, sleeping by oneself is looked on as a deprivation regardless of age. While familial cosleeping fosters a sense of security and communal closeness, it requires suppressing overt sexuality.

Sexuality and Physical Contact

Given group cosleeping, having sexual intercourse requires considerable discretion and constraint—and waiting for others to go to sleep. This is discussed in the early literature by Beardsley, Hall, and Ward (1959), Vogel (1967), Caudill and Plath (1966), Howard S. Levy (1971), and, more recently, Lebra (1976, 1984a). Statistical comparisons between Japan and the U.S. do not report significant differences in frequency of intercourse, according to decade of life or length of marriage (Shinozaki 1957; H. S. Levy 1971; Asayama 1974). They do, however, demonstrate a relative lack of foreplay and afterplay among Japanese lovers surveyed in some of these studies. Ideally, sex occurs after the children are asleep or before they awaken. Given the paper-thin walls and the close presence of small children, sexual union is attempted in a restrained and quiet manner. Despite these restrictions, intercourse is reported as mutually pleasurable (Shinozaki 1957; H. S. Levy 1971). Lebra's (1984a) interviews of married women noted that most wives were naive about sex before becoming married, although this was not accompanied by conflict or difficulty in enjoying intercourse following marriage.

These close sleeping arrangements raise the question of the possible effects of witnessing the primal scene on Japanese children. Reports from parents suggest the use of conscious denial, for example, "it's alright now, the children are asleep," "we are very quiet," or "they would not know what we are doing." However, it is not unusual for some little children to mimic the postures of the sex act, leading to prompt and embarrassed reprimands by adults (Garrick 1987, private communication). This suggests that dovetailing with their parents' denial, children may dissociate and eventually repress the recognition that their parents have intercourse. This repression is complementary to the caution exercised by the parents to minimize noise, which might break through the psychological blockade of their children. Thus, both parents and children eventually act as if "this never really happens."

In addition to cosleeping, there is a generous amount of close physical contact during daytime between infants, young children, and their mothers. Infants and small children are not allowed to fret very long, but are picked up to be nursed and rocked. The infant or young child accompanies the mother to various parts of the home as she works. Also, infants and children are allowed to nap on their own demand, and to fall asleep in various safe areas of the home adjacent to family members who are available to hold or divert them should they awaken. Probably because it does not involve being sent to another area of the home, Japanese children willingly accept naps, unlike some of their American counterparts. Special playpens and sleeping cribs are not used in Japanese homes, and are seen as cruel in forcing confinement and isolation. Security and safety are supplied by the direct, physical responsiveness of the Japanese mother or her surrogates. Japanese youngsters seem to encounter less frustration and more uninhibitedly learn to navigate within their home environment. Similarly, in outdoor expeditions the toddler is either allowed to walk or is carried on the back of a family member—usually the mother. The most popular and traditional form of transporting little children uses a cloth pouch (onbu suru) that positions the baby on the back and is connected across the shoulders and anterior neck. From this position the baby can see and participate in what is going on, while the mother's arms remain free to conduct other activities.

Infants and young children also maintain close physical contact with the family during the early evening. They are not placed on a strict sleeping schedule dictating that they be in bed at any precise, preestablished time. The Japanese mother develops strategies based on the child's own rhythm, with the hope that he or she will fall asleep at certain times of the day or nighttime.

Differences in various aspects of caretaking were shown among Japanese and American mothers and their youngsters by the frequently cited reports of Caudill and Weinstein (1969), Caudill (1972), and Caudill and Schooler (1973). These investigators confirmed that

the Japanese mother ... is present more with the baby, in general, and seems to have a more soothing and quieting approach, as indicated by greater lulling, and by more carrying in arms and rocking. (Caudill and Schooler 1973, 324)

This is readily observable in Japanese homes. Babies and children are adamant about requiring that their mothers be nearby and respond to their requests physically and emotionally. Conversely, mothers do not usually leave their infants and children "to play by themselves" (Garrick 1987, personal communication). In Caudill's studies, Japanese mothers did not initiate stimulation of their children as frequently as American mothers, but instead reacted to their children's activity levels. Similarly, the Japanese mothers vocalized, but did not verbalize as much as their American counterparts.[4]

In a psychoanalytically oriented cross-cultural study, Pavenstedt (1965) made comparisons between childrearing observed among youngsters and mothers in Boston and Kyoto. She commented on the high degree of body contact, mutual staring, and playfulness during feeding observed between Japanese infants and their mothers. She emphasized the close physical union between children and their mothers and the sentiment against having outsiders care for their children. In fact, the very idea of babysitting is anathema to Japanese (Wagatsuma 1985). Also, the notion of an infant or young child sleeping away from parents, or sleeping alone, is regarded as mean and frankly dangerous (Blood 1967, 180.) Both cosleeping and the reluctance to have strangers tend children are symbolic of the mothers' acceptance of total responsibility for child care. More defensively, it is related to avoiding any blame or condemnation if others sense that she is not fulfilling her appointed duties. Some mothers may even leave their children unattended while they go out on an essential errand, rather than reveal that they are not measuring up to the idealized standards of total caregiving (Garrick 1987, private communication).

Breast Feeding and Nutrition

Extended breast feeding has always been strongly advocated in Japan for a combination of nutritional, medical, and emotional reasons. The intimate interaction surrounding nursing symbolically characterizes the strongly interconnected infant-mother relationship. In the earlier literature (Lanham 1956; Dore 1967; and Vogel 1967), surveys of families reported that weaning usually was not initiated before eight months, or completed until fifteen months. Later studies showed somewhat earlier times for the beginning and ending of weaning, particularly in big cities. However, even with these changes, weaning is begun later and done more gradually when compared to the comparable surveys in the U.S.

In her study of five Kyoto families, Pavenstedt (1965) commented on the languid but emotionally intense nature of breast feeding in Japan. Fondling of the breast and nipple by the child was routine (also poignantly described by Lebra 1976). Both Lebra and Pavenstedt point out that the breast is not only a nutritional object, but also one of play and proximate connection to mother. Lebra (1976, 59) has exemplified this by citing folklore and songs that commemorate mother's breasts. The tactile availability of mother's breasts is enhanced by delayed weaning and cosleeping. Weaning may be begun earlier among mothers in large cities, reflecting the practical acceptance of supplemental or total bottle feeding. Bottle feeding is also used by mothers who are compelled to return to outside working situations—although this is discouraged unless absolutely necessary. Even following weaning, however, because of cosleeping the breast still is accessible for fondling and touching. Some Japanese children, usually boys, may be allowed to suckle while falling asleep, long after their nutritional weaning.

There is negligible embarrassment concerning nursing in front of other children or visitors. However, observation of women nursing in public—particularly in cities—is rare, principally through it being regarded as unsophisticated, not shameful. In a resume of folklore and interview research, Howard S. Levy (1971) reported on the subsidiary role breasts play in fantasy and sexual practices in Japan. The areas of highest erotization reported by men include the nape of the neck, ears, dorsum of the chest, breasts, abdomen, vulva, and thighs. Fascination with the breast is associated by the Japanese with the "pornographic" views of Westerners, where cultural stereotypes of generous endowment and high sexual appetites are combined in the idealization of prominent breasts.

Perhaps because of protracted weaning, cosleeping, and close tactile contact, the incidence of finger sucking and use of pacifiers is correspondingly low in Japan. Caudill and Weinstein (1969) demonstrated that Japanese youngsters indulged in more nutritional suckling and less use of transitional objects. They found a higher frequency of finger sucking and pacifier use among infants who were bottle fed both in Japan and the U.S., and they reported that

the average [finger sucking] for Japanese babies fed *entirely* by bottle is lower than the average for the American babies fed entirely by breast. (Caudill and Weinstein 1969, 30; italics original)

The introduction of solid foods for Japanese youngsters is qualitatively different than with average American infants. Although puréed foods are marketed, they are not as popular as rice and other bland table foods that are inconspicuously added to the infants' diets while they share meals with the family. A spoonlike implement is employed for feeding during early childhood. Manipulating chopsticks requires a high degree of coordination, and is not ordinarily mastered until age three or older. Touching food with the fingers is strongly discouraged, since Japanese consider handling food at the dinner table to be crude and vaguely disgusting. Playing with or spilling food is not regarded as amusing, and is avoided by removing any opportunity for spilling or messing. Generally, children are not forced to eat foods they do not like; hence, there is little implicit morality associated with having to eat certain foods or at certain fixed times (Frager 1971).

Bathing and Cleanliness

The custom of shared bathing also contributes to a sense of closeness and tranquility between children and parents. Although tiny infants are bathed in a special receptacle, very young children are bathed with their mothers (alternatively with fathers, grandparents, or siblings). Unlike Western communities where bathing is related to cleanliness and is done privately, bathing in Japan is socialized and connected to shared comfort, relaxation, and companionship. Bathing is divided into a preparatory sudsing and rinsing, followed by immersion into a clean tub of steaming hot water. Japanese are scrupulous about bathing daily, and use a small upright tub *(furo)* in which to relax and soak. This is used in sequence by members of the family, usually according to hierarchical status, accommodating two or, at most, three people at a time (one adult and two children). As in cosleeping, shared bathing continues long after such intimacy would be tolerable or comfortable in the West. Father/daughter bathing is discontinued around puberty, but mother/son bathing may go on indefinitely. Any latent sexuality present in bathing or in simple nudity itself is suppressed within the home. One exception occurs when married couples may take advantage of the comfort and privacy to enjoy intercourse (Garrick 1986, private communication). Same-sex bathing remains a common experience of special sociability among Japanese adults, and is associated with the nonerotic, sensual pleasantness of shared comfort and opportunity for chatting (Caudill 1972).[5]

In contrast to the close physical proximity, the intimacy of cosleeping and cobathing, Japanese parents and grandparents do not stimulate children through kissing, nuzzling, or tickling. Although infants and children are frequently picked up, held, and fussed over, kissing, especially on the lips, face, or neck, is rare (Wagatsuma and Lanham 1983). It is common to see a greeting between an adult and child celebrated with smiles, expressions of praise, and raising the youngster up to adult eye level—but not actually kissing. Little children touch each other, but adolescents and adults mostly avoid this. Married couples do not embrace or kiss each other except in private, and then generally as part of sexual foreplay. Little children commonly hold hands while walking to school, and young girls and boys are free to touch friends and classmates until reaching middle school, when this practice is limited to same-sex contact. Fathers can be tusseled with and touched until children approach age four, when his more formal and superior status reduces this possibility— unless *he* initiates contact. According to Barnlund's (1975) studies, there is a marked reduction in touching between father and children after age five. When contrasted with Americans, Japanese students reported only half as much touching. Also, nearly 20 percent of the Japanese sample registered very low levels of physical contact, and a considerable number reported remembering no physical contact with either the same- or opposite-sex parent. Japanese adults in public avoid touching each other during conversation or other interchange, although they tolerate this from foreigners, who "don't know any better."

As Barnlund states it,

Among Americans, communication through physical contact is much more common. . . . In Japan physical intimacy apparently decreases sharply after childhood, reducing reliance on touch as a means of expressing inner feeling. (Barnlund 1975, 109)

Early Socialization Regarding Aggression and Discipline

Reactions to crying reveal another contrast. Ordinarily, crying is responded to swiftly in Japan, both in public and at home. The close proximity of the Japanese mother tends to reduce fussing and crying. As Vogel and Vogel (1961), Caudill and Weinstein (1969), and Lebra (1976) all discuss, this rapid response to unhappy vocalization is a means of tacitly socializing the norm that crying is not an acceptable behavior. This prompt response also associates the reduction of tension with the physical presence of mother (Lebra 1976), and lowers the awareness of possible separation. Crying among children is seen as an unintentionally offensive act, in that it disturbs others. Because of this it is directly discouraged through injunctions about the impropriety of making a lot of noise. In public situations, children are directly instructed to remain quiet. They are also tacitly given the example of being impassive and unobtrusive through the behavior of their parents, siblings, and other people observed in natural settings. Often, this is initially difficult to learn for Japanese youngsters, who have become accustomed to the relative permissiveness at home, and are unaware of the indirect ways in which they have been diverted from crying or showing aggressive behavior. In public, the rules are not to disturb others, draw attention to oneself, or embarrass one's mother (or family) by fidgeting, or bawling—let alone being hostile or obstreperous. All mothers travel with little treats that are parceled out at the first signs of restlessness. A mother will even get off a subway or bus if her child's discomfort begins to escalate despite placation.

American mothers, in contrast, respond more to happy vocalizations of their infants, and engage in chatting and pretend conversations, particularly when the infant is in a good mood (Caudill and Weinstein 1969; Caudill 1972). Unhappy vocalizations—including crying—may elicit feeding, holding, comforting, or "changing" responses from the mother. Protracted crying, however, often leads to the infant being placed in a crib or playpen to "cry it out." Japanese mothers would regard this as very bad for the child, and as implying dereliction of their own responsibility.

In several studies, Caudill and Weinstein (1969) and Caudill and Schooler (1973) documented a higher activity level, more happy vocalization, and increased exploratory activity in American infants when compared to Japanese. They concluded that this occurred because of culturally differential responses, where the American mother accentuated small reunions during the day in an atmosphere of chatting during times of feeding and "changing," which stimulated and reinforced her infant to respond verbally. Contrastingly, the Japanese mother was seen as soothing and conditioning her child into becoming a more passive, nonverbal, contented observer.[6] Fisher (1964b), in commenting on cross-cultural linguistic socialization, noted the tendency of Japanese mothers to tolerate and mimic babbling and cooing, and to engage in "baby talk" longer than Americans. He suggested that such mimicry removed the incentive for more articulate speech and speculated that the mother's keen anticipation of her children's needs also postponed the incentive for verbalization. He observed that Japanese mothers, themselves, were less verbal than their American counterparts, which in itself could contribute to comparatively delayed verbalization. He also cited Dell Hymes in regard to a subtle aspect of linguistic socialization wherein "learning when not to speak is as important as learning when to speak" (Fisher 1964a, 109). As Lebra (1976) comments,

This cultural attention to the minimization of crying leads to two types of child behavior. On one hand, the child . . . learns that crying is not permitted under any circumstances and that whatever tensions he has will be satisfied by the nearby mother. (Lebra 1976, 143)

Lebra defines this kind of strategy as *appeasement* and regards it as a paradigmatic response pattern that produces a quiet, contented, and trustful Japanese child. She also comments that such socialization "may produce an undisciplined, spoiled child who knows that the most effective way of getting whatever he wants is to throw a temper tantrum" (Lebra 1976, 144).[7]

Spontaneous playful activity, including a limited amount of aggression, is permitted during early childhood. This is particularly true for boys, where stubborn or rambunctious behavior may be complained about, but actually is desired by the parents. Girls are taught not to be as assertive or aggressive as their brothers and are enjoined to be deferent, quiet, patient, and self-sacrificing.

The father's role in reinforcing distinctions in male and female behavior is indirect but effective. In his relative aloofness, immune from the forensics of home and child management, he is perceived in two ways. Intermittently, he is seen as a playmate. However, mainly he is regarded as a reserved, powerful and authoritative person, bestowed with high status and given solicitation by mother and the older children. His role in the outside world and the significance of his work status also reinforces their view of his authority. His potential for punishment is ironically inflated by the fact that it is not ordinarily used, except in brief expressions of displeasure. A popular aphorism likens the father to a volcano, in that he does not "erupt" very often, but when he does it can be spectacular. This may make even slight premonitions of displeasure frightening to mothers and children alike. As in many cultures, the mother reinforces this power by threatening the father's future intervention, as in saying that he will be told about their misbehavior unless it is corrected.

In contrast to the permissiveness toward some forms of spontaneous roughhouse, other kinds of controls are instituted in early childhood to teach youngsters to bow, to use proper honorific speech (keigo), and to be aware of assuming correct physical postures in various social situations. This combination of postural and verbal control explicitly acknowledges a hierarchy of authority relationships both within the family and in preparation for navigating in the outside world. Moreover, these skills are learned from parents and siblings whose own behavior reflects deference, use of honorific language, and controlled postures. The growing child also witnesses the outside society through direct experience, on television, or through overheard anecdotes. In these observations, courteous speech, deference, bowing, and studied pleasantness are displayed as a normative model for proper deportment.

The intensity and success of such training varies with the social position of the family and the amount of implicit reinforcement for such formality and politeness. Also, although formulas for ordinary public courtesy are routinely taught in the home ("Excuse me," "Thank you," "How do you do?") such pleasantries may fall into disuse under the influence of casual, tough-talking adolescent peer groups. Some parents have asserted that the *schools* should be held responsible for teaching basic social behavior, even including table etiquette (Garrick 1987, private communication). This lapse in the training of proper behavior either in the home or school is reflected in the policies of many Japanese firms that use orientation programs to introduce new employees to their institutional environment, but also to revive their sensitivity about formal, courteous behavior.

The precocious learning of postural control and honorific speech is ideally taught in a good-natured manner, accompanied by praise and encouragement. The goal of such training is to achieve a level of pleasant and alert unobtrusiveness—a sort of neutral impassiveness—both kinesically and verbally. Fighting, squirming, or moving around carelessly in public is regarded as discourteous, even when done by little children. In adults or adolescents, slouching or frequent shifting of posture is even more distracting and is interpreted as communicating uneasiness or distress. The most effective training takes place in extended families where standards are reinforced by grandparents in motivating both the parents and the grandchildren in the use of proper speech, bodily control, and politeness. In urban families, this may be less frequently emphasized and rehearsed. Direct chastisement for errors or omissions is also used. Another common measure for calling attention to unacceptable behavior is the swift initiation of a studied and rejecting silence. The frequent appearance of silence in Japanese communication itself provides a sociolinguistic context in which the child receives fewer direct cues, and must consider nonverbal and circumstantial features of the situation in order to formulate how to respond.

Kopp (1982) has discussed early childhood socialization as a series of developmental stages involving progressively more conscious and cooperative adaptation to caretakers' intentions—eventually leading to self-regulation. Early kinesic training by Japanese mothers teaches control through indirect techniques utilizing the sense of merger between herself and the young child. As Kojima (1984) notes, these indirect strategies blur the distinctions between *primary controls* (devoted to influencing others) and *secondary controls* (devoted to accommodating to others):

By indirectness of primary control strategy I mean the modification of existing realities, not through direct confrontation, but through deliberately using tactics that are expected eventually to modify behavior in the appropriate direction. (Kojima 1984, 972)

Later Language Socialization and Behavioral Discipline

Compared to North Americans, Japanese show a relative lack of idle conversation in the home, and a heightened attentiveness to nonverbal communication. With family and friends, lower levels of verbal interchange have the positive connotation that close relationships foster states of intuitive, mutual understanding in which speech is redundant. In fact, actually saying some things out loud may momentarily nullify the sense of special relationship, and be seen as demeaning or insulting to the other person. For example, adolescents may not verbally apologize for misbehaving or disappointing their parents, but instead demonstrate regret through actions that reverse or make up for the offending incident (Nagano 1985). Such strategies for indirect resolution are tacitly learned in early childhood, when silences and disapproving extralinguistic cues are displayed by parents or older siblings. Such pauses compel the youngster to reflect and deduce what happened, and examine what part he or she may have played in this apparently undesirable interlude. A series of such experiences gradually trains the child to avoid repeating mistakes through the anticipation of negative consequences.[8]

The use of silence, distraction, and indirect threats by Japanese parents are frequently mentioned as means for modifying childish behavior. The contrast between these Japanese methods and the verbal styles of many North American parents deserves mention. Mistakes or naughtiness among even very young American children often elicits extended "explanations" from mothers and fathers. These may review 1) what kind of wrong was done, 2) how this makes other people feel, and 3) what should be done in the future. These one-sided indictments later develop into dialogues as children acquire verbal skills and defensively counterattack with 1) their own justifications for action, 2) their own state of injured feelings, and 3) their own version of what might happen in the future. American children, therefore, tend to be socialized to become verbally adroit and to participate actively in confrontation and arbitration. At the same time they are tacitly trained to release counterassertions and counterstrategies. Through repeated small confrontations they are implicitly taught to argue and to defend themselves. Quite differently, Japanese youngsters learn that certain behaviors must be strenuously avoided lest they be exposed to humiliation and embarrassment, and be seen as causing pain to their mothers. Moreover, doing something wrong is bad enough; having to talk about it only adds to the ignominy.

The American mother builds upon the child's notion of his or her potentially being "willful," (i.e., irresponsible or "bad"), and in the process indirectly inflates the youngster's view of his or her own growing power and strength. Japanese children are led to the opposite conclusion by parents who believe that all children are basically good. Misbehavior is formulated as some kind of temporary quirk, or lapse of consideration—almost like an accident. Accordingly, children may be confused about the significance of their mistake.

During their early years Japanese girls and boys directly associate prohibitions and fears of punishment with specific rules connected to actual interpersonal behaviors within the family. These interaction rules are formulated on both direct and tacit instruction through incidents encountered on a case-by-case basis.[9]

Potent chastising forces are directly identified with both the mother and father. Through the parents' allusions to normative behavioral expectations in the community, these are extrapolated to even more powerful forces present in the outside society. Interestingly, however, these are not connected to a theological system per se, as is common in the Judeo-Christian or Islamic societies. Also, Japanese youngsters are socialized to feel that misbehavior not only threatens themselves with punishment, but can bring shame on their whole family—a threat that is less frequently felt or preventively used by American parents (Lanham 1956; Lebra 1976). The consequences of misbehavior are thus strongly interpersonalized rather than either reflected back onto the child or referred to some hypothetical, abstract system or "god." Moral awareness (Aaronfreed 1968) develops more in relation to the feared consequences of destructiveness toward the long-suffering mother (DeVos 1960, 1978, 1985).

In Japan, the internalization of behavioral controls is reinforced by orientation to social cues occurring outside of the home. These are gradually encountered through expeditions to stores, doctor's offices, parks, and public sidewalks. In observing the courtesy, bowing, and deferential speech of people in the outside world, children verify another dimension of support for behavioral controls. Moreover, children's natural apprehensions about the public environment may be exploited by the mother to reinforce conformity through fear of ridicule by outsiders. Threats of impending shame and embarrassment are commonly used to induce discipline on the basis that the child's inconsiderate behavior will be witnessed and disapproved by outsiders. Discussed by a number of observers, this has been referred to by Lebra (1976) as employing the use of a "third person" to reinforce discipline. For example, a visiting friend of the mother might be drawn into a conversation wherein the mother reports that the child recently did something wrong. Right on cue, the third-person visitor will display feigned astonishment that such an angelic child has misbehaved. The child, of course, is first startled, then upset and embarrassed by this unexpected disclosure. The result is a reinforcement to be good in the future in an effort to avoid embarrassment. In this transaction mother's friend acts like an outside personification of superego.

Similarly, the threat of separation is manipulated as a form of chastisement and correction. Many commentators (Vogel and Vogel 1961, 233; Lebra 1976; Reynolds 1976) report conversations between mothers and outside visitors where the mother (to the child's complete surprise) asks, "Wouldn't you like to take this little child; he's been so bad!" Also, as in Western societies, local or regional ghosts ("bogeymen") are used as fictional third persons to instill fears of separation, ridicule, or forthcoming punishment because of misbehavior (Lanham 1956). The threat of calling a policeman is another popular method of third-person intimidation, either to speak to the child or, in more serious instances, to "take the child away" because of some "naughtiness" or misbehavior. Fenichel cited this same superego stimulation used in European childrearing in the 1930s (Fenichel 1945, 103). Nowadays, Japanese children generally regard policemen as benign, protective authority figures, and are more threatened by the possibility of being shamed than being punished by them. Since the Japanese child is taught that the outside society is formidable and exacting in its expectations, the youngster is socialized into a continuing sense of need for security through contact and proximity to the mother. Later this dependency need is displaced to small social groups in school and the workplace.

Unlike their American counterparts, Japanese preschoolers do not threaten to run away from home to force their parents to comply with their requests for rights and entitlements. Quite the contrary, it is the Japanese parents who threaten to abandon or expel the child if he or she persists in disapproved behavior (Lebra 1976; Reynolds 1976, 103). This takes two forms. One is to place children into a dark closet within the home, keeping them confined until they have repented or at least calmed down. The second is more severe and involves actually pushing them outside the house (regardless of the weather) for an indeterminate time, allowing them to reenter only when they have shown evidence of sincerely acknowledging their wrongdoing. Such punishments are extremely effective, but constitute the reverse of the American situation where the child may be told, "OK, if you want to leave, we'll help you pack your things!"

Toilet Training, Orderliness, and Self-Control

In an early description of Japanese childrearing, Benedict (1946) noted that sleep and feeding were reactive to the child's own rhythm, rather than imposed as a discipline based on the parents' arbitrary schedule. A common comparative observation is that while Americans have discipline imposed on them during infancy and early childhood, they experience permissiveness in the form of increasing independence in later childhood and adolescence. The reverse of this takes place in Japan, where the high degree of permissiveness in the maternal/child relationship remains elevated until the child enters elementary school (at age five or six) and is subject to an increased need to conform to externally imposed schedules and discipline. A national celebration is held each November in Japan for all youngsters who have or will become three during that year (Beardsley, Hall, and Ward 1959). The age of three age is commemorated by discarding childish clothing and, symbolically, the behaviors of infancy and early childhood. Ideally, during their third year, children completely dispense with diapers, and enter a period where they are no longer considered "infantile." At this same age, many of them also enter some form of nursery or day-care setting. Expectations for increasing internalized control accordingly accompany this new status.

In regard to toilet training, the mother attempts to achieve this gradually, and especially to avoid conflict. Training the child involves anticipating his or her physiological awareness, staying in close physical contact, giving encouragement, and avoiding coercion, punishment, or moralization. A number of commentators (Benedict 1946; Lanham 1956; Beardsley, Hall, and Ward 1959; Vogel and Vogel 1961; Lebra 1976) cite that toilet training only seriously begins when the child perceives the social significance of controlling excretion. Attempts to increase the child's understanding or predict the child's rhythm may be initiated early, but if so is only half-heartedly expected to succeed. As Vogel and Vogel (1961) comment, toilet training is in large part mother training, "with her acceptance of the responsibility for anticipating the child, and gently leading him or her toward nocturnal and daytime control" (Vogel and Vogel 1961, 247). Furthermore, her close physical contact throughout this process is integral. She ordinarily does not leave the child on the potty alone, but tenderly supports the child while encouraging cooperation.

While the mastery of complete anal and urethral control is treated patiently, early socialization regarding cleanliness and orderliness is more rigorous and implicitly moralistic. Control of posture imparts a consciousness of social propriety in terms of the modulation of body movement in relation to other participants. This is accompanied by the control of facial expression, bowing, and accurate use of terms of address and other honorifics required in conversation with status superiors. Before serious attempts are made to achieve sphincter control, which involves both voluntary and involuntary systems, mothers train their children in the voluntary control of bodily posture. At home, babies are prompted into bowing toward guests by light pressure on the back of the child's head. Even while they are very young, children are periodically positioned into sitting up straight, with their legs neatly tucked under them. Little girls are taught to show propriety by sleeping on their backs with their legs straight and together. Girls are also taught to keep their knees together while bathing. Girls are instructed to walk gracefully, smile in a pleasant manner, and cover their mouths while laughing. While sitting in chairs in informal settings, boys may cross their legs, but girls should not. Neither should do so in any formal situation.

Children are allowed to move around the house freely, but correct posture is positively reinforced by periodically arranging the children's limbs and reducing fidgeting through distraction, encouragement, and praise. Gestural control emphasizes keeping the arms close to the torso and maintaining the lower extremities in contact whether sitting or standing. Random motions of arms or legs while sitting are discouraged, since they suggest restlessness or even irritation. These rules are reinforced by children witnessing the physical composure of their parents, grandparents, brothers, and sisters.

Similarly, orderliness and picking up after oneself are gently but consistently taught, in addition to being reinforced by the example of siblings and parents. Living in small quarters and using rooms in multiple ways lends itself to straightening up and storing personal objects. Psychoanalytically, it is interesting that the inculcation of kinesic controls concerning posture, vocalization, and avoiding messiness precedes the attainment of anal and urethral control. Speculatively, such kinesic controls might be more readily mastered on the basis of not being associated with dreads of failure and potential disgust, which commonly accompany premature and moralistic attempts to toilet train.[10]

There are several other important mechanisms observed in the early socialization of Japanese children regarding behavioral control. The verbal admonitions of the parents are generally abbreviated, and ideally uttered in mellow or encouraging tones. Usually these instructions are not repeated. Mothers particularly may use falsetto intonation as a way of mollifying any sternness in their attempts to induce new behavior. As another tactic, verbal admonitions are reinforced by systematically and promptly changing the environment. If children play with food, the container will immediately be placed outside their reach, indirectly demonstrating that such behavior is not acceptable. A third mechanism is the use of psychological isolation rather than physical segregation. If children do something especially naughty, adults and older children may suddenly shun them as a way of showing their displeasure—without actually saying anything.

Arguments are extinguished more or less before the fact, simply by the parents not engaging in them. As discussed in the previous chapter, direct verbal disagreement or confrontation is regarded as impolite and inappropriate in Japan except under compelling circumstances. Thus, negativity and disagreement must be displayed indirectly (that is, nonverbally) and commonly include the studied use of silence or thinly veiled indifference. Also, the clear recognition of the status hierarchy in the family reduces overt dissension, since the opinions of more senior persons, whether spoken or implicit, are acknowledged to be prevailing, and hence publicly unchallengeable.

In later childhood, sanctions for showing negative or incommensurate emotion include distraction, ridicule, or even frightening the child about the consequences of displaying too much feeling. Perhaps the most effective socialization, however, is through the example of the parents' own composure, and the reluctance of adults to stimulate negative emotion through arguments, confrontations, or "showdowns" between themselves, let alone with their children. More serious punishments include extensions of frightening, ridiculing, or bringing a "third-person" pressure on children to correct their misbehavior (Lanham 1962; Iga 1968; Lebra 1976).

Since Japanese support the social-philosophic belief that children are naturally and intrinsically good, then it is up to the parents to bring out this innate goodness. Misbehavior is causally explained as arising from some extraneous, outside influences, or from some "infestation"—often colloquially referred to as a *mushi* (worm). In the past, an effective punishment for recurrent and refractory misbehavior was to inflict a small burn on the surface of the child's skin through the use of "moxa" *(mogusa)*. Reserved for serious and repeated transgressions, this treatment consisted of igniting a pill-sized pellet of compressed fiber (like punk)—on the child's leg, forearm, back, or abdomen. Called "moxibustion," this was performed by an outsider, either a religious person or an indigenous healer. In the past, the rationale was to "burn out the bad worm" *(mushi)*, and is still explained on the superstition that severe tantrums, obstinacy, or disobedience are not intrinsic to the child, but constitute some "bad thing" temporarily residing in the youngster. Statistics on earlier or recent use of moxibustion are difficult to establish (Lock 1980). Parents are understandably defensive about revealing that their child may have shown serious behavioral problems. Also, although the procedure still is accepted as sometimes useful, it is considered old-fashioned and unnecessarily painful. Probably the threat of the procedure is still effective, and greatly supersedes its actual use (Lock 1980).

As mentioned before, Japanese society negatively sanctions the corporal punishment of children in the home and, to a certain degree, denies this when it does occur. Punishment constituting child abuse, however, is nearly nonexistent. As Wagatsuma (1980) indicates, there is very little literature on the subject, both because of its infrequency and because of the strongly negative connotations, which probably lead to underreporting. Child abandonment or even joint suicide of parents and children *(oya-ko shinjū)* occurs occasionally, and are publicized in the press. These tragedies occur as acts of desperation, usually on the part of mothers who are unable to raise their children because of severe economic distress, divorce, or unusual disability.

In fact, the reverse of child abuse, *parent* abuse, has become a significant problem in some Japanese families. This happens when a male adolescent physically assaults his mother and intimidates his father and other family members. Parent abuse occurs in middle-class homes where the father is unusually passive, and the mother incapable of discouraging direct physical aggression. Such adolescents may act well controlled in school or neighborhood settings, but remain ungovernable at home. Another Japanese problem involving aggression or physical abuse is reported where teachers or students are assaulted in a serious manner by individuals or groups. These acts are perpetrated by intermediate or high school students, and have raised the concern of psychologists, teachers, and administrators. Such incidents have increased in frequency, and generated considerable concern and publicity. In the opposite direction, there have been some reports of teachers inflicting physical punishment. Prior to the Occupation, corporal punishment was common and approved in moderation within public and private schools—as it was in British and American schools earlier in the century. In prewar Japanese classrooms, physical punishments used to be handed out for inattention, misbehavior, or laziness. More severe corporal punishment flourished in the military according to a hierarchical order, especially afflicting the lowest ranks and persons from outcast backgrounds (Minami 1971; Hane 1982).

As mentioned earlier, corporal punishment, such as spanking or slapping, let alone anything approaching beating or "thrashing," is normatively regarded as a serious weakness and evidence of defect in the parents. Some spanking occurs, but resorting to heavy physical force is regarded as evidence of failure in parenting. On the other hand, pinching is common, and frequently used with young children when they misbehave outside the home. Since corporal punishment is subdued, children's unconscious dread of dismemberment or castration is not stimulated by the real experience of bodily attack. However, at an unconscious level, these anxieties are presumably reinforced by the potential power attributed to both the immediate family and the outside society. As DeVos (1960) has reported from his interpretations of Thematic Apperception Test data, the child's concerns about potential physical harm are often projected onto worries about the destructive effects of misbehavior on the long-suffering, self-sacrificing Japanese mother. This awareness of dangerous, aggressive impulses becomes internally represented as a potential guilt, relating both to concerns about achievement and marital choice (DeVos 1960).[11]

Another important area of personal discipline involves socialization concerning envy, sibling rivalry, and respect for the possessions of other persons. Most Japanese youngsters do not celebrate birthdays, nor are they heaped with presents on festivals like Christmas or Hanukkah. Dolls and toys are given as individual possessions, but there is a restraint about avoiding ostentation, and an ethic about sharing possessions with others. As in most families, Japanese children are dissuaded from taking or abusing other youngsters' belongings. When this occurs, the return of the object to its owner may be negotiated by mother or teacher coaxing the child and appealing to fairness, rather than yanking something away from the offender. Children are instructed not to play with the toys of other children, unless freely offered the opportunity. Statements of envy about other children's possessions or privileges are opposed directly and indirectly—mostly through shame (e.g., "you should not ask for things we cannot afford"). Envy and sibling rivalry are reduced by the omnipresent awareness of status and gender distinctions, which dictate that younger children simply cannot have things that older siblings possess, or that girls are categorically not allowed to do some things that boys are permitted. Actually stealing things from others—and worse yet, being caught—is particularly shameful and reprehensible. Later, in school situations, efforts may be made by teachers to relocate stolen items, as if they were unintentionally picked up, to avoid humiliating the perpetrator.

The Conjugal Relationship, Narcissism, and Production of the "Ideal Child"

Psychoanalytically, the conjugal relationship in Japan stands in contrast to Western arrangements—at least in their idealized description as companionate, romantic, and exclusive connections. Although acknowledged to have important emotional and sexual features, marriage in Japan is normatively seen as a socially determined arrangement between families, solidified by public recognition and governed by stringent role-specific regulations dictating division of responsibility and obligations—particularly regarding the protection and development of children. Cultural inhibitions act to mute the significance of sexuality or romance between partners, while differential gender socialization reduces the areas of shared interests and experience among husbands and wives—although this is changing somewhat. From the child's standpoint, the continued availability of copious maternal nurturance through *amaeru* diminishes frustration and virtually eliminates envy toward the father. The lack of overtly expressed romantic activity between parents makes consciousness of competition for affection unlikely and rare. Also, general sanctions against envy are reinforced by the acceptance of ubiquitous status differentiations that modify and reduce rivalry toward either other siblings or father. Along with the prolongation of pregenital gratifications (in the form of cosleeping, cobathing, and high degree of skin contact), these factors all combine to change both the quality and timing of the oedipal resolution.

Moreover, these practices and customs work toward reducing the child's sense of personal narcissism, both through positive praise for being altruistic, and through strong condemnation for envying others or taking things from them. *Enryo* behavior (hesitation, reserve, modesty, and self-denial) is directly instructed and tacitly modeled after others; this becomes another mode of publicly renouncing personal narcissism or inflated entitlement. Reserve and modesty are taught through a sublimation of personal desire, where the pleasure of possession is replaced by the reaction formation of pride in simplicity, frugality, and austerity *(shibumi)*. As seen even more clearly in school and adult situations, the desire for recognition of individual worth and achievement is converted into a "group narcissism" that avoids personal praise in favor of recognition of collective achievement.

White and LeVine (1986) have composed a succinct summary of elements of Japanese childrearing that concentrate on producing "the good child" *(ii-ko)*. Their explanation emphasizes the cooperation of the mother in channeling the child's behavior toward optimal goals, and diverting rather than opposing willfulness. The strong ethic of "helping the child understand" *(wakaraseru)* is foremost in inculcating behaviors leading to smooth social adaptation. The mother's responsiveness to requests to *amaeru* (i.e., in spontaneously providing indulgence) is seen as cementing an interdependent, affectionate relationship where mother and child are allied in the arduous, cooperative endeavor of teaching and learning correct behavior. In their survey of ideal characteristics, White and LeVine (1986) noted that colloquial terms used to describe the ideal child *(ii ko)* naturalistically divided into two categories. One consisted of positive adjectives referring to the structural characteristics of *social embeddedness*, while the second described actual *social performance*. Terms in the first group were concerned with cohesiveness and defined the good child with words like "compliant," "gentle," "cooperative," "attentive," "swift in reaction," and "smart." The second group was concerned with social performance idealizing the virtues in both mother and child of "perseverance," "seeking understanding," and "capable of interdependence." Other virtuous characteristics will be summarized in a later chapter on Japanese selfhood. As did Murase and Johnson (1974), White and LeVine (1986, 57) commented on how there is no evidence of conflict seen "between goals of self-fulfillment and goals of social integration." Moreover, they identify the indulgent, nurturant, and interdependent *amae* relationship with mother as symbolically providing a bridge through which individual and social domains are interconnected.

Summary of Early Childrearing in Japan

In summary, the early socialization of children takes place in an atmosphere that diminishes aggressive behavior through strategies culturally based on the "average expectable environment" of Japan. These will be listed separately here but in reality express their effects through various combinations of approved behaviors.

1. *The permissive continuation of pregenital gratifications, including longer availability of the breast as a nutritional and tactile object, along with cosleeping, coeating, and cobathing.* Taken together, these provide increased physical contact with family members in response to the needs of the young child for security, warmth, and close proximity. These concretely and nonverbally signify emotional closeness and cherishment—particularly in the form of mother's prompt responses to requests for continued indulgence *(amaeru)*.

2. *The use of explicit strategies to teach the child habits of orderliness, postural control, and proper verbal and extralinguistic displays of respect.* These strategies combine to produce a pre-

cocious awareness of behavioral propriety and self-control along with a sensitivity concerning the hierarchical complexities of social roles and human relationships.

3. *The use of indirect strategies to ward off misbehavior, messiness, or undue aggression through distraction, silence, or the withdrawal of others.* These diversions focus the child's attention away from its own willfulness onto the needs, moods, and intentions of others. They also foster the acquisition of "empathy"—that is, the capacity to intuit and react to the feelings of others.

4. *The separation of sphincteral control from other dimensions of behavioral control.* Toilet training emphasizes tactile closeness and maternal participation along with the relative avoidance of moralization or high states of emotionality. Training the child to develop other controls (involving speech, posture, and emotion) is conducted with considerably more strenuous direction and moralization than the permissive atmosphere of toilet training.

5. *The channeling of superego punishment themes to an external society rather than to theological abstractions.* This reduces the development of a sense of individual "badness" in reference to purported supernatural phenomena. Superego dreads include the fear that misbehavior will reflect humiliation on the entire family. These are associated with potential guilt about hurting the mother as a consequence of personal transgressions or failures. Both guilt and shame tend to be interpersonalized rather than ambiguously theologized.

6. *The direct and tacit learning about social hierarchy is introduced through the immediate family.* This hierarchy fixes the statuses of fathers, mothers, siblings, and relatives in terms of their gender, age, birth order, degree of kindred, and accomplishments. Such stipulations reduce and channel narcissistic entitlement by way of ritualized and automatic submission to more privileged persons. This recognition also diminishes the expression of jealousy, envy, and inflated sense of personal specialness. However, a compensatory sense of special cherishment is preserved in the expectation for responses to requests for gratification of dependency *(amaeru)*.

7. *Learning about suppressing conflict, confrontation, or negative emotion is achieved through tacit example and direct instruction.* This is inculcated passively through the prompt respon-

siveness of the mother, who provides distraction from prohibited behaviors using a number of techniques, including silence, feigned rejection, or, if necessary, more punitive strategies. Punitive strategies include suggestions of outside ridicule, temporary but actual expulsion from the house, pinching, or the threat of moxibustion. Most terrifying, however, is the possibility of separation from the mother through being confined in a closet or locked outside the house.

8. *The oedipal transition is modified by the nonromantic nature of the parents' relationship.* The father is not seen as a serious competitor for mother's affection. Moreover, the mother's close attention to children during and following the oedipal period satisfies dependency cravings even after the children enter school. Continued physical intimacy in the forms of cosleeping and cobathing also stimulates and satisfies pregenital cravings, and at the same time extinguishes and represses recognition of genital, sexual drives.

The next chapter will summarize socialization practices centering on development outside the family in the context of school, neighborhood, and friendship relations. The consequences of these for the presence of protracted indulgent dependency *(amae)* will be noted.

Notes

1. As discussed by Hendry (1981), statistics concerning "arranged" versus "love" marriage vary considerably according to region of the country, size of the city, and age and education of the partners. Blurring the distinction between "love" and "arranged" marriages, many spontaneous dating situations are subsequently formalized through an appointed broker *(nakōdo)*.

2. In contrast to postindustrial city life, there is historical evidence of casual sexual behavior among adolescents in rural areas. Since sex has tended to be regarded in a nonmoral way (as a form of play and recreation), casual liaisons were ignored as long as these did not challenge issues of lineage.

3. As in any national group, the qualitative features of conversation vary widely in Japan between the home, workplace, or school. Within small groups in public settings, "small talk" abounds in situations where there is less concern with content than with sustaining innocuous and pleasant

discourse, conveying an atmosphere of shared positive feeling. While such characteristics typify "small talk" in any society, bantering among Japanese may seem more superficial to an outsider because of the amount of indirection and the stringent avoidance of conflict. In contrast, conversations between *two* persons in Japanese settings (working partners, friends, teachers and students) are less likely to be stylized, and more consciously devoted to looking for specific meaning and purposes (Garrick 1989, personal communication).

4. Chen and Miyake (1986) have looked more critically at some of Caudill's work, suggesting that the causes for behavioral differences between these two national groups were not sufficiently addressed. Citing Kojima (1979), they suggested that the Japanese mother's reluctance to stimulate her baby or to exert herself verbally was related to cultural values concerning infant development, and the high priority given to controlling emotion and to avoiding provoking or disturbing others.

5. In a comment about a Japanese graduate student studying in the U.S., Townsend (1979, private communication) reported that the student jokingly said, "I'll never understand the oedipus complex. When I go home to Tokyo on Christmas break, my idea of enjoyment is to take a bath with my mother and go out 'bar hopping' with my father!"

6. In a replication study, Shand and Kosawa (1985) showed significant differences in the amount of playfulness, spontaneous motor activity, manipulation of objects, and types of vocalization. However, quite opposite to Caudill's studies, the Japanese infants were *more* active while they were awake at three months, although they devoted less time to exploring objects in their environment and still slept more than the American subjects.

Also, their analysis of maternal behavior at three months showed a reversal of Caudill's and Pavenstedt's findings of greater physical contact between Japanese mothers and their infants. In speculating about these opposite findings, Shand and Kosawa wondered about the effects of culture change on these two groups during the interval between studies. Other findings were the same as earlier studies: American children continued to show more pleasant vocalization while Japanese infants cried more frequently.

7. Japanese youngsters' tantrums can be spectacular. The author witnessed a number of these involving children somewhere around the age of three. Two features were striking. First, the amount of noise and disturbance is incommensurate with the circumstance, and in radical contrast to the usually quiet and respectful behavior of children in public. Second, for an average Westerner, it is interesting to see how the parents respond with a passive and perplexed resignation to seeing their child go to pieces in public. Parents restrict their actions to crouching near the child, trying to distract it while softly and patiently pleading with it to be quiet. In the instances I observed, parents did not physically move their child or muffle

the outcry. As in the aggressive displays footnoted in the previous chapter, these tantrums can go on and on, and are both uncomfortable and bemusing to witness. Westerners are reminded of the usually swift combination of physical and verbal admonition unleashed on youngsters who begin to unravel in supermarkets, stores, or public transportation in the United States.

8. In her autobiographical account of Japanese girlhood in the late 1800s, Sugimoto (1934) reported the dread she experienced as a six-year-old caught carelessly shifting her posture during a tutorial session with her private instructor. Aroused by a fleeting indication of her restlessness, the tutor abruptly terminated the session, instructed her to leave the room, and encouraged her to meditate.

My little heart was almost killed with shame. There was nothing I could do. I humbly bowed to the picture of Confucius and then to my teacher, and backing respectfully from the room, I slowly went to my father to report, as I always did, at the close of my lesson. Father was surprised, as the time was not yet up, and his unconscious remark, "How quickly you have done your work!" was like a death knell. The memory of that moment hurts like a bruise to this very day. (Sugimoto 1934, 24)

9. Interaction rules (Goffman 1959, 1967) are complex, specified regulations that guide both the anticipation and evaluation of behavior. Unlike norms, which are more generalistic, interaction rules are influenced by situational variables and are concerned with governing interpersonal behaviors according to criteria regarding context, status, prior relationship, and propriety. Discussing a particular kind of interaction rule, Hochschild (1979) has explained the function of "emotion rules," which operate in the regulation of self-presentation and "impression management." Siegler (1983) has dissected the sequences connected to the dawning development of awareness concerning interaction rules during early childhood.

10. The basic difficulty of attaining bladder and bowel control involves the complex task of coordinating both involuntary and voluntary mechanisms. The reflexive urge to discharge the bladder or distal colon is an automatic reaction to distention and peristalsis, initially operating outside of consciousness. These automatic patterns of reflexive excretion are gradually opposed through the development of intentional, voluntary control. The relatively early, though permissive and nonmoralistic, training in Japan deemphasizes frustration and guilt fostered by more strenuous methods that attempt to impose earlier continence through humiliation and disgust.

11. Formulations attempting to explain distinctions between guilt and shame are complex even if formulated according to experience in a single culture. This author favors explanations that regard these two reactions as operating in a separate but overlapping manner depending upon the aggravating incident, the symbolical meaning of the event, and the extenuating

factors (as in Ausubel 1955). Most failures simultaneously elicit both emotional and cognitive components, but in various blends and intensities. Shame generally is more related to the interpersonal referents of a social audience, and elicits the basic emotions of embarrassment and surprise upon discovery. Guilt tends to pivot on intrapersonal or ambiguous referents, and unleashes the basic emotions of self-contempt and sadness. Some theories concerning guilt and shame have used dichotomized explanations (e.g., in Piers and Singer 1953) and have attempted to characterize cultures according to "deep" (superego) versus "superficial" (ego-ideal) reactions to failure. Both DeVos (1960) and Lebra (1971, 1983) have reexamined the manifestations of self-punishment among Japanese displaying the interplay between these two expressive systems in their simultaneous reflection of both (social) apology and (personal) mortification. This issue is complex and will be reexamined in later chapters.

CHAPTER 5

Japanese Education and Later Socialization

Educational institutions operate to provide graded instruction, furnishing students with skills in literacy and computation, along with information concerning science, history, health, and social studies. At the same time, schooling constitutes a context for progressive socialization confirming social and gender roles and reinforcing habits of self-control, courtesy, and discipline. At a more abstract level, schools provide a gatekeeping function for the selective induction of persons into specified work roles, materially dependent on the degree of success or failure in the school setting. Moreover, educational institutions operate as a transition from the family to the broader society, and are involved in fostering development that responds to the needs of the state, commercial institutions, industry, and the professions. All of these complex goals are achieved in conformity to prevailing cultural and ethical norms. In approaching these goals, Japanese education is notably efficient— even distinctive—in two ways. First, as discussed by Kiefer (1970), there is a high degree of conformity among norms operating within the family, the school, and the bureaucracy—and ultimately in the society at large. Second, in terms of achievement, Japanese schools have been notably successful in inculcating skills in reading, writing, and computation to virtually all citizens, and in retraining students in the classroom—particularly when compared with the American experience. For example, nearly 95 percent of Japanese adolescents graduate from secondary schools.

During the Tokugawa period, education was primarily available for the nobility and the children of privileged families. Curriculum was equally concerned with teaching didactic content and inculcating proper conduct. The content of courses accentuated literacy and mathematics along with information about Confucian and Japanese classics. In 1850, prior to the Meiji Restoration, it is estimated that nearly 40 percent of the population had acquired some education—mostly among males. Universal education, established in 1868 for boys and girls in all provinces, mandated four years of elementary schools, extended to six years after World War I, and three years of "middle school" following the American Occupation. National and prefectural universities developed alongside secondary education, selecting outstanding students for advanced studies leading to positions in government, industry, and commerce. Women's colleges—first established on a private, endowed basis—were set up around the turn of the century to produce elementary teachers, and to provide domestic skills and cultural refinement for young women from well-to-do families prior to marriage.

During the past 120 years, Japanese higher education has been carefully coordinated with national requirements for engineers, bureaucrats, executives, and professionals of various kinds. Overall, the educational system has been successful in creating a literate, disciplined, and socially cohesive citizenry, capable of filling diverse positions in a complex postindustrial society. Paralleling Japan's postwar economic development and political evolution, institutes of higher education have proliferated to provide collegiate and postgraduate preparation for increasing numbers of young men and women (32 percent as reported by Kumagai 1984, 195). Women now compete with men for positions in the most prestigious universities, but many more attend two-year colleges with the intent of seeking genteel employment prior to getting married.

Except for a brief postwar period, Japanese education has always been heavily centralized. The Ministry of Education maintains authority to regulate curriculum, select teaching materials, and standardize examinations on a national basis. Such a system is credited with producing graduates who at the high-school level show superior achievement in cross-national comparisons of competence in standard subjects—particularly in mathematics and science. However, critics of the system point to overstandardization, an emphasis on rote learning, and a lack of individualization or opportunity for electives. Another complaint centers on a regimented examination system that places a priority on the mindless accumulation of knowledge, and fatefully decides which students will track toward the most renowned high schools, colleges, and universities. There also is criticism of the lack of incentive in most baccalaureate programs, which often are lackadaisical in their requirements. Moreover, future employment is determined by the established reputation of institutions of learning, rather than the specific achievements of individuals who attend them. Thus, factors of institutional reputation and relations within an "old-boy" affiliation tend to dominate choices concerning the recruitment of graduates into the job market or to institutions for postgraduate study.

Preschool, Elementary, and "Enrichment" Schools

Education is taken very seriously in Japan, and is integrally connected to the maternal role. Mothers are both jokingly and seriously called *kyōiku-mama* or "education mommies." Even before installing the child in school, the mother will have given instruction in counting, memorizing names for objects, recognizing colors, and knowledge of some *kanji* (Chinese characters). Once involved in actual schooling, the mother continues as a tutor and supervisor for homework preparation. She responds to methodical reports given by teachers concerning homework and class performance.

Many Japanese children are enrolled in preschool settings—often as early as age three (C. Lewis 1984; Peak 1987; Hendry 1986; Hess, et al. 1986; Tobin, Wu, and Davidson 1989). There are two versions of this: *yōchi-en*, which are like nursery schools in the U.S., and *hoikuen*, which are more like day-care centers. *Yōchi-en* are licensed by the Ministry of Education and serve as a kind of "Head Start" program to prepare youngsters for both the academic content and social atmosphere of elementary school. The parallel system of *hoikuen* operates as a day-care placement for the convenience of working mothers, and is licensed by the Department of Welfare. Formerly, *yōchi-en* catered mostly to middle-class mothers seeking preparation and enrichment for their children prior to elementary school. *Hoikuen* originally served more of a custodial function for mothers who found it necessary to work. Recently these distinctions have become less evident. Both settings emphasize training in socialization and deportment over instructional content. Preschool training often begins at age three or four and continues until first grade, which is entered at age six. (There is no kindergarten in Japan.) Currently 92 percent of five-year-old Japanese youngsters attend privately operated preschools, despite the fact that attendance is not a formal prerequisite for entering primary school.

From a standpoint of socialization, preschools serve as a transition from the indulgent, child-centered home atmosphere where *amaeru* abounds, to navigating the chaos of a classroom of twenty-five to thirty individuals. Typically, the didactic content is not rigorous, although goals are set both by the licensing authorities and the schools themselves. However, as Peak (1988) reflects, the primary objectives for all children are "to live, work and play as a group, manage personal belongings, take responsibility for assigned tasks, and enjoy coming to school" (Peak 1988, 10). In many ways, particularly for the five-year-olds, these preschools function like American kindergartens, which were introduced early in the century to provide a partial-day social introduction to elementary school, but later became a compulsory part of the educational system.

In studying the development of "cooperative behavior" in Japanese preschools, Catherine Lewis (1984) has described some structural and procedural factors that she identified as fostering empathy, internalization of control, and an orientation of seeking mutual rather than individual benefits and rewards. Presaging the structure of elementary school, classes of twenty to thirty-five children are broken down into small, fixed-membership groups of six to eight students (called *gurūpu*). Groups are made up by the selection of the teacher, who distributes children with higher skills in leadership, athletics, or sociability among various *gurūpu* to equalize their assets. Cooperation among group members is developed through collaboratively working on academic and other projects designed to activate participation and to instruct students in the sharing of limited resources. Teachers deliberately minimize their own direct, overt controls over the children, preferring to have the preschoolers deal with these responsibilities themselves. Whenever possible, the teachers explicitly delegate control to the children in seeking completion of group projects, requesting assistance, or even intervening in arguments and fights (C. Lewis 1984, 1989).

Whenever possible, discipline is inculcated tacitly and indirectly, both in preschool and elementary school classes. Teachers are trained to avoid authoritarian measures, and instead make the children accountable for their own behavior. Teachers respond to problems and questions in a nearly Socratic manner by inquiring, "What do *you* want to do?" or "How did this happen?" or "Can you think of ways to do this better?" Children are also responsible for cleaning the premises and functioning in rotation as monitors to announce the opening of class, the beginning and end of lunch period, and the conclusion of class activities at the end of the day. Commenting on the preschool situation, Catherine Lewis (1984) describes the teachers' control strategies as "1) minimizing the impression of the teacher's control; 2) delegating control to children; 3) providing plentiful opportunities for children to acquire a 'good girl' or 'good boy' identity; and 4) avoiding the attribution that children intentionally misbehave" (C. Lewis 1984, 75).

This last strategy at times requires actually denying overt aggression or antisocial behavior, through seeking other definitions or explanations of intent. For example, teachers may try to control aggression by advising students how to intervene as fighting develops between two combatants. Teachers report that they are less interested in stopping aggression than in training the groups how to handle their own crises and arrange for eventual compromise and apology. Other forms of misbehavior are approached in the same way. Sometimes an errant student will be directly addressed by the teacher, but in a way that attempts to educate the student through asking a series of questions about his or her behavior. The teacher's purpose is to elevate the child's consciousness about the detrimental and dissocial effects of his or her behavior, while awaiting the development of internal control. This tactic consists of what Catherine Lewis (1989) calls "attributing children's behavior to benign causes." Through this process, teachers choose not to confront their students with interpretations or behavior that focus on malicious or aggressive intent, even when these motives seem transparent. Instead, they ask a series of guileless questions in seeking a nonincriminating explanation, while indirectly trying to modify the offensive behavior.

In their cross-cultural survey of preschools Tobin, Wu, and Davidson (1989) observed that in Japan, the United States, and the People's Republic of China issues of misbehavior and control centered on mostly minor physical assaults, primarily involving boys. These authors concluded that this in itself was a reflection of the differential socialization of gender roles, where boys are allowed to be challenging and physically aggressive, while girls are drawn into placating and breaking up fights. In their study, the explanations for fighting were registered by teachers from all three national groups who observed videocassette illustrations of preschool behaviors in three cultural settings. Many of the Japanese teachers who reviewed the tapes believed that fighting is "natural" for boys, and that allowing it is essential in order to cultivate its eventual control. They felt that suppressing aggression would lead to more explosive behavior at a later age. It was believed that children in general, but mostly boys, should have some experience with physical aggression, to know "what it feels like." Most important, it is necessary to learn how to contain the urge to aggress against others through actual experience. Other Japanese preschool teachers, however, felt less comfortable with indirect systems of control and stated that they favored direct intervention:

we quickly separate the children and tell them that fighting is wrong, that it doesn't settle anything, and encourage them to apologize and settle their problems without violence. (Tobin, Wu, and Davidson 1989, 51)

However, neither of these reactions to physical aggression introduces the child to the idea of opposition through *counter*aggression. The idea that "if you hurt other people, someone is going to punish or hurt *you*" does not ordinarily get socialized in Japanese youngsters as a determinant against aggression. This will be discussed in a subsequent chapter on modal Japanese personality.

Catherine Lewis (1987) also has reported on representative first-grade classrooms, confirming her observations made in the preschool setting. Here again, the emphasis was on the training of procedural skills, fostering smooth peer socialization, and achieving a sense of positive identity and loyalty within the small social groups (now called *han* or *kumi*) and the overall classroom. In her experience, repetitious and patiently spoken instructions regarding personal habits, the need for cooperation, and assumption of more control received as much emphasis as did content-based teaching. Placing responsibility for both their deportment and their learning on the children themselves puts the teacher in the role of a benign authority figure who furnishes advice about how the groups can manage their social interaction and demonstrate competence in their studies. In the elementary school environment children continue to be rotated through situations where they are responsible for beginning a class, supervising projects, monitoring luncheon, and intervening in disputes.

In a detailed description of the Japanese elementary school, Duke (1986) accentuates the significance of the small, fixed-membership work group *kumi*). As in the preschool *gurūpu*, the *kumi* operates to build loyalty, cooperation, and empathy for others and to promote mechanisms for shared problem solving, conflict resolution, and moderation of individual competition. He sees group participation as a crucial element in consolidating habits and modes of relating, which later become predominant traits of social interaction affecting the nature of friendship patterns, work associations, and institutional identifications. Classes of thirty-five to forty-five youngsters (large by U.S. standards) are divided into groups of eight to fifteen students preselected by the teachers to represent a balanced cross-section of the class. Regardless of aptitude or skill, all students proceed at the same pace. Each *kumi* is responsible for its own members keeping up with assignments and projects. Mothers are directly engaged in being aware of assignments and helping their children with homework and preparation for exams.

Students are collectively responsible for controlling the activity level in classrooms, distributing food at luncheon, and straightening the classroom. The strong sentiment that develops in these classes is reflected by the frequency of elementary school reunions, in addition to the celebrations held by former high school, college, or professional school classmates.

In contrast to many American classrooms, students are not segregated into graded sections according to levels of proficiency in reading, writing, or other skills. Also, there are no "remedial teachers." Virtually all children attain required baseline levels of competence in reading, writing, mathematics, and other subjects through routine instruction, the help of their *kumi*, and their mothers. Standardized texts, workbooks, and examinations regulate the content and organization of teaching. Japanese children are consistently given demanding homework assignments and are expected to complete and submit these to teachers for correction and return. They attend classes five and one-half days a week for 230 days a year, contrasted to five days a week for an average of 180 days in the U.S. (In both systems a number of holidays, exams, and preparation days diminish this total.) As Duke (1986) points out, the curriculum itself induces a discipline that is intrinsic to the content of coursework. For example, the Japanese language uses four different writing systems to represent words: *katakana*, which is a phonetic, square, block-style system; *hiragana*, which is a cursive, phonetic syllabary; *Romaji*, which is a cursive (romanized) set of inscriptions; and *kanji*, which is a Japanese adaptation of Chinese

ideographic symbols, which individually represent specific phonemes, words, and terms. Learning to recognize *kanji* by sight is
demanding and rigorous; learning to reproduce *kanji* is even more
grueling. Transcribing these complex ideographs slowly, let alone
rapidly, requires greater precision than printing or cursive script in
most other languages.

Similarly, instruction in mathematics emphasizes the development of mental and spatial comprehension through performing simple
problems in one's head. The abacus *(soroban)* is introduced early
(third grade) and becomes a rudimentary but effective calculator for
performing complex mathematical operations. Unlike an electronic
instrument, the abacus concretely displays its operations through a
series of digital indicators (one to ten) that are swiftly moved about.
Duke (1986) concludes that the Japanese thoroughness in teaching
mathematics and writing is implicated in producing adults who
almost uniformly develop a high capacity for mental concentration
and manual precision, preparing them for competence in a variety
of eventual work settings.

The relatively high achievement of Japanese youngsters in elementary school is also explained by the attention given to the
feelings of the students—although mainly in a collective rather
than individual way. Merry I. White (1987) discusses how Japanese
teachers methodically address the emotional reactions of students
as they anticipate learning new and challenging procedures, particularly in mathematics. Dealing with these apprehensions preventively fosters learning with minimal anxiety.

From preschool to postdoctoral level, Japanese education is divided into public, private, and a few "elite" or experimental schools.
Public secondary education itself is divided into academic and vocational (i.e., commercial or technical) schools. Academic schools
are stratified in degrees of excellence, judged according to the historical reputation of the school, the nature of the faculty, the qualities of the students, and the track record for placement of graduates.
Attendance is partly based on geographic location; however, successful passage of stiffly graded entrance examinations is required
for admission. Most preschools are privately operated, many by
various denominational churches—as they are in the U.S. Private
elementary schools are not numerous. Sometimes they are sought
by parents whose children do not qualify (by residence or entrance
examination) for admission to a "good" public school. Private schools
at the junior and senior high levels are sometimes preferentially

sought because of their connection to a college or university. However, more commonly these are selected by affluent parents when their children have not been successful in gaining admission to the better public schools.

The physical facilities of both private and public schools are austere, perhaps even a little grubby and utilitarian, in comparison to average American school buildings. Faculties are small and teachers are expected to supervise after-class activities in sports, music, dramatics, and various clubs on a voluntary basis. Fewer gadgets and amenities are provided. Athletic contests and seasonal festivals are sponsored as all-school events, but dances or mixers for coeducational socialization are not. Female teachers predominate in preschools and in the earliest elementary grades. Male teachers begin to be encountered in the upper primary grades, and most administrative positions are filled by men. Teachers at all levels enjoy relatively high status and respect in Japan as compared to the U.S. Entry-level salaries are competitive with those in industry and commerce, and consistently attract well-prepared and motivated young people for careers in education.

Alongside the public and private schools, a parallel system of commercially operated "enrichment schools" (called *juku* or *yobikō*) are available for extracurricular development at preschool, elementary, and secondary levels. Some of these cater to preschoolers and focus on sports or artistic endeavors (ballet, music, Japanese fencing). Other *yobiko* introduce youngsters to basic skills in writing, using numbers, and drawing. Enrichment schools for older children focus on intense training in the standard school curriculum (math, languages, science, English) and either are used remedially or to prepare youngsters to compete more successfully on entrance examinations, while qualifying them for admission to superior middle schools (seventh to ninth grade), high schools (tenth to twelfth grade), and universities.

Summary of Pre-Adolescent Socialization

Working in collaboration with the "education mama," both preschool and early elementary training are devoted to weaning boys and girls from a self-centered, permissive home environment toward the demands of the outside, social world. This is achieved by setting a series of fixed responsibilities toward managing time, working in small cooperative groups *(kumi)*, and consolidating internal controls over behavior.

Preschool and early elementary teachers—almost exclusively female—take over the maternal role through being benign directors of activities. Their vigilance about carefully observing students' behavior and development is superficially disguised by their apparent indirection, agreeability, and feigned passivity. Strategies to emphasize interdependence among small group members and to enhance personal responsibility for control are patiently inculcated and reinforced. These early school contexts also function to provide a moral force endorsing the merit of orderliness, industry, academic skills, and proper deportment. The opposites of these virtues are not so much repudiated as denied, diverted, or "reinterpreted." Teachers offer encouragement, praise, and reward for conformity and cooperation, and tend to ignore, redirect, and eventually extinguish undue aggression, misbehavior, inattention, or indolence (as discussed by C. Lewis 1984, 1987).

The strong *amae* relationship established with the mother (and to a lesser extent toward other family members) is both split and modified in the school situation. Some cravings for special cherishment *(amaeru)* are satisfied through the teacher's genuine affection, permissiveness, and interest in students. This is accompanied by a degree of tolerance for indiscretions, laziness, contentiousness, or uncivilized behavior as long as efforts are made to reform. Teachers make a conscious and persistent attempt to define their students as "good," and to elevate their self-esteem on the basis of actual performance. Another part of *amae* becomes diversified in the close interpersonal relationships within the *kumi*, where fellow students reciprocally respond to each other's needs and work together to experience the satisfactions and rewards of group achievements. *Amae* is even more directly implicated in the formation of selective personal attachments and friendships within and outside of their *kumi*.

As in the family, socialization pressures operate to convert individual (personal) narcissism into a collective pride achieved through group identification. This diffused pride is associated with the *kumi*, the whole class, and for that matter the entire school—preparing the young citizen for collective identifications later in life.

Confidence concerning presentation of self is directly rehearsed and reinforced through requirements for public speaking to the entire class, responsibilities for directing programs (opening and closing class sessions), and publicly reiterating standard forms of polite salutation and responses to persons of higher status.

Along with this socialization concerning social interaction, there is a serious and demanding requirement for mastering study habits, completing assignments, and keeping up with others. Even at the elementary school level it is emphasized that all students meet basic standards in a tightly regulated and standardized curriculum.

Adolescent Socialization in Japanese Middle and High Schools

Rohlen (1983) has characterized the first six grades of primary education in Japan as relatively egalitarian in offering nearly all students an equivalent opportunity for achievement. Although admission to public schools is determined partly on a geographic basis, neighborhoods in Japan are more diversified in socioeconomic strata than in the U.S. Thus, schools are not sharply differentiated according to levels of affluence or class position based on geography alone (as they tend to be in American cities and suburbs). Wearing uniforms is universal in public schools, and restrictions concerning ornamentation and jewelry act to reduce discrimination according to the class status of the parents.[1]

Also, teachers strive to show impartiality and to gloss over differences in talent, ability, presence of outside resources, or even minority status (DeVos and Wagatsuma 1967). Despite this, children from minority groups, such as *Burakumin* or those of Korean descent, are congregated in certain neighborhoods and attend schools that consistently show lower achievement in examination scores and admission into better middle and high schools.

During the first six years of schooling, the atmosphere of learning is serious, but individuals are only moderately pressured about reaching high standards of performance (Rohlen 1983). However, with each progressive year, teachers, parents, and students demonstrate an increasing awareness about the relationship between academic achievement and occupational future. This builds steadily until the point of admission to intermediate school (grades seven to nine), when the atmosphere changes suddenly. Attending intermediate school begins the preparation for examinations taken during the ninth grade to qualify individuals for entrance to a hierarchy of desirable high schools (grades ten to twelve). Acceptance into a well-regarded high school requires students to prepare, sit for, and excel in competitive examinations that divide students into cohorts based upon numerical achievement scores. These test results are accompanied by the written recommendations of their middle school teachers, but are considerably more significant in determining selection than are personal qualifications. Such selections fatefully determine students' ultimate opportunities and achievements within the adult society—except for a small cadre of affluent children whose parents may be able to place them in a good private school alternative irrespective of their test scores.

A large gap in future opportunity exists between the application to vocational versus academic schools. However, even within the public academic schools, there are significant differences in quality, reputation, and prospects for the future. As Rohlen (1983) states it, "students are shunted out into a hierarchy of schools, each with its own sub-culture. Education has many tracks at this point as there are high schools in a particular locality" (Rohlen 1983, 134). School reputations are based on the records of examination scores of recent graduates, and the reputations of the colleges and universities to which they have been admitted. The emphasis on grades and test performance becomes crucial, and pivots on the mother's participation, the availability of help at home, the ability to pay for outside tutoring, and the economic resources and motivation within the family. Social stratification affects this in that parents from professional or white-collar positions offer more direction and modeling for achievement and, moreover, possess financial resources to provide outside tutoring and *juku*. The more affluent families also tend to have better social connections, which can be mobilized to find alternative pathways for enrolling their youngsters in private schools, or providing special arrangements for remedial study.

High School Socialization

Both in vocational and academic high schools, students are divided into home rooms that continue to be diversified and represent a range of individuals with various levels of academic capability and class backgrounds. Students from minorities also are distributed rather than segregated. This guarantees a blending of abilities within each classroom. However, students no longer function in fixed, small *kumi*, although they tend to retain the same set of classmates for three years. Unlike American high schools where students circulate to classes, students remain in their home rooms while teachers rotate to provide courses within a fixed curriculum set by the centralized Ministry of Education. Relaxed sociability is present in the home room before and between classes, but these settings do not function as a social club for holding parties or other independent extracurricular events. Contacts between the sexes are friendly, but are accompanied by shyness and rarely become publicly romantic.

Students continue to be responsible for basic janitorial care of their classrooms and work settings. Although the curriculum offers virtually no electives, students are encouraged to participate in club activities after 3:00 p.m. Clubs are devoted to sports, music, photography, (spoken) English, practical sciences, and dramatics, and are supervised by teachers who have skills or interests in these areas. Particularly in sporting clubs (volleyball, baseball), older students display authoritarian dominance over novitiates. Rohlen (1983) describes hazing as part of the ordinary socialization and solidarity in athletic groups—both male and female. Hazing includes forcing an exaggerated deference to older players, along with responsibilities for cleaning up and doing ignominious tasks. At times, hazing exceeds this and occasionally can be quite cruel and physically excessive.

Discipline is uniformly expected in the school situation. This requires maintaining orderliness, completing assigned school and homework, and meeting scholastic qualifications. Beyond this, dress codes are enforced and tardiness and truancy are not condoned; smoking and antisocial behavior toward other students are promptly and seriously punished. As a moral institution, the high school extends beyond the confines of the classroom and playing fields, into the neighborhood and general society. Students are not supposed to be seen in "outlandish dress" on the streets, or be observed "wasting their time" in coffee houses, pool rooms, or other "flesh pots" (Rohlen 1983). Most students go directly home after school or following club activity, generally to complete homework, watch television, listen to music, or attend *juku*. Students from vocational campuses are characteristically more casual toward homework assignments, and spend less time at serious study. Interestingly, Rohlen reports that they are required to do more chores at home than are academically oriented students, who are pampered—particularly males. Girls and boys leave the school campus separately, usually in small groups. Romantic boy-girl relationships occur, but are clandestine, and are not approved by the faculty or sanctioned by other students. Although boy-girl friendships may be formed, formal dating on a one-to-one basis is still relatively uncommon. Coeducational "group dates" are the norm. Friendships are formed in clubs as well as the classroom, but are less exclusive than during elementary school days. Students commonly live in diverse areas of the city, making the opportunity for after-school socialization more difficult (Rohlen 1983). Compared to their American counterparts, Japanese teenagers have much less after-school contact with friends, and even less social contact with members of the opposite sex.

Maintenance of proper behavior both on and off the school grounds is framed in terms of each school's reputation. Teachers and administrators believe that they are responsible for behavior within both the school and the general community. Students from schools lower in academic-quality hierarchy or from vocational settings characteristically are more lackadaisical, and may take the opportunity for having coffee dates or strolling together in coed pairs and groups. Such behavior among students from the more elite schools would be looked on as a detriment to the schools' reputations, as well as potentially scandalous for the individuals. Thus, moral pressures against open romantic pairing not only creates risks of embarrassment or derision for the individuals, but also a fear of exposure and condemnation by the school authorities. Unchallenged overt pairing may invite criticism of the school's reputation and lead to comparisons with schools of lower achievement, where nonconforming behavior may be more common.[2]

As reported by Rohlen (1983), high school teachers conceptualize and treat their students as children rather than young adults. The ideal teacher—male or female—is described as "industrious" (indefatigable) and "self-sacrificing" (like mother). They provide a calculated mixture of affirmation, affection, discipline, and nurturance toward their students—but not in a uniform manner. Teachers respond differentially to students according to their attractiveness and achievements.

While admission to high school is a critical juncture in the Japanese student's life, examinations for selection into colleges and universities are even more auspicious. For the majority of students who look forward to postsecondary education, this process will determine their eventual societal and occupational role, based on the reputation of the institution and its connections to the job market.

Both earlier and more recently, critical commentators have written about the psychological consequences of this examination system, called "examination hell" or *shiken jigoku* (Vogel 1962; Kiefer 1970). Kiefer describes the system as displacing the sense of interpersonal competition onto the general society and suggests that "the education system [is] a continuation of socialization trends begun in the family, and is a bridge between the family and the socializing agencies of the educated adult, namely bureaucratic peer-groups" (Kiefer 1970, 346). He sees the habits of loyalty, small-group cooperation, and identification with the family and school group as being eventually transferred into the "bureaucracy": that is, into corporations, businesses, and other workplaces. In a parallel manner, he describes a transfer of the emotional dependency *(amae)* from both family and school life into relations with office groups, bosses, and fellow employees.

Summary

The content of this and the previous two chapters has responded to Pelzel's (1977) suggestion that Japanese indulgent dependency *(amae)* should be illuminated by a systematic attempt to list its connections to specialized history, culture, childrearing, and socialization. The summaries composed here are intended to provide this background. They also permit comparisons to generalizations from traditional psychoanalytic theory—in this case regarding the implications of child and adolescent development.

Central to the theme of this book, the naturalistic observations of Japanese infantile development offer ethnographic evidence for the persistence of a strong nonsexualized desire for affiliation, cherishment, and dependent indulgence *(amae)* that is in conflict with traditional psychoanalytic explanations of dependency and affiliation as secondary drives (as in Parens and Saul 1971). This will be more systematically addressed in subsequent chapters. Following a comprehensive and critical presentation of the concept of *amae* (chapters 6 and 7) and the psychocultural view of the Japanese self (chapter 8), a more thoroughgoing application of these ingredients to psychoanalytic theory will be made in chapter 9.

Notes

1. The subject of social class is difficult to discuss with Japanese. In the author's experience, a number of research subjects, informants, and col-

leagues at first responded to questions about "class" by playing down the significance of social differentiations in Japan. When pressed further, individuals apologetically indicated that certain "lower-class" positions are occupied by persons of Korean ancestry and "outcasts" *(burakumin)*. These informants also divulged that the Ainu (an indigenous non-Japanese ethnic group residing in Hokkaido) and *gaijin* (foreigners) are separated from the ambiguous mainstream. If prodded further, some informants may talk about "regional differences" (e.g., Okinawans) or about persons working in "the water trades" (hostesses, bar girls, prostitutes). What is most apparent, however, is that Japanese are reluctant to talk about class differentiation.

As another interesting tendency, inquiring about stratification often becomes diverted into an itemization of *moral* characteristics, suggesting a perception that the prestige hierarchy of "class" depends more on the quality of ethical conduct than on educational background, status, area of residence, family of origin, or economic power.

One Japanese informant who had lived in the U.S. for nearly ten years reflected on her degree of awareness about the socioeconomic backgrounds of friends while attending high school in Illinois, and later while living in a sorority at an American university. She contrasted this awareness with the paucity of information she had about the families of her closest friends and fellow graduate students in Japan. Other informants added that they often were not very knowledgeable about their own father's work or income, partly due to the tendency among Japanese to segregate work and family roles.

Enryo (ritualized modesty) also operates to conceal the particulars of social background, and to avoid embarrassing persons by inquiring about private matters concerning educational achievement, work status, possessions, or other manifestations of affluence (travel, recreational patterns, size of residence). Taken together, all of these factors tend to make the discussion of class differentiation vague and difficult.

2. Even with the strictures about dress code, rules against indolent after-school behavior, and discouragement of adolescent heterosexual pairing, opportunities for mildly defiant behavior are available. Perhaps the gaudiest of these is the weekly tradition for some teenagers from the Tokyo area to congregate on Sunday in the business section and boulevards near Harajuku Station. Dressed in "punk" costumes, these young people parade, dance, sing, play portable cassette recorders, tease, and flirt in a noisy but generally harmless fashion.

PART TWO

Psychocultural Aspects of Japanese Dependency and Self

CHAPTER 6

A Multilevel Analysis of Doi's Theories of *Amae*

A Psychosocial Analysis of *Amae*

The formulations of Takeo Doi and the commentators who have responded to his writings concerning *amae* provide a central framework for a multidimensional description and explanation of dependency. Summarizing Doi's published work, however, gives rise to complications that must be addressed. In the evolution of his writings, he initially focused on dependency as a psychological motive passively expressed during infancy and childhood, but also observable in later life. This was described in terms of individual psychology, sometimes as a "drive," need, or "desire" (Doi 1956, 1962a, 1962b, 1964, 1969). From the beginning, however, Doi's explanations also furnished a semantic and sociolinguistic analysis of meanings attached to terms describing manifestations of dependency among Japanese. These explanations have explicitly involved cultural factors, many of which have been systematically discussed by Doi himself. He has also discussed *amae* in terms of its clinical manifestations, and in the quality of psychotherapeutic transactions. Beyond this, Doi has made allusions to historical, mythic, and nationalistic aspects of *amae* that relate to a Japanese ethos, and to prevailing ideologies concerning national identity and the self-perceived "uniqueness" of the Japanese.

There are a number of problems involved in trying to summarize *amae*. One of these is that dependency behaviors can be conceptualized as points along a behavioral continuum, ranging from less-than-average to "normal" to excessive to pathological. Moreover, pathological may be clinically abnormal in a diagnostic sense, or merely strongly eccentric. Another complication lies in distinguishing *amae* as a particular form of dependency—specifically one involving indulgence and nurturance—from a spectrum of other dependent motives and interactions (Lebra 1976).

As discussed in previous chapters, the behavioral applications of dependency are most extensive, and are highly influenced by cultural, situational, and circumstantial factors. Another difficulty in summarizing the effects of *amae* concerns the manner in which states of Japanese dependency are interdigitated with other Japanese norms and interaction rules, particularly those that regulate conventions such as status, gender, social relationship, age, and position in the lifespan. A final complication involves the conceptual levels at which dependency and interdependency may be examined: 1) as an individual, organismic trait; 2) as an interactional phenomenon occurring between two persons; 3) as a relationship of an individual with groups and family; and, finally, 4) as a series of relationships between large groups themselves.

This chapter will confront some of these difficulties by discussing the writings of Doi and his commentators in terms of various conceptual levels, including cultural and developmental differences. Taken together, these will be organized into a multidimensional depiction of *amae*. Specifically, these will be discussed as 1) psychological and metapsychological characteristics, 2) psychocultural features, 3) social-psychological patterns, 4) clinical and psychotherapeutic implications, 5) interactional and phenomenological formulations, 6) psychoanalytic critiques of "indulgent dependency," and, finally, 7) social-philosophic allusions to *amae*.

Psychological and Metapsychological Characteristics of *Amae*

As a psychoanalytically trained academic psychiatrist, Takeo Doi was the first to draw attention to the psychological implications of the word *amae* (Doi 1956).[1] While a commonly understood expression in Japan, *amae* has no concise counterpart in the English language. As defined earlier, it is a noun, derived from the intransitive verb *amaeru*, which describes the "ability to depend and presume upon another's benevolence, basically to be catered to or waited on." M. Masuda (1959) lists a number of vernacular English equivalents: "to be babied, to act like a spoiled child, to coax, to be coquettish, to request favors, to avail oneself of another's kindness." Other colloquial approximations include the "desire to be pampered" (Lebra 1976), "to seek the goodwill of others . . . flirt with, take advantage of, or butter up" (Pelzel 1977). Doi himself suggests the word "wheedle" as an equivalent English expression. Tyler (1983) has added the definitions of "to play baby," or "to coquet" in the sense of tease. Doi comments that expressions of *amae* possess an aura of sweetness and permissiveness that are not connotated in the English approximations of the word.

In his original work, Doi commented on Michael Balint's (1952) psychoanalytic observations about the absence of the linguistic distinction in most Indo-European languages between the active and passive experiences of love. In the English language, the state of desiring to be the passive object of cherishment is not given a distinctive etymologic term, but instead requires the gerund: "*being* loved." In contrast, the Japanese term *amaeru* denotes the promotion of security and cherishment sought through another person. There is no corresponding word for this in the English language.

The words *amae* and *amaeru* may be examined both in their intrapsychic and interactional dimensions. Intrapsychically, *amae* is present as a motive or "desire" that becomes expressed as yearnings and expectations to be held, fed, bathed, made safe, kept warm, emotionally comforted, and given special cherishment (Doi 1973a). This is similar to what Bowlby (1960, 1969) identified as a drive toward "primary love" or attachment. Interactionally, *amae* is manifested by the transactions of such yearnings in numerous culturally acceptable situations in Japan. Doi has used the word "merger" to describe the relational quality of these primary and selective object relations and has sometimes substituted the word "love" for cherishment (Doi 1972).

Although verbal requests for *amae* may be made directly, they ordinarily are not. Requests for *amae* are usually negotiated through nonverbal expressions of need (Doi 1973d, 1989a, 1989b). Subtle, gestural indicators for nurturance and cherishment are generated in a passive, infantile manner and are designed to be picked up and acted upon by the nurturing partner.

Many of the English equivalents for *amae* have negative connotations, for example, "whining," "sulking," "coaxing," "pouting," "wheedling," "being spoiled or pampered." In the West these expressions are often used pejoratively to describe states of helplessness in what are considered to be age-inappropriate demands for assistance or undue attention. Disparagement of excessive or inappropriate *amae* also exists in Japan, but is counterbalanced by a manifestly higher acceptance of overt dependency when compared to the U.S. (Kumakura 1984, private communication).

In Doi's early writings (1964, 1969), *amae* was specified as a strongly expressed, internally structuralized drive striving for affiliation, security, succorance, indulgence, cherishment, and love. Such organized strivings were held to constitute a basic and essential part of human personality—specifically as an ego-instinctual drive for object relations. In stating this, Doi joined a series of schismatic psychoanalytic writers who have stressed the significance of seeking human affiliation as a nonlibidinous "instinct" (notably as in Fairbairn 1954; Winnicott 1965a; Bowlby 1960, 1988). However, unlike Doi, these latter writers have explicitly formulated dependency to be of central consequence in a revised theory of psychoanalytic object relations and human affiliation. In contrast, Doi has not advocated a radical revision of theory, but has more moderately suggested the addition of dependency to existing metapsychological theories of primary drives (Doi 1969). Although his statements concerning dependency are constructed in the context of Japanese culture, he clearly states that these motives are universal, albeit modified or disguised in Western societies.

Unlike Bowlby, Doi has not methodically assembled ethological evidence as a presumptive background for suggesting a sociobiological precedence given to a primary affiliative drive. However, such biologically directed motives are conspicuous among primates and lower species, where programmed bonding and attachments are essential for establishing an infant/mother partnership guaranteeing nutrition, body temperature regulation, cleansing, and refuge from predation.[2]

Although Doi identifies the precursors of *amae* as originating in the unconscious "ego instincts," his definition of *amae* is that of a human *psychological* phenomenon that becomes manifest after four to six weeks of infantile life. This occurs when the incipient ego shows an awareness of the separateness from the mother. It is conjectured that a dawning sense of separation constitutes a prototypical psychological position, which eventually evolves into an internal-object representation of the mother—or, more likely, of the mother/infant relationship. Conceptually, Doi's description parallels traditional psychoanalytic explanations that constitute the earliest weeks of human life as psychologically ambiguous, characterized internally as "oceanic narcissism," and relationally experienced as "symbiosis" (Mahler and Gosliner 1955). Originally described as passive and separated from its environment by a "sensory screen," the neonate is currently regarded as actively participating in a two-party, interactional system (Emde 1983; Stern 1983, 1985).

Although Doi's earlier formulations concentrate attention on the internal structuralization of the desire to *amaeru*, his descriptions have always been implicitly interactional, and have involved some form of reciprocal partnership—specifically within the infant/mother dyad, but also in other significant partnerships, where the desire to lean on and be cherished is prominent. *Amae* is thus conceptualized both as an intrinsic trait and as a series of complementary interactions based on the infant/mother paradigm.

Psychocultural Features of *Amae*

Many of Doi's descriptions of *amae* are simultaneously psychological and cultural. His psychocultural emphasis methodically relates *amaeru* transactions within a matrix of other culturally specified norms organized around ritualized self-denial and modesty *(enryo)*, around variations in status and obligation *(on, giri)*, and involving the fluctuating mutuality and feelings *(ninjō)* intrinsic to these relationships (see chapter 4). The desire to depend on, affiliate, and be indulged is shown by Doi to be opposed and regulated by *enryo*, which imposes a hesitation and restraint onto attempts to *amaeru*. *On* and *giri* are also regulatory in restricting or thwarting *amae* according to the structural features of specified, nonintimate social relationships. The quality of feeling *(ninjō)* is expected to wax and wane situationally, and presupposes the underlying but unexpressed desire to affiliate, lean on, or claim special attention and affection. These social-psychological manifestations, although channeled by cultural conditioning, can be seen as patterned interactions carried out to achieve goals concerned with security, nurturance, deference, affiliation, maintenance of "face," and attainment of normative social competence.

In looking at behavior through a psychocultural lens, *amae* emerges as a balancing of needs according to an interplay of action possibilities enacted during real-life situations. The needs to affiliate and to

avoid being rejected or humiliated are prominent in the consciousness of average Japanese concerning their presentation of self (Doi
1973a, 1986). Closely related to norms regulating *enryo*, the social
presentation of self requires a balancing of the projection of self at a
public level *(tatemae)* with an awareness of unexpressed thoughts,
emotions, and strivings *(honne)* that are *not* directly transacted (Doi
1973b). The presence of these inexpressible feelings and thoughts
is not disreputable per se, but is associated with a potential lack
of propriety if directly disclosed. The individual's ability to shift
between the "inside" *(ura)* and "outside" *(omote)* dimensions of
social-psychological awareness is regarded as a crucial achievement,
without which effective social and personal competence cannot be
sustained (Doi 1973b, 259).

Paralleling these psychocultural dimensions of Japanese experience, the metapsychological implications of desires for dependency,
indulgence, and affiliation have been exposed by Doi. Unlike Fairbairn (1954), who makes dependency the centerpiece of his theory
of object relations, or Bowlby (1960), who makes separation the
psychological pivot for his developmental formulations, Doi more
modestly formulates the significance of an affiliation/separation
tension within a psychoanalytic, dynamic explanation of behavior
—particularly in his publications of 1962a, 1964, and 1969. He sees
the basic drive for affiliation seeking expression independently, in
combination or even in competition with other drives—including
ego-instinctual, libidinous, and aggressive motives (Doi 1969). All
of these drives would be defined as "psychodynamic" in providing
explanation for a variety of overt actions and behaviors on the basis
of unconscious, activating forces.

Although consistently described in his writings, Doi's psychoanalytic formulations are clearest in a 1969 publication (335–38). Here
he proposes a separate dependency drive, intertwined with other
primary drives, but having a special connection with libidinous
drives. This is illustrated by him through the ethological studies of
Harlow and Harlow (1962), who demonstrated that the deprivation
of a primary, desexualized dependency in infantile monkeys inter-
fered with their normal development and expression of adult affiliation, including subsequent competent sexual performance. In asserting the hypothetical autonomy of a dependency drive, Doi
identified it as the basic motive for the establishment of object
relations. As such, these earliest affiliations establish a pattern for
subsequent connections to persons, things, and the general environ-

ment that are potentially independent of attachments instigated by libidinous or aggressive motives. Although the processes concerning the development of internal object representations are not detailed by Doi, they are presumed to be based on the generally accepted models explaining early psychological *incorporation*. As he states it, "identification and assimilation are psychological mechanisms with which the inhabitants of the world of *amae* are very much at home" (Doi 1973a, 45).

Doi also directly criticizes Freud (1914, 1931), and Hartmann, Kris, and Loewenstein (1951) for understating the significance of nonsexualized, ego-oriented dependency, even though all of these authors commented on needs for affiliation and acknowledged them to be of importance—outstandingly during childhood. The traditional explanation for the omission of dependency as a freestanding drive is that Freud hypothesized the primacy of the *libidinal drive*, which consigned dependency to the derivative status of a "secondary drive." Doi (1969) also cites the general cultural bias against dependency in Western societies, which downplays both its significance and manifestations. Doi (1964) suggested that Freud's comparison of juvenile helplessness with "irrational" adult desires for security through religion also tended to disparage dependent motives (Freud 1927). At a more personal level, Freud (1931) stated that the initial attachment to mother seemed "elusive" to him. This suggested to Doi (1969) that Freud overlooked the significance of dependency, perhaps out of his own repression of early nonsexualized affiliations. In a later statement (1990a), Doi speculated that Freud's ambivalence about authority (Freud 1914, 49) also tended to disguise overt dependency in the psychoanalytic situation, through analyzing such needs as anachronistic and neurotic, rather than as evidence of unconscious motives for indulgence and cherishment.

Social-Psychological Enactments of *Amae*

Throughout Doi's work there has been an explicit concern with descriptions of indulgent dependency demonstrated as exaggerated or distorted expressions of *amae*—illustrated by him in numerous cultural examples using common Japanese words and expressions. Some of these expressions have been mentioned previously but will be listed and tabulated here, summarizing Doi's (1973a) descriptions of "the pathology of *amae*."

Table 6.1 summarizes a spectrum of behaviors described by Doi (1973a) occurring in various forms of maladaptive, exaggerated, or pathological manifestations. Paralleling Ekman's (1984) description of "normal" and "disordered" manifestations of emotion, these illustrations can represent 1) momentary distortions of *amae* occurring in the form of *evanescent feelings,* 2) more persistent reactions over time (minutes or hours) constituting a *mood,* 3) consistent presentation of these reactions (as "traits") that attain a *characterologic status,* and, finally, 4) exaggerated, intense, and persistent displays that signify *clinically pathological conditions* of overdependency.

This spectrum of dependency states can be clarified by examples. A momentary expression of *amae* might consist of a student's feelings and behavior involved in requesting a special favor from a professor (e.g., assistance in procuring a teaching position). A more persistent mood might involve that same student brooding for a period of minutes or hours over frustration in failing to elicit an indulgent response from a patron. A more characterologic example of exaggerated *amae* might define a student who chronically appears frustrated, helpless, and whining in his or her relations to professors, fellow students, parents, and people in general. At the end of this dependency spectrum one might see a student whose helplessness and indecisiveness progress to the point of the student becoming depressed, missing classes, failing to complete assignments, and avoiding contact with friends and teachers.

Age and developmental factors also affect the significance of dependency cravings. Fleeting reactions to deprived *amae* shown by whining and pouting are universally normal for youngsters, but peculiar or even pathological in adolescents or adults, simply through being age-inappropriate. Relational factors also affect the transaction of dependency. For example, in Japan, persons in an established subordinate relationship may make appropriate attempts to *amaeru* with their bosses or supervisors; however, these same demonstrations would be obnoxious or presumptuous with new or casual acquaintances. Similarly, different settings and contexts affect the pathological designation of distorted *amae.* For example, it may be normal to *amaeru* one's mother in the home, but inappropriate to attempt this while riding on public transportation. Or it might be permissible for a graduate student to *amaeru* her professor in eliciting help for a grant application, but inappropriate in discussing a highly personal problem with another graduate student. Bearing these variables in mind, a number of behavioral terms related by Doi to the frustrations, exaggerations, denials, and conversions of *amaeru* will be reviewed. This list (see table 6.1) is assembled operationally and is not meant to be comprehensive.

The first of these reactions, *suneru*, involves the straightforward expression of "sulking" as a communication of anger following the frustration of *amaeru*. Although an active response, it is insidious in not confronting the frustrating partner with direct hostility, but instead displaying an internal mood state that has no apparent object. Commonly this is seen in children or young adults who go from "all smiles" to a petulant uncooperativeness. Sulkiness and petulance may also be seen in adults who are miffed about expressed or unexpressed needs not being attended. A man may pout because his wife did not collect his suit from the cleaner's, or did not return from a social outing in time to prepare his meal. Nurses on a surgical service who discovered that they had not been invited to join the doctors at a Sunday picnic may refuse to greet the doctors the following week, and work slowly or uncooperatively as a means of venting their displeasure. The doctors might say that the nurses are *sunete iru*, or sulking.

Uramu is an intense but concealed reaction to frustrated *amaeru* that focuses unspoken resentment or even hatred toward the non-gratifying partner who is perceived to be the cause of a grievance. *Uramu* is experienced as a hidden internal awareness, as the frustrated individual strives to deceive his or her offender. In Japan, it is not uncommon for a low-status person to feel *uramu* toward an ungracious person of higher status. Status difference and social distance between the resenter and the perceived offender may mean that the resenter cannot realistically achieve revenge and that the target of the grudge never becomes aware of the resentment.

The word *uramu* may be used to identify several gradations of resentment, some of which are mild and petty. However, it most often applies to a persistent grudge festering over a long period of time, and relates to a desire for revenge that remains deeply hidden until a final moment of opportunity. Thus, in its most florid representation, *uramu* may ultimately be revealed in a public outburst that results in a scandal or humiliation for the astonished offender. Characteristically, the outburst is totally unexpected and unpredicted by the target of concealed animosity. Sometimes the person who harbors a long-standing grudge may be able to effect revenge in a completely secret manner, while the offender remains ignorant of

TABLE 6.1
Psychological Conversions of *Amaeru* (after Doi 1973a)

Japanese Expression	English Translation	Psychological Mechanism
suneru	To pout, sulk, or demonstrate petulance	Frustrated desire to depend or seek cherishment is converted into a thinly disguised hostility
uramu	To harbor a grudge or resentment	Failure to achieve gratification leads to a smoldering sense of injury and desire for revenge
futekusareru	To show open defiance toward others in behavior or speech	Perceived narcissistic injury turned into petulance, defiance, and noncooperativeness
hinekureru	To act in a perversely negative and suspicious manner	Unsuccessful attempts to *amaeru* converted into suspicious, obstinate, and peculiar behavior
sumanai	Expression of apology, regret, or remorse	Overt craving for dependency and cherishment disguised by self-abnegation and excessive apology as a strategy for getting attention and establishing empathy
kodawaru	To be finicky, difficult, overly concerned or distracted by details	Denial of needs for reciprocal *amaeru* by acting difficult, inaccessible, and difficult to engage
toraware	Caught up, preoccupied, obsessed	Fears of rejection of *amaeru* converted into repetitive thoughts, overconcern with one's body, and hypersensitivity in social situations
yakekuso ni naru	To lose control; to respond to frustration with irresponsible behavior	Failure to achieve gratifying responses leads to histrionic and masochistic demands for pity, recognition, or favor

Term		
wagamama	Selfish, egocentric, willful, "spoiled"	Cravings to seek favors and special regard are exaggerated in a perpetual demand for attention and entitlement
higamu	To feel unfairly treated; to be prejudiced against, biased; to be warped or suspicious	Inability to enjoy *amaeru* gratifications leads to pervasive suspiciousness and distrust of others' motives or favors
higaisha-ishiki	Feeling or awareness of having been the injured party	Chronic sense of victimization leads to nearly insatiable demands to *amaeru*
kuyashii	Mortified, frustrated, vexed	Failure to achieve gratification of *amaeru* leads to an ill-defined sense of outrage
amanzuru	To be resigned to an undeserved state or situation	Actual needs are disguised or temporarily denied through pretending to accept an altogether unfair condition
wadakamaru	To feign indifference in order to disguise a negative emotion	Disruption of *amaeru* due to unresolved insult or injury leads to anger that is concealed by an indifferent manner
toriiku	To ingratiate, "set up," place in emotional debt	Craving for *amaeru* disguised by allowing others to become gratified and hence indebted
tereru	To be excessively shy or unusually bashful	Desire to *amaeru* is deflected by incapacity to relate smoothly to others

the instigator or the reason behind the damage. For example, a professor who has harbored a deep and enduring *urami* (noun form) against his chairman may learn of an attempt to enroll his boss's son in a distinguished private high school. The secretly resentful man may use his personal influence with the dean of admissions to orchestrate the rejection of the boy's application. A milder manifestation of *uramu* could involve a secretary who has developed a smoldering but obscured resentment toward a work partner because of what she believes to have been a series of slights and impositions. Her grudge is never expressed directly, but is shown through increased silence, studied politeness, diminished solicitation, or other subtle and indirect manifestations. The person who is the target may be dimly aware that something is the matter, but not be able to resolve it, because both the resentment and its cause remain concealed. These reactions mostly occur in long-standing relationships rather than casual connections. At an unconscious level, in substituting anger for emotions expressing the desire for indulgence, *uramu* may successfully disguise the underlying craving for *amae*.

Two more overt forms of frustrated *amae* seek expression in clearly recognizable hostile behavior. These are *futekusareru* (to have a fit of the sulks, to become spiteful) and *hinekureru* (to act unduly negative or suspicious). As with *uramu*, these at once serve to disguise the yearning for dependency and to punish the nongratifying partner through the release of aggressive speech or behavior. The defiant behavior of *futekusareru* occurs as a result of incompletely suppressed anger or indignation. For example, an engineer who feels his technical advice has not been properly heeded might become pointedly uncooperative and refuse to participate in a new project. The psychological strategy of sulking or displaying lack of cooperation covers over his underlying need to be appreciated by substituting a display of anger.

Hinekureru (literally meaning "twisted" or "warped") is a word applied to persons who react to frustration in a perversely suspicious and negative manner. Even when they are gratified, such persons may show unwarranted suspicion and distrust toward their benefactors, and behave as soreheads or ingrates. Such a response superficially rejects gratification and thereby denies the need to *amaeru*, and at the same time psychologically projects the responsibility for feeling unsatisfied onto the erstwhile benefactor—even while the subject is being indulged or placated.

The Japanese word *sumanai* is used to express both apology and gratitude. The word means to "feel sorry, regretful, conscience-stricken, or guilty" and is a commonplace Japanese expression, sometimes used to communicate remorse at not having fulfilled expectations. The use of apology among Japanese is complicated and often includes exaggerating one's own guilt. A primary function of exaggerated self-blame is to deflect or minimize any actual blame that might be inflicted upon the self. A corollary of accepting exaggerated responsibility is to act as a self-designated scapegoat, deflecting punishment and blame from other sources while simultaneously protecting other persons who may have actually been responsible. Thus, the assumption of exaggerated self-blame may function to make another person feel obligated. Exaggerated self-blame also may constitute a denial of the individual's own needs through a lavish but insincere apology for not having fulfilled others' requirements or expectations.

Expressions of apology are conspicuous in Japan, and have many ritualistic characteristics, even beyond the automatic and conventional indications of politeness, such as "excuse me" or "pardon me" as they are used in English. The use of *sumanai* can express regret that may not actually be felt; however, completely sincere remorse may be conveyed using this same phrase (Nagano 1985). Nevertheless, among the Japanese, it is routine to find the use of apology as a social-interactional strategy that predisposes the direction of an encounter toward a seeker/gratifier relationship, in a manipulative gesture to cultivate *amae*. An example of an exaggerated acceptance of blame might be when the president of a corporation publicly accepts total responsibility for an explosion in one of his company's factories and hands in his resignation, even though he realistically could not have caused the catastrophe. His assumption of responsibility for damage, injury, and death serves to focus guilt and blame that might otherwise have been more destructive if it were diffused throughout the corporation.

Another defensive conversion of *amaeru* is illustrated by the verb *kodawaru*, which means "to cause difficulties, to obstruct, or to habitually oppose people." Referring to a person in this state, Doi observes, "Even more than the average man, of course, he would like to be permitted self-indulgence, but the fear of being rejected prevents him from giving it straightforward expression" (Doi 1973a, 30). Used in its adjectival form, *kodawari* describes the behavior of persons who are "finicky," "difficult," and perfectionistic. By being "sticklers," they continually cause trouble for others. Such people make themselves unavailable or inaccessible to potential *amaeru* by being aloof, officious, and preoccupied with details. For example, a woman who is eligible for marriage and in the process of reviewing suitors may be unable to settle on an appropriate match because her attention is fixed on trivial imperfections noted in a series of potential candidates. In being distracted by nonessential details (such as a prominent adam's apple, shaggy eyebrows, or large ears) this young woman is unable to make a reasoned choice based on more fundamental qualities regarding marriageability. As defined by Doi, *kodawari* means to be "sensitive to minor things . . . and . . . inwardly disturbed over one's personal relationships" (Doi 1962a, 133). His interpretation of this condition is that it originates in a failure to achieve the capacity for mature negotiations of interdependency. Clinically, the term *kodawaru* may be used to describe an obsessional state where a person gets stuck in a pattern of thinking, shows a fascination with minutiae, and loses perspective concerning ongoing social interaction. Such persons are perfectionistic, easily distracted by petty details, and low in their capacity for warm, affiliative relationships. In Western clinical terms some of these individuals would qualify for a DSM III-R classification of "obsessive-compulsive personality disorder" (American Psychiatric Association 1987).

Toraware, meaning "to be caught up or bound," is another word that refers to individuals who are obsessive, easily distracted, and hypersensitive. It is commonly used as a colloquial expression, but is employed also as a psychiatric term for what in Japan is a clinical condition featuring repetitious worries, hypochondriasis, disturbances in concentration, and overreaction to sensory and social stimuli. Originally formulated by the Japanese psychiatrist Shoma Morita (1922), this condition is roughly comparable to a "mixed psychoneurosis" in the older American nomenclature (DSM II classification, American Psychiatric Association 1968). On a nonclinical basis, *kodawari* is also used to describe being unable to escape from the clutches of tradition, fate, or custom. This form of obsession is closer to what might pass for being "possessed" or overdedicated to a conviction or idea—as in "a magnificent obsession."

Another indirect reaction to frustrated *amae* may be seen to follow especially severe frustration or failure. This is called *yakekuso ni naru,* which refers to "throwing oneself away" in the sense of deliberately abandoning self-control. As the imagery suggests, this can be used to describe a tantrum in an adult or adolescent. For example, a man who has been trying to repair a toaster may explode into a rage and demolish the appliance. Alternately, a would-be suitor whose attentions have been ignored may get drunk and collapse on his wished-for girlfriend's doorstep. In both examples, the underlying strategy is that such drastically dramatized frustration may elicit or even force sympathetic and caring responses.

Wagamama (meaning "selfish and egocentric; insistent on having one's own way") is a pejorative term defining a person whose demanding behavior shows a persistent and naked desire to *amaeru*. Such willfulness and manipulation are regarded as revealing detrimental, age-inappropriate dependency, and usually exasperate rather than endear. *Wagamama* also exhibits an inflated sense of entitlement that attempts to force indulgence. This word is often used to criticize the demanding, clinging, and obstinate behaviors of growing children. By adolescence the term is more selectively applied to young women to criticize socially disapproved assertiveness, which for Japanese females, especially, is interpreted as willfulness or opposition. Behavior that disregards societal norms or expectations or demonstrates eccentric individualism may also be perceived as *wagamama*. In this sense, *wagamama* is a generic expression used as a means of social control from a higher-status to a lower-status person: parent to child, boss to employee, husband to wife, male to female, older to younger person (Garrick 1989, personal communication). For example, the Japanese noun *amaekko* is equivalent to the English terms "big baby" or "spoiled"—and similar in connotation to the English word "brat." Using this expression implies that certain children, or even older persons, have been brought up in a way that allows them to display excessive needs for assistance or special recognition. A significant dimension of *wagamama* is that such self-centered behaviors are accompanied by a lack of sensitivity for the needs and feelings of others. Severe instances of *wagamama* may suggest the presence of narcissistic personality disorder.

As an illustration of adult "spoiled" behavior, a woman who displays *wagamama* may agree to meet a boyfriend for dinner, but only if he will travel out of his way to a location designated by her (fully knowing this is inconvenient). Although he explains why he would prefer to meet at a more central point, the woman insists that he meet her at the particular place she has selected. Thus, she blatantly seeks to be indulged while simultaneously dominating the partnership. The boyfriend indulges the woman by giving in to her insistence, in spite of sensing that he has been unfairly manipulated.

Doi also describes a spectrum of mild to moderate paranoid reactions that convert the hostility of frustrated *amae* into states of suspiciousness toward others, sometimes accompanied by a sense of victimization. The first of these is *higamu*. Like *hinekureru*, this is a word meaning "twisted or deformed," and is used to describe behaviors reflecting undue suspiciousness toward the motives of others, accompanied by cynicism toward their potential goodwill or capacity to nurture. A more characterologic version of *higamu* is called *higaisha-ishiki*. This describes a chronic sense of having been unjustly wronged, whereby a person displays intense hurt and feelings of being victimized. A third and somewhat intermediate expression, *higai-teki*, defines a kind of momentary defensiveness aroused by a misinterpreted sense of being attacked or criticized by others. Doi (1973a) describes these three low-grade states of suspiciousness and anger as unconscious projections of the individual's own mistakes or inferiority, which are then converted into the seeming unresponsiveness or coldness of others. While relating these overreactions to deficient early socialization and unduly frustrated *amae*, Doi categorically differentiates these from other, more severe paranoid conditions. Although clearly nonpsychotic, these milder "pathologies" engender isolation and lack of social integration. Because of the central significance of group interaction in Japan, such isolation is more maladaptive than it might be in individualistically oriented societies. Underlying all of these states of victimization is a component of powerlessness, suggesting that the individual feels chronically at a disadvantage and unjustly overwhelmed by superior forces.

Doi also discusses some normally encountered reaction formations to feelings of degradation and victimization using the term *kuyashii*. *Kuyashii* means "vexation, chagrin, and self-reproach." It is used as an adjective that describes the mortification of a person who has failed in some conspicuous, public manner. Doi defines *kuyashii* as an ill-defined sense of personal outrage characterized by both outwardly directed anger and self-punitive feelings at the same time. Japanese do not conceal *kuyashii* feelings, but readily give vocal expression to such feelings. Associates easily identify with the experience of *kuyashii* and offer sympathetic, supportive, and bolstering encouragement, thus fulfilling *amaeru* cravings.

Doi describes a series of milder reactions that he relates to frustrated *amae*. *Amanzuru* is a word meaning "to feign apparent satisfaction in the face of manifestly unsatisfactory circumstances." This amounts to putting up with conditions that are clearly undesirable and, by inference, undeserved. Strategically, such calm acceptance may at once win admiration from others, and call attention to the unfulfilled needs. For example, a stoical resignation after being unfairly passed over for promotion will draw stronger sympathy and support than griping, blaming others, or trying to mobilize the sympathies of coworkers.

Also in this spectrum of moderate reaction formations, several other descriptions of overt denial of *amaeru* are implicated in displaying thinly concealed desires to gain assistance. One of these is *wadakamari*, a noun that describes a feigned indifference that is generated to disguise underlying resentment about failing to be gratified. This usually involves long-standing misunderstandings that create resentment, ill-will, or "bad blood" between various partners: two brothers, two companies, or even two countries. Doi notes that *wadakamari* "is used when an ostensible indifference conceals a lurking resentment towards the other" (Doi 1973a, 30). This may occur following a temporary or trivial misunderstanding among close friends, and sometimes can readily be resolved.

Another version of deflected dependency gratification is called *toriiru*. This involves the conscious restraint of *amaeru* behaviors, which are replaced by a display of excessive self-humility. *Toriiru* is defined as "to curry favor with another," and is manifested by actively ingratiating oneself and being obsequiously attentive to another person in order to obtain one's own goals eventually. Doi describes *toriiru* as "a method of permitting oneself to *amaeru* while appearing to allow it to the other man" (Doi 1973a, 30). This approach is enacted defensively out of the concern that a direct exposition of *amaeru* might not be acknowledged, and that emotional needs may be met best by manipulating the indebtedness of others. A more open and straightforward strategy for receiving attention is defined by the word *tanomu*. This refers to making polite, direct requests of another; to ask for something, or to rely on someone for favor or nurturance.

In describing a superficial denial of *amae*, the word *tereru* stands for excessive shyness or social awkwardness, which becomes so severe as to thwart the individual's ability to *amaeru*. This occurs in intensely bashful people who are inept in interpersonal relations, and hence unable to transact their dependency needs with other people. Effective communication in Japan requires a certain amount of confidence based upon the careful rehearsal of how to behave in public situations. Persons who are excessively shy simply do not "push the right buttons" in trying to elicit attention. Worse yet, their shyness continually announces that they are probably incapable of fulfilling the dependency needs of others.

The definitions of these terms (also listed in table 6.1) have involved both direct and indirect responses to motives designed to achieve satisfaction for dependency cravings, as these take place-in ordinary two-party encounters. The following terms and situations are more globally related by Doi (1973a) to manifestations of-*amae*.

The experience of love (discussed also in chapter 7) is seen by Doi as crucially connected to the potential or actual projection of one person's emotional needs onto another, and as directed toward a hoped-for acceptance and cherishment. Although this love may be sexualized in some instances, Doi describes it as primarily embedded in the provision of security, warmth, and cherishment as provided in the earliest, desexualized infant/mother relationship. Also, homosexuality, in the generic sense of craving intimate attachment to same-gender partners, is described by Doi as embedded in *amae* —whether or not it ever becomes overtly sexual. The persistence in Japan of same-gender, intimate relations with selected friends throughout life may be partly explained by the cultural acceptability of reciprocally transmitted and received *amae* among members of the same sex.[3]

At a similar level of generality, the adjective *sunao* and the noun *sunaosa* represent idealized Japanese personal characteristics that incorporate factors of guilelessness, openness, and amenability. *Sunao* includes the ability to resonate with and enhance other people's intentions in an apparently effortless manner. Also, the desire to be malleable to others' self-expression is part of this definition. Described earlier by Doi (1973a), the term *sunao* has been extensively dissected by Murase (1982) in an attempt to make the term more cross-culturally comprehensible. In an idealized presentation of self, the qualities of obedience, acceptance of what comes, and the capacity for relating both unegotistically and interdependently are combined with the avoidance of pettiness or antagonism. Persons who are *sunao* also have a superior capacity to be candid, warm, and genial toward others. Such characteristics imply a high level of competence in balancing the tensions connected to the need to depend and the ability to forestall dependence, the need to dominate and the ability to defer to others, the need to be close and the ability to disarm tension in close interpersonal relations. The characteristic feature of *sunao* is being able to transact with other persons in a way that averts subterfuge, does not produce disruption, and focuses minimal attention on oneself (Murase 1982).

Similarly, in several publications, Doi (1973a, 1986) has described the development of self as a psychosocial achievement—relying critically on the balancing and channeling of *amaeru* into acceptable, creative transactions involving a balance of giving and receiving. In contrast, various pathologies of the self are associated with failures in *amaeru* transactions—for example, as witnessed in narcissistic persons' inability to "give" of themselves, or in adults who display a persistent and nearly total inability to depend on others. Their incapacity to establish smooth, sustaining, and reliable interdependent relationships may be due to disruptive development in early childhood, caused either by psychological trauma or constitutional factors involving both the child and the mother.

Doi's descriptions constitute a summary of psychological and social-psychological terms organized around the concept of *amaeru*, in regard to the basic, lifelong desire to seek and, later, to furnish indulgent dependency.

In putting together his survey of descriptive terms defining the various "pathologies of *amae*," Doi (1973a, 101) composed an emic taxonomy of various reactions to excessive or conflictual manifestations of *amae* using common, and mostly nonclinical, Japanese words to define these ordinary life situations. When these appear in exaggerated and protracted forms, they may be considered pathological. In milder manifestations they may represent plans for strategic interaction that directly or indirectly relate to *amae*. However, Doi does not claim that these descriptions constitute a tight or comprehensive explanation of "personality"; rather, he has organized them in an attempt to articulate a spectrum of behavioral situations emphasizing indulgent dependency. Rather than displacing other causal-motivational explanations, his formulations may be seen as a complementary system that acknowledges the primacy of a drive for object relatedness, and the corresponding conditions that accompany frustrations or diversions of this drive. At no point in Doi's writing is *amae* suggested to be a monolithic motive underlying all human behavior, although some critics have accused him of this. As in any speculation concerning causal explanations of behavior, the concept of *amae* has distinct limitations.

For example, William Tyler (1983) has commented on some of the limitations of *amae* in explaining Japanese behavior.

The degree of manipulative behavior involved may vary, but Japanese provides other vocabulary such as *nedaru* (to importune), *toriiru* (to take in) and *kobiru* (to seduce) to describe actions arising from ulterior motives. *Amae* may receive approbation as childlike, cute or coquettish or be rejected as childish, infantile or self-centered. . . . Although etiquette normally requires reticence and self-effacement, there are occasions when one unabashedly imposes on a friend or even a stranger. Underlying this license is a recognition that the majority of human relations rest upon a calculation of shared interests, and that to be overly conscientious in asking and receiving favors . . . is unfriendly and stand-offish. (W. Tyler 1983, 48–49)

Clinical and Psychotherapeutic Aspects of *Amae*

In a descriptive manner, Doi has also written about both the normal and distorted qualities of *amae* observed in a variety of clinical psychiatric conditions (Doi 1973a, 1977). In schizophrenia, for example, the ability to establish and retain complex interdependent relationships is severely compromised. In a fundamental way, the process of schizophrenia leads to an exaggerated lifelong dependency on family, treatment institutions, or professional caregivers, as a result of the individual's incapacity to relate cooperatively to others or to navigate within the complexity of ordinary social interactions. Wynne, et al. (1958), have discussed this deficit in object relations using the concept of "mutuality" in a manner that is equivalent to the psychological sense of "merger" in *amae*. Similar to Doi, these authors make the assumption that the movement toward mutually satisfying interpersonal relations is fundamental in human behavior. Such a motive furnishes a basis for establishing primary object relations and for subsequent socialization experiences. They use the term "pseudomutuality" to define the noncomplementary qualities that afflict schizophrenic persons in their relation to others. In their opinion, pseudomutuality leads to disjunctive role playing that is unaccompanied by any genuinely intersubjective process. In a similar observation, Doi's commentary about schizophrenia parallels that of these authors and suggests that while deficiencies or distortions of *amaeru* do not cause schizophrenia, the need to depend is exaggerated at the same time that the individual is severely compromised in establishing creative, adult interdependencies.

The preceding section and table 6.1 have summarized social-psychological descriptions of various states of frustrated or exaggerated attempts to maintain primary, dependent connections with other people. In explaining these behaviors in terms of a fundamental, ego-instinctual drive, such descriptions represent a spectrum of disorders paralleling various "adjustment reactions," "psychoneuroses," and "personality disorders." As in Western psychiatric nosologies (DSM III-R, ICD-9), such behaviors would only qualify as clinical conditions according to criteria of unusual persistence and intensity, accompanied by serious social maladaptation and subjective suffering. Also, although Doi (1973a) has used Japanese words to typify these behaviors (in *emic* terms), these do not constitute a series of indigenous, "exotic" syndromes, but are the basic elements of which such maladaptations and misery occur universally.

His descriptions of the indulgent and dependent qualities of psychotherapeutic relationships have been published in a number of articles and presentations (Doi 1962a, 1964, 1969, 1973e). The relationship with the analyst in Western psychoanalytic procedures is cited as an example where the reexperiencing of an infantile "passive love" is fostered through the calculated regression in the transference neurosis (Glover 1956; M. Balint 1952; F. Johnson 1988a). Citing Michael Balint (1952), Doi concluded that the emergence of this form of early relatedness at once documented the universality of the need for indulgent dependency, and illustrated the manner in which such needs are concealed, disguised, or defined as "infantile" in the West. Even in psychotherapies that are less intensive and protracted than psychoanalysis, overt desires to depend upon, feel helpless with, and yearn for special cherishment commonly emerge. For that matter, these tendencies are routinely observable in the doctor/patient, healer/client relationships. They also are present in a number of asymmetric role sets where the unequal status of the partners (professor/student, minister/parishioner) is combined with the potential for developing intensified feelings and awareness of needs *(amaeru)*. Psychoanalytically, these would be seen as reevoking the features of early infantile dependency, which has been termed "primary object love" (M. Balint 1952).

Doi (1964) also discusses the differences in the quality and processing of transference in Japan and the Western nations. Basically, in the U.S. such heightened dependency is regarded as a necessary but transitory *distortion* that later will be replaced by a mature independency. That is to say, formerly helpless persons learn through insight and experience to be less dependent on their therapists or mentors. Deferent and insecure graduate students complete their degrees, or a devastated widow eventually "works through" the ambivalence of grief and reinvests herself in new relationships. However, in Japan, the cultural acknowledgement of *amaeru*, and the overt declaration of this need, acts as a governor to keep such yearnings from becoming exorbitant. In contrast to Western explanations, however, such needs are not expected to evaporate, but are allowed to remain because of the normative acceptability of such strivings and feelings throughout the lifespan. Because of this, Japanese students characteristically remain deferent and obligated to their professors and teachers *(sensei)* throughout life. Patients customarily retain a belief in their physicians' or psychotherapists' superior powers and wisdom.[4]

Doi (1984, 1990a) sees this difference in the cultural acceptability of dependency to be one explanation for the relative unpopularity of traditional Western psychoanalysis in Japan. Although many Western psychotherapies are based on identifying and reducing intrapsychic conflicts, traditional psychoanalysis is particularly devoted to seeking resolutions that create an awareness of liberation from the neurotic strictures of childhood and the consolidation of adult autonomy. These goals seem culturally peculiar to average Japanese. In fact, a number of Japanese psychotherapies and revitalization techniques actively pursue resolution through a sense of atoning for prior guilt and achieving a deferential reaffiliation with others—nearly the opposite of Western models of therapeutic restoration (Murase and Johnson 1974; Reynolds 1976; Rohlen 1974a; D. K. Kondo 1987).

Interactional and Phenomenological Formulations of *Amae*

Earlier, the interactional formulations of dependency highlighted by Lebra (1976), Hisa Kumagai (1981), and Kumagai and Kumagai (1986) were mentioned. Writing as a social and cultural anthropologist, Lebra (1976) analyzes dependency experience in Japan as an addition to her structural observations concerning the asymmetric aspects of obligation inherent in *on* (Lebra 1969). She has analyzed dependency in terms of four categories. The first category is a *dependency of patronage* and fits into her 1969 analysis of *on* as an asymmetric obligatedness that defines dependency experienced within unequal status relationships. In these instances, reciprocity is chronically unbalanced, and the debtor feels permanently bound by undischargeable obligations. Her second category is that of a *dependency of attendance* and addresses the opposite side of the coin, by depicting the subtle needs of the higher-status partner, which are instrumentally and emotionally supplied by the inferior partner's indebtedness and fealty. She sees *amae* as falling into a third category of a *dependency of indulgence (amae)*, where the emotional aspects of affiliation are foremost, and are developmentally related to the infant/mother paradigm. She describes a fourth category of *dependency of pity*, which designates relations established on the basis of disability and helplessness, gratified through consolation and helping responses to inflated states of need accompanying illness, disability, or catastrophe. Although described separately, these categories may overlap or be present simultaneously. For example, a dependency of indulgence may be deepened by the recipient partner becoming disabled. Although capable of defining dependency in any society, Lebra's categories have a special application to categorizing dependency in Japan. Indirectly, she criticizes Doi's descriptions of *amae* as being applied too ambitiously to social phenomena where indulgent dependency may not be the most salient explanation, for example, in macrosocial phenomena in postwar Japan. Other critics raise this same issue, which will be addressed subsequently.

Lebra (1976) also added an explicit interactional description of *amae* as a role complementarity between two partners: one who displays *amaeru* and another who furnishes *amayakasu*. *Amayakasu* is the verb denoting the responsiveness of the nurturant partner who provides *amae* to one who signals the need to depend *(amaeru)*. Moreover, she distinguishes two versions of this partnership —"active" and "passive"—which yield four types of possible *amaeru/amayakasu* transactions. In acknowledging this same role complementarity, Doi (1986, 1988b) prefers to use the reciprocal, interactional terms *amaeru/amaesaseru*.

In a complex, interactional analysis of *amae*, Hisa Kumagai (1981) has built on the work of both Doi and Lebra in putting together a phenomenologically based description of reciprocal *amaeru/amay-akasu* illustrated in a series of symbolic interactions. These encounters between two partners relate manifest, implicit, and latent objectives to the gaining and giving of affection, support, and affirmation in interdependent associations. Paralleling Doi's descriptions of the "vocabulary" and "pathology" of *amae*, Kumagai lists examples of strategic interactions (for example, "asking favors," "feigning helplessness," or "expressing anger") whose objectives are related to the confirmation of *amae* between two participants. She uses the term "bipolar posturing" to capture the fluctuating and interchangeable role playing that characterizes indulgent, interdependent transactions both in intimate and nonintimate encounters. Building on this, Kumagai draws a parallel between the way *amayakasu* (giving indulgence) shapes and channels *amaeru* in intimate relationships, whereas *enryo* (as discussed by Doi 1973a) performs the same governing function in nonintimate relationships. She sees both *amayakasu* and *enryo* as postures that involve the withdrawal of egoistic motives in favor of gratifying or serving the *amaeru* of the dependent partner.

At several junctures (1981), she criticizes Doi's emphasis on defining *amae* as "passive love," and discusses the Western difficulty of understanding the underlying, strategic *activity* involved in seeking indulgent dependency. It is evident from her writings that giving and receiving *amae* are potentially both "active" and "passive" possibilities in *amaeru/amayakasu* behaviors. This is also implicit in Doi (1973a) and explicit in Lebra (1976). However, in using the terms "active" and "passive," Kumagai inadvertently falls victim to the contextual ambiguity of these terms.[5]

Despite these terminological problems, Hisa Kumagai makes a good case for the underlying presence of an active, self-aware, and intentional self in Japanese persons, even when the egoistic, striving self is momentarily withdrawn or hidden—notably in *enryo* or *amayakasu* behaviors (as in Kumagai and Kumagai 1986). Within Japanese culture, such withdrawal of an overt, assertive self is clearly understood to be a conscious suspension of egoistic motives, and when appropriately used, actually testifies to the presence of self.

Francis Hsu's (1971b) discussion of the cultural variation in levels of awareness addresses this same issue—illustrated by him in what he calls the "unexpressed conscious" layer of personality functioning. Looked at quantitatively, this conscious but inexpressible self is prominent in planning and executing social navigation among Japanese. As noted before, this is exemplified in the abundant use and awareness of nonverbal communication, added to the calculated significance given to silence, ambiguity, and indirection —all of which operate to disguise, but not completely conceal, the inexpressible self and its submerged intentions.

In a quantitative, interactional direction, Hiroko Minami (1982) has examined *amae* in relation to a network of social supports observed in Japanese women college students. Mitchell (1976) has deductively studied the manifestations of *amaeru* in the interpersonal and corporate workings within Japanese politics and law. In legal proceedings the quality of interpersonal relationships and sensitivities of the interactants are prominent. Compared to the United States, there are relatively few practicing attorneys in Japan, and there is a strong disinclination toward engaging in adversarial actions or litigation. Every effort is made to seek resolution of differences through informal or court-supervised conciliation. Disputes that arise are expected to be resolved by the participants themselves rather than through formal adjudication. Even having to consider suit or litigation represents a potentially shameful failure in the mechanisms of maintaining or restoring harmony. Conspicuous among these mechanisms is the recognition of reciprocal interdependency, and the need for meeting obligations through fulfillment of mutual indulgence.[6]

In another analysis involving the reactions of Americans living in Japan, Tobin (1982) comments on the subjective tensions experienced when persons socialized to be independent find themselves living within complex webs of reciprocal obligation and interdependency. Using interviews, observational data, and his own monitored introspections, Tobin documents the high degree of ambivalence produced by living in Japan.

> The dependence Americans perceive in Japan awakens in them unconscious dependency issues and stimulates repressed dependency longings which [they] find unacceptable and threatening. (Tobin 1982, 37)

Psychoanalytic Extensions and Critiques of *Amae*

Historical Features

A number of commentators have addressed the adaptation of psychoanalytic theory and practice in Japan. Prior to Doi's formulations about *amae,* Muramatsu (1949) described some of the psychological consequences of the strong *gemeinschaft* and familial orientation flourishing in Japan. Writing in the immediate postwar period, Muramatsu discussed the consequences of social status and life-course trajectory within an authoritarian Japanese ethos. Incorporation of these cultural baselines promised security for those who were obedient and who conformed to a limited range of expectancies. As an American psychoanalyst stationed with the occupation forces, Maloney (1953, 1968) raised critical questions about Japanese culture, socialization, and political subordination as these combined to produce (in his view) persons who were denied personal significance, individuality, and the opportunity for "freedom." He also was bewildered by the derivative Japanese versions of Western psychoanalysis, which stressed the significance of a desexualized maternal/child relationship and placed a distinctly negative value onto excessive personal autonomy and individualism.

Various attempts to explain these differences in theory and practice revolve around the contrasting cultural suppositions in Japan and the West. Miyamoto (1973) has commented on the relative lack of interest in psychoanalysis in Japan, except at an abstract, intellectual level. He cites the fact that Freudian metapsychology is posited on a close and competitive relationship with an authoritarian father, and a sexualized relationship to mother that together give rise to internal conflicts emerging in the Oedipus complex. However, he observes that in the Japanese family the emotional relationship with father is relatively weak, and the dominant instrumental and affectional connections pivot on the strong, close, and desexualized dependency furnished by the mother (also mentioned in Caudill 1962b). Under these conditions there is a relative absence of drive to eliminate or displace the father, who is already displaced, or to seduce the mother, who remains "possessed," albeit in a nonsexual way.[7]

Although attracting attention among Asian specialists, social scientists, and some psychologists, Doi's formulations have not had much direct impact on psychoanalysis per se. More recently, however, a panel at the American Psychoanalytic meetings (Panel 1984) and a presentation at the International Psychoanalytic Association served to publicize his views on dependency drive (Doi 1987a). Also, Wisdom (1987a, 1987b) has commented on the significance of *amae* as both an "unquestioning demandingness" and an "introjective identification" arising out of the earliest infant/maternal connection. He sees Doi's formulations as addressing the problem of how the ego transforms the self-love of primary narcissism into object love.

The idea of *amae* obviates this difficulty altogether, since it presumes that the baby is born with an attitude conducive toward "*amaeru-ing*"— which indeed is phylogenetic as well as ontogenetic—and one must suppose that it is of evolutionary value. (Wisdom 1987a, 264; italics original)

Culturological Critiques and Extensions

Three American-based psychoanalysts originally from Japan (Takahashi, Nakakuki, and Taketomo) have offered critiques and extensions to Doi's formulations concerning *amae*. Takahashi (1980, 1983, 1984) acknowledges the primary significance of *amae* as a basic and positive dynamism fostering early object relations. He adds an equivalent negative dynamism operating to limit the expressiveness of *amae*, and uses the Japanese word *gaman* to characterize this balancing feature. As he defines it, *gaman* is a "curtailment of egoism for the sake of others" or, more simply, a "self-control over egoism." He sees both *amae* and *gaman* becoming manifest through the mechanism of "projective identification." Psychoanalytically, Takahashi describes *amae* as potentially being both the projection and introjection of good internal objects created through a process of "libidinal projective identification." Conversely, he sees the reintrojection of "bad projections" as inducing *gaman*, and suggests that this process be termed "aggressive-projective identification." Using cross-cultural illustrations, he sees Japanese childhood socialization as accentuating *amae*, but thwarting aggression, which thereafter becomes represented partly by its reaction formation of *gaman*. Conversely, he sees American child-rearing as stimulating "aggressive-projective identification" while punishing or restricting the projection of dependency onto others (Takahashi 1984).

Nakakuki (1984) has organized an examination of *amae* against the background of the transformation of primary narcissism as elaborated by Kohut (1966, 1971). He conceptualizes the overt whining and petulant reaction to frustration of *amae* (in the form of *suneru*) as a distinctive emotion repetitively expressed in passive-aggressive behavior. Thus, he sees the simultaneous awareness of desires to *amaeru* and the frustration of *suneru* as constituting an ambivalent state of both wishing to merge and wishing to separate from others.

This creates what he calls an aggressive-dependent relationship. Paralleling other critics, he feels that Doi has attempted to apply *amae* to sociocultural phenomena in a manner that may be confusing.

Nakakuki's (1984) overview of Doi's work introduces yet another "balancing concept" to *amae* using the Japanese word *shibumi* (literally meaning "astringent" but also "restrained") to characterize behaviors that counterbalance *amae*. These include "resignation," "alienation," and "humility." These constraining tendencies represent a conversion of *amae* through the unconscious mechanisms of repression and projection, manifestly operating through self-discipline, denial, and reaction formation. Like Takahashi (1983, 1984), Nakakuki suggests that early projective identification operates in two directions: first, as a narcissistic, positive identification with others in terms of an affiliative *amae*, and second, as a masochistic identification representing an inversion of the aggressive instinct.

Both Nakakuki and Takahashi reinforce and expand Doi's explanations of the reciprocal relation between *enryo* and *amae*. Nakakuki (1984) also suggests classifying *amae* into "primitive," "infantile," "pathological," and "normal" states, paralleling Kernberg's (1982) classification of *narcissism*. Seen in this light, *amae* is explained as ultimately being channeled into a mature, narcissistic drive sustaining a sound self-esteem. Additionally, Nakakuki suggests an operational psychoanalytic definition of *amae* classifying it first as a drive to merge with others, second as an entitlement for permissive behavior, and third as a defense against aggressive feelings toward others.

Another psychoanalytic commentator, Taketomo (1984, 1986, 1988, 1989a) has raised serious criticisms of Doi's work and suggested a partial reconceptualization of *amae*. He accuses Doi of formulating a monolithic psychological theory that is overgeneralized and ambiguous, and suggests that Doi has failed to sharpen up the discontinuity between infantile and adult manifestations of *amae*. He then criticizes Doi for emphasizing *amae* as an individual craving for passive love and indulgence, while ignoring the transactional features of interdependency—similar to the objections of Lebra (1976) and Hisa Kumagai (1981). He also faults Doi for studying *amae* using "object language" rather than "metalanguage," and for looking at motivational rather than metacommunicative aspects of dependency.

At a fundamental level, Taketomo (1984, 1986, 1988, 1989a) argues that Doi has emphasized the wrong etymologic definitions of *amae*, particularly neglecting those meanings that implicate the semantic and connotative features connected to "playfulness" and what Taketomo terms "coquetry" (as mentioned earlier by W. Tyler 1983). To illustrate this, he describes that many *amae* interactions take place under the metacommunicative rubric of playfulness. Such playfulness signifies that the *meaning* for the behavioral situation is extrinsic to the concrete interaction, and must be found in the context of a kind of coquetry—that is, a kind of flirtation or even teasing. In fact, Taketomo feels that this metacommunicative meaning of *amae*—as playfulness or coquetry—is a common denominator in all *amae* transactions.

He describes three different forms of *amae* relationships: 1) infantile, 2) adult coquetry/playfulness, and 3) adult noncoquetry. He basically agrees with Doi's description of the earliest infant/mother indulgent gratification as prototypical of children's desire to *amaeru*—although with the distinction that even this is transacted as a mimicry of an earlier state—with both partners aware of a certain playacting. In the second case, the adult may teasingly attempt to influence a potential gratifying partner to supply gratifications, "as if" in quest of a return to the unburdened and easy indulgence of childhood. He sees this as "a mimicry of a mimicry" (Taketomo 1986, 532). The third and nonplayful attempt to *amaeru* during adulthood is described as a manipulation to trespass on another's benignity and kindness. This occurs when the conscious aim is not to regress to the prototypical infant/mother situation, but rather to trespass on another and force gratifications and concessions that are only symbolically related to infantile *amaeru*.

Having suggested the common denominator of an "as-if" mimicry underlying *amae*, Taketomo structurally extends this into a theory of *amae* that centers on the metacommunicative aspects of diverse interdependent transactions. By "metacommunicative" he means that regardless of the manifest behaviors, the underlying intentionality and meaning revolves around the implicit understanding that *"this interaction is under a mutually agreed-upon suspension of some ordinary restraint(s)"* (Taketomo 1986, 541; italics mine). Although such strategies are often playful between juveniles and adults, they could also be conceptualized generically as a kind of "gamesmanship" among adults, in the sense of attempts to achieve strategic, interpersonal domination as discussed by Haley (1958), Berne (1978), and Potter (1978). Taketomo is also concerned with what he sees as the overgeneralization and ambiguity in Doi's writings about *amae*, and his failure to define developmental continuities and discontinuities in dependency experiences (Taketomo 1986). Since others (Lebra 1976; Kumakura 1984) have raised these same issues, they will be collectively addressed in the conclusion of this chapter.

Doi's published response to Taketomo's criticism (1988) expresses surprise at what seems to be a global attempt to discount Doi's formulations. He sees this criticism as attempting to discredit his etymologic speculations concerning *amae*, and accusing him of inflating a vernacular word into a technical conceptualization. Moreover, Doi notes that Taketomo is suggesting that *amae* is properly conceptualized at three specific metalinguistic levels, all of which incorporate a conscious understanding of coquetry or playfulness. In defending himself, Doi (1988a) suggests that all Japanese have an intuitive understanding of the various meanings of *amae*, and that his attempts have been to refine these commonly acknowledged meanings through a metapsychological, interactional, and metalinguistic analysis. Doi has taken pains to distinguish between the vernacular use of *amae* and a more technical "vocabulary" expressing a number of higher-level applications (as in Doi 1973a). He concludes his response to Taketomo's criticism by regretting the confrontational aspects of Taketomo's critique, but endorsing the fact that discussion "will have an impact on people who have an interest in *amae*, on some issues in Japanese culture and furthermore the methods in psychiatry and psychoanalysis" (Doi 1988a, 5).

In this author's opinion, the phenomena of dependency, attachment, and interdependency constitute a range of behavioral possibilities that readily permits a variety of explanations. Admittedly, there are difficulties in combining intuitively derived interpretations of emic information with more rigorously organized, etic observations of dependent behaviors. However, this difficulty does not suggest that the understanding of *amae* may not be enriched through a combination of emic and etic approaches. This author also feels that Taketomo's emphasis on coquetry is a useful extension, but not an eclipse, of Doi's work. The criticism that Doi does not acknowledge metalinguistic aspects of *amae* will be discussed later. However, Taketomo's suggestion that a self-conscious awareness of playfulness in *amae* transactions is always present seems difficult to apply to the infant or very young child. Presuming such a degree of cognitive sophistication in the prerepresentational child is not plausible. Also, Taketomo's comments about nonverbal aspects of *amae* transactions inaccurately accuses Doi of missing the significance of extralinguistic communication. In many publications (1964, 1973a, 1973d, 1986, 1989a, 1990b), Doi has stressed the ubiquitous nonverbal, gestural, and metalinguistic components in *amae* transactions.[8]

A Documentary Summary of Doi's Work

Kumakura and Ito (1984) have comprehensively examined Doi's work in a book-length Japanese publication of sympathetic and critical commentary.[9] Their book is concerned with organizing and summarizing Doi's published work against the background of Western psychoanalytic theory, and includes a detailed examination of Doi's methodical approaches to language, to clinical experience, and to theory formation. Moreover, the authors have constructed a developmental chart that relates Doi's work to a series of intrapsychic and social-interactional stages, including characterologic positions that represent fixations, regressions, or failures to progress in normal development.

They acknowledge that there is an ambiguity in the common word *amae* that is traceable to differences in its vernacular meanings and connotations. This is contrasted with *amae* as it is used by Doi and others, as a formal social-psychological term. Doi's technical use of *amae* is additionally complicated in its application as a psychoanalytic (metapsychological) term standing for a primary affiliative drive, and at the same time as a Japanese cultural term identifying a spectrum of indulgent/dependent transactions portrayed as acceptable prerogatives that seek expression in selective encounters throughout the lifespan. Two other applications of *amae* also contribute to the ambiguity of its meaning: specifically, Doi's use of the concept in clinical descriptions (diagnostic and therapeutic) and in more social-philosophic reflections. Kumakura and Ito reconcile some of this ambiguity in terms of the personal and professional development of Doi in his contact with Western cultural experience, conceptual orientations, and psychoanalytic studies. These Western perspectives are contrasted with his personal and professional familiarity with Japanese life and clinically based explanations of human behavior.

Using Doi's published work, both in Japanese and English, these authors trace his conceptual commentary on psychoanalytic theory regarding both metapsychology and technique, directly compared to conventional definitions taken from Western literature. The most significant difference emerges in Doi's hypothesis of *amae* as a freestanding drive to affiliate and to establish dependency, which has been obscured in Western psychoanalysis and defined as a secondary motive—related to libidinal rather than ego drives. Another significant point is that the cultural makeup of Japanese—particularly in regard to *amae*—creates an interactional situation in which a number of aspects in the therapeutic situation are crucially altered (critically discussed by Maloney 1953, 1968; Peter Dale 1986).

Chronologically following the publication of Kumakura and Ito, Doi, in *The Anatomy of Self* (1986), discusses qualities of subjective consciousness concerning ego identity, called *jibun* (self) in Japan. Paralleling the psychocultural commentary of numerous commentators on Japanese subjectivity, Doi sees the self as more conspicuously defined *in its connections to others* than in Western societies. Both subjectively and in real interactions, the consciousness of self is experienced in a flow of activities and identifications in conjunction with other persons. In fact, sharp differentiation of self from others is regarded as unnecessary, and even unhealthy. Doi (1973b) also provides an understanding of this in discussions concerning the degree of consciousness among Japanese concerning *omote* (outside) and *ura* (inside). This is accompanied by a more articulated sense of relational aspects of the self within intimate *(miuchi)* and "midrange" encounters *(seken)*, and the emotionally neutral contacts with the "faceless crowd," or strangers *(tanin)*. The smooth operation of this dual consciousness (Doi 1973b) in social transactions is regarded as constituting an attainment of healthy narcissism, and parallels Erikson's (1959) concepts of successful identity formation achieved following the attainment of psychosexual and psychosocial competence.

Kumakura and Ito (1984) then conduct a survey of what they call Doi's "linguistic theory." Some of this pulls together his lexical and semantic examinations of *amae*, both alone and in juxtaposition with other Japanese terms summarizing salient aspects of normative behavior (e.g., *on, giri, ninjō*). Other lexical explanations involve a glossary of Japanese terms that stand for predictable types of social transactions and psychological states that illustrate the effects of Japanese culture both on individual and collective behaviors (as summarized in table 6.1). These aspects of Doi's "theory of language" are seen as simultaneously ethnographic and clinical, and as contributing to an indigenous, descriptive explanation of the social psychology of average Japanese.

However, at a different level, Kumakura and Ito see Doi imposing a more abstract, interpretive, and scientific meaning on both individual states of consciousness and actual social transactions connected with *amae*. This amounts to a symbolical interpretation of individual consciousness and, simultaneously, an anthropological analysis of the normative significance of Japanese interactions. Contrary to Taketomo's criticisms (1984, 1986), these authors specifically describe Doi's etic formulations as a metalinguistic enterprise that examines not only what is said, but also "that which is above and beyond what is verbally expressed" (Kumakura and Ito 1984, 171). Some of these metalinguistic explanations address a psychocultural understanding of conventional Japanese behavior as it occurs among typical representatives. Another level of meaning is described in the context of metalevel interpretations of behavior in clinical psychotherapeutic encounters. Here the acceptance of a drive for indulgent dependency is implicitly recognized by both the therapist and the patient, and is thus more accessible for the purpose of intervention, interpretation, and the deepening of insight.

Political and Social-Philosophic Aspects of *Amae*

Doi's writings also have extended into a realm of commentary concerning *amae* as a national character trait whose expression is revealed in a variety of social and political activities. Sometimes his illustrations of *amae* at a national or collective level constitute extrapolations from simple examples of individual and small-group behaviors. For example, in several publications Doi commented on the student unrest, apathy, and radicalism of the early 1970s in terms of postwar loss of social cohesion, the sense of victimization, and the diminishing influence of the father in the Japanese nuclear family (Doi 1973a, 1973c, 1974). Some of his speculations were based on a reported increase in school phobia, and on psychological changes observed among Doi's clinical contacts and general information from the news media. In other instances, his commentary has related contemporary social trends to Japanese transactions in politics, esthetics, or literary themes (Doi 1973a, 1973c, 1983a, 1983b). Although *amae* is mentioned in a number of these, other issues are examined as providing understanding of general social behavior. Some of these are in the form of short articles and focus on a few particulars—like an understanding of *yutori* ("leisurely state of mind") or modern Japanese identity as *zeitgeist* (Doi 1970, 1983a, 1983b). Other essays involve looking at political phenomena or literary sources against a background of historical, cultural, and psychoanalytic explanations.

Doi (1973a) also discussed *amae* in modern society through an informal review of historical and sociocultural factors that he attributed to a "balancing of *amae*." In prewar Japan, the imperial family served as a model symbolizing the interconnectedness of obligation and dependency within the home, neighborhood, workplace, and nation. The emperor's divine nature and mythic ancestry personified the uniqueness and destiny of the Japanese nation. Embedded in this relationship to the emperor and nation, the obligations and responsibilities of ordinary persons became potentially exalted, in the service of both divine as well as more mundane objectives. Doi sees the postwar transformation of this dedication to destiny and national development as continuing in a heightened consciousness about national objectives, but now in the absence of any conscious supernatural attributions. This persists in the forms of maintaining national interests against outsiders, a sense of specialness and superiority, and a continuity between the historic, contemporary, and future Japan.

Doi has speculated about factors in honorific language that intensify awareness of potential indulgent dependency. Such language rules impose a consciousness about the statuses of conversational partners, and act to regulate the limits and direction of indulging or being indulged. Additionally, Doi has reflected on the effects of ancestor worship and superstition in reinforcing connections with deceased family, local gods, or "restless souls" that purportedly guide the destinies of individuals. The dependency aspects in these fictive relationships acknowledge how ordinary individuals should deal with overwhelming natural and supernatural forces—essentially through depending on the benignity of these forces to avoid misfortune or catastrophe.

These and other social-philosophic speculations have raised criticisms from a number of sources concerning the overgeneralization of *amae* in its application to national character, and as an explanatory principle for collective behaviors (Pelzel 1977; Lebra 1976; Peter Dale 1986; Taketomo 1986). To this author, such criticisms overlook the inherently rhetorical nature of social-philosophic writings, which do not purport to test specific hypotheses through methodical study nor use deductive reasoning based on tightly organized observations. This distinction between social-philosophic and more rigorous theoretical writings is one response to Doi's being criticized for overgeneralization. Other explanations will be offered in the following chapter.

Notes

1. Doi's education and training in psychoanalysis (described in Doi 1956) began in Japan through a postwar psychoanalytic study group. This conceptual introduction was expanded during a fellowship in the United States at the Menninger Clinic, where he received training in psychoanalytic theory and psychotherapy (1950–52). Upon returning to Japan, he was accepted for a training analysis with Heisaku Kosawa, who had studied with Freud during the 1930s and was a senior psychoanalyst in Japan. Doi later became a candidate for training in the U.S. at the San Francisco Psychoanalytic Institute (1955–56). Personal considerations dictated his return to Japan, where he continued a self-analysis conducted along with intellectual development gained through reading, clinical work, theoretical synthesis, and scholarly writing (1956 until the present). Doi is a member of the International Psycho-Analytic Association and has established a conspicuous reputation as a theorist, academician, clinician, and teacher. His scholarly and popular writings have earned him a secure place in the international intellectual community.

2. As mentioned in Cairns (1976a), the ethological evidence among primates and lower animals for bonding and attachment is profuse. Correspondingly, certain human neonatal reflexive behaviors (e.g., crying, grasping, suckling, smiling, etc.) are functionally connected to affiliative needs and display obvious survival features. However, beyond the immediate neonatal period, human behaviors relating to attachment or dependency become complicated by factors associated with social learning, culture, and the variable characteristics of nurturers. The presence of such factors makes any direct comparison of human attachment behaviors with attachment in lower species tentative and difficult to establish.

3. As mentioned earlier, in Japan sexuality tends to be considered as one of a number of positive physical pleasures (Caudill 1962a). There is relatively little guilt about the *physical* aspects of sexual pleasure, whether these are experienced in autosexual, homosexual, or heterosexual contexts

(DeVos 1978). However, sexuality that promotes scandal, social distress, or personal indignity is strongly sanctioned. Because of this, homosexuality that is facultative, occasional, and (above all) discreet is relatively ignored. Men who are unmanly, regardless of their sexual preference, may not be respected. Male homosexuality has recently become more of a public issue because of the possibility of transmission of acquired immune deficiency syndrome (AIDS).

4. In actual practice Westerners may often feel strong, even exaggerated, gratitude toward their physicians, mentors, or psychoanalysts. However, such residual feelings are regarded as extraneous, perhaps embarrassing, and even potentially as evidence of unresolved positive transference or anachronistic motives—including "leftovers" of unconscious, frustrated sexual desires.

5. There are several problems in using "active/passive" terminology. One is the difference between a manifest, behavioral description of events versus a proactive, intentional *direction* of events. The latter may appear to be passive behaviorally, but actually be intentionally active. Another problem is that active/passive descriptions often attribute activity to the initiator of action, or at other times to the participant who is most active. Thus, these terms constitute relative rather than absolute judgments about activity/passivity, even at a behavioral level. This is especially evident in describing interactions where activity/passivity is a product and function of both interactants. In this author's opinion, it is more methodical to concentrate on the differential intentionality involved in these superficially "active" or "passive" participations. At an intentional level of explanation, both partners may be actively pursuing the same objectives but through different, even opposite, means. For example, as Kumagai and Kumagai (1986) suggest, amae can be an active strategy of passively accepting indulgence.

6. Wagatsuma and Rosett (1983) have critically looked at the practical experience with contract law in both the United States and Japan. Americans are typically more concerned with legally binding, written agreements and may pursue adjudication in the event of problems. However, they commonly use out-of-court resolutions or compromise after having threatened suit. Also, while Japanese are punctilious in their amaelike relations with in-groups, their negotiations with strangers, competitors, or antagonists may be quite defensive and adversarial and take full advantage of written contracts, outside arbitration, or litigation.

7. The differences in cultural suppositions about the strength and duration of primary affiliation between infants and their mothers is not restricted to Japan. Other examples in some Indian and African societies will be discussed in chapter 9.

8. Although not using the word "coquetry," Doi (1972, 389) illustrates an *amae* transaction in a cross-cultural context, where the dying heroine

in Erich Segal's *Love Story* uses "language of mock aggression," which simultaneously conceals her feelings of weakness and indirectly conveys warmth toward her desolate husband.

9. The summary of this book is based on a translation of portions of the text by Regina Garrick, as well as consultation with Kumakura himself (1984, private communication). Yasuhito Kinoshita (1985) also reviewed some of the untranslated text. The following commentary represents a synthesis from these three sources; however, this author is responsible for any errors or misrepresentations in the interpretation of these materials.

CHAPTER 7

A Summary and Synthesis
of *Amae* Theory

Recent Commentary on Takeo Doi

Since the mid-1970s, Doi's publications concerning *amae* have received increasing attention from researchers and scholars within developmental psychology, psychoanalysis, and Asian studies. This is reflected by the number of citations in other scholarly works and both supportive and critical commentary from various sources. Thus, it seems timely to summarize Doi's major conclusions and to synthesize *amae* according to an interpersonal model (as outlined in Hsu 1971b).

Recent Publications and Presentations

In addition to the publications already cited, some spontaneous comments generated in a radio interview with Hiroshi Wagatsuma entitled *"Amae* and Personality" were subsequently transcribed (Doi and Wagatsuma 1984).[1] In this interview, Doi emphasized the importance of the interactional nature of *amae,* saying, "essentially it is necessary to have someone to *amaeru* toward. If you do not have another person there, you cannot *amaeru.* Moreover, that other person has got to be able first of all to accept you, yourself, in order for *amae* to be established" (Doi and Wagatsuma 1984, 2). Doi also emphasized that *amae* is fundamentally concerned with establishing connections to things and persons in the environment—conventionally called "object relations" *(taishō kankei).* Doi observed that the mother-child relationship in Japan seemed to have changed qualitatively during the past forty years, and that mothers recently were not as forthcoming in supplying security and dependency needs. He speculated that this might represent an ambivalence concerning their roles as mothers in the face of work-role identifications formed outside the home during part of their adult lives. He wondered about this apparent loss of confidence in the singular identity of motherhood, occurring paradoxically at the time that the mother-child relationship has potentially become more intense due to the smaller size of the Japanese family. Greater numbers of young Japanese families now reside in large cities, work at salaried occupations, and live in apartments. Both mothers and fathers commonly reside away from their families of origin. This changes the quality of traditional family life, through the absence of a multigenerational family and kin group. Also, because of their absorption in work, fathers are reported to have become more removed from the emotional and instrumental activities of the home, giving rise to the term "fatherless families" (Wagatsuma 1977). Both Doi and Wagatsuma commented that children are no longer simply regarded as "blessings from heaven." The number and timing of pregnancies are carefully planned in relation to other family and personal objectives (Coleman 1982). Children are more liable to be considered as projections of parental egotism, and when contrasted with prior generations, are now regarded as being waited on and spoiled. Doi commented on the heavy involvement that many Japanese mothers now have in their children's education and enrichment, in contrast to prior generations.

In his book *The Anatomy of Self* (1986), Doi again reinforces the nonverbal qualities in *amae* transactions, saying,

Amae itself is an emotion that is constituted tacitly. It is telepathic, prelinguistic, and does not need the medium of language. It is communicated directly from heart to heart. Certainly it is an emotion of intimacy, but it is also fundamentally related to secrets of the heart. (Doi 1986, 138)

In a presentation concerning the psychoanalytic implications of *amae*, Doi again stressed the significance of the intransitive nature of *being loved*, and the manner in which Japanese normative experience makes this distinction more conscious than in societies that do not differentiate between active and passive love. He sees *amae* from its inception to be object-relational, and therefore connected to secondary narcissism. He also relates *amae* to the process of psychological identification, gradually developing as the infant differentiates from its mother. He describes an *ambivalence* fostered through *amae* reflecting the alternation of total acceptance and partial rejection by the nurturing object. Emotionally, the child feels and experiences a sense of high desirability coexisting with a dread of possible rejection tinged by the fear of lowered esteem.

Doi (1987a, 1987b) has also made observations concerning the cultural conceptualization of psychoanalysis pivoting around what he felt was Freud's own ambivalence about authority. As mentioned previously, Freud anchored his notions about authority in the clinical situation as being based on the analyst's expertise and objectivity, rather than on any magical imputations or needs for dependency felt by the analysand. Doi comments on Freud's determined effort to separate psychoanalysis from religion in creating a systematic, technical procedure that scientifically analyzed the conflicts of patients and avoided stimulating the subject's desire for magical restitution. As stated in earlier publications (1962a, 1969), Doi feels that Freud ignored the significance of dependency needs because they stemmed from ego instincts rather than from libido. This partly explains why Freud consistently overlooked the primary importance of dependency in establishing object relationships, even when this clearly imposed the perception of dependence of a (subordinate) analysand on the (superior) analyst. Paradoxically then, in trying to evade aspersions of psychoanalysis as a "belief system," Freud defensively backed into a position of being inadvertently *authoritarian*.[2]

Failing to identify and signify dependency as a basic ego instinct has paradoxically led to increased mystification both about the psychoanalytic process itself and about some aspects of institutional psychoanalysis that continue to foster a pious adherence to some of Freud's writings in a way that is incongruent with his own repeatedly stated desires to create a scientific metapsychology.

In other recent commentary, Wisdom (1987a) has composed a supportive critique of Doi's (1973a) exposition of dependency. He comments that traditional psychoanalytic theories have encountered problems in establishing the nature of earliest object relations and that the concepts of primary and secondary narcissism still beg the question of what psychological processes are connected in the transformation of self-love into object love. He sees the concept of *amae* as obviating this difficulty, "since it presumes that the baby is born with an attitude conducive toward '*amaeru-ing*'—which indeed is phylogenetic as well as ontogenetic—and one must suppose that it is of evolutionary survival value" (Wisdom 1987a, 264).

Critique of Doi's Work by Dale

Some reactions to the excessive expression of Japanese cultural chauvinism *(nihonjinron)* were introduced in chapter 3. Peter Dale (1986) has devoted a chapter, satirically titled "Omnia Vincit *Amae*," criticizing Doi's formulations about the significance of indulgent dependency in Japan. As previously mentioned, Dale first criticizes Doi's conjectures about the root derivations of the word *amae*. He next finds Doi's significance of the "intransitively-expressed, passively-experienced love" of *amae* to be a misinterpretation of Michael Balint's (1952) conclusions about the absence of words in Indo-European languages for this experience. Dale's reading of Alice Balint (1965) suggests to him that the early infant is not simply a "passive object" in the maternal-infant transaction. However, the infant's capacity for reciprocal participation—now quite generally accepted—does not refute Michael Balint's earlier point about the lack of common Indo-European words expressing the instigation of behaviors that might gain indulgence and cherishment. Nor do Doi's speculations about certain archaic meanings of *amae* invalidate his other etymological or psychocultural hypotheses concerning the significance of *amae* as a basic human motive.

Dale (1986) also criticizes Doi for expanding the meanings and significance of common Japanese words, for the purpose of giving a proprietary and "unique" significance to ordinary things. Dale compares this activity to the prewar manipulations of *kokutai* ("national polity") and *kokusui* ("national essence"). Both of these propagandistic trends declared specialness and superiority for all things Japanese. However, in social science and psychology, Dale sees the use of emic Japanese words as perpetrating this same kind of national chauvinism, especially when these expressions are used to characterize technical terms or to substitute for more general social-scientific expressions. Dale consistently analyzes the writings of Doi and other "Japanologists" as illogical, lacking in sophistication concerning Western philosophy, and devoted to reifying Japanese versions of vertical relatedness, social solidarity, and indulgent dependency. Dale (1986) criticizes a number of Japanese terms that Doi has used to characterize both intrapsychic and interpersonal phenomena. He concentrates on two issues: first, Doi's exposition of *amae* as a prototypical human motivation; and second, his view that Doi has attempted to overturn Western psychology and psychoanalysis by his formulations concerning the psychology of the Japanese.

Admittedly, Doi has devoted most of his scholarship to examining aspects of dependency and interdependency as they manifestly appear in Japanese society and in the consciousnesses of individual Japanese. He has written extensively about the different levels at which dependency can be witnessed in Japanese life—sometimes in connections that seem elliptical or strained. However, his broad investigation of the concept of *amae* can be looked on as an attempt to look for themes that exert influence on both individual and group psychology in a variety of transactions. In this author's reading of *amae* theory, Doi has not attempted to insinuate that *amae* is a pandynamic underlying all aspects of Japanese behavior. Also, in his cross-cultural commentary, he has disavowed any implication that dependency experience is somehow exclusive to Japan. In fact Doi sees it flourishing in the West despite cultural tendencies to disguise and even extinguish patently interdependent behavior under the ideological shroud of preferences for independence, individualism, or "narcissism" (Lasch 1979). Similarly, it is difficult to see Doi's recommendations for the *addition* of a basic drive for affiliation and nurturance as a radical overturning of psychoanalytic theory that would expunge previous definitions of basic drives.

Finally, in his scathing analysis of Doi and other Japanologists, Dale virtually destroys consideration of cultural speciality. In denying the significance of Japanese cultural specificity, he assumes a polemical position that only a scientific, logical, and deductively reasoned approach to intrapsychic and behavioral events can be sustained. Although not denying the existence of cultural forms, he appears to regard these as only demonstrating superficial curiosities of language and custom superimposed on universal traits.

Despite these exaggerations, some of Dale's arguments concerning *nihonjinron* are engaging, and draw attention to the problems of hyperbole that do in fact afflict uncritical, indigenous explanations of cultural speciality. It is useful to expose the tendency to make invidious comparisons between cultures through asserting that "indigenous" means "superior." Ironically, however, Dale (1986) does this in a manner that ignores intrinsic cultural variability in favor of arguments for the essential truth and primacy of Western European philosophic and behavioral explanations of human personality. Unfortunately, what emerges through his critique of writers on Japanese "ethos" is a nihilistic and destructive superiority—concerning Western normative criteria—the same sort of ethnocentric bias he seeks to expose in the Japanology literature.

Amae *as Love and "Charity"*

In most of Doi's writings, the definition of *amae* has centered on the feelings of helplessness and the passive, infantile desire to be cherished and indulged. In earlier publications he substituted the word "loved" for "cherished" and translated *amaeru* as "to depend and presume upon another's love." Somewhat later, Doi (1972) centered a discussion about the infantile craving for indulgence on an interpretation of Erich Segal's (1970) novel, *Love Story*. More recently, Doi (1986) devoted a chapter (titled "Secrets in Love") to analyzing several types of adult, intimate relationships in terms of a sublimated "Christian love" theologically called "charity." He also discussed his insights concerning the effect of the psychoanalytic situation in developing and exaggerating the feelings of both sexualized and nonsexualized love that routinely make their appearance during clinical treatment.[3]

Doi describes romantic love as requiring a quality of secretness, which relates to a special experience that cannot (and should not) be shared except between the lovers themselves. Even when mutual love is public and explicit, lovers typically feel that their feelings and experiences are not completely knowable to others except by extrapolation or projection. Also in a recent presentation, Doi (1987a) agreed that *amae* might be considered a kind of love but went on to say, "However, what distinguishes *amae* from the ordinary meanings of love is that it presupposes a passive stance towards one's partner, as it invariably involves a dependence on the receptive part of the partner for its fulfillment, though it is quite possible to pursue such a passive stance actively" (Doi 1987a, 4).

There are two factors in Doi's general use of the word "cherishment" rather than love. For one thing, in Japanese life the terminology of love is usually not used in spoken or written communication. Love is assumed, implied or conveyed nonverbally rather than stated openly. Second, the term "love" itself is a convoluted and complex expression susceptible to multiple definitions and meanings, even if confined to one particular cultural context and historical era. Perhaps because of this, Doi has preferred the word "cherishment," referring particularly to the kind of admiration and nonsexualized affection that is lavished on infants and children. Nevertheless, the contrast intended by Doi distinguishes the pregenital and manifestly nonsexual love of the early infant-parent relationship from later, overtly sexualized relations. Such pregenital love also involves future platonic relations between intimate family members, close friends, companions, and confidants.

Doi's occasional alternate use of the word "love" can engender confusion simply because of the ambiguity of the expression as having both an affectionate *and* sexual denotation. Pelzel (1977) also suggested that love subsumes dependency as part of an irrepressible desire to relate intimately to others. Michael Balint (1952) correspondingly used the phrase "primary love" to describe the emotional quality of merging with another.[4]

Gould (1963) has examined the issue of love in the three hypothetical cases of *Christian love* ("charity"), *platonic love*, and *romantic love*. Theologically, Christian love is defined as the unconditional love of a creator for the "created," which then becomes imitated by humans in their charitable regard for each other. Platonic love is a love for beauty and truth that may be reflected toward actual people, as well as toward ideals or perfect standards. Romantic love, although potentially sexual, expresses the precarious consequences of a passion that in its "romance" is doomed to frustration and failure, or even associated with death or destruction. Contrasted to these three forms of love, Gould sees Freudian, sexual love as concentrating more on the physiological expressions of sexual passion and immediate pleasures than on these more refined or sublimated forms.

Gould's (1963) philosophical analysis of platonic love testifies to some of the complicated issues embodied in the deceptively simple term. One of the differences he sees between Freudian and platonic notions of love is that Freud saw sexuality as craving promiscuous and indiscriminate satisfaction, and thereby potentially selfish and antisocial. Such destructiveness was thought to be held in check by the inhibitions of society, intrapsychically represented by the restraining and potentially punishing superego. Plato, on the other hand, represented the intrinsic desire to affiliate with others (sexually or not) as universal, and saw this desire as being channeled by a counterbalancing desire to abide by the corresponding *rational order*—present as a system of ideals in the prevalent society (as a conscience, rather than superego).

Interestingly, this philosophic difference between Plato and Freud parallels the division between ego-instinctual appetites for simple affiliation, and the sexual appetite for orgasmic satisfaction that characterizes part of psychoanalytic theory. Clearly, Doi's postulate of a primary, freestanding dependency need is closer to the platonic model. However, Doi does not thereby deny the significance of libidinal motives, nor their migration during early childhood, latency, and adolescence. However, he joins other theorists (Fairbairn, Bowlby, Winnicott, Sullivan) who stress the existence of ego drives emerging from the life-preserving instincts that become associated with an independent mode of binding and clinging—demanding nurturance, and cherishment.

Kernberg (1972) has also attempted to integrate theories of object relations with theories concerning drive, which have previously been divided. He believes this division has existed partly due to developmental and life-historical reasons:

In more general terms, instincts are expressed *first* as inborn behavioral patterns that relate in an "average, expectable environment" of mothering functions and interpersonal interactions; and *later* are expressed as internalized object-relations, that in turn, are a crucial organizer of all other psychic structures. This conceptualization represents an attempt to integrate psychoanalytic instinct and object-relations theories. (Kernberg 1972, 233)

In this explanation Kernberg is suggesting that the infant's instantaneous, neonatal attachment to mother may be the result of a primitive ego-instinctual drive that only later (perhaps as early as ten weeks of age) becomes psychologized and gradually takes on the features of a psychic representation. This explanation coincides with Doi's speculations about the dawning of the psychological consequences of *amaeru* in the infant at about that same time. Kernberg's ecumenical suggestion retains the traditional explanation that visualizes the progression of libidinal focus according to "a first stage, when the early capacity for sensuous stimulation of erogenous zones (particularly oral and skin erotism) is integrated with the later capacity for establishing a total object relation; and a second stage, when full genital enjoyment incorporates earlier body surface erotism in the context of a total object-relation, including a complementary sexual identification" (Kernberg 1974, 486).[5]

Kernberg's attempted resolution of this issue uses an explicit interactional framework to explain the nascent beginnings of the first stage of object relations. However, this still employs the language of libido theory ("erotism"), implying that the intrapsychic drive behind this goal-directed behavior is *sexual*. As with Mahler's theory on separation/individuation, the drives for social affiliation ("object hunger") are still attributed to being activated by libido.

Summary and Conclusions

This and the previous chapter have involved a complex review of Takeo Doi's publications plus critical and supporting commentary from other scholars. This subsection will list the present author's view of this information, and conclude with a synthesis concerning the complicated concept of *amae*.

1. Amae *is part of a larger domain of dependent and interdependent relationships.* In stating this, this author is endorsing the clarifications made by Lebra (1976), dividing dependency experience into categories of *obligation, patronage, indulgence,* and *pity.* Doi himself has never suggested that *amae* is coterminous with all dependency experience. To the contrary, his descriptions of indulgent dependency consistently expose the intertwining and complementarity of *amae* with other norms that regulate the quality and intensity of human associations. Although Doi has concentrated his writings on indulgent dependency, this does not suggest that *amae* is hierarchically fundamental to all other dependency experience—either developmentally or logically. One might, however, raise such a possibility. Perhaps *amae* does represent a sociobiological drive for strong, dependent affiliation and indulgence, which is later modified by factors of status, power, gender, and situation, leading to a spectrum of qualitatively varied states of dependency.

2. Amae *(or indulgent dependency) is identified by Doi as a basic desire, motive, or "drive."* In psychoanalytic terms, Doi describes *amae* as a metapsychological construct representing an innate "ego instinct" associated with the primary need to affiliate and establish a dependent connection with a maternal object. Although behavioral manifestations are present at birth, evidence for a psychological basis for *amae* only becomes observable during the phase of early differentiation—gradually defined between six weeks and eight months of infancy. Structurally,

this takes the form of a drive operating to gain the instrumental objectives of physical contact, support, warmth, and protection as well as emotional responses in the form of tenderness and cherishment. This drive for maternal connection is transacted nonverbally, takes place in the grossly asymmetric situation of infantile helplessness, and serves as a paradigm for future modes of *amae* relationship. In a psychoanalytic sense, Doi has described *amae* as an underlying drive, coequal to libidinous and aggressive drives, which produces a variety of manifestations depending on the situation, the interactants, and the position in the life cycle. It arises from the self-preservative ego instincts and from its first appearance is concerned with object relatedness. It coexists and blends with both aggressive and sexual desires—again depending on various circumstances and conditions. As with the other basic drives, the expression of *amae* is channeled through unconscious mechanisms that operate to filter, convert, or repress direct expression. *Amae* is also transmitted through a screen of various conscious executive and adaptive ego mechanisms that modify its direction and may alter the forms of its behavioral manifestations. Although Doi has not constructed a comprehensive taxonomy of the effects of unconscious defenses on *amae*, such dynamics are implicit in his descriptions of a series of frustrations, exaggerations, and omissions involving the attempted transaction of indulgent dependency (as summarized in table 6.1 in chapter 6).

3. Amae *constitutes a Japanese cultural expression of indulgent dependency; versions of this universal dynamism take on different forms in different cultures.* This conclusion states that the ego-instinctual drive for affiliation and cherishment is universal, but that the patterns, characteristics, and conventions connected to its expression show broad cross-cultural variability. In Japan and some other societies, these interdependent patterns are quite visible. (Some of these will be examined in chapters 8 and 9.) This suggests that basic drives might be analogous to the basic emotions: present in all humans but varied in their *overt* expression according to different "display rules" or "emotion management" varying with specific cultural groups.

4. Amae*like dependency and interdependency are observable throughout the lifespan.* Both the manifestations of dependency and the allowable situations in which these may be transacted change throughout the lifespan, according to culturally defined

norms and interaction rules. Doi believes that the desire to seek some form of indulgent dependency is distinguishable throughout the lifespan, although appearing in a variety of modified forms. Although he does not discuss this rigorously, negotiation for establishing asymmetric, indulgent dependency takes a number of different forms and intensities according to social, historical, and cultural factors (as well as contextual and circumstantial features). Nevertheless, selective opportunities for gratification of needs for indulgent dependency are available that take into account cultural definitions of age-appropriate behaviors during childhood, adolescence, adulthood, and old age.

5. Amae *is not a simple or unitary phenomenon; it may be examined at several different levels of subjective and behavioral experience.* Part of the confusion in reading Doi's extensive writings on this subject centers on the need to make distinctions concerning *amae* occurring at four levels of behavioral analysis. The first of these is *amae* conceptualized as an intrapsychic disposition: "drive," "trait," "motive," or "desire." At this level *amae* is heuristically defined as an intrinsic and distinct motive, seeking a particular kind of attachment or affiliation, typified by the urgency of the infant/mother relationship. In Doi's opinion this motive is freestanding (i.e., "basic" and separate), connected to the ego instincts, and not primarily libidinized. Although structurally separate, this motive works in combination with other primary and secondary drives.

The second level of *amae* is interpersonal and becomes interactionally expressed through a dyadic transaction between asymmetric partners where one is concerned with seeking gratification *(amaeru)*, while the other is reciprocally providing gratification *(amaesaseru* or *amayakasu)*. In addition to occurring in dyadic partnerships and small groups, *amae* may also be allegorically construed as occurring between larger groups where features of asymmetrical interdependence are conspicuous and where the partnership includes both instrumental and sentimental dimensions.

At yet another level, *amae* is experienced as a series of social-psychological transactions centering on culturally approved behaviors that engage mutually understood expectations, follow regulated directions, and achieve a range of predictable objectives.

At a more microscopic level, *amae* can be examined according to linguistic features, including not only lexical and semantic properties communicated in dependent encounters but also their sociolinguistic manifestations, which reflect the verbal and non-verbal conventions regulating the forms of allowable interdependent transactions in particular societies.

In his own differentiation of these various levels of *amae* experience, Doi (1973a) has divided them into "the vocabulary of *amae*," "the ideology of *amae*," "the logic of *amae*," "the pathology of *amae*," and, finally, "*amae* and modern society." His classification helps to segregate these categories for purposes of analysis. However, Doi does not suggest that these levels do not overlap and complement each other, both in real-life experiences and in speculations regarding their significance.

6. *Doi's theory of* amae *does not specify sharp continuities and discontinuities in regard to indulgent dependency.* Although Taketomo (1986) has raised this as a criticism, Doi has not attempted the formulation of a strict, phase-specific progression of indulgent dependency. There is no systematic developmental psychology of *amae*, although Kumakura and Ito (1984) have examined aspects of *amae* theory alongside traditional psychoanalytic explanations of development. Except for speculating about the gradual appearance of indulgent dependency between the first six weeks and eight months of infantile life, no other age-discriminating points are articulated. This contrasts with the highly chronological psychoanalytic developmental theory, which imposes a series of discontinuities representing the evolution of an unconscious sexual drive through oral, anal, phallic, and, finally, genital zones. Also, Mahler's (1972) description of separation/individuation stipulates the existence of overlapping but discontinuously expressed attachments through a behavioral evolution of changing relationships to both self and other objects during a thirty-six-month time frame. Other developmental theories impose a discontinuous, phasic interpretation of human development during childhood, adolescence, and adulthood. Many of these deal with defining both behavioral and structural characteristics in speculating about the relation between the unfolding appearance of drives, and consequent behavioral changes over time.

Continuity in this sense refers to the perseverance of hypothetical drives that exert a persistent effect upon behavior; *discontinuity* refers to both the intrapsychic and behavioral changes denoting qualitative differences between present, preceding, and subsequent phases of development. Some of the difficulties of providing proof for such descriptive theories have been mentioned in the first two chapters.

To return to Doi's treatment of this, it is explicit in his writings that indulgent dependency is connected to leaning upon others for the satisfaction of what psychoanalytic theorists would describe as *pregenital* satisfactions. These would include gratifications relating to nonsexualized situations wherein human comfort is achieved through pleasure and relief of frustration, both in childhood and throughout the life cycle. Although Doi does not specify the discontinuous manner in which these gratifications appear or disappear during various points of the lifespan, it is implicit that this drive undergoes qualitative changes.

His failure to specify these changes raises the criticism that his theory of *amae* is "monolithic" and applied in an overgeneralistic manner. However, Doi takes pains to endorse the presence of other motives activating human behavior, and in no way attempts to establish a "pandependency" explanation of human personality. Nor does he suggest that *amae* has a primacy over other motives except perhaps in its chronological appearance. Moreover, there is nothing similar to the pansexualism that has been the object of criticism in Freud's theories of "instinct."

7. Amae *can be productively applied to psychotherapeutic and clinical encounters.* The forms of asymmetrical interdependency described by Doi may be readily observed and applied to the understanding of therapeutic situations, particularly those involved with intensive and extensive examination of subjective personal history, as in psychoanalytic psychotherapy and psychoanalysis. The appearance of a primary object love in Western psychoanalytic situations (M. Balint 1952) has been mentioned repeatedly by Doi as an illustration of the universality of the motive for indulgent dependency. Moreover, in Japanese culture, the acceptance of the need to relate in an indulgent, dependent fashion to physicians gives rise to a different atmosphere in psychotherapy and psychoanalysis than in the United States.

8. Amae *may be examined through a study of language and culturally specific terminologies.* Kumakura and Ito (1984) have examined Doi's published work partly as a "theory of language." Taketomo (1986) has quite oppositely seen Doi's formulations as inaccurate and lacking in recognition of the metacommunicative dimensions of *amae.* Peter Dale (1986) has more devastatingly

concluded that Doi, and other Japanologists, have become involved in an attempt to impute "unique" and special lexical significance to mundane Japanese words and expressions. In this author's opinion, Doi creates not so much a theory of language as a theory of *meaning*. This is illustrated by his examination of language and language use in numerous publications. Some of his analysis of words is at a lexical, referential, and semantic level, and surveys the denotations and connotations of terms and expressions used to describe interactions among Japanese. Since so many *amae* transactions are conducted nonverbally and depend crucially upon gestures, status relationships, and interactional contexts, it is implicit, but not specified, in Doi's writings that *amae* is analyzed as a semiotic transaction—that is, one wherein the one who appeals and the one who gratifies conduct this negotiation partly or even largely through signalized, nonverbal communication.

Although not a linguist, Doi has deductively listed psycholinguistic explanations of various meanings associated with certain Japanese words, terms, and phrases having to do with indulgent dependency. Some of this description comes from clinical as well as cultural observations, and can also be considered to be informally sociolinguistic. In these instances he is involved in a level of analysis that examines the social and contextual characteristics of dependent interactions, teasing out the putative intentions of the participants as well as the directions and objectives entailed in the action process. As in his clinical descriptions, these are rendered informally in terms of an analysis of discourse involving the psychological and psychoanalytic interpretations of underlying meanings.

Contrary to Taketomo's criticism, Doi clearly imposes a metalinguistic analysis concerning what he calls the "*amae* sensibility," present in the participants whose actions he describes. His analysis is metacommunicative in that it pursues an interpretation of the sense and meaning of these situations at a different level than in the concrete substance of the encounter. Thus, the actual words or actions in the encounter require a higher level of understanding in terms of what Goffman (1969) called "strategic interaction." "*Amae* sensibility" defines a psychological set among participants who will be capable of deciphering strategic metalinguistic meanings that accompany superficially neutral conversation.

9. *Doi's social-philosophic commentary concerning* amae *is a use-*

ful contribution to the understanding of modal Japanese person-ality. At this point in time, the dangers of overgeneralization of national character have been well publicized and warn against making biased or stereotyped descriptions of societies and cultures. Such warnings, however, do not erase evidence that most societies and national groups display features that reflect the effects of their particular cultural history, physical environment, prevailing belief systems, language and socialization practices. These specialized features have an aggregate impact on members of those societies in their public interactions among themselves as well as with members of contrasting national or cultural groups. In that light, Ruth Benedict's early descriptions of salient factors in Japanese life are still informative, even forty years after their appearance in the literature. However, three caveats are prominent: one, that such generalizations apply differentially to various segments of the society; two, that some of these generalizations apply to other societies (i.e., they are not proprietary or "unique"); and three, that some of these characteristics may change over time.

For example, although *amae* is conspicuous in Japan, and in some other Asian societies, it must be examined in comparison to the expression of analogous transactions in similar and contrasting cultures. Also, any notion that elements of a fictive "national character" are uniformly experienced by all parts of the population is, of course, completely untenable. A more tempered interpretation that some traits are more apparent in certain societies is a realistic and even testable hypothesis. The other fact is that whatever else national character is, it consists of a blending and accentuation of universal traits that are expressed in ways that are observable and predictable among certain members of these groups.

In this spirit, Doi's commentary about the significance of *amae* in political, literary, and historical aspects of Japan falls in the realm of social philosophy. This is parallel to Christopher Lasch's (1979, 1984) discussions of "narcissism" in American life. Such commentary in no way suggests that all Americans are narcissistic in either trait-psychological or social-interactional aspects. It merely suggests that the ideological support for self-actualization, self-interest, and self-indulgence are strongly endorsed in the Western ethos and have reached a prominence among affluent, secular Americans. Doi's examination of student riots or reactions to postwar change are of the same genre —offered as attempts to illuminate some of the possible underlying cultural themes that partly explain these social phenomena. As mentioned before, the problem is in distinguishing between Doi's speculations about aspects of Japanese ideology and public mentality, as opposed to his psychological and metapsychological descriptions of indulgent dependency in other contexts.

Synthesis

This chapter has been devoted to a summary of *amae* ("indulgent dependency") according to various commentators and critics. *Amae* has been related to other forms of dependent affiliation and examined in normal and pathological contexts at intrapsychic and extrapsychic, structural levels. In concluding, it may be helpful to draw these observations into a coherent whole where some of the variety and complexity of dependency relations may be visualized using Hsu's (1971b) "Psychosociogram of Man" (see figure 7.1). As discussed in an earlier chapter, Hsu's (1971b) publication challenged the prevailing and popular Western models of "individual personality" by diagramming a model of human functioning based on psychosocial organization. His graphic depiction begins with the innermost layers of unconscious and preconscious structures, and continues through four intermediate layers of interpersonal relations, finally extending to two peripheral layers of more vague association to a larger mass society. In constructing this diagram, Hsu integrated structures from Freudian psychoanalysis using Parsons and Durkheim as a bridge between the conceptual areas of "personality" and "culture." Hsu also built onto the *cognitive* base of Kaplan's (1961) "social personality" and the *semantic* base of Anthony Wallace's (1961) "Mazeway." Hsu's contribution was to add an *affective* base, which he saw functioning through a dynamic "psychosocial homeostasis."

In his scheme, human function is diagrammed as a series of irregular, concentric circles, which loosely signify the structural divisions among the unconscious self, the subjective self, and various levels of socially communicative relationships—implicitly including the relationship to one's own self. His psychosociogram also deals with the levels of social association and the range of

FIGURE 7.1
Levels of *Amae* Experience (Examined against Hsu's Psychosociogram)*

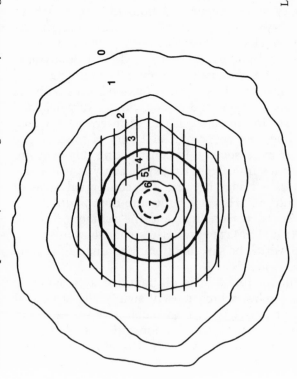

Level 0: *Outer World* (The deindividualized foreign world)
Amae is insignificant and "felt" in its absence.

Level 1: *Wider Society and Culture* (the faceless crowd and strangers in mass society)
Amae not available except in unusual circumstances of of distress, disability, or emergency.

Level 2: *Operative Society and Culture* (Distant kin, coworkers, acquaintances, shopkeepers, casual neighbors)
Amae is not conspicuous because relationships are based on role playing and governed by protocol of *giri, enryo,* and formal politeness.

Level 3: *Intimate Society* (Family, close friends, favorite teachers)
Amae is common and is negotiated in terms of mutual needs in an atmosphere of potentially high emotion within symmetrical and asymmetrical partnerships.

Levels 4 & 5: *Expressible and Inexpressible Consciousness* (Preparatory and proactive *planning* for close, distant, or ambiguous encounters)
Amae regulated by reviewing realistic and appropriate opportunities to seek or gratify needs for indulgence.

Levels 6 & 7: *Preconscious and Unconscious Elements* (Psychic organization ordinarily out of awareness)
Amae as a basic drive intermittently seeking gratification and cherishment.

7 Unconscious ⎫
6 Preconscious ⎬ Freudian
5 Unexpressed Conscious
4 Expressible Conscious

⎱ Jen (Personage)

3 Intimate Society and Culture
2 Operative Society and Culture
1 Wider Society and Culture
0 Outer World

* Adapted from Hsu 1971b, 25.

functions implicit in these operational layers. For our purposes, the capacity of these layers to support *amae* has been superimposed on the original diagram, illustrating Hsu's concern with "homeostasis" as a dynamic affective mechanism.

Hsu's *Layer 0* represents the deindividualized, vague outside world, which is only dimly comprehended by the individual. This consists of foreign countries, exotic societies, or even unfamiliar and unvisited parts of one's own society. The next level, *Layer 1*, consists of the wider and general society (mass society) in which one moves but is not directly known. It is represented by "the faceless crowd," strangers, or *tanin*. In both of these layers *amae* is ordinarily neither present nor potential, but in fact may be felt in its absence—as in the isolation and craving for company experienced while alone in large public areas. Contacts, if they are made, are governed, almost out of awareness, by automatic courtesy. Some indulgence may be extended to strangers in distress, or disabled people, but rarely involves *amae* per se.

Hsu's *Layer 2* is the realm of operative society and culture inhabited by the recognizable faces of coworkers, shopkeepers, acquaintances, casual neighbors, fellow club members, distant kin, etc. These consist of regular, nonintimate propinquity based on the relationships made at school, workplace, club, or neighborhood, engaging nonintimate behavior. In Japan these relationships are regulated through *enryo*, *giri*, and *ninjō* according to the nature of the role sets, the duration of relationships, the degree of closeness, and the requirements of specific situations. Opportunities for either requesting or furnishing full-blown *amae* may develop, but ordinarily are incongruent because of the nonintimate relationship. Favors, mutual help, and interdependency are restrained by courtesy and protocol, whereas rewards and indulgence are attenuated. During these transactions, emotionality and sentiment are present but restricted. Attempts to extract extensive and special indulgence would be regarded as gauche, manipulative, and grossly inconsiderate.

Hsu's *Layer 3* is the realm of intimate society and culture occupied by the nuclear family, special kin, close friends, intimate work associates, childhood chums, and confidants. Role sets in these relationships routinely offer potential for reciprocal *amaeru/amaesaseru* interactions. In real life, such relationships are not uniform, and the propriety for seeking indulgent dependency varies with the circumstances, the nature of the association, the individual interaction style, and the intensity of needs. The complex, unspoken negotiation of reciprocal prerogatives also varies according to the factors of age, gender, status, and longevity of relationship. Although they involve a numerically small number of intimates, the quality of these relationships is of the highest significance and emotional consequence to the participants.

Hsu's *Layer 4* is a transitional zone characterizing the contacts between the individual and his/her social environment. This is the area of "expressible conscious," which is engaged in the assessment of the social environment and concerned with the successful navigation with other individuals in a manner that is simultaneously self-conscious and readily observable to others—what Goffman (1959) termed "the presentation of self" (Goffman 1959; Rosenberg 1979). In contrast, Hsu's next level *(Layer 5)* is called the "Unexpressed (or "inexpressible") Conscious," where the individual carefully monitors direct communication out of fear of undue disclosure, communication of impropriety, or transmission of extraneous thoughts. However, this layer can be involved with eliciting indulgent dependency by way of either deliberate or "leaked" communication through gestures or other nonverbal behavior. At this level of "Unexpressed Conscious," the presence of the desire to *amaeru* may be intuited or guessed by others, even if it is "concealed" and not explicitly conveyed.

This layer constitutes a subtle but significant potential for empathic communication between sensitive partners. Japanese are socialized to be aware of the presence of "dual consciousness" in themselves and others (Doi 1973b, 1974, 1986). This posits that part of the meaning of communication must be deduced or inferred from subtle, contextualized extralinguistic clues. Thus the possible motives and feelings of others may be apparent, and accurately guessed even when they are not or cannot be directly expressed. Since *amae* is characteristically promoted in an indirect, nonverbal manner, this mutual understanding about what may be lurking in the inexpressible conscious is a crucial although silent part of transacting indulgent dependency in Japan.

Hsu's final levels *(Layers 6 and 7)* relate to the Freudian *preconscious* and *unconscious*, which by definition are intrapsychic, and not ordinarily associated with direct or unfiltered communication to the outside world. However, although not detailed by Hsu, psychoanalytic theory posits the presence of dynamisms operating through structures interacting *within* the unconscious itself, some of which have an effect on the "Unexpressed Conscious" through a vague awareness of drive pressures, conflicts, fantasy, emotions, and memories. However, within Layers 6 and 7, *amae* would be represented in the form of an innate (unconscious) drive seeking strong dependent affiliation with objects. These drives for affiliation would be seen as operating in complex ways alone or in concert with other drives having differential effects on subjective awareness and actual behavior. Visualized in this way *amae* can be identified as an unconscious (primary) drive, operating alone or along with other drives to seek affiliation with external objects—specifically in encounters involving security, indulgence, cherishment, and nonsexualized affection. As with other drives, *amae* would be present as an uninhibited drive, but also as filtered and modified by ego mechanisms acting to repress, deny, rationalize, project, or otherwise alter the original motive.

At the level of subjective awareness, *amae* would be present both as "inexpressible" and "expressible" motives, representing intentions and strategies leading toward drive satisfaction and tension reduction. At the interactional level of intimate association, *amae* would be present as a potential for various kinds of reciprocal gratifications through direct expression with a limited number of close associates. In the less intense association of secondary relationships, the potential for *direct* expression of *amaeru* is more limited, and may be seen in attenuated and indirect versions, moderated by *enryo* and *giri*.

In less consequential social relations with strangers or the general public, *amae* is virtually nonnegotiable—except under dramatic or emergency circumstances.

At all these levels, *amae* operates as a kind of desexualized "object hunger," preferentially seeking contact with indulging, nurturing partners but pragmatically settling for less than this.

In concluding this "synthesis," one final dimension of *amae* deserves reemphasizing—namely the manner in which motives for indulgent, dependent affiliation have their diffuse effects in regulating relationships and in channeling the direction of the action process. Again, using Hsu's "psychosociogram" as a panoramic example, one can visualize the multiform ways in which the desire to seek dependency constitutes an integrating design for interaction. Although universal, dependency cravings are more overt and responded to among Japanese. This is because of the heightened awareness of prerogatives for special indulgence, and the exqui-

site consciousness concerning status relationships that permit-
amae.

Notes

1. Portions of the transcript of this broadcast were translated by R. J.
Garrick for the purposes of review in this chapter.

2. In a comment criticizing the American cultural exaggeration of independency, Basch (1980) has remarked on the suppressed consciousness
concerning interdependence:

In Western civilization a pejorative connotation is attached to any relationship in
which child-like dependence has not been concealed sufficiently to let us deceive
ourselves about its existence. In fact, however, society is basically a collection of
life-support systems. Our relationships with other people, our profession, our country, our Church, and so forth, are all opportunities to meet dependent needs in
situations that have at least the illusion of timelessness. . . . The old and the infirm
often feel disreputable and blameworthy because they can no longer function independently. Physicians who care for patients in need of continued therapy—allergists
and dermatologists, for example—are often looked upon as if their activities were
on the borderline of acceptable practice, and their patients are sometimes depre-
ciated for continuing treatment that helps but does not cure. (Basch 1980, 118)

3. Theologically, the word "charity" (Latin, *caritas*) has been used to
characterize "Christian love." This is defined as "the virtue or act of loving
God with a love that transcends that for other creatures . . . or for loving
others for the sake of God" (Gove 1966, 378). Alternately, the word "charity" stands for "a kind disposition to help the needy." In both of these
meanings, "charity" is clearly a nonsexual term, and one that tends to be
applied in asymmetrical relationships. However, the application of the
term "charity" to define behavior or feelings between individuals can also
occur in more egalitarian contexts, and roughly stands for a platonic (i.e.,
nonsexualized) mutual caring, typified by kindness and consideration—
but, again, devoid of sexuality.

4. Words and terms for "love" in Japanese are used economically. Feelings of love are preferentially conveyed through nonverbal signals, and
sympathetically picked up by the loved one—without being directly told.
The word *aijō* is used to define feelings of affection and devotion, while the
word *koi* stands for sexual attraction and romantic feelings. As mentioned
before, *amae* is a word representing the desire to be cherished or loved in a
nonsexual contextualization.

5. Kernberg (1972) sets down four stages concerning the development of
internalized object relationships. The first of these is constructed under the
influence of pleasurable, gratifying experiences and interactions with
the mother sometime between the fourth and twelfth week of infancy. The

second stage involves the consolidation of undifferentiated self-object representations of diverse sensory experiences that are affectually distributed into "all-good" or "all-bad" rudimentary self-objects (ten weeks to six months). Following that a third stage appears when the self-image and object-image have been sufficiently differentiated within the core of "good" self-object representations. The differentiation of self occurs later and is complicated by the process of positive and negative projections. The fourth stage evolves after the first year and extends through the second year. During this last period *cognitive* "object permanency" and *emotional* "object constancy" are reached while "good" and "bad" partial objects become integrated. Following this the gap between the child's self concept and his or her actual presentation of self becomes reduced (Kernberg 1972, 234).

CHAPTER 8

Psychocultural Characterization of the Japanese Self

The Concept of Self

Indigenous descriptions of Japanese personality and attributions of self abound in documentaries from anthropological, psychological, and literary sources. These can be summarized and integrated into a psychocultural picture of the Japanese self—based primarily on *emic* terms and descriptions. Other social-scientific formulations concerning modal personality styles can be examined as combinations of emic and etic formulations.

The concept of self in Western psychology may be topographically divided into "inner self," "interpersonal self," and "public self" (as summarized in F. Johnson 1985). The *inner self* is associated with a fluctuating flow of consciousness, including anticipation of actions and the subjective awareness accompanying solitary introspection. The *interpersonal self* involves actual communication encountered in pairs or small groups taking the form of direct, reciprocal interaction. The *public self* operates in a more impersonal realm where expectancies are vague, are less reciprocal, and take place in the context of larger groups and congregations. In real-life situations, attention flows back and forth through these levels of awareness of "self" and social connection, while consciousness shifts to accommodate the ongoing action process.[1]

Johnson (1985) has summarized conceptualizations from a number of disciplines concerned with the contemporary Western understanding of self. The self is currently seen by some theorists as a social construction, symbolically and signally created between and among social beings. The self is described as a phenomenological object, examined in a series of evanescent actions in real-life settings. In these contexts, the self is immanently situational and specified in its adaptation to the fluctuating circumstances of real-life encounters. The self may be productively studied in terms of communicative process—including communications with one's own self. Although defined in these social-constructional terms, the self is intimately connected to the raw reality of bodily experience, both genetically and in contemporaneous awareness. The self is also seen as operating in the realms of memory, recognition, and intention—only part of which is consciously accessible at any given moment. Thus, unconscious trends and motives not directly observable are conceded to contribute to the purposeful direction of self in the action process.

Most outstanding, the self is both an immediate, phenomenal object transacting in the evanescent and specious present, and an archive of prior actions, events, dreams, and hopes. In this sense, the self is simultaneously instantial and historic, social and personal, conscious and unconscious.

Given this structural background, certain characteristics of the Japanese self will be reviewed through a series of psychocultural descriptions. Commentary from ethnographic, literary, and personal accounts will be assembled in an impressionistic view of personhood among Japanese. In seeking generalizations about the Japanese self, this chapter will metaphorically resemble a series of drawings or sketches rather than an album of fine-grained photographs, susceptible of precise measurement and conforming to some nomothetic, fixed reality.

Cautions about the limitations of descriptions concerning national character have been raised repeatedly. Neither scholars nor intelligent laypersons take stock in caricatures that purport to define large groups according to specialized or unique patterns typifying all culture bearers at all times. As Befu (1986) has commented, comparative differences between cultural groups are self-evident, although these can readily lead toward stereotyping (for example, the intense and persisting maternal indulgence within most Japanese families). As Befu states it,

It may be impossible to eliminate stereotyping altogether even from scientific discourse. The question is, therefore, how to use stereotypes and how to interpret them when used by others. That Americans believe in free will, for example, does not mean that they will exercise it all the time or that their actions are based exclusively on it. Similarly, the truism that the Japanese are group oriented does not mean that all Japanese are; or that group orientation is the only form of relating Japanese recognize. (Befu 1986, 13)

Hsu (1971b) also has confronted criticism of generalizations about national character by stating that neither the observable ranges of personality style nor in-group, regional variation wash away persistent and recognizable differences between cultures:

> For no matter how much we are bogged down by . . . eschewing questions of national character, there are fundamental differences, on a probability basis, between individuals originating from different societies and cultures. . . . Whether we examine interpersonal details or the patterns of national affairs and development, we are bound to come face to face with drastic differences of approach. . . . For example, any American anthropologist dealing with his Japanese counterpart must admit that, in most cases, he is likely to find cultural differences over and above individual differences. (Hsu 1971b, 24)

Japanese Conceptions of Personality and Selfhood

In this discussion, the term, personality, will refer to systematic attempts to codify human behavior through the use of empirical measurement. It will also refer to "personality" in the more emic and colloquial sense, depicting the ways in which both individuals and groups display clusters of characteristics in their social presentations that set them off from other persons and groups. The descriptions of selfhood in Japan to be summarized here originate from folk, scientific, medical, and mythic sources (e.g., in Pelzel 1970). Speculations concerning the internal, structuralized aspects of personality, such as "motive," "intention," or "will," are included along with explanations of performance based upon presentational aspects of self that are behavioral and objective.

Descriptions of both subjective and presentational dimensions of the self involve interpretations of culturally regulated performances —either implicitly or explicitly. Explanations of subjective experience are available in transcripts of communication in clinical settings, in expository writings, from personal diaries, and from social-philosophical sources that describe features of inner awareness.

Explanations are also deduced from interpretations of social-psychological accounts of interaction based on experiences shared by two or more interactants. Taken together, these constitute psychosocial formulations (as in Hsu 1971b) that describe and structuralize dimensions of personal functioning from the most interior and ordinarily unconscious elements, through an intermediate level of face-to-face interaction, out to the most superficial, routine, and banal interchanges.

As mentioned in the previous chapter, Hsu's (1971b) model constitutes a social-anthropological "field" that captures the dynamics of interpersonal function in terms of both intrapsychic content and social relationships. He points out that the Western concept of personality has heuristically been weighted toward explanations of individualism. As an antidote to this tendency, Hsu substituted the Chinese term *jen* (which generically means "man" or "personage") to embed the locus of personality in interpersonal transactions.

As demonstrated in the analysis of *amae*, Hsu's psychosociogram constitutes a model that topographically depicts different cultural and personal styles according to variations in interaction rules that accentuate or diminish certain forms of communication, and either encourage or forestall relationships at these various levels. For example, some prominent Japanese interaction rules operate to inflate the awareness of *unexpressed* (or "inexpressible") *consciousness*, in a way that is lavish compared to average American rules regarding disclosure. Similarly, the lack of a sharp sense of boundary between one's own identity and the collective identity with parents, intimates, and selected small groups is another way of expressing that the average Japanese has more a sense of "social self" in conjunction with others than a strongly individualistic personal identity. In fact, Hsu's basic premise of looking at the interface of self with others is compatible with prevailing (emic) explanations of the self in Japan.

Inside and Outside: The Nexus of Japanese Selfhood

In a repetitive manner, emic depictions of Japanese selfhood concentrate on the delicate connections between an internal, inexpressible awareness and the consciousness that accompanies the direction of external action in the real world. Basically, these emic descriptions of awareness focus on both the boundaries and inter-sections between interior information (subjective or "private" data) and exterior information that is communicatively interactional and "public." Doi incisively described this awareness in Japanese persons through what he termed a "dual structure of consciousness" (1973b). Using this term he portrayed the coexistence of a heightened awareness of distinctions between the interior and exterior "worlds" among Japanese. In formulating this awareness, Doi used the commonly expressed, culturally meaningful words of *omote* (meaning *"front,"* "straightforward," or "overt") and *ura* (meaning *"back"* or "concealed"). *Ura* also has the nuances of "dark," "insincere," or "sinister."

Omote *and* Ura

Doi's (1973b) exposition was extended in his book on *The Anatomy of Self* (1986), and the present summary owes much to his lucid description of Japanese selfhood. In his publication, the dialectical relationship between what is publicly accessible versus what is concealed or private is emphasized through a series of ordinary Japanese words referring to the emic awareness of outside and inside dimensions. Parallel terms are introduced that represent this same dialectic: for example, *uchi*, which means "close relations," and *soto*, which stands for "outsiders" or peripheral relations. These terms have direct sociological applications. *Uchi* defines the intimate relationships individuals have with family, close kin, intimate friends, and some special neighbors or coworkers. It specifies close, primary relationships established by factors of propinquity, loyalty, fixed obligation, or strong affection. *Soto*, on the other hand, refers to distance in human relationships and connotes the absence of intimacy. These nonintimate relationships require formal protocol, regulated politeness, and calibrated degrees of deference and restraint.

Tatemae *and* Honne

Paralleling these terms are the important words *tatemae* and *honne*, which also describe relationships according to an outside/inside dimension affecting both subjective awareness and objective social behavior (Doi 1973b, 1974, 1986). *Tatemae* is an "exterior" term that refers to cultural conventions and consensually accepted regulations for proper behavior. In this sense *tatemae* is parallel to the word *omote*—in the scope of its social-psychological relations. *Tatemae* is based upon principles and normative rules well understood within the culture. Doi compared *tatemae* to Max Weber's concept of the "legitimate order" (Weber 1964). This "public" and normative *tatemae* is contrasted and balanced against a "private" *honne*, which represents the nondisclosed subjectivity of individuals whose underlying motives and intentions are obscured beneath the formal, social-presentational aspects of *tatemae*. In this sense, *honne* is parallel to the concept of *ura* or, as Doi says, "it is concealed in *ura.*"

All of these paired terms—*omote/ura, soto/uchi, tatemae/honne*—constitute hypothetical poles of objective and subjective experience operating in a dialectical and reciprocal manner. As such, they divide human experience into relative degrees of inside and outside awareness accompanying human performance.

As mentioned in previous chapters concerning childrearing, Japanese youngsters are socialized to become highly sensitive to interaction rules concerning the normative regulation of behavior *(tatemae)*. These rules require their conformation through the control of speech, nonverbal gestures, facial expressions, and kinesics. At the same time, children become aware that these external manifestations serve as a cover for undisclosed awareness, involving frustrated expectations for action, furtive desires, concealed wishes, and unexpressed feelings. Such awareness is experienced as an ongoing recognition of the difference between internal urges and external performance. Also, this "dual consciousness" is projected onto other persons, predicating that they are also aware of the *tatemae* and *honne* dimensions of their own subjectivity. Thus, both Japanese interactants are concerned with gauging the impact of their communications through carefully observing the *tatemae* of the other partner.

Deducing what may lie underneath the normative *tatemae* in Japanese communication requires a high degree of empathy and intuition, in order to estimate the dimensions of undisclosable motives and emotions in other people. As Doi (1973b, 1986) points out, the ability to navigate successfully between these levels of internal self-awareness and external self-presentation is a measure of psychosocial competence and sophistication in adult Japanese life. Authenticity, in individual selfhood, is exemplified by the degree of fit between self-awareness and self-presentation. This consitutes an area of persistent misunderstanding for Westerners, who conclude that the external, *tatemae* formalism of Japanese comunicative style implies a kind of stereotyped insincerity at a social level, and a personal inauthenticity at a subjective level. However, from within the culture, Japanese communicate in ways that penetrate through the ambiguous, courteous, or even ritualistic conversation to estimate the underlying feelings and intentions of *honne* in the other partner. The degree to which this takes place reciprocally and smoothly varies with the familiarity of the participants as well as their sophistication.

The high awareness among ordinary Japanese of these dialectical dimensions of experience and communication draw attention to something that is present, but not as pronounced, in Western life. For example, the formal/informal or explicit/implicit distinctions concerning communication in Western social relationships in many ways approximate *tatemae/honne*. Also, the notion of "open" versus "hidden" (or open versus secret) conveys a similar awareness of public and private dimensions accompanying human performance. Thus, the differences between Japanese and some Western communication styles are not categorical but quantitative, in terms of the prominence and frequency of awareness of this outside/inside dimension among Japanese. Westerners typically become more conscious of these dimensions in situations where potential or real conflict is imminent, or where the need to guess at underlying intentions is raised by a sudden misunderstanding, argument, or impasse. Also, the need to penetrate beyond the formal meaning of communication is introduced in contexts where protocol is high (such as in diplomatic negotiations) or where self-serving subterfuge might be expected (as in testimony during a trial or interrogation of a suspect). Looking for submerged intentions and feeling in Western life is also standard in psychotherapeutic treatment, and in the interpretation of literature or poetry. Thus, it is not the case that Westerners lack the capacity for "dual consciousness," or that they lack categories for stipulating inside/outside or public/private dimensionality. Rather, it is the case that such awareness is more discontinuous, and less intense than among average Japanese.[2]

Public and Private

A common form of discussing the dimensions of overt and covert communication in Western life explores the difference between "public" and "private." "Public" refers to things that are in the general domain of understanding, are relatively objective and accessible to observation—similar to the normative explications of *tate-mae*. "Private" refers to functions, possessions, ideas, or fantasies that "belong" to the individual and are not readily accessible to other persons. The terms "public" and "private" also have moral connotations in Western personal interaction. Things that are deliberately hidden or secret may be regarded as ulterior in the pejorative sense of potentially concealing information against the interests of other people. This reflects the Western ethical preoccupation with *sincerity* in communication (as in Trilling 1962), which holds that the greatest good is ideally served when persons communicate in a forthright, direct manner. Thus, there is a potential invidious dichotomy between overt versus covert, exterior versus ulterior, honest versus dishonest (as pointed out in Doi 1986). The Japanese also attach significance to sincerity *(makoto-sa)*, which is established when there is a congruity between internal purpose and external presentation (Garrick 1990, personal communication). Despite this similarity, Japanese forms of sincerity are filtered through discourse rules that discourage directness, restrain emotionality, and scrupulously avoid conflict. In this sense, there is more recognition of the inevitability of discrepancy between inside and outside. In the Western world discrepancies between public and private are moralistically regarded as potentially associated with hypocrisy, deception, or phoniness. The idea of private is also more extensively substantiated in Western constitutional and civil law, protecting the ownership of material goods, property, inventions, and original ideas to a degree that is not as prominent in Japan.[3]

As Doi (1986) has noted, another Western term referring to two-dimensional awareness is *ambivalence* (Bleuler 1924; Freud 1912). This psychological term is used to indicate the simultaneous presence of conflicting feelings, thoughts, or reactions to specific people, ideas, memories, or behaviors. Such conflicts are represented at both unconscious and conscious levels. In psychoanalytic theory, such conflicting emotions and ideas are partly explained on the basis of stratified early experiences involving encounters that require the repression of feelings and memories containing intrinsically inconsistent emotional experiences. As mentioned earlier, Japanese have a higher tolerance for accepting inherent contradictions in themselves, in other persons, and in nature itself (Nakamura 1964). In this sense, their capacity for tolerating ambivalence or paradox is high when compared to average Westerners.

The Japanese expressions for "public" (*ōyake* and *koritsu*) are reasonably parallel, although more restricted than the English-language meanings of "public." The words stand for institutional, socially observable functions and processes that are part of a commonwealth of objects, experiences, and ideas and cover the notions of "public buildings," "public acclaim," or "public awareness." "Private" is not so easily translated, although the words *watakushi* and *shi* may be understood as "I," the first-person, singular pronoun. Both of these words convey the connotation of strong personal subjectivity. *Shi* is also used as a word stem that, combined with symbols (cognates) for other terms, directly conveys the sense of personal subjectivity or privacy. Such combined expressions parallel the more explicit use of "I," "myself," "personal," or "private" in English. What is evident, overall, is that compared to the rich applications of the word "private" in American life, the concept is relatively hypocognated in the Japanese language (R. I. Levy 1984). As an alternative for avoiding the brash connotations of first-person expressions, some Japanese recently use the English loan-word for "privacy," pronouncing it as *puraibashi.*

Doi (1986) also concluded that *ōyake* and *watakushi* do not precisely align with their English equivalents. In his analysis of these words he does not detect the psychologic dimensions of outside/inside that are central to *omote/ura, soto/uchi,* or *tatemae/honne.* The word *watakushi* ("I"), while denoting and emphasizing a particular person, does not carry along the Western connotation of sharp individual identity, which is so strongly suggested by the words "private" or "myself" in American life. Also the words *ura, honne,* and *uchi* simply do not transmit connotations of a strongly individualized personhood in Japan. Moreover, in American life, public and private are prominently represented in legally defined rights, privileges, and responsibilities, reinforcing American notions of strong individuality, personal ownership, and responsibility. Individualism is ideologically supported as a basic and fundamental value, where self-determination and autonomy are guaranteed even though in the real world, relative deprivations of both are ubiquitous.

Conflict Resolution and "Face"

In looking at situational adjustment in Japanese interaction, Lebra (1976) also examined the dimensions of *omote/ura* and *uchi/soto.* Ishida (1984, citing Doi 1973b) applied these dialectical pairs to a study of conflict resolution, largely in the context of formal organizations and social institutions. Here again, *tatemae* and *honne* were presented both as technical terms concerning self-presentation and subjectivity, and as colloquial expressions defining a conventional and commonly expressed sense of outside/inside dimensionality.

The issue of *face* is another corollary of the sharpened "dual consciousness" described by Doi (1973b). "Face" has received popular attention as a significant concern among Japanese and Chinese. However, as illuminated by Goffman (1959), the maintenance of face is a common concern in Western interpersonal connections, although not so explicitly recognized. At a social-interactional level, "face" is concerned with the maintenance of a harmonious equilibrium between two interactants during both prosaic and significant encounters. In Japan, "face-work" (Goffman 1967) strives for smooth, polite encounters ensuring dignity and emotional balance among interactants. Subjectively, face is concerned with the conscious monitoring of smooth social navigation in which the avoidance of being embarrassed or, alternatively, causing embarrassment for others is central. Numerous commentators have addressed the precautionary aspects of self-presentation in Japan. In both mundane and auspicious encounters, interactants seek action possibilities that carefully follow cultural protocols, are designed to avoid open dissension, and, at the same time, authentically carry out the intentions and desired options of the interactants.

Lebra (1976, 110–35) has examined three domains of situational interaction among Japanese, differentiating intimate, ritual, and anomic situations. Depending upon which of these is involved, behaviors vary according to a baseline that regulates interactions according to the social context, the nature of the interaction, and the quality of the relationship. Central to her systematic descriptions of conflict, the maintenance of harmony *(wa)* is an uppermost consideration. This is achieved through trying to maintain a balance between spontaneity and inhibition. Within most encounters, the preservation of face is crucial, and interactants use a number of communicative strategies to preserve the appearance of agreement and positive feelings. Lebra (1976) first lists the mode of *mediated communication*, where direct interaction is avoided, and a third person is selected to broker communication on behalf of the first interactant toward a second party. Her second category of *refracted communication* also uses a third party to change or improve a situation that would be difficult to navigate on a two-person basis.

A third category involves using *anticipatory communications* chosen in a preventive way to forestall difficulties, or to alter communication, before the fact. A fourth mode uses *self-communication* as an introspective rehearsal of possible future events. A fifth mode uses *written communication* to convey explanations concerning possible interpersonal problems—again, avoiding face-to-face encounter.

Two other modes of communication use *understatement* and *unobtrusiveness* to minimize conflicts through reducing involvement or denying significance. The final mode that Lebra lists is *ritual communication*, where highly formalized patterns of speech and gesture are employed in publicly established, consensually understood role playing. Lebra (1984b) later added the mode of *self-aggression* as another way of resolving dissension, through becoming a self-incriminator and offering a way out for the other party either to share the blame or to evince sympathy. One final mechanism of conflict resolution is also advanced—specifically, *acceptance*. Previous chapters have discussed how childhood socialization prepares individuals to accept adversity fatalistically, and to develop the capacity to endure even in unbearable situations. This also can be used as a mode of conflict resolution, as observed by other commentators (e.g., in Hiroshi Minami 1971).

Another well-publicized process of minimizing conflict and preventively smoothing out differences is called *nemawashi*, which figuratively means "taking care of the roots." Prominent in corporate and political settings, *nemawashi* consists of informal maneuvers with persons or constituencies to develop policy through conversing with separate participants prior to the time of any official meeting. This allows individuals or power blocs to express their potential objections before the fact, and to adjust their position to what is perceived to be the direction of the ultimate decision. This process operates as a rehearsal for the formal meeting where consensus is assured, thus avoiding any appearance of confrontation, dissatisfaction, disloyalty, or challenge to others. As van Wolferen (1989, 338) indicates, actual consensus is often subtly coerced by the feared consequences of appearing to be recalcitrant or divisive.

Kokoro, Hara, and the Japanese Self

Kokoro (meaning "heart") is perhaps best known in the West as the title of a sensitive Japanese novel (Soseki 1957 [1914]) that examines the protracted experience of guilt in a university professor concerning the suicide of a young friend many years previously. *Kokoro* metaphorically stands for "heart" in the sense of subjectivity and deep intentionality in the hidden areas of concealed motives. *Kokoro* is a commonly used term loosely defining some functions of the self that are not readily apparent to others, except through intuition or deduction (as in Hsu's "Unexpressed Consciousness"). Doi (1986) connects *kokoro* to the notion of "secrets" *(himitsu)*, which have to do with the mystery and privacy of subjective life natural to all persons. Since such subjectivity is ubiquitous, *kokoro* is taken for granted as a mostly hidden and deep part of personal functioning. Although not used as a formal psychological term, at a folk level *kokoro* has the informal status of a motivational system that activates behavior through true feeling and sincerity. As mentioned in Lebra (1976), the idealization of having a pure heart *(magokoro)* amounts to cultivating a guileless and unegotistical state of mind, while radiating a pure "true-heartedness." She comments that the "inner self" is structurally symbolized by both *kokoro* (the heart) and *hara* (belly or "gut"), while the "outer self" is metaphorically located in the face or mouth. She also speculates that the awareness of *kokoro* is discovered at around age two and a half, and undergoes progressive refinement both through the feedback of personal introspection and through actual reality testing with others. Later in life, disturbances in personal function or disability in social relations are connected with the need to "rediscover one's *kokoro*," and to keep it intact in the face of outside disturbance and stress.[4]

As Doi (1986) has discussed, the secrecy connected to one's own *kokoro* can also involve hypocrisy or deception. In any society, it is understood that the presentation of self at times is seriously at odds with internal feelings or intentions. Doi points out, however, that "the fact that *kokoro* is hidden is not what makes hypocrisy and deception evil. Rather, it is the fact that the person has pretended that there is something in his or her *kokoro* that is not there" (Doi 1986, 107). This again points to *kokoro* as an internal guideline for authenticity, integrity, and sincerity. Discrepancies between actual behavior and underlying intentions are expected. However, protracted disparity or falseness would indicate a need for change or resolution, partly because of the practical difficulty of obscuring one's real feelings or intentions over long periods of time.

As a colloquial term for "belly," *hara* is only slightly similar to the word "guts" in American slang in such expressions as "my gut reaction" or "gut feelings." However, *hara* is a more complicated term than "guts," and is frequently used in colloquial descriptions of behaviors that are more complex. As an emic expression, *hara* represents another underlying "locus" of internal dispositions, held responsible for activating certain behaviors. At a folk level this source of power is associated with two kinds of activity: promoting unusually complicated strategies of interpersonal navigation, and striving for exceptional achievement. As with *kokoro*, *hara* is a metaphorical (obviously not anatomical) region of the "gut," alleged to be the repository of deep personal integrity and strength of purpose. Through concentrated training and cultivation, these inner resources may be mobilized in planning for strategic actions with or against other individuals. As Lebra (1976) has commented, there is an awareness of "the duality between the heart-belly sphere and the . . . 'face-mouth sphere' [where] . . . the individual occasionally succumbs to an irresistible temptation for masochistic self-exposure." This can take the form of an unwitting release of strong opinion, a tactless comment, or an uncouth expression that comes straight from the *hara* in an unexpurgated form. Thus, in comparing *hara* and *kokoro*, *hara* is less accessible to observation and functions as an internal, secret place for energizing strategic actions.

In a recent description, Matsumoto (1984) defines the "art" of managing *hara* (called *haragei*) illustrated through a series of prescriptions governing social navigation. These are based on a model of deception and intrigue, although Matsumoto disclaims this— probably because denial of any invidious purpose is part of the *haragei* strategy. Nonetheless, *haragei* emerges as a series of hidden designs to control interaction, and to disguise and deceive through confusing or forestalling action. For example, Matsumoto (1984) lists twenty rules to avoid saying "no," including "not answering," "keeping the other person hanging with vague answers," "exuding false politeness," "evading questions," "diverting conversation," "feigning pity," "blaming *karma*," or merely "acting dumb." *Hara*, then, is a word that is colloquially used to speculate about the hidden or ulterior intentions of other persons. These intentions are not necessarily adversarial. Some are involved in the concentrated mobilization of interior strength for a variety of neutral or even altruistic purposes. Also, it would be misleading to suggest that *haragei* is a preoccupation of all Japanese persons. However, it does constitute another colloquial distinction between the external self-presentation and the "true," interior nature of the self in regard to intentionality and the display of emotion.[5]

Matsumoto (1984) cites the dictionary definition of *hara* as "the verbal or physical action one employs to influence others by the potency of rich experience and boldness; or alternatively the act of dealing with persons and situations through ritual formalities and accumulated experience" (Matsumoto 1984, 17). In the systematic treatment of *hara*, he graphically diagrams this as the most internal source of human energies—in some ways roughly equivalent to a system of drives "operating at the very core of personality." This core of *hara* is surrounded by a more superficial layer of "heart" *(kokoro)*, which represents another internal repository of intentions and emotions. A yet more accessible layer is termed "mind" *(chi)*, and has to do with *conscious* proactional strategies under the influence of voluntary behavior, that are concerned with following a logical and rational order.

As Passin (1982) indicates, the translations of "mind" into Japanese raise the possibility of applying a number of terms that refer to different operational categories, including intellect *(chi)*, reason *(risei)*, consciousness *(shōki)*, attention *(chūi)*, and intention *(ito)*, along with terms associated with emotion or temperament such as *kidate* (disposition), *kanjō* (emotion), *kokoro* ("heart"), *ki* (spirit), and *hara* ("belly"). As in English, the word for "mind" incorporates a conglomerate of conative, cognitive, perceptual, and emotional functions. However, it is interesting that there is no single equivalent word that stands for all these functions—as there is in English. Passin (1982) has also diagrammed the overlapping psychological realms of "heart," "belly," "spirit," and "intellect" subsumed under the Japanese conception of "mind." Taken together, these descriptions constitute a folk (emic) topography of *personality* that depicts "drives" *(hara)* filtering through "true feelings" *(kokoro)* and eventually through the conscious and proactive, executive ego ("mind"). Another significant dimension of consciousness called *ki* will be explained subsequently.

Matsumoto also describes potential conflicts and paradoxes in the interconnections among these various folk categories. For example, one may have a true heart *(kokoro)* and yet not tap into *hara* (or "guts," as it were). Similarly, individuals might display keen and clear thinking (that is, "a strong mind"), but be ignorant of how to mobilize the deep forces of *hara*. According to Matsumoto, Westerners might be able to grasp the intellectual significance of *hara*, but without training would not be able to master *haragei* as an effective interpersonal strategy. However, in seeking parallels to *hara* and *haragei* in Western contexts, it is easy to discover methods that are used to develop states of highly concentrated consciousness in perfecting musical performance, dancing, graphic arts, or athletics—such as weight-lifting. Also, in the West, there are both religious and secular methods involving intense meditation, prayer, or trance undertaken to achieve heightened levels of awareness or emotional tranquility. What is lacking in the West, however, is a commonly consulted model for actions—with or against others—that depends on hidden strategies, and that draws its special power from internal resources, as in the formulaic use of *haragei*. Also, the Western use of contemplation or trance is not organized into folk description of personality. Moreover, trance is not associated with a topographical locale (outside of the *brain*) as it is in *haragei*.

Interestingly, Matsumoto (1984) disavows *haragei* as a form of "gamesmanship," as described in the West by Goffman (1959), Berne (1978), or Potter (1978). He concludes that gamesmanship is conscious, superficial, and even frivolous. However, his illustrations of the strategic objectives for which *hara* is mobilized are directly analogous to the general operations of gamesmanship.

Ki, Jibun, Ikigai, and the Japanese Sense of Self

In his publication on *amae*, Doi (1973a) composed a cultural and etymological examination of the Japanese word *ki*, defined as "the movement of the spirit from moment to moment" (Doi 1973a, 97). This simple word stands for the normal flow of conscious thought and feeling that accompanies action in the immediate and evanescent present. *Ki* is concerned with the anticipation of potential enactments in the instantly encountered reality. In Doi's view, this awareness is basically pleasure oriented, insofar as it optimally seeks objectives leading to tension reduction, and harmonious relations with other people. As such, the term pivots on conscious, proactive planning, but is conspicuously connected to emotion and temperament. Thus *ki* is associated with defining a spectrum of feeling states and dispositions that accompany action. Doi enumerates a number of Japanese expressions utilizing the stem word *ki*, which denote the apprehension of "guilt," "capriciousness," "peculiarity," "craziness," "irritability," "narrow-mindedness," "depression," "reluctance," "geniality," "impatience," "generosity," "frankness," and so forth (Doi 1973a, 96). He also makes the point that *kokoro* and *hara* are more deeply embedded "structures" underlying observable behavior, while *ki* is descriptive of the proactive awareness that anticipates immanent social interactions. The emotional dispositions of *ki* may or may not be observably connected to basic, underlying drives.

Peter Dale (1986) has strongly criticized Doi for his analysis of the significance of various expressions using the stem *ki*. He sees this as an unscientific attempt to substitute ambiguous, indigenous expressions for established technical terminologies in order to claim a specialized and unique meaning. Dale (1986) suggests that Doi has embarked on a "linguo-gymnastic enterprise in the rewriting of psychoanalytic theory" (1986, 132), and that Doi's substitution of vernacular words for complex scientific expressions is a bankrupt and dubious undertaking.

It is quite true that in their explanations of *ki*, Doi (1973a), Rohlen (1974b), and Margaret Lock (1980) all agree on its special signification and prominence. However, none of these authors suggests that the emotions defined in terms of *ki* are exclusive or unique to the Japanese. Rather, it is the case that the use of these and other vernacular Japanese terms indicates something about the consciousness of emotion that accompanies various kinds of human performance. Also, these three commentators did not deductively invent expressions concerning *ki*, but were involved in a linguistic and metalinguistic analysis of expressions present in the ordinary speech of average Japanese. Reporting colloquial, emic terms used for emotional experience does not invalidate using scientific terms for these same emotions, nor does it displace other common words that may be valid in their own descriptive and connotational power. Especially in terms of emotional expression, Dale's critique seems naive. It is axiomatic in the Sapir-Whorf hypothesis that the specialized denotations, connotations, syntax, and grammar of any language reflect the subjective perceptions and interpretations of reality by members of particular language groups. Moreover, in the realm of adjectives that define *mood states* (as opposed to more neutral discriminations, such as color recognition) it is difficult to capture actual meanings without accepting the indigenous expression. This is nicely illustrated by Robert Levy's (1973, 1984) discussion of the lack of terms for "depression" among Tahitians.

In terms of *self theory*, *ki* is significant in that it testifies to the consciousness of average Japanese concerning the fluctuating states

of emotional awareness, and is displayed both emically and etymo-
logically in the glossary of terms that Doi has illuminated and
interpreted. In Lock's (1980) description, *ki* is connected with the
understanding that "change in a person is seen as transient oscilla-
tions about a hypothetical norm, which is in a state of balance"
(Lock 1980, 85). Within her conception, humans are seen as constituted through cultural definitions that interact with the immediate
environment. In this sense, the term *ki* includes what in Western
circles has been called "impression management" (Goffman 1959,
1967; Hochschild 1979) or the regulation of "feeling rules" (Ekman
1984). Both of these "scientific" Western terms represent how the
mobilization of feelings is coordinated with the interpersonalized
action process. In psychoanalytic terms, *ki* would be part of both
the adaptive ego, in responding to the *ki* of others, and the executive
ego, concerned with carrying out reality-based objectives in interpersonal situations.

Hisa Kumagai (1988), in an essay on the subjective Japanese self,
has also illuminated the structural consequences of the word *ki* in
signifying an internalized locus of energy and feeling connected to
self-awareness and emotions:

Of conceptual interest here is that in the word *ki*—used as a root word to
indicate and connect elementary feelings and thought processes—the Japanese have reified "energy" into a subjective entity that moves the individual *to become* both activator and respondent of interactional processes.
The general awareness of *ki* by the people themselves is evidenced in
various facets of their personal consensual life—from socialization practices to formal presentation. In closing, the author . . . concludes that (a) *ki*
is more *substantive* and *active* than "impulse" in the movement of the
social act; and (b) . . . the Japanese model provides an *explicit* conceptual
demonstration of the substantive roles of the "I" as well as affective elements in social interaction. (H. Kumagai 1988, 175; italics original)

In contrast to *ki*, the word *jibun* (which translates as the "true
self") has cultural characteristics that relate to a broader experience
of self in Japanese mentality. The word *jibun* is used to indicate
identity and to define a personal selfhood. Also, the word *jishin* is
not equivalent to the generic Western meaning of self, but is ap-
pended to other words (e.g., *watakushi-jishin*) to indicate a special
emphasis or subjectivity. *Jibun* is not equivalent to the generic
Western meaning of "self," but is closer to what Masterson (1985)
psychoanalytically calls "the real self." *Jibun* does not represent a
multiplicity of empirical "selves" that collectively make up a socio-

logical composite of a particular individual (as in William James 1950 [1890]). *Jibun* in Japanese life is more selective and must be "discovered" (really, *re*discovered) at moments of crisis, through a process of contemplation, introspection, religious experience, or, less commonly, psychotherapy. The "true self" is not only ego-syntonic, but is supposed to facilitate proper and congenial relations with others. In this sense, *jibun* is close to what some Western authors have loosely termed the "authentic self," representing a comfortable approximation somewhere between what the individual would like to be, and what he or she actually is.

In Masterson's (1985) psychoanalytic description, the "real self" (like *jibun*) is synonymous with "healthy," "normal," or "rehabilitated" and implies a congruence between internal self-objects and the reality of the extrapsychic world. Ideally, the "true self" includes the capacity for commitment and productivity, along with a maintenance of identity and self-esteem and a desirable balance between *tatemae* and *honne*. The "true self" is released from any need to either be defensive or unduly aggressive in the conduct of interpersonal negotiations.

In Western life, the therapeutic process of psychoanalysis is credited with redirecting the individual from both narcissistic and neurotic handicaps of early childhood, toward a rehabilitated discovery of a mature "true self." In a parallel way, some Japanese psychotherapies (particularly *Morita* and *naikan*) are associated with reestablishing pure and smooth relations with others. However, contrary to psychoanalysis, these are achieved through reinforcing humility and refreshing the patient's sense of obligations and responsiblities toward others. These therapeutic methods have been discussed by Murase and Johnson (1974), Reynolds (1976, 1980), and Reynolds and Kiefer (1977) as indigenous procedures that promise restoration and rehabilitation. However, these approaches have been critically characterized by Peter Dale (1986) as "instrument(s) of coercion and punishment for those who break down under the weight of disindividualizing socialization" (Dale 1986, 172).

The ideal self in Japan is also addressed by Dorinne Kondo (1987) in her examination of indigenous aspects of selfhood related to family, school, and work place. She describes the function of revivalistic "ethics retreats," which are conducted by businesses and corporations to reawaken a dedication to work and to the improvement of interpersonal relations (also described in Rohlen 1974a). Rehabilitative goals are attained through a tightly scheduled regimen involving lectures, meditation, exhortations, physical exercises, and symbolical purifications. All of these operate toward restoring the "true self." As in *naikan* method, these retreats explicitly inculcate the development of sincere gratitude toward others fostered through the experience of self-denial, mortification, endurance, and meditation under the direction of a retreat master.[6]

In terms of the ideal self in Japan, the word *ikigai* (denoting the "meaning of one's life") functions as a core expression for the notion of both private and public identity. As discussed by Garrick (1988), *ikigai* is a common expression symbolizing personal identity. It implies the existence of a primary social definition of an adult person signifying "this is what really makes me tick—really moves me." Such a centralized focus undergoes change, accommodating to the lifespan, and may concentrate on aspects of familial, occupational, or avocational roles. Thus, for many women, their *ikigai* would surround their preoccupation with mothering, maintaining a home, and marriage. Correspondingly, men's *ikigai* is frequently focused on their occupational role and identification with work group and company. As Garrick (1988) points out, *ikigai* may at other times involve crafts, hobbies, intellectual interests, or ideological causes to which the individual is intensely attached. As in Western situations, these core identifications may be inconspicuous in one's public role or life style, and only apparent to family or intimate friends. Regardless of its observability, *ikigai* subjectively furnishes a crucial point of reference to "true" or "ideal" self.

The Self in Linguistic Socialization and Ordinary Speech

Dorinne Kondo (1987) has summarized features of spoken Japanese that simultaneously address the semantic content of messages and the metacommunicative markers concerning the status relativity between conversational partners:

In terms of the self, one can say that these distinctions presume the existence of a social self and an emotional self: the self as concatenation of social roles, on the one hand, and the individual as a sentient being, on the other. The premises underlying this . . . *omote/ura* structure of selfhood (Doi 1986) assume the existence of a self that is sensitive, vulnerable to hurt, and exceedingly emotional, but they also take for granted that a person is constantly suspended in a web of social relationships. In comparison to archetypal notions of Western individualism . . . the most striking contrast is the connectedness of self and other, the relational quality of self. (D. K. Kondo 1987, 245)

Kondo noted Smith's (1983) analysis of honorifics in their tendency to make distinctions between the "internal self" and "social self." These are more complex than in English-speaking countries simply by virtue of the language rules regarding the explicit observation of status. Smith describes that by age three most Japanese youngsters have mastered the use of six terms of self-reference that define the relational characteristics of themselves to others (girls need only five). This is in contrast to American children, who only need to make the rudimentary distinction between "I" and "you" as pronominal discriminations between self and others. Testifying to the complexity of Japanese socialization, additional terms relating to kinship, and denoting other degrees of social distance, are subsequently learned. Hearing and using these terms repetitiously make youngsters conscious of the complex status relativity regulating social interaction. Moreover, as Smith points out,

The acquisition of personal referents does not end in childhood in Japan, but instead continues throughout adult life . . . the calculus is first learned in the family . . . where children quickly discover that they may not use personal referents directly referring to any person senior to them. (Smith 1983, 79)

As mentioned previously, proper names are not customarily used in Japan; instead, formal titles are selected that take into account the social position of interlocutors, the context of conversation, and pertinent situational factors. These all act to emphasize a linguistic tendency toward relational rather than individual identification of self.

Because the Japanese concept of self is so intensely relational and infused with social cohesion, there is a tendency to imagine that Japanese do not experience a sense of "true" or "authentic" self outside these multiple social contexts. This does not seem to be the case, however. As Smith speculates,

It seems to me that the Japanese possess a very clear sense of self, although it differs from our own, and that they regularly behave as though persons are indeed individuals. Western observers are often blinded by [the] inability to perceive the locus of self in Japan, and by our unwillingness to accept the low priority given its expression. (Smith 1983, 89)

Lebra (1976) has also reinforced this point by suggesting that the discrimination concerning self involves understanding the proper navigation within situations. This facility is regarded as a mark of maturity among Japanese. Epitomized by the word *kejime* (which means "discrimination"), this identifies the individual's capacity to maintain status and positional awareness in the varying situations occurring in intimate, public, and ritualized encounters. As she comments,

Actual situations vary from case to case, but the cultural principle governing cross-situational interaction is simple and clear; one situation should not be mixed with another. Situational mixture is avoided by giving priority to one situation over another, by ignoring one and dealing with another, or by sequentially arranging one situation after another. . . . This concern for maintaining *kejime* (discrimination) may contribute to the Japanese person's keen awareness of the discrepancy between *honne* and *tatemae*. (Lebra 1976, 136)

Suzuki (1986) has also analyzed the Japanese emphasis on blending the "self" into the "other," illustrated by the abstemious use of pronouns in conversation and writing. This low use of pronouns results in the self being specified *secondarily*, that is, according to the person who is being addressed. In contrast to the frequent use of the first-person singular in many European languages, the Japanese ordinarily avoid "I" *(watakushi* or *boku)* and instead substitute a status term that describes or in some way defines the speaker, as in "someone's student," "someone's teacher," "such and such a university's professor." Even in the instances where an adult Japanese may consciously select to use the first-person singular pronoun for the purpose of emphasis, the choice will be made according to the perceived differences in power and social distance factors.

Seen in this light we may even say that the Japanese self is an undefined, opened-ended state until the appearance of . . . a specific addressee. This may well be the explanation for the unease and discomfort Japanese experience when dealing with people we cannot define. (Suzuki 1986, 149)

Suzuki (1986) states that while in other languages the distinction between self and other is a priori and basic, there is a contrasting tendency among Japanese to blend and incorporate the observing self *into the observed object*. Suzuki sees this sociolinguistic centering on the addressee as creating "a culture of anticipatory perception" or a "culture of consideration" (Suzuki 1986, 167).

In a more personal disclosure, Passin (1982), who speaks English,

French, Spanish, and Japanese, reflected that the learning of a foreign language involved for him a

> vast transformation of the self. The self in effect is reprogrammed, and this process is not only psychological but, it seems to me, physiological as well ... when I speak Japanese I am always surprised at how polite a person I can be, something that I do not particularly think about myself when I speak English. (Passin 1982, 81)

Kumagai and Kumagai (1986) also focused on the psychological conjunction of "other" and "self" in Japanese persons, through examining what they called the "hidden-I," identified by them as an indistinct selfhood revealed within a series of transactions of indulgent dependency. Examining both *amae* and *enryo*, they pointed out the assertive manifestations underlying these superficially passive, interpersonal strategies. Behind the attempt to generate indulgence on the one hand, or the obsequious denial of significance on the other, the "hidden-I" emerges (also observed by Reynolds 1976).

Ego-Ideal and the Japanese Self

Erikson (1950, 1959) extended psychoanalytic ego psychology by discussing the attainment of identity and psychosocial competence as basic developmental goals during adolescent socialization. Similarly, Geertz (1976) described the process of investigating developmental competence in his use of an ethnographic method where informants define themselves as persons through a gradual process of self-disclosure, even though their realization of what constitutes their selfhood may be rudimentary. Parallel to the notion of competence, Kiefer (1988) has examined the attainment of maturity through different cultural approaches that identify idealized characteristics attributed to adult exemplars in various societies. Some of these idealizations in Japanese life have already been mentioned in White and LeVine's (1986) review of "the good child" (or *ii-ko*).

In all societies, adjectives used to describe exemplary characteristics of idealized members consist of words referring to observable behavior, but at the same time implying the underlying presence of certain desirable, inherent traits or qualities. Also, the meanings attributed to these adjective clusters clearly exceed the ordinary semantic signification of these words, and connote special degrees of achievement and desirability.

Sunao

A number of idealized Japanese qualities have been discussed in previous chapters, including such temperaments as "harmonious," "gentle," "restrained," "modest," "pleasant," "cooperative," "grateful," "empathetic," "subtle," "enduring," "achieving," "pure," and so forth. Alone or in combination, these traits are regarded as exemplary of mature Japanese selfhood—although clearly understood to be *ideal* rather than routinely encountered or consistently achieved.

As mentioned in chapter 6, the Japanese word *sunao* is a powerful cultural term depicting a high degree of competent social navigation based on the combination of outstanding personal strength, flexibility, and resourcefulness. Literally defined as "compliant, obedient, and cooperative," the connotations of *sunao* are more extensive than this. Murase (1982) conducted an analysis of this exemplary term as being "upright," "genuine," and "undistorted." In the interpersonal realm, *sunao* stands for "obedient," "accepting," "passive" (i.e., non–self-assertive), "unselfish," "open-minded," and "free of antagonism." At a more personal or trait level he sees *sunao* as "relaxed," "gentle," "unconflicted," "unprejudiced," and "reflecting joy and gratitude." Murase (1982) connects this idealized term to the disingenuousness and innocence of childhood, and discusses *Morita* and *naikan* as two forms of Japanese psychotherapy that may restore *sunao* through a calculated acceptance of guilt, gratitude, and desire for harmony—parallel to the rediscovery of *jibun* ("true self").

Although the positive dispositions associated with *sunao* would be desirable in any culture, the Japanese consolidation of this particular cluster seems distinctive. For example, ideal personality characteristics in American children (and adults) cluster around "independent," "self-reliant," "assertive," "flexible," "considerate," "obedient," "ambitious," "energetic," and so forth. As another contrasting example of cultural idealization, Geertz (1976), in studying Balinese selfhood, has analyzed the "proper ordering" of social action condensed in the Balinese word *alus*. This word stands for "pure," "refined," "polished," "exquisite," "ethereal," "subtle," "civilized," and "smooth"—all of these operating in what Geertz called an (internal) "felt realm" and an (external) "observed realm" of experience.

Similar to Doi's (1972) distinctions of social navigation within a "dual consciousness," Geertz characterizes this same essential feature:

> The goal is to be *alus* in both the separated realms of the self. In the inner realm this is to be achieved through religious discipline . . . in the outer realm it is to be achieved through etiquette, the rules of which . . . are not only extraordinarily elaborate but have something of the force of law. (Geertz 1976, 227)

Barnlund (1975) has addressed the attitudes behind optimal self-presentation through a cross-cultural study of Japanese and American college students. One of his instruments used a roster of adjectives permitting subjects to register their endorsement of these as typical or atypical of themselves. The Japanese emerged as endorsing "reserved," "formal," "silent," "cautious," "evasive," "serious," "distant," and "dependent." Contrastingly, Americans described themselves as "self-assertive," "frank," "informal," "spontaneous," "talkative," and "self-expressive" (Barnlund 1975, 54–56).

Japanese Self in *Hansei, Kan,* and the "I-Novel"

Counterbalancing the strenuous concentration on protocol in Japanese interpersonal behavior, there are a number of activities connected to private exploration, secret introspection, and communion within the inner self. *Hansei,* meaning "reflection and self-examination," is an institutionalized version of this that encourages both children and adults to allocate some time looking into themselves. Such introspection is encouraged to search critically for weaknesses or imperfections, and to rehearse strategies for self-improvement and betterment of interpersonal relations. As reported in White and LeVine (1986), *hansei* exercises in grade-school classrooms are conducted as a group activity in self-criticism undertaken to improve performance, resolve problems, and refine plans for superior achievement and social harmony.

Kan, which literally means "observing oneself," is another term used for constructive, methodical introspection. As Doi (1988b, private communication) explains it, *kan* has the quality of both Freudian free association and a "detective story," insofar as the individual is searching for hidden understanding through which to reorganize behavior or improve communication with others.

The common Japanese practice of keeping some form of diary is another way of privately recording thoughts and events. Also, a number of aesthetic pursuits highlight the internal and private appreciation of beauty through writing poetry *(haiku)*, practicing calligraphy, performing music, doing flower arrangement, or perfecting the ritual tea ceremony. Additionally, the enormous amount of reading by the Japanese in public and private settings constitute a way of secluding themselves or retreating from the rigors of protocol and face-to-face performance. Reading fiction has diverting and escapist qualities in any culture. In Japan, however, it would seem to satisfy a stronger need for privacy, and a temporary shutting off of the machinery devoted to self-presentation. Observing Japanese in waiting rooms or on public transportation, one sees individuals of all ages who appear to be completely absorbed in reading newspapers, novels, or school books—seemingly observing none of the activities or conversations going on around them.

The "I-Novel," Masks, and the Self

Keene (1956), Morris (1962), and Miyoshi (1974) have commented on the significance of what is called the "I-novel" in Japanese literature. These pieces of fiction constitute a genre of pseudoautobiographical accounts rendered in first-person singular, which painstakingly report life experiences through the unsuppressed account of the author's feelings, thoughts, and proactive schemes. Arising around the turn of the century, these confessional and naturalistic narrations are considered to have attained their popularity because they diametrically oppose the Japanese constraints placed on the expressions of egoism, strong emotionality, and self-disclosure. Keene (1956) sees the fascination with these novels as an attempt by both authors and readers to capture an otherwise prohibited sense of individuality. Morris (1962) reflects that the "I-novel" has recently lost some of its popularity, but still captures the interest of many Japanese readers. Often the self-exposure of the "I-novel" is monotonously negative and tortured. As one example of this, Osamu Dazai's No Longer Human (1958) is a pseudobiographical account of a young man who feels devastated by a chronic inability to reveal himself or to be truly accepted by parents, servants, teachers, or friends. In a series of diary entries, he reveals his central problem of insincerity, and the consequent emptiness experienced in his meetings with others (DeVos 1979). Along with this, the hero suffers from a terrible sense of loneliness, and the grim realization of his inability to transmit authentic feelings.

The actual use of masks with stereotyped facial expressions is a central factor in the traditional Japanese *noh* theater. The imagery of masks is frequently used in fiction, symbolizing the conflict over the awareness of disparity between "inside" and "outside." In many novels, this dialectical tension is exemplified by focusing attention on the difference between what is socially portrayed—as shown through a mask or facial clues—and what actually is felt—usually some mixture of torment, pain, or sense of alienation. Many examples are available, but the works of Yukio Mishima (1925–70) are especially revealing. Notably in *Confessions of a Mask* (1949), the painful imbalance between subjective awareness and social performance is prominent. This is poignantly related in the thoughts of his eleven-year-old protagonist, who feels the pressures for correct social presentation:

> The reluctant masquerade had begun. At about this time I was beginning to understand vaguely the mechanism of the fact that what people regarded as a pose on my part was actually an expression of my need to assert my true nature, and that it was precisely what people regarded as my true self which was a masquerade. (Mishima 1949, 27)

Even more tragically, these conflicts were abundantly apparent throughout Mishima's lifetime (as in Nathan 1974), during which he precariously balanced success, international reputation, and literary productivity against a fugitive carnality, reactionary militarism, and a sense of failure. Craig (1970) has cited Mishima's own reflection of the self as likened to a stage assistant in a *Kabuki* play "who dressed completely in black, seems to be scarcely more than a shadow, and who periodically disappears through turning his back toward the audience" (Craig 1970, 18).

In his commentary on the Western self, Mishima (1964) amusingly declared that Americans sometimes "tend to overexist." His comment illustrates the cross-cultural difference in self-presentation wherein the average Japanese is concerned with concealing personal egotism behind a mask, while the average American is concerned with generating at least a modicum of visible individuality, lest he or she be regarded as shy, conflicted, devious—perhaps even retarded.

Kobo Abe (1966) created a particularly vivid portrayal of disturbed self-presentation in his novel, *The Face of Another*. His protagonist had been severely disfigured in an accident and left with a deformed, repelling countenance. Abe's protagonist describes how his scars and oozing sores are covered by a mask of bandages and plastic contraptions. In using the image of a mask, Abe allegorically focuses on the face as a conduit of contact with society. At one point his hero states,

I who had lost my face was destined to be shut up forever in a solitary cell ... with no roadway.... I suppose facial expression is an adequate communicating roadway.... Isn't it a preconception derived from habit to suppose that the soul and the heart are in the same category and can be negotiated only through the face? (Abe 1966, 31)

Fumiko Enchi (1983), in a novel simply titled *Masks*, uses the images of *Noh* theater to concretize the shifting moods and intrigue carried out by her central characters. In a more global use of mask imagery, Buruma (1984) has collectively described the Japanese as consciously "living behind a mask" that selectively filters the perceptions of both cultural insiders and outsiders. For persons inside the culture there is a release in getting beyond the mask of decorum, reserve, harmony, and propriety in order to glimpse the underworld of exuberant passions and forbidden delights. In the opposite direction, these masks prevent outsiders from witnessing the disordered and abandoned side of Japanese life. Activity in bars or life among "the water trades" *(mizushōbai)* is an outstanding example of behind-the-mask behavior. Here, propriety may be abandoned. One can drink, flirt, speak out, show anger, argue, and be naughty or rude. One may complain about a callous boss, a neglectful wife, indolent children, or problems in getting promoted. Similarly, women's decorum dissolves when they get together in the privacy of small groups of intimates to joke about their husband's infirmities, the pomposity of their mothers-in-law, and the strictures imposed in being "all things to all people" (Garrick 1986, private communication). However, to outsiders this masking and compartmentalization appears inconsistent or even reprehensible.

Buruma sees the difference between "outsider" and "insider" reactions to masked behavior as being connected to the issue of *nihonjinron*. By this he means that Japanese entertain a conspicuous tolerance for contradiction, partly as evidence of their "uniqueness." Outsiders, on the other hand, may judge this acceptance of contradiction and lack of inhibition as hypocrisy.

In all of these literary instances, the figurative use of mask imagery directly addresses the balancing of outside and inside (tate-mae and honne) and exhibits discernible cultural differences in the management of sincerity. As Hochschild (1979) noted, Trilling (1962) defined "sincerity" as a congruence between inner emotions and outward display of feelings signaling certain intentions. Trilling (1962) then contrasted "sincerity" with "authenticity," which he defined as the congruence between the subjective awareness of self (as an emotion manager) and the actual quality of specific internal feelings—irrespective of how they might be perceived by others. Trilling's point was that in Western life, an historically earlier concern with sincerity had slipped from a focus on the need for external consistency into a need for internal consistency and a more privatized integrity. Wagatsuma (1970, 1984) has also discussed this in terms of the tendency of Americans to repress ambivalence in order to create a sense of personal integrity, and to avoid the cognitive dissonance inherent in the awareness of ambivalent emotions. Japanese, on the other hand, were seen as having a high tolerance for ambivalence regarding emotions, opinions, or ideas. Thus, a consciousness of internalized honne coexists with the awareness of carefully controlling feelings that will be observed externally. This is another way of explaining the need for "masks" (deception, restraint, control) at the tatemae level of interpersonal action. One might parenthetically comment that Westerners "mask" their ambivalence at an intrapsychic level (through repression), and thus are less concerned about the problem of inadvertent leakage of ego-dystonic emotions or ideas.

Japanese, on the other hand, have a more explicit concern with Trilling's sense of sincerity as experiencing a congruence between tatemae and honne, and feel potentially more at risk if serious discrepancies emerge. This offers a partial explanation of some forms of suicide among Japanese that occur when public behavior (especially failure, or exhibition of cruelty to others) produces intense and unbearable guilt leading to destruction of the self (as explained in DeVos 1973). The novelist Mishima (1964) illustrates this in his response to an American reporter who asked him for his explanation of why Japanese choose seppuku (ritual disembowelment) as a form of suicide. By way of explanation, Mishima quipped words to the effect, "But this is how we show we are sincere!"

Categorical and Cultural Descriptions of Japanese Personality

Older Literature on Personality and Self

A number of social-psychological and cross-cultural studies of Japanese conducted during the 1950s and '60s examined differences in group mean scores regarding trait-psychological categories such as authoritarianism (acquiescence), dominance (deference), aggressiveness (passivity), and assertiveness (unassertiveness)—as in Arkoff (1957) and Arkoff, Meridith, and Iwahara (1964). These and other studies consistently found both Japanese males and females to be comparatively high in their needs for deference, abasement, and submissiveness while low in expressed needs for aggression, exhibitionism, dominance, independence, and leadership. In a review article concerning the influence of social structure on human behavior, Caudill (1973) listed common themes reported by both Japanese and Western commentators. Among the twelve themes listed, several pertain to this current chapter:

a. A strong sense of obligation and gratitude.
b. A sense of sympathy and compassion *(ninjō)* for others.
c. Devotion to parents, and especially a strong, long-enduring tie in almost its childhood form to the mother.
d. An emphasis on self-effacement, and a tendency to attribute responsibility to others rather than taking responsibility for one's own actions.
e. An attitude of deference and politeness toward one's superiors, and toward those with whom one has a tie, coupled with not so much rudeness as obliviousness toward those with whom one does not have a tie.
f. A tendency for understatement, and an emphasis on nonverbal communication. (Caudill 1973, 349–54)

In a summary of literature on Japanese national character, Yamamoto (1964) also composed a list of traits abstracted from a number of cultural commentaries. Of some eighteen descriptive clusters, the following seven pertain to the characterization of self:

1. Politeness, courteousness, respectfulness, delicacy and sensitiveness to interpersonal feeling, fulfillment of promises, sycophancy, well-intentioned lie, dislike of flat confrontation.
2. Diligence, sincerity, patience, self-control, self-sacrifice, perseverance. . . .

3. Order, discipline, and self-sacrifice in the family, utmost importance of filial piety. . . .
4. Thinking much of prestige, dignity, and honor, fear of being mocked, maintenance of dignity. . . .
5. Paternalistic benevolence in social contacts, boss-and-follower relations fictitiously identified with father and son, submission and nonresistance to authority. . . .
6. Having proper place in the social system, importance of honorifics and self-abasing expressions in the language. . . .
7. . . . social ties of *on* (favor flowing down) and *giri* (sense of obligation created by *on*) . . . endurance of the feeling of gratitude. (Yamamoto 1964, 17–22)

In seeking to define a cultural model of interaction, Bennett, Passin, and McKnight (1958) employed the following "features" characterizing Japanese:

articulate codification of the norms; strong tendencies towards a face-to-face, or "primary group" type of intimacy; an emphasis upon hierarchical status positions; concern for the importance of status; relative permanence of status once established; and "behavioral reserve" or discipline. (Bennett, Passin, and McKnight 1958, 44)

A number of early writings on the psychology of the Japanese were concerned with issues of national character, sometimes using psychoanalytic characterizations of childrearing and psychohistorical reconstructions to interpret ethnographic findings (as in Ruth Benedict, James Clark Maloney, Geoffrey Gorer, and Weston La-Barre). These contributions have been extensively and critically reviewed.

Caudill and Scarr (1962) also contributed a cross-cultural comparison of Japanese value orientations, again as a reflection of "personality" dispositions, displayed through the comparative preference among Japanese for *collaterality* in both work and family relations when compared to Americans.

Indigenous Psychological Literature

Hiroshi Minami (1971) published an early, Western-style compendium of the psychology of the Japanese, written in 1953 and later translated. In his discussion of the Japanese self, he listed submission to authority as most conspicuous, describing it in historical and current frames of reference. Relating this to Confucian models of filial status awareness, he illustrated reactions to authority through allusions to military authority. These protocols dictated not merely submitting, but submitting mindlessly and swiftly. Thus response to authority is judged not only in terms of compliance but also in terms of the speed with which commands are responded to and obeyed. This quality is not restricted to military settings, but is evident in Japanese classrooms, where prompt and cheerful compliance to instructions is expected and rewarded, although by no means always seen. Such hearty responsiveness is also encountered in routine public situations, particularly in retail sales. Behind this swift superficial compliance, Minami sees submission and affirmation cloaking a form of masked egoism, and even acting as a smokescreen for egocentricity. He states that the mastery of appearing to conform to outside requirements may paradoxically increase the individual's inner awareness of a contrasting subjectivity that is *not* transmitted to the social world.

Minami's description of this secret subjectivity is an eloquent contribution to what Doi later defined as "dual consciousness." Developmentally, Minami sees the combination of overt submissiveness and covert unsubmissiveness as a way of learning to harbor contradictory actions and thoughts comfortably. Minami (1971) also contributed insights concerning happiness and unhappiness among Japanese. In his view, happiness should not be celebrated, but cautiously acknowledged through an almost underplayed appreciation. He describes the demonstration of satisfaction itself as hazardous, and cites folklore that illustrates how pleasure may be swiftly followed by remorse. Many folk stories and aphorisms not only stress the transitory nature of happiness, but worse, suggest the premonition of pain upon experiencing joy. Minami's descriptions of unhappiness are connected to a spectrum of lonely, sentimental feelings, where the perception of imperfections, and the anticipation of misfortune seem ego-syntonic—almost a kind of comfortable masochism. From Minami's viewpoint there are four solutions for unhappiness: first, to accept the situation; second, to rationalize it as inevitable; third, to divert oneself consciously from the feeling; and fourth, to blame and reproach oneself for falling into such an unfortunate condition. The capacity to endure disappointments and accept pain is exemplary of a virtuous character, and paradoxically can be experienced as "positive." Being content with small rewards is also recommended. Expectations should not be inflated, and one should be grateful for being spared severe adversity.

As mentioned before, the impermanence and dangerousness of romantic love has been reiterated in literature, folklore, popular songs, and drama. Marital relations strenuously avoid public romantic display and base their stability on more secure and permanent grounds than sensuality or romance. Minami (1971) also notes the Japanese normative concern about the shallowness of accumulating money or ostentatious possessions. Economic success or worldly reward are preferably encountered as incidental to virtuous endeavors featuring perseverance, industriousness, and dedication to high performance. The cultural message is that it is all right to make money, but this should be secondary to higher motives.

In another commentary written in the postwar period, Ishida's characterization of self concluded that Japanese were less concerned with universal principles governing human action than with a highly developed sensitivity toward interpersonal and situational ethics (Ishida 1974). He also underscored the development of tacit, intuitive sensitivity toward other persons as a prominent dimension of Japanese subjectivity. The strategic use of silence, and the capacity for deducing implicit, nonverbal communication was described as pervasive in ordinary Japanese interaction. Ishida also pointed out parallels between Zen Buddhism and the tendency to regard the denial of self and the attainment of selflessness as a virtuous achievement. The presentation of self in a modest, ostensibly passive, and quiet manner was acknowledged as desirable—regardless of one's status.

American Contributions

Befu (1970) has also called attention to some Japanese aesthetic styles clustering around the ego-syntonic experience of melancholy, sadness, and suffering. Looking at self-presentation, he interprets the process through which intuitive understanding is learned as ultimately affecting both subjective awareness and performance. One gradually learns the necessity of looking for what is hidden, and attempting to intuit the feelings and intentions of other persons. Discussed earlier, the development of a finely tuned sensitivity to the feelings and latent intentions of others is a crucial part of early childhood socialization. Described as *omoiyari*, this sensitivity involves an acute understanding of status hierarchy and privilege, which govern the direction of the action process. Accurately intuiting the wishes, feelings, and needs of superiors, equals, and subordinates is essential, and requires a high degree of concentration and discrimination of social contexts *(kejime)*.

In a later publication, Befu (1986) has discussed *personhood* in Japan. As an expression, "personhood" is parallel to, but quite different from, Western terms centering on individualistic definitions of personality or the self. Like Hsu's (1971b) term, *jen*, "personhood" refers to an *interpersonal self*, which is conceptualized through "interpersonalism" rather than through individualism. Befu defines interpersonalism as a broad, normative orientation whereby persons characteristically refer to, and think of themselves in terms of, various dyadic role sets. Thus, persons are defined in terms of reference rather than in terms of independent existence and isolated subjectivity. He sees interpersonalism as requiring a highly discriminating sense of status relationships used to define the nature of the relationship, the consequences of commitment, and the extent of dependency and reciprocity. He also sees interpersonalism as connected to potentially intense states of mutuality and trust, varying according to the relative statuses, length of the relationship, and frequency of interaction. In addition to personhood and interpersonalism, a third characteristic of "interdependence" is emphasized by Befu (1986) as defining the range of options for symmetric and asymmetric obligatedness within particular role sets.

The characteristics that constitute self-discipline are also identified by Befu as a conscious part of idealized self-presentation, demonstrated overtly by overcoming hardships, displaying endurance, and exerting a high expenditure of effort. Subjectively, self-discipline requires a mental attitude of intense concentration in order to mobilize internal strengths and resources. Befu (1970) cites the Japanese word *seishin* ("spirit") as incorporating an intense determination and high degree of motivation similar to the vernacular descriptions of *haragei*. However, *haragai* is a tactical, interactional relational skill that mobilizes deep internal resources. In contrast, *seishin* constitutes an immutable quality of individual spirit or mentality.

The category of "role perfectionism" is identified by Befu as an inherent part of conscious Japanese personhood. This term approximates the psychoanalytic concept of ego ideal. At a conscious level, the individual is motivated to improve skills, particularly those connected to work activity and family expectations. Regardless of one's social role (janitor, professor, housewife, bureaucrat), the effort to meet the highest possible standards within the potential of this role is a conscious expectation and should be visible to other persons. Similar to DeVos (1960), Befu feels that this role perfectionism is solidified by the example of the long-suffering Japanese mother, whose role expectation of being a super-provider and nurturer is incorporated by her children in the form of inflated standards for performance. Later, these ego ideals also may function in the generation of guilt based on failure to achieve these goals. Befu sees the attainment of such objectives as frustrating. However, the attempt to improve is perhaps more important than the actual skill level achieved:

Surrounded by adults with these cultural conceptions of the self, children are bombarded daily by stimuli manifesting them. Since these are cultural concepts within inherently positive values, children are necessarily rewarded by accepting, internalizing, and acting in accordance with them. Concepts of the self must, therefore, be powerful molders of the adult the child will become. (Befu 1986, 26)

DeVos, in a series of publications, has illuminated various aspects of Japanese selfhood and personality. In one of his earliest analyses, DeVos (1960) described the motivation toward achievement connected to potential guilt toward parents, particularly the mother. In terms of socialization, he saw this as related to Japanese mothers' calculated permissiveness, conspicuous indulgence, and self-sacrifice for their children. During early socialization, these become incorporated as superego elements, and later overpower the willfulness of the child, but also constitutes a *mentorship* "that teaches causality in behavior and the consequences of action" (DeVos 1985, 150). Through example, Japanese mothers tacitly direct their children toward learning to postpone and sublimate impulse gratification. By observing their mothers, children also learn endurance as a reliable strategy for ultimately achieving behavioral objectives. As described before, this constitutes a powerful "push-pull" sensitization that inculcates discipline and conformity at the same time that the child is lavished with indulgence and permissiveness. As DeVos expresses it,

The mother's teaching style and expressions of appreciation and praise, and the emotional climate created in the mother-child teaching efforts are singular for the Japanese context and feeling because they constrain the child's own behavior. Given the sensitivities . . . and the cultural emphasis on social dependency, one . . . finds that the Japanese internalize their experiences in such a way that a potential for guilt acts as an internal constraint on any tendencies toward behavioral deviation. (DeVos 1985, 151)

In other publications DeVos (1981, 1988) has indirectly addressed the *tatemae/honne* consciousness in his observations about the internal "field independence" of Japanese. He states that "the Japanese do not fit the generalization that a sensitivity to social approval and cooperative attitudes is more characteristic of a field-dependent cognitive pattern, while field-independent individuals tend toward competitive interaction patterns in individualistic social goals" (DeVos 1985, 168). What he points out is that the perception of internal feelings and intentions in Japanese is highly "field *in*dependent," and that the visible, self-presentational conformity only superficially appears to be "field dependent." He also comments on the relative lack of ambivalence and shame about the body, which is socialized as a positive object deserving comfort and satiation through interaction with the intimate, indulgent, and nurturant relationship with mother. This is also evident in the relative lack of guilt concerning sexual gratification. Guilt is more related to the fears of potential role loss than to sexuality per se (DeVos 1978, 237).

Reaching beyond the conventional descriptions of harmony and avoidance of confrontation, DeVos (1985) discusses the introjective displacement of aggression, which, following internalization, then becomes transformed into what might be considered an ego-sytonic "moral masochism." In addition to this internalization, DeVos comments on the projective use of the outsider as a target for diverting aggression onto persons defined as not belonging to the in-group. He looks on this as partly explaining the chronic disparagement of foreigners in Japan, and the periodic violence toward those perceived as being lower in status and thus inferior—notably in minority populations (Wetherall and DeVos 1975; DeVos and Wagatsuma 1967, 1973).

In commenting on the awareness of guilt, DeVos (1985) infers that the copious manifestations of shame, which are consciously related to interpersonal referents, act as a screen to conceal the undischargeable sense of guilt relating to serious personal transgression—particularly that which has involved destructiveness toward others. He makes the distinction that in cross-cultural comparisons of Thematic Apperception Test stories, the Japanese evaluation of achievement takes the form of anxieties concerning the capacity to carry out functions—without questioning whether the challenge is necessary or realistic. In contrast, American subjects related their anxiety to whether or not they should assume responsibility for certain achievements—without considering much about the actual execution of such achievements. Obviously, both experiences of guilt can be arduous and overpowering. DeVos's point is that the Japanese feel fundamentally accountable in terms of their capacity to achieve, whereas the Westerner agonizes more about whether or not the decision to undertake achievement has been authentically committed.

In a number of works, DeVos (1960, 1973, 1978, 1985) has dealt with motivations connected to *achievement* as one of five basic, instrumental dimensions of interpersonal roles: achievement, competence, responsibility, power, and mutuality. At a conscious level he relates the conspicuous achievement orientation among average Japanese to socialization procedures that reinforce the continuing need to engage in cooperative endeavors within hierarchical family and work groups in which interdependency and mutual obligatedness are highly articulated. At an unconscious level, he sees the validation of the self as crucially connected to "sustained work activity . . . being transmitted into modern goals" (DeVos 1973, 185).

He sees this combination of motivations as tapping into both instrumental and expressive factors leading to achievement within the context of collaterality, mutuality, and strong affiliation. He contrasts this with McClelland et al.'s (1953) Western-based, social-psychological formulations for achievement, where individualistic (egoistic) motives are foremost, and the *absence* of affiliation is conspicuous.

The psychological interconnection between affiliative object-cathexis and social cohesion is illustrated by DeVos in his complex discussion of role narcissism and suicide (DeVos 1973, 445). He uses Durkheim's (1951) conceptual typology to examine the psychocultural aspects of various forms of Japanese suicide. While agreeing with Durkheim, DeVos feels that adding a consideration of unconscious motives reduces the difference between Durkheim's categories of "altruistic" and "egoistic" self-destruction:

When examined psychodynamically . . . many cases of altruistic suicide may be found to spring from primitive motives rather than from a well-developed and differentiated sense of adherence to mature human values. (DeVos 1973, 448)

This is particularly observable in instances where failure in objectives or sudden loss of social connectedness may thrust the individual into a mode of self-destruction as a reaction to a sense of overwhelming ignominy or void. DeVos (1973) thus adds to Durkheim's classification an "egocentric" typology that is paired against "anomic suicide." He sees egocentric suicide as occurring because of abrupt severance or change in narcissistic gratifications resulting from specific, interpersonal disruptions—as opposed to the more diffuse sense of retreat and disconnection in anomic suicide. He speculates that egocentric motives represent disruption at a more differentiated level of development than the objectless and schizoid position accompanying anomia. Such speculation coordinates with Doi's assertions about how protracted states of infantile affiliation provide continuing sustenance and narcissistic reward, but carry the profound risk of potential interpersonal disconnection.

DeVos and Wagatsuma (1967, 1973) have also illuminated Japanese selfhood through their ethnographic study of minority populations. As in marginal populations elsewhere, the psychocultural characterizations of the minority group often become the polar opposites of idealized normative values in the general culture. Moreover, such characterizations are assimilated by both the dominant majority and the minority themselves, as illustrated by a *buraku* ("ghetto") informant.

Buraku persons are usually identifiable . . . at least for other *Buraku* members. . . . Living conditions within the outcaste community are terrible—torn-down houses, unsanitary conditions, distasteful occupations, dirty food, bad language, violence, fighting, laziness—everything that is bad and ugly is found in outcaste districts. . . . This something horrible permeates the people who are born and reared and live in this area, something like a bad body odor. Even when an individual leaves the community, wherever he may go there is something horrible, which is discernable and always accompanies him. (In DeVos and Wagatsuma 1973, 408)

DeVos (1985) has given an exposition of the Japanese self through both etic and emic dimensions. He mentions the historical tradition that explicitly requires exemplary behavior on the part of parents and teachers. This high expectation for punctilious role modeling by adults facilitates the tacit, implicit learning of standards for public behavior that is so prominent in Japan. He also emphasizes the background effect of Confucianism in its deep cultural influence on ideology, family configuration, and hierarchical status. The significance of nurturant dependency *(amae)* is also repeatedly stressed by DeVos in a number of writings. Moreover, he has described how the expectation of nurturance is inherent within the operation of internal control (DeVos 1989; private communication).

The Japanese Self as Revealed in Clinical Psychoanalysis

Alan Roland (1988) has examined some characteristics of the Japanese self through a comparison with American and Indian "selves." Partly through examining the communicative features of the psychoanalytic situation in Japan, he discusses the use of intuition and innuendo to facilitate disclosure in otherwise unexpressive analysands. Roland also comments on the heavy investment in a "familial self" (both in Japan and India) provoking an identification with what he calls "we-self" as well as "myself." The presence of a severe restraint against expressing or even acknowledging anger is mentioned as a serious therapeutic resistance, as is the oversensitivity to criticism, which is evident in a number of defensive strategies (flattering the analyst, becoming obsequious, not replying). He reinforces DeVos's (1980) speculations about the unsuitability of traditional Western psychoanalysis for average Japanese due to both communicative and ideological factors. As mentioned earlier, psychoanalysis is ideologically influenced by notions of individualism and autonomy. The procedure employs a method that stimulates unedited, free-associative disclosures and promotes the discharge of socially prohibited emotions. Moreover, the procedure is subjected to an intellectual *analysis* of various aspects of the therapeutic process itself—notably "resistance" and "transference." This is conducted in an atmosphere of candor and strict confidentiality facilitating the production of insights about previously repressed and painful realizations. None of these are part of ordinary communicative style among average Japanese.

Despite this, Roland (1988) believes that the recognition and utility of psychoanalysis is slowly growing in both Japan and India, although accommodating to indigenous social, cultural, and psychological patterns. Roland makes the interesting point that even with the emphasis on collective social identity and avoidance of individualism, this paradoxically promotes the formation of an extremely secret and private "internal self." Citing a personal communication from a Japanese psychoanalyst (Tatara in Roland 1988), Roland states that this intensely secret self can only be revealed indirectly, even in psychoanalytic treatment situations (also see

Tatara 1974). In these Eastern settings, Roland suggests the analyst must avoid being intrusive and using blunt interpretations or interventions that pry into this secret self. Instead, the existence of the secret self can be indirectly acknowledged, but not confronted as "resistance."

Psycholinguistic and Emotional Aspects of the Japanese Self

Some of the sociolinguistic aspects of subjective awareness have already been discussed, particularly in terms of first-person singular pronoun usage. This section will concentrate on broader aspects of communication, discussing both self-presentational and subjective perspectives, particularly in regard to the selective demonstration of emotion.

Nakamura (1967) has discussed historical, philological, and linguistic aspects of what he calls the "consciousness of the individual in daily life." He comments that Japanese scholars did not undertake a logical dissection of the relationship between "the universal," "the particular," and "the individual" prior to the introduction of Western philosophic writings. Within the Japanese language, the "individual" is designated in ambiguous ways. Because of this, Nakamura concluded that

the Japanese wanted to locate the individual in experience, not in the abstract. Largely because of the Japanese emphasis on concrete immediacy in experience, the individual was grasped as a living thing, and not as a bloodless, inanimate thing in the realm of the abstract. The living individual is always located in various kinds of human relationships. (Nakamura 1967, 182)

Dorinne Kondo (1987) also uses a sociolinguistic exposition of the Japanese language to provide an especially clear insight into conceptions of selfhood. As she states it,

especially in the Japanese case, one can say that attitudes toward the self and its relationship to the social world are crystallized in language. . . . In Japanese, one cannot utter a sentence without communicating at least two things: one) the actual content of the message itself, the referential meanings; and two) the meta-message about the relationship between the speaker and the listener. . . . A striking feature about Japanese is that the latter message most often assumes greater importance . . . in short, Japanese expresses a series of successive layers of intimacy and distance, formality and informality . . . these levels of language are sifted out into (their) purest forms [and] leave us with two endpoints of a continuum; on the one hand the world of indirection, duty, distance, surfaces; and, on the other, the world of emotion, "true" feeling, intimacy, depth. (Kondo 1987, 243–44)

It is difficult for someone who doesn't speak Japanese to simulate the subjective process that accompanies using status and relational markers that are constantly required in conversation. Honorifics not only impose the proper selection of word endings, but also require vigilance concerning the status implications of discourse rules that regulate the initiation of topics, the permissible length of statements, and the intonational patterns expressing emphasis (Gumperz 1982). Acknowledgment of role differences also involves the modulation of proper levels of emotion indicated through facial and gestural expression, again governing these according to both status and situational factors.[7]

Morsbach (1973) has compiled a documentary of the significance of nonverbal communication among Japanese. This includes the calculated use of silence, an economy of spoken words, and the attention given to both the generation of emotion and the calibration of other people's emotions based on extralinguistic cues or intuition. Both subjective and presentational aspects of the self participate in the planning, execution, and interpretation of facial expressions, gestures, intonational patterns, and the calculated use of silence itself.

Saville-Troike (1985) has discussed how various indexical meanings in Japanese conversations are communicated through the conscious use of nonutterance—or at times the calculated incompletion of sentences. Gender differences in Japanese communication have been addressed by Hall (1984) that implicate women as conveying relatively more emotion in spoken language than men. The nuances of Japanese women's language have been analyzed and categorized by Shibamoto (1985). Although primarily interested in syntactical differences, she also comments on the gender differences in conveying emotion. Women's speech is more "emotional" as demonstrated by the tendency to lengthen vowels and consonants. Women's speech also involves a subtle deviation from the more metronomic, regular enunciation of spoken Japanese. Higher and greater range of pitch are also characteristic of women's speech, along with more contrasted pitch/stress patterns. Finally, there is a tendency to end sentences with higher rising intonation (Shibamoto 1985).

For both males and females, communication of emotion in Japan is considerably more stylized than in Western cultures. Influenced by self-presentational, subjective, and situational factors, the disclosure of emotions is considerably more calibrated, packaged, and formalized. Moreover, the nonverbal and extralinguistic accompaniments of emotion are consciously controlled as a kind of prosodic "music" that accompanies the semantic "lyrics" of communication. Two general rules apply: first, along an emotional spectrum of negative/neutral/positive, Japanese attempt to sustain a slightly positive, phatic emotionality;[8] second, Japanese persons characteristically portray a formal control of speech even in friendly and nonconflictual conversations. The presentation of self in neutral conversations modulates emotionality by conveying a pleasant disposition, facially manifested by a slight, stylized social smile. More conspicuous with women than men, this is common during ordinary discourse. Because it is so frequently present, at times smiling occurs in what would be paradoxical contexts by Western standards. Thus, Japanese adults commonly display a slight smile in discussing things that are quite unpleasant or even sad. Such a signal is not misinterpreted in Japan, although it may be regarded as peculiar by outsiders. Also, laughing occurs not only in regard to mirth or jocularity, but also may be used to cover embarrassment or emotional overload. In those instances, laughing is used as a filler to disguise momentary embarrassment or confusion. Hearty laughing is approved, in fact encouraged, as a positive response to situations or the acknowledgment of another person's attempt to amuse.

Sadness is often displayed either by an impassive expression or merely the withdrawal of cues displaying slight pleasantness. Actual crying, of course, occurs, but interestingly may be signified only by tearing—unaccompanied by facial cues connoting sadness or changes in phonation or breathing—for example, "sniffling" or sobbing. The transmission of aggressive feelings also may be conveyed with an impassive facial expression. Anger, or even the suggestion of slight aggression, will often be signaled through the stilted enunciation of words, or a generally increased assertiveness. While direct verbal markers of aggression may be used, a haughty silence and furrowed eyebrows can be just as effective in communicating anger or potential aggression.

From an extralinguistic standpoint, the general economy of bodily movement and the calibration of gesture and facial expression are prominent in public settings. Also the extralinguistic status indicators, which regulate bowing, deferential speech, and subordination of one conversational partner to the other, tend to suppress and stylize the kinesic manifestations of emotion. What is not understood, however, is that amid this stylization and control, the emotionality of conversations among Japanese is high. Despite formalities, conversational partners are vigilant in detecting the emotional cues that accompany the semantic content of conversation, or are implicit in the situation. As D. Kondo (1987) has observed, "the ideal is an accommodation of the social and emotional selves, where powerful emotionality creates a self which is sensitive to others not by social fiat, but out of caring and love" (Kondo 1987, 246).

Kiefer (1980) has captured the high degree of underlying emotionality in Japanese communication using the term "feeling orientedness."

The traits which I have lumped together under "feeling-orientedness" include a general recognition of the emotional (as opposed to the rational) nature of man: a taste for nuances of subtle expression well documented in Japanese arts and well expressed in the language; a high value placed on anticipating and gratifying the feelings of others with a minimum of direct communication; and the elaborate cultivation of emotionally titillating experiences. (Kiefer 1980, 429)

The capacity for Japanese to transmit and receive feelings is persistently misunderstood by Westerners. The hackneyed observation that the Japanese are "inscrutable" or incapable of being understood is in large part sustained by Westerners' tendencies to attend to the lyrics rather than the nonverbal "music" of Japanese communication. The problem is also one of scale: the indicators for expressing feeling in Japanese involve subtle changes in intonation, facial expression, and gesture. The delicacy of this transmission of feeling and intent may be lost on the average Western conversational partner. Comparatively speaking, the Japanese capacity to focus simultaneously on the emotional concomitants of the relationship and the content of communication emerges as very high when contrasted with average Western persons in comparable situations. Concentrating on these nonverbal factors produces a certain amount of free-floating tension and concerns about making mistakes. Many persons who are bilingual in Japanese and English comment on the tension that accompanies communication in the

Japanese language, because of having to remain alert to so many dimensions of the interactive process, and being nagged by the thought that they may make some kind of error. In contrast, when speaking in English, conversations are less fraught with anxious expectation or the fear of doing something "wrong." Also, it is common for bilingual speakers to mention the comparative easiness of speaking English rather than Japanese in not having to monitor honorific considerations, or to worry about the transmission of emotion (F. Johnson 1984).

Taijin-Kyōfushō and the Breakdown of Self

Taijin-kyōfushō is a relatively common psychiatric syndrome appearing among adolescent and young adult Japanese, mainly affecting males. It is characterized by blushing, apprehensiveness about being with people, fear of eye contact, concerns about sweating and giving off odors. Such diffuse concerns are often accompanied by lowered social performance and fear of failure. The Japanese term itself can be translated as "anthrophobia," literally "a fear of people." As a diagnostic term, *taijin-kyōfushō* has been present in the Japanese psychiatric nomenclature since the 1920s and, in its full-blown state, may qualify as a culture-bound disorder (Yap 1969). Since its original description by Morita (1922), other Japanese clinicians have contributed to its understanding and commented on the evolution of its symptomatology. The severity of this symptom cluster is variable in both young men and women. Milder cases are clinically equivalent to "adjustment reactions" (DSM III-R; American Psychiatric Association 1987) or "neurotic disorders" (as described in World Health Organization ICD-9 1979). Some uncomplicated cases approximate the DSM III-R diagnoses of "avoidant disorders of adolescence," "avoidant personality disorder" (in adults), or "social phobia" (American Psychiatric Association 1987). In the U.S., the latter two conditions occur mainly in males, but are not encountered as frequently as in Japan.

Among Japanese, more severe cases of *taijin-kyōfushō* develop when free-floating ideas of standing out in public become organized into delusional preoccupations and involve disturbances in reality testing (as noted by Kasahara and Sakamoto 1971; Tanaka-Matsumi 1979). Although manifested by diffuse symptoms relating to the body image, *taijin-kyōfushō* is centrally concerned with the social presentation of the self. Patients are apprehensive about encountering other people, fearing that they may be unable to restrain the disclosure of unwarranted intentions or feelings—as exemplified by obsessive concerns about blushing, transmitting odors, or not being able to resist staring at others. In the opposite direction, individuals fear being looked at and being an object of attention. These symptoms converge around the issue of the integrity of self-presentation, particularly in threatening a loss of control over the "inexpressible conscious." In this sense, *taijin-kyōfushō* may be regarded as a threatened breakdown of the presentation of self, and as a distortion of the ordinarily well-monitored balance between outside and inside *(tatemae* and *honne)*. Symptoms of avoiding people and social situations are secondary to more fundamental fears of being unable to navigate in routine encounters because of the fears of leaking information about ordinarily undisclosed topics or feelings.

Another way of looking at *taijin-kyōfushō* is as a generalized weakening in the capacity to sustain role sets. The ability to react creatively and promptly within a series of role sets is strongly emphasized and rehearsed in Japanese socialization throughout the lifespan. Any change or attenuation in this facility generates conspicuous anxiety, along with the wish to flee interpersonal situations. These disorders characteristically occur during late adolescence, when pressures for mastering competent adult roles are paramount. One might speculate that in Japan the apprehension concerning failure to achieve maturity concentrates on the smooth execution of roles. Similar stresses among Western adolescents more commonly produce anxiety and depression concerning the inability to measure up to age-appropriate expectations or appearing sophisticated.

Summary

Before summarizing characteristics associated with the Japanese self, some underlying factors concerning Asian psychology should be mentioned. As noted by Walsh (1984), various Asian psychologies have developed in close association with Buddhism, Hinduism, Taoism, and Sufism. Although conventionally regarded as religions, these systems are more concerned with elaborating philosophical principles of "correct thinking" and existential awareness of "being in the world." Psychologies derived from Eastern systems are viewed by Walsh (1984) as addressing three levels related to "normality" and health: first, in the depiction of psychopathology; second, in the definition of existential subjectivity (including proactive planning); and third, in a concern with "transcendence" or control of various levels of consciousness. Asian psychologies typically have been less concerned with taxonomic descriptions of psychopathology or the hypothetical structuralization of what underlies such conditions. Instead, they have centered on the phenomenological understanding of the immediate, ongoing action process, and on cultivating methods through which the disciplining of consciousness is mastered—as in contemplation, trance, or Yoga. In contrast, Western psychological remedies extol the development of insight in the service of superintending personal action based on an individualistic model of self-control. In a nearly opposite direction, Eastern psychologies emphasize the understanding of human nature through renouncing the egoistic self in favor of acquiring a sense of universal relatedness to other persons and things. Walsh (1984) quotes a Zen Master: "To study Buddhism is to study the self, to study the self is to forget the self, to forget the self is to be one with others" (Walsh 1984, 91).

In contrast, the Western depiction of self is pursued through analytic and deductive modes of thinking, and attempts a materialistic, rational, and logical evaluation of various structures, traits, dynamisms, and functions (F. Johnson 1985). Individualistic, structural properties that operate adaptively and defensively are examined for their power to explain normal and abnormal thought, moods, and behaviors. Abnormal or atypical behaviors are conceptualized as "disorders," representing clusters of maladaptive, inflexible, or disorganized traits accompanying states of exceptional subjective stress or interpersonal discord—technically compiled in various diagnostic manuals.

Several summaries of characteristic Japanese personality traits or versions of selfhood have already been listed (as in Caudill 1973; Yamamoto 1964). In concluding, the present resume will accentuate some of these. In a private communication, Befu (1989) has restated the chronic problem of differentiating "cultural descriptions" from "behavioral descriptions." As stated at the outset, the present psychocultural characterization of the Japanese self is in the form of a *collage,* composed of various pieces of commentary, observation, and scientific investigation. What emerges is an impressionistic image of both the subjective and presentational self within a range of introspective and social activities. As in looking at a collage or painting, the potential meaning of this chapter requires the reader to superimpose operational questions and speculations about actual behaviors in the real world. In this sense this "collage" is inert and incomplete; it can only be invigorated by posing hypothetical questions about actual behavior and looking for comparative clarification. Moreover, such clarifications are not ordinarily measurable in any strict scientific sense and are heavily influenced by the "eye of the beholder."

The following statements represent a condensation of some of the generalizations reviewed in this chapter:

1. *Japanese Self and Asian Psychology.* Both emic and etic portrayals of Japanese self inevitably carry along the historical, philosophic, religious, and folk aspects associated with Asian psychologies and religions—notably Confucianism, Buddhism, and Shinto. This is just as evident as the traditions that underlie Western psychology and have influenced the exposition of personality and self in analytic, logical, and deductive modes that stress ontological individuality, intricate internal structuralization, and a concentration on personal rather than social selfhood.

2. *Japanese Selfhood as Interpersonalism and Interpersonal Awareness.* Numerous commentaries emphasize that individual awareness and self-presentation among Japanese yield to a self that is conceptualized in terms of relational role sets, interactional performances, and social operations detailed in highly circumstantial and specific contexts. This is not the equivalent of saying that Japanese have no sense of individuality, or that they do not make discriminations that recognize specific, ontological existence. However, the fact is that in their subjective lives and self-presentation, the awareness of personal existence and potential action is framed in terms of interpersonal conjunction to others in the context of specific situational contexts.

3. *Japanese Self and the Phenomenon of Group Narcissism.* There is extensive documentary evidence that Japanese children and infants are socialized to transform primary narcissistic entitlement and personal vanity into group pride and collective narcissism in the context of family, school, workplace, and nation. The egocentricity of early childhood is confronted and diminished through the early acquisition of status awareness (specifi-

cally of one's relative insignificance), and modified by learning ritualized humility, modesty, and denial of self-aggrandizement *(enyro)*. However, as a trade-off, an important continuation of narcissistic rights remains in the prerogative for receiving special indulgent attention, preserved in the form of a consciousness concerning *amaeru*. Psychologically, this encourages the projection of needs for entitlement, praise, and pride onto larger social groups rather than the individual. Socialization that diminishes envy, discounts personal possessions, and routinely renounces the prominence of self accompanies this altruistic projection of vanity into larger social configurations. Pride in groups is also manifested in the exclusiveness that many Japanese maintain about the innate superiority of their language, culture, and "race"—chauvinistically expressed in exaggerated versions of *nihonjinron*.

4. *Social Discriminations Affecting Japanese Selfhood.* Although status and gender stipulations are universal in human groups, the ways in which these are finely graded and consciously direct the action process are conspicuous among Japanese. Awareness of deference and subordination are exquisite in comparison to other national groups—particularly in contrast to the pseudoegalitarian ethos flourishing in the United States. Qualitatively, for Japanese this constitutes an awareness of a world of persons within a kind of naturalistic sociology of action possibilities, based upon the discriminating factors of age, gender, position, and relative power.

5. *The Outside/Inside Dialectic of Japanese Selfhood.* Repeated cultural descriptions testify to the high degree of awareness among Japanese concerning the dialectical opposition of internal feeling states and the proactive strategies that operate in the external social environment in which these are transacted. Thus, behavior appears relatively stylized, formal, and, to the naive observer, stereotypic and ritualized. However, this stylization occurs in the context of an internal subjectivity that cautiously monitors outward performance while attempting to intuit other people's hidden subjectivity. The emphasis on phatic and emotional communication often predominates over actual semantic, conversational content. Conversation itself is prone to be indirect, unassertive, and relatively ambiguous when compared to communication in analogous Western situations.

6. *The Connection between Discipline and the Japanese Self.* Dis-

cipline is socialized early in Japanese childhood through the calculated control of the body designed to minimize obtrusiveness and inculcate restraint concerning the exposure of undue emotion. Throughout early development, discipline and perseverance are patiently taught in association with accepting responsibility for orderliness and completion of simple tasks. Precision is also taught in mastering honorific language and complex social-relational terms. Pre- and elementary school instruction continues this socialization process in patiently fostering industriousness, emotional restraint, and internalized control.

7. *The Minimization of Conflict in Japanese Self-Presentation.* At the level of both group and individual behavior, the suppression of conflict is a major issue in Japanese life. The development of internal control over aggression is carefully socialized during infancy and childhood, through both tacit example and a concerted effort to make the child empathic and alert to the sensitivities and feelings of others. Strategies of action are learned that move encounters toward cooperation and harmony whenever possible. The combination of avoidance of conflict and emphasis on the importance of interpersonal connection leads to an ethical focus on the situational, contextual, and circumstantial regulation of conduct—rather than on generalistic, abstract norms outside of the immediate situation. Positively, this concentration on interpersonal behavior potentiates smooth and fair relations between persons, who bring equivalent sensitivity and concern to their encounters. Less desirably, such a situational focus exempts individuals from responsibility or fairness based on more general moral principles that operate irrespective of circumstantial or status factors.

8. *The Secrecy of "Inner Self" in Japanese Subjectivity.* The heightened concentration on presentational aspects of self, and differentiation between "inside" and "outside," is accompanied by an awareness of what is *not* being transacted or directly disclosed to others. The significance of this inner and secret self is testified to by numerous colloquial expressions indicating the presence of suppressed thoughts and feelings that reach consciousness but do not directly emerge in actual performance. The presence of such a secret and unknowable self pervades relationships even with intimates, where hidden intentions and emotions may be intuited but not seen. More invidiously, such secrecy may involve willful deceit, duplicity, and disguise in the

service of furtively achieving goals or controlling the actions of others through subterfuge or denial. In a more neutral manner, ritualized humility or disavowals of egoistic motives may represent denial used in the service of reducing tension, avoiding conflict, and preserving smooth interpersonal relations. Paradoxically, however, the ritual denial of egoistic purposes in Japanese life leads to an elevated sense of a nontransmitted and exquisitely "secret self."

9. *The Regulation of* amaeru. Throughout the lifespan, the prerogative to seek opportunities to depend upon others is consciously retained. While exhibited lavishly during childhood, the capacity to seek dependence and special cherishment is abridged in later life, becoming attainable in more limited circumstances and prohibited in others. Such limitations, however, do not remove the conscious desire to create such conditions—and alternatively to provide nurturance to persons who qualify for such entitlement. Contrasted with Western settings, adults readily make demands for help that would be regarded as gauche or inappropriate in the United States.

Also, quite beyond the satisfaction of instrumental needs, the continuing prerogative to *amaeru* is connected to basic desire for intense affiliation and nurturance, which are ego-syntonic and culturally approved in Japan. Finally, the prerogative for *amaeru* is more conspicuous among men than women. As in most societies, women are socialized to be more responsive in providing rather than receiving instrumental and emotional support.

The following chapter will summarize other cross-cultural information illustrating the presence of culturally reinforced acceptance of motives for dependent affiliation. It will also reintroduce some of the problems present in the dialectic between universalism and relativism.

Notes

1. This phenomenological division of ongoing consciousness is based on the philosophical writings of Husserl (1952) and Heidegger (1927). Later these division of existential awareness were framed by Binswanger (1963) into the realms of *Eigenwelt* ("own world"), *Mitwelt* ("middle world"), and *Umvelt* ("world around"), signifying three subjective frames of reference with their corresponding modes of orienta-

tion and potential for interaction. Metaphorically constituted as "worlds," these are naturalistically experienced as states of consciousness featuring different degrees of awareness, attention to sensory stimuli, and preparation for action. Although capable of conscious, internal direction, shifts in awareness and concentration predominantly follow cues signaled by contact with physical and social objects in the external world.

2. Making judgments about relative differences in consciousness between cultural groups is based upon a combination of participant observation and informant testimonials—methods germane to anthropology. However, a more methodical attempt to compare such phenomena cross-culturally would require using instrument-oriented questionnaires capable of capturing specified semantic and connotational differences between groups of representative subjects from each culture (as in Szalay and Maday 1973).

3. In the Western world, concerns with privacy are conspicuously raised in the confidential relationships between physicians and patients, attorneys and clients, clergy and parishioners, journalists and their sources of information. These constitute special relationships where the disclosure of sensitive or intimate information may take place in a manner that cannot become publicly accessible, and hence is protected by law as "private." An even more delicate confidentiality is present in the psychoanalytic situation, where the therapeutic method emphasizes the spontaneous "free association" of highly secret, ordinarily uncommunicated information disclosing private thoughts, offensive feelings, and embarrassing happenings in both real life and fantasy. Such an access to the "inexpressible conscious" in the process of free association is contradictory to Japanese rules for disclosure and constitutes another explanation for the relative unpopularity of traditional Western psychoanalytic treatment for average Japanese.

4. The psychological distinction between external objects and self objects are hypothesized to begin with the earliest substages of individuation (Mahler 1965, 1972; Lee and Noam 1983; Daniel Stern 1985; Masterson 1985). However, the consolidation of a unified *self object* is theorized to occur only after the establishment of the capacity for representational thought (Piaget 1970). The differentiation of the "secret" nature of personal thought is speculated to occur following this period, and has been linked to the awareness of "disinformation"—that is, the capacity to mislead or lie to others. Some of the developmental consequences of the awareness of lying among young children have been addressed by Peterson, et al. (1983) and Kohut (1966) (summarized in Ford, King, and Hollender 1988).

5. By way of documenting the significance and versatility of the term, Matsumoto tabulates twenty-six colloquial expressions that use the stem word *hara*. In his view the potential for *hara* is universal, but the cultivation of skills to employ it are prominent among Japanese—and primarily accessible to *males*. In response to a question about women's acquisition of *haragei*, his answer is that "it is possible for a woman to grow up to be a

woman of *hara*; but it is not probable that a woman will develop . . . *hara* unless she really tries harder, or the Japanese tradition tries hard to accommodate change" (Matsumoto 1984, 28).

6. These Japanese methods of personal restoration are effective because they respond to cultural patterns that extol compliance, conformity, humility, and social solidarity. *Morita* (A. Kondo 1953) consists of a custodial experience over a period of three to five weeks during which the patient is detached from all but the most mundane activity. Under close supervision, former levels of functioning are slowly resumed in an incremental manner, pausing if there is any recurrence of "nervous" symptomatology (called *shinkeishitsu*). The method requires maintaining a diary and meditating on important life events, which are then reviewed with the *Morita* therapist. *Naikan* (Murase and Johnson 1974) is a more abbreviated method (five to seven days) that enforces a partial separation from the environment along with a guided meditation that focuses on the rediscovery of gratitude and a sense of closeness with significant persons from both the past and present.

A less individualized method involves employees attending group spiritual training, sometimes called "ethics retreats," which take place in remote settings and are sponsored by corporations, banks, or businesses. These function as revivalistic workshops that intend to improve self-discipline, often in the context of becoming better adapted to the institutional policies and directives of specific organizations (Rohlen 1974a; D. Kondo 1987).

All three of these rehabilitative and therapeutic methods involve submission to outside authority, and to an arduous series of tasks voluntarily undertaken in the service of restoring social functioning. These methods studiously avoid the use of rationalistic, analytical reinvestigation of the past—an element that is conspicuous in many Western psychotherapies. Such use of introspection is regarded as counterproductive, or even "sick" by standards based on Asian psychologies (Walsh 1984). Also, the amount of submission to authority and regulation of activity in these Japanese procedures is alien to most Western therapeutic procedures, although present in some religious or "inspirational" group techniques.

7. The public, social-psychological atmosphere in Japan is thick with automatic affirmation cues, formalized "heartiness," and superficial indicators suggesting compliance. To enter a place of business or stroll into a section of a department store commonly sets off a welcoming chorus of melodious, enthusiastic voices. When something is requested (for example, in a restaurant or store), clerks instantaneously punctuate the request by saying, "*Hai!*" (yes). Also, in ordinary conversation, the partner who is listening to the principal speaker emits rhythmic affirmation sounds (called *aizuchi*)—sometimes including "*hai*," but often merely using encouraging noises or soft grunts. These sounds become exaggerated in telephone conversations (in the absence of visual affirmation cues) and are often delivered

in a stacatto fashion—serving to indicate assent or understanding toward what the speaker is saying. Other nonverbal, extralinguistic signals are used to indicate compliance and agreeability. A Japanese secretary may move with swift small steps to announce a guest's arrival to her boss—suggesting the importance of the visitor or occasion. Waitresses respond with speed and dexterity to place beverages and food carefully in front of the diner. Clerks bow and scurry off to find the right-sized shoes or article of clothing. The semiotic metacommunication in each instance is that the person being served or accommodated is important, and that whatever needs are expressed will be swiftly satisfied if at all possible.

8. Phatic communication consists of the nonsemantic dimensions of speech used for the fundamental purpose of revealing or sharing emotion, and for creating an atmosphere of sociability in which the exchange of actual information or "content" may be more agreeable. In all societies, small talk and "bantering" are basically connected to the transmission of emotional understanding of pleasantness and security, rather than content per se. What is significant among Japanese is the high degree of consciousness about this function, and the tendency to be indirect, elliptical, and ambiguous in the actual content of conversation. This ambiguity itself lends to focusing attention on underlying, phatic transmission concerning the monitoring of emotion during various interactions.

PART THREE

Conceptual and Theoretical Dimensions

CHAPTER 9

Modifications of Psychoanalytic Theory by Cross-Cultural Evidence

The purpose of this chapter is to compare anthropological evidence concerning juvenile and adult behavior with some prevailing psychoanalytic theories of human development and personality. Psychoanalytic theories have traditionally emphasized intrapsychic topography and unconscious dynamisms evolving through an unfolding series of relationships to a complex extrapsychic object-world. Until recently, theories based on anthropological descriptions have exclusively proceeded in the opposite direction: heuristically defining the "structures" and functional dynamisms of the social environment in terms of their extrapsychic and collective characteristics. The effects of the cultural environment on individual persons are conceptualized as socializing processes operating through the agency of particular persons toward infants and children. The focus of this chapter's discussion will center on the reported behaviors of parents and other exemplars involved in the socialization and training of infants and children in several Asian societies. Using mainly Japanese materials, the author will make some general observations and raise questions concerning the relationship between psychoanalytic and anthropological theories.

Concerning psychoanalytic theory, it should be emphasized that psychoanalysis is based on a number of theories that attempt to explain human development and function (Wallerstein 1987). Often viewed as dogmatic, psychoanalysis from within exhibits lively debate, self-criticism, and controversy concerning aspects of both theory and practice. The field continues to undergo progressive changes based on clinical and experimental observations.

Although controversy exists about many aspects of metapsychological theory, traditional practice is based upon some generally accepted axioms. Probably the most prominent of these is the tripartite, structural view of intrapsychic personality (id, ego, and superego) dynamically activated by largely unconscious mechanisms. These three structural domains are psychodynamically interrelated and respond to the extrapsychic world through instinctive drive systems operating to achieve pleasure, obtain relief of tension, and seek a level of psychological homeostasis. The attachment to objects, including the object of self, is attributed to the effects of a primary libidinal drive. Sexual and aggressive drives are heuristically explained as being connected to the outside world through psychic representations called *internal objects*. Causal-motivational explanations of behavior are formulated as attempts to reach intrapsychic equilibrium amid conflicts emanating between and among ego, id, and superego, mediated through the unconscious mechanisms of defense. Such explanations also take into account conscious adaptations to reality and execution of performance. Thus, human behavior is seen as reflecting the consequences of intrinsic —that is, structurally originated—conflicts that seek resolutions at both intrapsychic and extrapsychic levels. Also, psychoanalysis has traditionally portrayed an antagonistic relationship between the innate drives and the outside real world.

Such axioms concerning psychoanalytic theory are deceptively straightforward; however, their ramifications are complex. For example, the relationship of extrapsychic, "real-world" objects to internal need satisfaction is at once highly technical and hypothetical. These interconnections are examined through constructs involving processes of "incorporation," "introjection," "identification," and "imitation." Seen in this way, the taking in of cultural ingredients (specific languages, socialization rituals, beliefs, and ideologies) occurs as a fusion between internal and external systems. The term for such a combination in psychoanalytic theory is the partial or complete *internal object*, displaying simultaneously intrapsychic and extrapsychic characteristics. Although considerably more complex in its intrapsychic formulations, the process for the fusion of external and internal environments parallels the Piagetian dialectical model of assimilation and accommodation (Piaget 1970).

Generally, within psychoanalysis there is a distinction made between the need for an open-ended approach to metapsychological theory, and a more dogmatic adherence to empirically established and time-tested principles of actual treatment. Treatment is founded on a clinical method that has evolved over nearly a century of practice. Although a distinction can be made between the domains of "theory" and "practice," metapsychological principles (as summarized in the preceding paragraph) are continually used to explain and formulate the significance of actual treatment encounters.[1]

Psychoanalytic Theory, Universalism, and the "Japanese Problem"

As mentioned in the introduction, some of the tension between psychoanalysis and anthropology has historical roots partly centering on the issue of universalism versus particularism (or cultural relativism). Currently, polemical positions are not given much credit—for example, psychoanalysts who feel that the consequences of cultural variability are trite, or anthropologists who allege that the outstanding differences observed among various cultures makes any kind of universal structuralization unlikely. However, even with some accommodation, serious problems remain. Some of these revolve around the factors of *depth, timing,* and *significance.*

Questions concerning *depth* inquire about the putative levels at which cultural diversity differentially affects performance. For example, do specialized cultural rules affect "deep structures" in a permanent or protracted manner, or do they merely account for superficial differences—analogous to the range and number of words used for classifying color in different cultures?

Questions of *timing* are raised to inquire into chronological factors associated with the infant's or child's readiness to be influenced by the impact of the cultural environment. For example, what are the age ranges and phasic periods during which the transmission of various kinds of cultural specificity may effectively take place?

Questions of *significance* constitute the broadest category and inquire into the specialized meanings and consequences that cultural variables impose on both behaviors and subjective awareness in particular societies. For example, do the culturally diverse symbolisms concerning the incest barrier constitute *categorical* differences, or merely superficial nuances in the naming or labeling of universal tendencies? Manifest differences in depth, timing, and meaning are apparent in cross-cultural studies regarding parent and kin configurations, weaning, sleeping arrangements, toilet training, rules for bodily contact, patterns of vocalization, regulation of discourse, and so forth. Attempts to interpret such diversity readily expose the tension between universalism and relativism. Some recent efforts to bridge this controversy have been listed by Gehrie (1978), summarizing the theoretical contributions of Hartmann (1958 [1939]) and Hartmann, Kris, and Loewenstein (1951). In an earlier reflection, Caudill (1972) cited Hartmann's depiction of "exogenous" cultural factors in their effects on conflict-free executive ego in the developing child.

Hartmann (1958) speculated on the significance of culture, which he parsimoniously termed the "average expectable environment." He described this environment as being impressed on the individual through ordinary, standardized, and predictable stimulations—that is to say, stimulations that were "average" or modal within any given culture. He also saw the child being influenced by capricious and unexpected events that were not culture-specific, but germane to all human group living. These included the ubiquitous stresses and conflicts that produce intrapsychic disturbance: separations, interpersonal strife, losses, lifespan crises, severe physical impairment, or accident.

As a psychoanalytically trained anthropologist, Caudill (1962b) saw Hartmann's (1958) position as addressing the issue of universalism versus particularism. As quoted in the introduction, Caudill specified the "average expectable environment" as influencing the forms of both biologically determined patterning and phenotypically learned performance. He also accentuated the differentiations in development that influenced the manner in which culture channeled human behavior according to maturational phases. Caudill's response to the implicit question raised by Hartmann's speculations about culture critically challenged the basically structural, intrapsychic formulations in traditional psychoanalytic theory.

Writing from a structuralist position, Freud was initially concerned with generating a deductive metapsychology based on clinical observations, along with formulations derived from symbolizations in dreams, myth, and literature. He was especially interested in defining the nature of universal structures that underlay manifest human behavior and would ultimately constitute a "scientific psychology." These hypothetical structures are parallel to, but more complicated than, the deep structures hypothesized by Chomsky and his associates in regard to the innate basis for generative grammar formulated some sixty years later (DeGeorge and DeGeorge 1972). The parallel is that deep language structures putatively consist of irresistible universals present in each intact infant, furnishing the innate potentiality for the comprehension and expression of spoken language. Thus, the capacity for language develops irresistibly and spontaneously, given ordinary opportunity for growth, socialization, and maturation. However, the particular characteristics of various spoken languages (selection of phonemes, morphemes, syntax, and grammars) are highly plastic, and channeled by culture, socialization practices, discourse rules, and status and gender differentiations. Although more complex than language acquisition and speech competence, the acquisition of behavioral competence raises the same question. How much of human interaction is governed by universal structures that potentiate and channel the acquisition of standard behavioral repertories? This also raises the question of how and when cultural conventions, norms, belief systems, formulae for personal interactions, and display rules are shaped through both deep and superficial structures.[2]

As cited in Tobin (1982), LeVine (1973b) updated the universal/relative controversy some twenty-five years following Caudill:

I have long argued that cross-cultural evidence will eventually pose a fundamental challenge that psychoanalytic theorists must face, and that in dealing with it they must revise their conceptions of what is normal, necessary, and adaptive in the psychic development, structure and functioning of humans. This is what I call "the Japanese problem." (LeVine in Tobin 1982, 2)

As mentioned in the introduction, in using the term "the Japanese problem," LeVine was simultaneously concrete and metaphorical. Stated concretely, "the Japanese problem" consists of attempts to account for the manifest differences in socialization, normative standards, interaction rules, and the quality of subjective awareness among Japanese when compared to other cultural groups. Metaphorically, the "Japanese problem" signifies a more general challenge to psychoanalytic universalism through behavioral and subjective evidence testifying to diversity in content, timing, and significance among various human groups.

Japanese culture presents an optimal context for examining universals and particulars addressing this question. By all accounts Japan is a complex, postindustrial society with high levels of literacy, educational attainment, technological sophistication, and economic development. Moreover these developments have unfolded during the relatively short period of 120 years, and reflect coordinated national planning and growth (see chapters 3 and 4). However, despite these remarkable innovations, there has been relatively slow change in cultural norms, beliefs, and interaction rules that govern gender distinctions and childrearing and regulate patterns of social relationships, communication, and the presentation of self.[3] Also, the particulars of Japanese culture have been the subject of extensive scholarly and popular commentary during the past forty years, reflecting the contributions of both outside and indigenous specialists.

Cross-Cultural Studies of Child Development

The history of the cross-cultural and cross-national study of personality has been summarized by Tapp (1981). The "culture and personality school," influential during the 1940s and 1950s, used a psychoanalytic developmental model, searching for causal connections between early socialization practices and culturally distinctive adult behaviors variously defined as "modal personality," "configurational personality," or "national character." This emphasis waned, partly due to methodological difficulties, and to a wave of criticism concerning unacceptable, stereotypic generalizations. Also, by the 1950s, evidence from experimentally controlled, fine-grained studies of early development seriously questioned some of the pat assumptions of earlier psychoanalytic theory. As noted by Tapp (1981), cross-cultural studies during the 1950s and 1960s became more statistically oriented, used directly translated Western instruments, and concentrated on social-psychological constructs comparatively examined as a spectrum of "personality traits." During the 1970s, cross-cultural investigation began to use instruments that were differentially sensitive to cultural and language factors.

Tapp (1981) cites the landmark influence of a series of critical reviews (Hsu 1961; Kaplan 1961; Child 1968; Milton Singer 1961; DeVos and Hippler 1969) that redirected workers to more sophisticated field methods. These accentuated the need for fastidious attention to linguistic and conceptual translation, consideration of response bias, comparability of sampling, and distinctions between group- versus individually derived data.

In two contributions, LeVine (1970, 1973a) attempted to rehabilitate "culture and personality" as a legitimate area within cross-cultural studies. He recommended the intensive study of individual informants based on combined psychoanalytic, ethnographic, ecologic, and developmental approaches. His strategy was premised on "an unequivocal mandate from the clinical practitioners of psychoanalysis, but not at the loss of attention to such processes as perception, cognition, learning and memory" (LeVine 1970, 213). His psychoanalytic approach was also concerned with accounting for the subjectivity of the ethnographer through looking at both the conscious and unconscious biases of the observer (also promoted by Devereux 1969). LeVine reintroduced the legitimacy of making tentative causal and etiological connections in explaining aspects of cross-cultural diversity, and emphasized the need for longitudinal studies in order to reexamine the stability of findings and interpretations over time.

The Blending of Relativism and Universalism

A number of attempts to define universal needs and functional systems have been composed by a series of psychologists and anthropologists (as in Kluckhohn 1950; Becker 1962; Lonner 1981). Lonner has systematically summarized approaches to the conception and definition of universals from a number of disciplines. An early anthropological model developed by Malinowski (1944) listed "basic needs" along with their concomitant cultural responses. A more complex catalog was composed by Murdoch (1945, 1949). Most well known, the Human Relations Area Files (HRAF) has functioned as a repository of detailed information derived from reports of over two hundred societies distributed among seven hundred categories of specific needs and functional activities. A later compendium, The Ethnographic Atlas (Murdoch, et al. 1962), used a series of behavioral codes to examine over one thousand social groups, facilitating comparative study on a large number of independently investigated societies. However, as mentioned by

Munroe and Munroe (1975), the potential of such vast banks of information is often compromised by the problems of incomparable or inaccurate data, as well as the intrinsic restrictions of the original field work itself. Data banks of this sort also represent investigations taking place over a period of years, but reporting on only one time frame of investigation. Hence, these do not address the question of variability over time (as illustrated by Geertz 1990).

In extending the conventional division between biologically standardized "nature" and culturally differentiated "nurture," LeVine (1973a) offered his description of contrasts between personality genotype and phenotype. He described the *personality genotype* as

a set of enduring individual behavioral dispositions that may or may not find socially acceptable expression in the customary (or institutionalized) behavioral population. Its major characteristics are early acquisition, resistance to elimination and subsequent experience; incapacity for inhibition, generalization and other transformations under the impact of experiential pressures. (1973a, 116)

In contrast he saw the *personality phenotype* as the

observable regularities of behavior characterizing an adult functioning in a variety of settings comprising his environment. [This] . . . includes his patterns of performance and social roles in formal and informal settings, in interaction and alone, in coercive and free-choice situations, under stressful and relaxed conditions, in verbalization and actual behavior. It includes his conscious attitudes and values, skills, competence and knowledge, and his preferences in tastes in recreational and hedonistic activities. (1973a, 122)

Freedman (1968, 1970) added ethological comparisons to developmental and cross-cultural information in an attempt to tease out possible biological universals underlying human performance. Leach (1972) has discussed certain nonverbal markers that are universally associated with human behavior. Irrespective of cultural specificity, these are seen as falling into five main categories: 1) markers of *interpersonal domination* (those connected to status hierarchy, including power relationships based on superior physical size or social role); 2) markers of *gender discrimination and social age* (those categories of gender and age differentiations affecting anticipatory responses); 3) markers associated with the distinction between *life and death* (those qualities distinguishing animate from inanimate objects on both a real and a symbolical basis); 4) markers associated with *food choice* (those factors associated with edible versus inedible, or even poisonous objects); and, finally, 5) markers connected to *threat or vulnerability* (based on anticipation of real or imagined danger from other persons or things).

Two other areas of biologically based universal behavior have been clarified in the past twenty years: those that verify a fixed biologic substrate regarding the universality of *basic emotions* (Ekman, Sorenson, and Friesen 1969; Izard 1971, 1977; and Ekman 1984) and for *color perception* (Berlin and Kay 1969). The validation of these universal patterns of recognition in no way extinguishes the rich diversity demonstrated in the highly differentiated naming and significance of color tones among various cultural groups. Nor do these conclusions challenge the widely differential meanings and "display rules" (Ekman 1984) connected to the expression of emotion in various societies (also discussed by Robert Levy 1984).

Universals in Language and Evaluative Behavioral Terms

Building on the work of Lenneberg (1967), both Chomsky (1965) and Philip Dale (1972) have considered language to be both species-specific and species-uniform. This "innateness hypothesis" has been tested in studies regarding the acquisition of language and the characteristics of adult speech examined both monolingually and across various languages and cultures. Despite high variability in the use of particular phonemes, morphemes, grammar, and sociolinguistic practices, evidence of deep structures has been advanced as a biologically based capacity underlying the organization of all spoken languages. Formats for the operations of language exist despite variations in word order, sentence construction, or the cultural specialization that channels and regulates ordinary discourse. Acknowledgment of a basis for universal deep structures does not invalidate the conclusion of linguistic relativists who have asserted that immersion in particular languages induces a distinctive world view, and accounts for differences in subjective perception and interpretation of reality, based partly on the intrinsic features of languages themselves.

In another specified context, Geoffrey White (1980) has examined cross-cultural evidence for universal factors involving the attribution of personal and temperamental characteristics, based on an analysis of naturalistic behavioral categories examined in several societies. His findings reinforce the frequently cited conclusions of

Osgood, May, and Myron (1975), whose statistical examination of a number of cultural groups showed the consistent emergence of three factors concerning the significance of affective meaning generated in spontaneous conversations. Using semantic differential techniques, Osgood (1964) found the recurrent appearance of a factor of *evaluation* (a good/bad distinction), a factor of *potency* (a strong/weak dichotomy), and a factor of *activity* (a hierarchy of fast/slow). Taken together, these three accounted for a disproportionate amount of variance in the analysis of affective meaning when examining a number of culture and language communities.

Universals in Childrearing

Closer to the central issue of this book, lists of universals regarding childrearing have been composed. One by LeVine (1977) includes the following as universal goals of parents vis-à-vis their children: 1) the physical survival and health of the child, including the normal development of reproductive capacity during puberty; 2) the development of a behavioral capacity for economic self-maintenance in maturity; 3) the development of capacities for discriminating cultural values regarding morality, prestige, wealth, religious piety, intellectual achievement, personal satisfaction, and self-realization—symbolically elaborated in culturally distinctive beliefs, norms, and ideologies (LeVine 1977, 20).

Melford Spiro (1978) has looked at cross-cultural regularities in family systems seen as responses to what he terms "irreducible biological characteristics of human existence." Among these he lists 1) bisexual human reproduction effected through sexual intercourse; 2) the helplessness of the human neonate in its protracted physical and emotional dependence; 3) the requirement that caretakers attend to dependency, security, and educational needs commensurate with cultural tradition; 4) the presence of relatively permanent pair bonding; 5) the strength of the child's prepotent dependency needs, connected both to affection and security; and 6) the presence of mixtures of gratification and frustration in the course of early human development.

Against this brief survey of universal functions, some psychocultural aspects of Japanese childrearing and personality will be reviewed.

Japanese Childrearing, Personality Development, and Psychoanalytic Theory

One of the purposes of this book has been to look at the impact that Japanese childrearing practices produce on the subjectivity and behavior of individual culture bearers. The following section will examine aspects of Japanese socialization alongside traditional psychoanalytic theories of development. This involves looking at what influence the "average expectable environment" of Japan may have on the channeling of intrapsychic structures and dynamisms as well as overt behavior. The basic question is an old one: to what extent are theories in psychoanalysis based partly on the "expectable environment" of those societies connected with its institutional and intellectual history—notably, Western Europe and North and South America? This section will raise questions concerning this by examining Japanese culture and childrearing—in an attempt to identify the appearance of dynamic processes (for example, separation-individuation) or structures (for example, ego ideal and superego) in light of traditional Western psychoanalytic metapsychology. Such questions can only be partially addressed here in terms of logic and deduction. Definitive answers will require careful attention to clinical psychoanalytic and developmental studies of Japanese adults and children, plus empirical studies using depth interviewing and observations of normal infants, children, and adults in Japanese society.

Japanese Culture and Psychoanalytic Drive Theory

Some conceptual limitations of psychoanalytic drive theories have already been mentioned. First, reflecting the turn-of-the-century generalizations, drives were defined as innate, irrepressible, and relatively unmodifiable biological substrates. These forces were held to activate behaviors connected to *survival* (through ego instincts), to *objects* (through an evolving expression of libidinal instincts), and *dynamic interaction* within a personal and impersonal world (through the aggressive instincts). Within the biological sciences the term "instinct" (or "innate drive") has been abandoned—except in nostalgic or literary allusions. Even the successor term "fixed action pattern" has been highly qualified because of evidence that degrees of modifiability persist in behavioral patterns present in lower species, let alone in humans.

Second, the dual (really triple) theory of psychoanalytic drives does not sufficiently address, let alone explain, the phenomenological complexity of human cognition, emotion, and social behavior. Such a reductionistic system does not seem sufficiently comprehensive or adequate to account for the diversity of human motivations and performances.

Third, of the three basic drive systems, only *libido* has been given extensive treatment in its developmental, clinical, and existential aspects. Although Freud vacillated in his theorizations about other drives, libido retained its central significance as an ascendant and primary "instinct." In developmental terms, libido was depicted as the primary drive evolving through oral, anal, and phallic stages preceding the attainment of genital primacy. Such a generalistic definition has elicited outside criticisms of becoming a vague and inordinate "pansexualism" (Jung 1956 [1912]; Mandler 1963).[4]

The narrowness of the dual instinct theory will be confronted in a concluding chapter. However, even taken as it is, cross-cultural evidence from Japanese society adds to deductive arguments by Adler, Horney, Fairbairn, Sullivan, and Bowlby for the primary significance of an additional elementary drive centering on a desexualized attachment, affiliation, and interpersonal connection. Such a drive for indulgent dependency is vividly apparent at birth, but is also identifiable in modified forms observable throughout the lifespan (as discussed in chapters 6 and 7). Against this background, the Japanese cultural documentary strongly emphasizes the central significance of *amae,* and constitutes an experientially based argument for a nonlibidinous, primary drive closely connected to rudimentary systems having the goal of "individual" rather than "racial" survival. Other comprehensive theories of development (summarized by Maccoby and Masters 1970) routinely implicate the outstanding evidence of needs for affiliation, nurturance, and security operating alone or in concert with other drives or dispositions, described in systematic formulations concerning reciprocal needs and behavioral objectives.

The Japanese and the System Unconscious

In regard to the ordinary Japanese awareness of inner and partly hidden sources of motivation, there are both similarities and contrasts to Western psychoanalytic explanations of patterned unconscious and preconscious systems. As discussed by Doi (1990a), Rohlen (1974b), Wagatsuma (1983b), Smith (1983), and Hisa Kumagai (1988), the highly generalized Japanese concept of *ki* is used to designate the consciousness of the individual's emotions and desires—something of his/her subjective flow, combining both feelings and intentions. *Ki* is a complex term that globally stands for a reflection of the personal psychic interior composed of what can be classified as conscious, preconscious, and (some) unconscious elements (see chapter 8). Within a broad, emic definition of *ki*, many different feelings, thoughts, intentions, and impulses operate to affect subjective consciousness and overt behavior in ways that are only partly under conscious, executive control. These elements include illogical and irrational thoughts, associations, feelings, and motives that may conflict with the compunctions of social reality and the normative order. However, unlike in psychoanalytic theory, where primary and secondary processes are depicted as stratified levels of mental functioning, the Japanese visualize this irrationality as originating *outside* of the self—something that is, as it were, imposed on the self or only temporarily residing within the individual. According to Wagatsuma (1983b), the actual "performing self" may be strengthened or trained in such a way as to exert increased mastery and control over the intrusion of these incoherent elements. This may be achieved through a variety of experiences or procedures—including ordinary socialization and discipline, religious practices, Zen Buddhism, or (more rarely) psychotherapy. As witnessed in literature and folklore, mastery and discipline may also be gradually achieved through the lessons of personal experience, including misfortune.

Perhaps indirectly influenced by Judeo-Christian theology, psychoanalysis portrays human nature as a mixture of morally "good" and "bad" elements, but with an emphasis on the blemished nature of humankind. Freudian metapsychology depicts the individual as primarily motivated by strongly selfish, aggressive, and hedonistic drives. These drives are either oblivious to or antagonistic toward collective society, and are only reluctantly tamed. In the reverse direction, Japanese theories of human nature (Pelzel 1970; Lebra 1976; Wagatsuma 1983b) report that human nature is basically good, and if unimpeded seeks to achieve harmonious relations with other persons, and reach a comfortable accommodation to nature. Although not expounded in a syllogistic philosophical manner, moral "badness" in human beings is seen as representing either momentary imbalances (for example, omissions of basic goodness) or as due to the effects of poorly defined, outside forces that pervert ongoing human interaction. As Lebra (1976), Wagatsuma (1983a), and Doi (1973a, 1986) explain, the common, colloquial metaphor used to explain both misbehavior and illness colloquially is the word "bug" or "worm" (mushi). Instead of implicating the child's naughty intentions, the mushi is metaphorically held accountable for unwanted, ego-dystonic thoughts or feelings. Using similar reasoning, if persons are notoriously or persistently "bad," they may then be considered so wretched and odious as not to be truly human and called hito de nashi, as explained in Wagatsuma (1983a).

Other emic terms that define internal and partly unconscious forces have been summarized in earlier chapters. Discussed in chapter 8 as hara ("belly," "gut," or stomach) and kokoro ("heart" or "essence"), these constitute reservoirs of energy that in a causal-motivational manner are alleged to produce their effects on both private consciousness and public performance.

Unconscious Aggressive Drives. Japanese cultural sensitivity concerning the suppression of aggression and the channeling of assertiveness have already been mentioned. These attitudes implicate the surfacing of overtly aggressive behaviors as unpleasant and ego-dystonic, betraying elements that are foreign to the idealized "inner self."

Aggression may be defined as the application of force or hostility toward others, and involves both real and threatened physical domination or punishment. Assertiveness, in contrast, implies verbal (i.e., symbolically mediated) domination, which may or may not be accompanied by physical aggression. Normatively, aggression is accepted in Japan as a natural, although regrettable, occurrence in both individual and group behavior. Among Japanese, the awareness of aggression either as a latent force or as actually appearing in real-life enactments is intimately associated with the need for *control*. In Japan, such control optimally takes the form of suppressing or disguising aggression in favor of more graduated and subtle strategies designed to achieve one's objectives, without generating hostility or causing violence. Because of this, strategies that are both passive and aggressive are prominent in Japanese interaction when disagreement or displeasure threatens to arise.

Moreover, assertiveness is ordinarily regulated through the explicit recognition of differential statuses, and embedded in protocols governing honorific speech and the fastidious consciousness concerning superior/inferior social hierarchy. The emphasis on sustaining an atmosphere of harmony among people is surrounded by norms that disguise or deny the wish to unleash power or mobilize hostility. For example, the cultural norms for ritualized humility and politeness *(enryo)* act to remove and neutralize the possibility of overt aggression. Also, the careful accommodation to age, gender, and positional statuses operates to mute aggression, through predicating that individuals have only limited power to apply force or influence situations according to their social positions. Hence, aggressive strategies or responses are suppressed in recognition of the inevitability of following the dictates of the hierarchical social order.

Even when rationalized, violence toward others must be justified as the last possible alternative when grievance is severe and other resolutions have proved unworkable. Normatively, violence toward the young, weak, or unprotected is particularly offensive, while a controlled counteraggression—for example, toward rioting students or violent persons—is permitted. Violence in the form of military aggression in Japan—as everywhere else—is justified in terms of defense against outside aggressors, compelling needs for expansion, or revenge for past injuries or national humiliation. Forms of rationalized violence are also symbolically woven into a romanticization of the *samurai,* or former warrior class. The conspicuous aggressiveness of *samurai* is idealized as being unleashed in the protection of their patrons, or for other well-intentioned purposes.

As mentioned previously, aggression is carefully suppressed through socialization procedures that strongly deter and divert its expression (Nakakuki 1984; Takahashi 1984). Also, as DeVos (1960, 1978) has illuminated, aggression may be dealt with through rationalization and projection onto others. It may also be extinguished through suppression and denial—always with the purpose of maintaining the appearance of harmony and peacefulness. Fostering these same defense mechanisms, Japanese children are socialized to be personally unaggressive more through tactics of distraction and shaming than through direct counteraggression from parents or teachers. Some counteraggression does occur, but the most favored strategy is to make children aware of the pain and humiliation caused by their behavior (Catherine Lewis 1989; DeVos 1960).

Unconscious Sexual Motivations. Some of the ways in which sexuality is dealt with behaviorally and culturally by the Japanese have been described in previous chapters. Basically, motives for sexual activity are regarded as positive and natural inclinations that strive for expression and satisfaction. Optimally, such satisfactions are encountered as simple pleasures, preferably sought in circumstances that do not compromise the dignity and integrity of others. As in most societies, sexuality is dealt with ambivalently by Japanese. Public displays of affection between courting or married persons are strongly prohibited. However, physical touching, overt flirtation, and provocative behavior are approved of in the bars or drinking places. While open expressions of tenderness between husbands and wives are strongly contraindicated, nudity in the context of bathing or dressing is regarded as unremarkable. Given the sleeping arrangements, the potential exposure to the primal scene is higher than in societies where parents and children sleep more privately.

As in Judeo-Christian and Islamic societies, homosexuality is a complex issue in Japan. Because of the severe difference in socialization, the inclination toward same-sex relations is strongly stimulated and results in long-standing friendships among both men and women. Such intimate relationships are commended, although only on a platonic and nonsexual basis. Relationships that actually involve physical contact and passion are regarded as deviant for both sexes. Persons who are homosexual are generally extremely cautious about keeping this part of their life secret. As Garrick (1991, personal communication) has noted, if homosexual behavior is discovered or briefly publicized, family and friends act as if nothing is amiss and essentially ignore the behavior. As she says,

The model is: conformity to heterosexual norms is expected and enforced; homosexual behavior is secretive; exposed homosexual behavior is strongly disapproved and ignored; blatant homosexuality meets with active avoidance and social ostracism. (Garrick 1991)

Similarly, attitudes about extramarital affairs parallel Western experiences. Since the shift to a nuclear family structure, modern wives expect fidelity and are likely to demand this. However, because there is compelling social pressure to maintain an intact marriage "for the children," and few wives can remain self-sufficient in a divorced status, some wives may reluctantly accept philandering out of necessity.

In regard to other aspects of sexuality, masturbation does not generate much commentary, presumably being considered to be an insignificant, private act. Prohibitions against sexuality—including autosexuality—are not publicized as part of a theological or folk system regarding reprehensible behaviors. Because of this, it would be difficult to hypothesize that sexual drives or "instincts" would ever be given the central significance among Japanese imputed in Western psychoanalytic theory, based on either manifest or latent features of Japanese life. Instead, as mentioned in prior chapters, the dominant and basic motive for object relations is connected to amae: that is, through an affiliation stressing indulgent dependency and social connectedness throughout the lifespan.

From a comparative, anthropological standpoint one might conclude that the heavy significance given to sexuality in psychoanalytic theory can be partly attributed to a Western theological emphasis about carnal desires, embedded in biblical and dogmatic renditions concerning the inflated significance of shame and guilt associated with some manifestations of sexuality (onanism, fornication, adultery, nudity, and so forth). If psychoanalytic theory had originated in Japan, the unconscious operations of suppressed aggression or the terrifying fears of separating from others plausibly might have been accorded the highest significance. This speculation does not suggest that unconscious sexual strivings would not be accorded a place in the submerged motivations of Japanese, but not as an undercurrent constituting an exclusive hypothesis for the creation of object relations in general. In fact, as Hsu (1971a) has commented, the high degree of sexualization of the exclusive marital unit in Western societies probably has its cultural roots in monotheism and individualism.

Monotheism stresses the nonpluralistic relationships between individuals and their divine creator. Individualism similarly tends to emphasize the personal over the familial bonding between marital partners. Combining with traditions of courtly love and romantic selection of spouses, such cultural trends are connected to heightening the exclusiveness of married individuals. Because of this, the normal and gradual development of independency by children is associated with awareness of sexual rejection accompanying the renunciation of juvenile dependency. This is in marked contrast to Japan, where the emotional aspects of a sexual relationship between parents is culturally obscured, and the quality of continuing, available dependency (amae) is not so abruptly or completely renounced.

Japanese Childrearing and
Separation/Individuation

Ethnographic information about Japanese childrearing demonstrates a close and continuing physical attachment between mothers and infants, a nonscheduled feeding routine and continued contact during various times of the day, evening, and nighttime. The physical architecture as well as the emotional nature of close interpersonal nexus extends this intimacy, including the customs of sleeping and bathing together. Japan is characterized by the protracted attachment of infants and mothers in the context of a highly developed postindustrial society. Speculations concerning the implications of these factors for the development of internal representations and the characteristics of cognitive functioning will be discussed later. However, the evidence for temporal protraction of an intimate connection between mothers and children is prominent in Japanese childrearing compared to modal North American practices. This documents that the infant-mother relationship is both more intense and more persistent; it also suggests that both physical and psychological separation take place more gradually and less completely.

Mahler's substage of differentiation depends critically on the perceptual maturation of the infant and is associated with increasing discrimination of sensory awareness, and the integration of visual, spatial, auditory, and temporal orientations. This progressively includes the recognition of favored objects, the appearance of stranger anxiety, and other features chronologized by experimental investigations in a number of different cultures. Also, early in this period, an exploratory hunger becomes more pronounced, presumably representing drives that seek adaptive and executive ego expression.

The most obvious speculation to raise concerning comparative degrees of individuation in Japan is that, given the protracted contact between infant and mother, psychological individuation develops more slowly and to a less conspicuous degree than in most Western European and nonethnic American children. The child is raised in an atmosphere of extended physical and psychological closeness, which modifies the sense of sharp individuation. At the same time, this close association is reinforced by cultural values that conceptualize individuals in relation to a hierarchically arranged family and social system (Nakane 1970; Lebra 1976). In the face of relatively little direct opposition to the youngster's wishes, a higher degree of primary narcissism ("entitlement," "omnipotence") is sustained in the closeness to mother and the relatively unresisted expression of pregenital needs. However, as in all societies, primary narcissism is modified during the first thirty months of life by both direct and tacit pressures to suppress whining, crying, and other exhibitions of strong emotions and demandingness. In terms of individuation, this might suggest that diminished direct frustration and confrontations with the parents would tend to retard the progression and extent of individuation. Also, if the mother continues to be nurturant and seemingly permissive, individuation would not be as strongly stimulated by the development of ambivalent recognition of the "bad mother" through the experience of a series of frustrations, nongratifications, and confrontations that are more common in Western childrearing practices. Moreover, the fact that the child is less physically isolated would tend to diminish a sense of individuation.

According to Mahler, the substage of "practicing" begins at about seven to ten months and lasts until fifteen to sixteen months of age. Practicing is characterized first by the infant's crawling, climbing, and righting itself, with a second substage demonstrated by independent, unaided standing. In Mahler's view, this period is accompanied by parallel psychological maturation, which allows ambulation away from and returning to security contacts, accompanied by the progressive utilization of ego drives connected to curiosity and exploration.

Comparative data regarding the median ages for crawling, standing, toddling, and walking between youngsters in Japan and the United States do not reveal statistically significant differences. The assumption is that the biological capabilities of these two groups of children are essentially equivalent. Unfortunately, comparable cross-cultural studies specifically examining practicing behaviors are not available. Pavenstedt's (1965) psychoanalytic observations in five Japanese homes extended into the second year of life. However, her focus was not systematically involved with a study of practicing. She did, however, comment on distinctive aspects of separation-individuation.

We saw, then, children who, by and large, were happy and peaceful, seldom frustrated, practically never exposed to anger, seldom without an adult "in devoted attendance." Almost nothing was done to encourage independence of a self care variety, although opportunities for choice in the expression of will, autonomy if you like, were not infrequent. They were offered few avenues for the displacement of aggressive, libidinal drives—there was little opportunity to hit and pound, to water play, no chance to play with sand, mud or paints. Motor activity, which may be an avenue of discharge, was present but nowhere near to the degree that is indulged in our culture. . . . Separation anxiety was prominent.

What seemed to me least in evidence was Margaret Mahler's separation-individuation phase. I wondered whether in this culture, where for generations the importance of the family superseded the importance of the individual, an individual ever reaches the degree of differentiation that is desirable in Western culture. This, too, may have a bearing on the expression of aggression. (Pavenstedt 1965, 425)

By inference, Pavenstedt's comments suggest that during both early and later childhood, practicing behaviors are less encouraged, and that the "refueling experience" is more constant and present as a continuous aspect of *amae* behavior.

Mahler's next substage of *rapprochement* appears between sixteen and twenty-five months. It is signaled by the mastery of independent locomotion and is psychologically accompanied by heightened anxiety concerning the mother's presence and accessibility. Mahler deduces that the child now becomes "more and more aware, and makes greater and greater use of his awareness of physical separateness." She also describes that, as a consequence of this awareness, the child becomes more manifestly frustrated.

Regrettably, the systematic, longitudinal research reported by Caudill and Weinstein (1969) and Caudill and Schooler (1973) did not specifically examine subjects during the subphases of practicing and rapprochement. Their reports of Japanese and American youngsters at two and one-half years reflect behavior toward the end of the rapprochement stage. In terms of activity, differences were found between Japanese and American mothers as well as the infants. They reported the activity level of the American mothers as higher, both in vocal and physical interventions. Japanese children were reported to be less active at this age compared to their American counterparts, although not at a statistically significant level.

Using the concept of *amae*, these investigators coded children's activities at two and one-half years in terms of "self-indulgent behavior" and in the verbal/nonverbal request to be cared for, carried, and comforted. Their interpretation stated,

Analyses of dependency-related behavior indicate that at the 2–1/2 year age level there is significantly more *amae* behavior displayed by the Japanese child, and significantly more encouragement and support of *amae* behavior by his caretaker. . . . The Japanese child is also more likely to seek reassurance from his caretaker than is his American counterpart, and the Japanese mother is more likely both to carry and to hold her child than is the American mother (at that age). (Caudill and Schooler 1973, 333)

They furthermore described

more verbal activity and physical independence than their Japanese cohorts and that such behavior was shown in expressing unwillingness . . . to comply with another's demands, in making demands on their caretaker, emphasizing their personal possessions, and taking care of their own bodily needs. (Caudill and Schooler 1973, 333)

American mothers were thus seen as stimulating their children to greater physical activity through encouraging verbalization and exploration, while the Japanese mothers were soothing their children into relatively more passivity in regard to their interpersonal environment. In any society, rapprochement coincides with the introduction of the child to the standards and norms of the adult world, and is heralded by increasing requirements for responsibility and internalization of behavioral controls. Colloquially, this period is called the "terrible threes" in the United States. The Japanese call this era *mitsugo no tamashii*—literally, "the spirit of a three-year-old"—implying the same contest between the imperious demands of the child colliding with the mother's strategies for gradually reducing these.[5]

Speculatively, the rapprochement crisis in Japanese children might be expected to be different because of the following distinctions in childrearing and culture. First of all, some narcissistic gratifications are continued rather than abridged, or even shut off, as they are in many Western societies. Hence, an atmosphere of nurturance and indulgence continues along with cosleeping, cobathing, and a high degree of close physical contact. Second, outright prohibitions, sanctions, or verbal confrontations are avoided in favor of appeasement strategies (Lebra 1976). Third, sanctioning behavior is inculcated in the control of posture, use of proper speech, and modulation of emotion. Compared to average American children, Japanese youngsters are more likely to be quiet and even demure in situations outside the home. Although highly attentive to the social and physical environment, they ordinarily do not fight, speak loudly, or call attention to themselves in public situations when adults are around.

Japanese youngsters can be seen as preserving some of the "symbiotic" connectedness modeled after the infant-mother relationship. Some elements of this closeness continue into latency, adolescence, and even adulthood—albeit in attenuated forms. Accordingly, psychological individuation is modified, partly due to the continued physical as well as interactional contact with the largely positively identified maternal object. Individuation, furthermore, is accompanied by a socialization process wherein the awareness of impulses, thoughts, and emotions that are *not expressed* is accentuated during the early years of development.

Japanese Childrearing and the Psychosexual Stages of Development

The originality of Freud's hypotheses concerning psychosexual development was threefold. First, he not only postulated the existence of a sexual drive during infancy and early childhood (which had been previously suggested), but he also defined this as a primary motivational component. Second, he described a phasic, zonal migration of sexual concentration evolving during early years of development. Third, he formulated a "biphasic" human sexuality where, following the oedipal transition, manifest sexuality was interrupted by the moratorium of latency.

Oral Stage. Traditional psychoanalytic theory has emphasized the nutritional and gustatory aspects of the *oral stage* and has relatively ignored the significance of input involving contentment, discomfort, and other stimulations associated with kinesthetic, sensory, and motor systems. These latter systems involve attentional states and affects connected with cutaneous sensation (temperature, stroking, being fondled or bathed); perception of space (being rocked, held, moved, confined); auditory input (responding to murmuring, singing, environmental sounds); visual recognition (tracking objects, identification of faces, mutual gaze); olfactory sensations (odors emanating from self, environment, or person objects). In addition to these, there are kinesthetic and interoceptive sensations that accompany and amplify other solitary or shared experience. Although not given much significance in traditional theory, these sensations contribute to the psychic representations associated with this earliest stage of development.

In comparison to the U.S., Japanese infants are uniformly reported as enjoying more protracted and permissive opportunity for breast (or bottle) feeding, as having tactile contact with their mothers' nipples and breasts, and as enjoying increased physical connection ("skinship") with the mother during both day and nighttime (Beardsley, Hall, and Ward 1959; Vogel 1967; Caudill and Weinstein 1969; Lebra 1976, 1984a). Mothers establish a close and nearly exclusive connection to their young children. Babysitting is virtually unheard of, and the use of day-care or custodial facilities during early infancy is unpopular. Children are not stuck away with a bottle, or placed in cribs or playpens. Infants are generally not left to cry themselves to sleep. Moreover, infants and small children are incorporated into the general family life, where they are socialized into the rhythm of family activities and relations to other persons.

There is a decided difference in the use of transitional objects between North American and Japanese children. The reported low incidence of thumb sucking (Caudill and Weinstein 1969) or of inanimate sleeping companions (dolls, "teddy bears," or blankets) constitutes a significant psychological as well as cultural difference. Although Japanese youngsters are given stuffed animals, such dolls or "security blankets" are not supplied to substitute for the real maternal object (see footnote 6 in chapter 2).

Both cross-cultural studies (e.g., Caudill and Weinstein 1969) and other observations (Caudill and Doi 1963; Lebra 1976; Pavenstedt 1965) demonstrate that Japanese mothers show prompt responses to infantile distress (fidgeting, crying). In a society where individual noisiness and commotion are avoided, it is consistent that infants and children would be discouraged and distracted from crying. Thus, in addition to permissive feeding, and a high amount of physical contact, frustration is avoided by swift responses to crying or other signs of discomfort.

Because the infant's demands elicit prompt responses, it is suggestive to speculate that less ambivalence may be built in during the oral stage among Japanese infants. This is paralleled during juvenile development where the moralization of eating (or not eating) does not become prominent among Japanese youngsters and their mothers. Another factor is that the socialization of eating with others, including early introduction to table foods, imposes uniform regulations concerning eating, rather than a specialized feeding schedule for the youngster.

In summary, the cultural features of the oral stage of development are comparatively permissive, generate low frustration, and manifest less ambivalence concerning the incorporation of food. Psychoanalytically, the oral stage has been identified as being crucially connected to preoccupations with giving and taking, dependency and independence, closeness and distance to others, symbiosis and individuation, trust and mistrust (Fisher and Greenberg 1977; Mahler 1965; Erikson 1959). Studies of Japanese children indicate the extension of a strong interdependency *(amaeru/amaesaseru)* between mother and child, a socialization that stresses the consequences of collateral relationships together with permissiveness and indulgence fostering an atmosphere of trust. Although prominent during the oral stage of development, these qualities continue during subsequent phases.

Anal Stage. Benedict's (1946) observations concerning the generally permissive nature of oral indulgence have been sustained by subsequent studies. In contrast, Gorer's (1943) and LaBarre's (1945) early speculations about the "anality" of Japanese personality, purportedly related to severe toilet training, were overturned by the empirical work of Sikkema (1947), Beardsley, Hall, and Ward (1959), Lanham (1956), Vogel and Vogel (1961), and Vogel (1967). These and subsequent reports have consistently demonstrated relatively relaxed bowel training accomplished in a nonmoralistic way among both rural and urban Japanese.

As discussed in chapter 2, one of the problems of the psychoanalytic interpretation of the anal stage of development (age one and a half to three) is the distinction between the specific erogenous zone itself (i.e., sensations connected to excretion) and the more general issue of acquiring a progressive awareness and control of the social and physical environment. Embellishing Abraham's (1927) drive-related concentration on anal preoccupations, later authors have argued for the designation of "anal-muscular stage" to emphasize the more distributed concerns and pleasures connected to bodily movement, coordination, and early physical autonomy. Even beyond the acquisition of muscular control, the psychic components of attaining behavioral control are most significant. These formulations are only incipient during the prereflective period early in the anal stage. However, they become more conscious as the child's observations about the directions of social behavior begin to suggest the presence of intentions, motives, and goals initiated by participants in these interactions. Based upon their observations of the social and physical environment, children gradually begin to conceive themselves as intentional actors. During the anal stage, the development of systems concerning self-control hypothetically derive some of their qualitative features reflecting the issues of sphincteral as well as other muscular control. However, this is progressively more concerned with ego-level, executive monitoring of social interaction, based on emotional and other communicative cues in the social environment. Therefore, although Japanese bowel training is relatively benign, the emphasis on control of posture, emotion, speech, and physical activity during this period are rigorous, and operate to stimulate early superego prohibitions over fears of not displaying proper control.

Two other psychoanalytic elements are significant during the anal-muscular stage: namely, aggression and autonomy. As mentioned in prior chapters, ordinary and intermittent displays of aggression in Japanese children are preferentially handled by "appeasement" or mediation rather than direct opposition or confrontation. This constitutes a paradox—specifically, that in a society highly concerned with the suppression and avoidance of overt aggression, the earliest behavioral rules for this pivot on distracting or even gratifying the child in order to thwart aggression. As mentioned previously, this socialization also includes absorbing aggression from other children on some occasions, rather than responding with physical retaliation or restraint. The expectation is that children will eventually learn to restrain their own impulses on the basis of a developing empathy for others, and through realization of the painful consequences of their aggression. This realization is accompanied by an attempt to avoid embarrassment and guilt at being seen as the perpetrator of aggression. Such indirect socialization continues in the preschool and elementary school environments, where painstaking explanations of the consequences of hostility or violence toward others are favored over counteraggression or simple authoritarian control (as discussed in C. Lewis 1984).

As mentioned earlier, communication in the Japanese home focuses children's attention in a psychologically decentered manner onto the social interaction going on around them. In the relatively quiet atmosphere of the Japanese home, where silences are frequent, children are induced to be attentive to verbal and nonverbal indications of the partially hidden intentions, intuitions, feelings, rights, and prerogatives of others—including those of the more powerful people around them. Unlike the more verbal and ideologically oriented childrearing among nonethnic Americans, Japanese training tends to make children concentrate on observing the reactions of other people, rather than connecting behavioral adaptation to threats based on "principles" or "regulations" extraneous to the immediate interaction. Thus, Japanese socialization fosters a gradual internalization of control that is situationally variable, and punished by humiliation. Additional threats of expulsion from the home, or punishment by outside "referees" may add to fears of potential embarassment or humiliation. Although physical punishments are avoided, they do occur and naturally reinforce fears concerning bodily pain or injury.

Throughout this socialization, the ideal Japanese mother patiently conducts rehearsals of behavioral tasks, which are inculcated through demonstration and explanation. This is done by painstakingly telling the child what must be done before, during, and after certain performances (e.g., playing with toys, putting objects away, not soiling things, not touching the floor, being careful of people's feelings, not demanding undue attention). Whenever possible, admonitions are made in a warm and encouraging tone of voice.

The concentration on muscular control and the necessity of responding to others facilitates a heightened sensitivity and empathy about other people's feelings, at the same time that prerogatives for closeness, permissiveness of expression, and gratification of needs are continued. This constitutes a push-pull situation where some aggression is tolerated by the absence of direct opposition, but also may be directly punished through embarrassment and humiliation. Since this is continued in later socialization, such experiences leave the Japanese youngster (and eventually the adult) relatively unrehearsed for navigating situations involving directly aggressive interpersonal behavior.

Some behavioral effects of this are interesting to witness. When children do get into playground fights, these may be protracted because peers do not seem to know how to respond, intervene, or end the aggression. Although youngsters are instructed by teachers concerning making interventions to stop fighting, most of these techniques of mediation are verbal, and avoid direct physical attempts to separate the combatants. Similarly, in public situations, preschoolers occasionally produce tantrums that become Wagnerian in scale, partly because the parents themselves seem helpless to control the exorbitant emotionality in a direct manner.[6]

Although aggression is thwarted indirectly during the anal stage, training in orderliness, cleanliness, and neatness are methodically socialized in both boys and girls. As in all societies, distinctions between clean and dirty are inculcated in the supervision of daily activities, including cleanliness rules regarding not only excretion but also the handling of food, the avoidance of certain objects, and in routines of bathing and washing. Considerations of pollution and contamination are reinforced in admonitions about avoiding contact with soil or dirt, distinctions between the floor and furnishings, the lower and upper portions of the body, and the potential offensiveness—even dangerousness—of bodily products. Orderliness is taught by both tacit example and explicit rules. Objects are to be handled carefully and replaced after being used. Injunctions against displaying or abusing others' possessions are prominent in the home; these injunctions are continued in the school, and eventually in the work environment.

Psychoanalytically, the qualitative effects of the anal stage as influenced by Japanese childrearing reinforce learning habits concerned with orderliness and general cleanliness. While the control of proper posture and of emotion are directly and explicitly instructed, the control of aggression is mostly taught indirectly, and regulated by evasion, diversion, or subtle forms of suppression. During this stage, psychological individuation and autonomy proceed within the context of a continued closeness to mother along with socialization practices that repeatedly remind youngsters about the feelings, intentions, and prerogatives of others. Fears of contamination are related both to the real environment, where they may be potentially controlled, and to the internal, psychological environment, where they function as superego elements foreboding potential humiliation and guilt. Inherent fears of bodily harm and disfigurement are relatively unstimulated or reinforced by childrearing practices that strive to avoid physical confrontations and corporal punishment. On the other hand, threats of potential separation are frequently employed to promote compliance using fears of rejection or emotional isolation.

Phallic-Oedipal Stage. This stage of development takes place between four and six, is mastered differently by boys and girls, and is divided into two main periods: a dyadic, phallic-narcissistic substage, and a triadic (i.e., competitive) phallic-oedipal period. According to traditional psychoanalytic theory, this stage is concerned with the early consolidation of gender identification with the same-sex parent, and the repression of heterosexual strivings for the opposite-sex parent leading to a submergence of heterosexuality during latency. Ideally, this facilitates the eventual reappearance of relatively unconflicted sexual awareness during adolescence. In psychoanalytic terms, successful navigation of this period for boys involves dealing with castration anxiety through renunciation of competition with father followed by a friendly, or at least nonthreatened, acceptance of him as an exemplar. Again, in psychoanalytic terms, since girls objectively lack a penis, their concern with castration is explained as centering on fantasies concerning prior mutilation and status inferiority, conceptualized psychoanalytically as penis envy.[7]

By definition the early phallic stage is reached when the genital region becomes the predominant locus of conscious sexual gratification. This is usually coterminous with a beginning consolidation of gender role in its social consequences—namely, the gradual assumption of characteristics that define functional gender roles in the society—regarding both present and anticipated functioning. This period is termed phallic-narcissistic (Edgecumbe and Burgner 1972) because it is initially egocentric and preoccupied with bodily self in terms of identification with the same-sex parent. The second stage involves the more stressful *triadic* resolution, accomplished by first acknowledging the consequences of attraction to the forbidden, opposite-sex parent, then repressing and resigning to the loss of that parent as a possible sexual object. Although the appearance of a prohibitory superego is conceptualized as being developed during prephallic phases—largely in connection with the control of aggression—prohibitions activated by the oedipal resolution are alleged to have more far-reaching effects on subsequent personality style and sexual adaptation (Hartmann and Loewenstein 1968).

Speculatively, the "average expectable environment" of children's socialization in Japan produces differences that qualitatively affect the phallic-oedipal stage. The most basic of these pertains to both sexes and consists of the continued preoedipal closeness to the mother in terms of her relatively undiminished accessibility for nurturance, emotional security, and a close, functional, interdependent partnership *(amaeru/amaesaseru)*. This close connection is manifestly more extensive than would be encountered in most Western childrearing. Even earlier, but particularly following the phallic period, girls relinquish some claims for nurturance by way of sublimating their needs and taking on the social role of caregivers who serve others. Japanese boys do not do this, and are allowed to continue a closeness to mother that would be defined as potentially pathological in many Western families. In comparison, Japanese girls gradually become less dependent on their mothers in making demands; however, their emotional connectedness continues to pivot on the special cherishment expected as part of *amae* (Garrick 1989, private communication).[8]

The psychological position of the average Japanese father is also different from that in modal, nonethnic American families. Traditionally, he does not participate much in nurturing or childrearing, and is identified as a person of vague but high status whose authority is witnessed in the mother's deference to his presence, and reinforced by normative rules that confer power on adult males. Thus, quite irrespective of his personality style, the Japanese father may be pictured as a potential threat—whether he actually is involved in punishing the children or not. He is also available as a role model for the early phallic male, who is encouraged by example not to talk too much, to act in a decisive manner, and, at times, to intimidate others—including mother. Some girls may take on some of these male, "tomboy" *(o-temba)* characteristics, but only to a limited and playful degree. Also, some girls may get closer to their fathers through using boyish affectations—especially endearing if there are no boys in the family. They may also ingratiate fathers by capitalizing on their sweet femininity—however, on a preoedipal level and not involving physical contact as might occur in the West. In fact, another crucial difference in the Japanese oedipal transition is the general lack of emotionally expressive physical contact in the home. As mentioned earlier, little children are not kissed on the lips, tickled, or nuzzled by either parent. This creates a paradox, where physical closeness, cobathing, and cosleeping are accompanied by an almost phobic avoidance of other physical contact—especially behavior that is latently sexual in adultomorphic terms. Also, Japanese parents do not hug, kiss, tickle, or playfully touch each other in view of their children.

The progression of Japanese youngsters through the later phallic-oedipal phase is culturally influenced by the high priority placed on status propriety, the suppression of envy or rivalry, and the nonromantic and low sexual stimulation in the home. Since the oedipal resolution involves a triadic relationship among mother, father, and child, this putatively requires a redistribution of libidinal drive and a more firm consolidation of gender role. However, in the Japanese family, the mother's prior status as a preoedipal intimate partner does not change radically for either the boy or the girl—although girls sublimate some of this through their increasing identification with her. The mother does not, however, become an adultomorphic love object who because of this stimulates a superego prohibition in order to deny any latent sexuality. What this seems to mean is that sexual feelings are both suppressed and repressed, with their developmental resolution delayed. The continued provision of preoedipal gratification makes any latent, adult sexual strivings inconspicuous.

In their triadic relationship to father, children view him as a high-status competitor for nurturance from the mother. He is not, however, perceived as a competitor for intense affectionate or romantic feelings. Children retain a consciousness of the priority given to their needs in eliciting preoedipal indulgent gratifications. Also, rivalry itself is suppressed by cultural proscriptions learned through repetitious instruction about not coveting other people's possessions or privileges. Individuals are accorded prerogatives according to their age, position in the family, gender, and perhaps special conditions—such as unusual talent, need, disability, or infirmity. Certain superego constraints are connected to the social reality of the status characteristics within the Japanese family. The rights and prerogatives as well as the power and possessions of individuals are justified by relatively unchallengeable conditions of status occupancy. Juvenile drive expressions for seeking attention collide with the superego prohibitions of status differentials that operate to reduce and suppress individualistic and selfish desires. Accompanied by the overt admonitions against exhibiting anger or envy, these act to reduce the expression of competitiveness in general.

What is not successfully neutralized by these preoedipal restraints may be swept under the rug of "dual consciousness." This exemplifies the acute awareness of the difference between proper, allowable social presentation of self and the conscious yet inexpressible feelings, desires, or intentions that are inappropriate or even dangerous to communicate. Although not unique to the Japanese (see Hsu 1971b; Doi 1987), the early emphasis on control of musculature, speech, and emotion tends to heighten the distinction between "expressible" and "inexpressible" among Japanese youngsters. In terms of the oedipal transition, this control might act to suppress overt sexual cravings that could lead to ridicule, embarrassment, or even physical punishment.

Against this background, the phallic-oedipal phase would seem to be less tumultuous and involve lower arousal of superego referents related to the denial of sexual feelings for the opposite-sex parent. This may explain why Japanese are not disturbed by ordinary family nudity, or their dim awareness of primal scene, since the oedipal resolution does not entail a highly charged denial of adultomorphic fantasies toward the parents as sexual objects per se.[9] Also, in terms of actual social interactions, heterosexual contacts are suppressed and discouraged not only during latency but also in early and midadolescence. Traditionally, young Japanese men and women gain comparatively little experience in precourtship situations of dating, going to dances or parties together, although this is changing somewhat in the larger cities. Most socialization among middle and late adolescents occurs in groups, without emphasis on a one-to-one basis.

As mentioned previously, *overt* individual competition is discouraged both in the home and in society at large, except in academic achievement, games, or play. Even in ritualized contests, winners are enjoined to be gracious and modest. Encouragement of exemplary performance or chastisement for failure focuses on the individual child's own capacity for performance. Comparison with older siblings or fellow students may be made, but not in a way that emphasizes head-to-head competition. Socialization into collective efforts also channels potential envy and jealousy into an identification with group achievement—for example, how well the entire class did on certain assignments or in cleaning up the classroom. This induces a sense of cooperation in group achievement, partly through helping those whose abilities are not outstanding. The conspicuousness of individual achievement is also discounted through *enryo*, which operates to produce a ritualized modesty and self-deprecation among those who are outstanding.

Of course, such socialization does not extinguish the perception of individual competition, envy, or jealousy. Life both inside and outside the family takes place within a meritocracy, where differential recognition and rewards are given on the basis of successful striving, the possession of unusual skills, and the mastery of culturally endorsed repertories. Certain individuals are rewarded more in the home, school, and workplace, but in a manner that minimizes interpersonal competition. In general, salaries are primarily calculated on length of employment, and bonuses are distributed partly on a per-capita basis. Superior achievement is recognized through promotions to positions of higher status and responsibility. While such promotions are routinely accompanied by indirect benefits, they are not necessarily accompanied by a rise in income.

From a psychoanalytic standpoint, however, a more important factor in diminishing oedipal jealousy and competition is the lack of an open romantic bond between the parents. Since the emotional intensity of this relationship is downplayed, children are not stimulated to feel excluded through an asymmetric triadic relationship with either mother or father. Caudill (1962a) commented that the Japanese son is not a rival with his father, since he already "possesses" the mother and will continue to do so as long as he does not make any direct, adultomorphic sexual claims. Caudill also suggested that this sense of possession required a splitting of erotic feelings between a son's preoedipal tenderness for his mother and his dawning awareness of sexual passion. He concluded that the unambivalent provision of indulgence and care in Japanese child-rearing diminished both the expression of aggressive drives and the intensity of the oedipal conflict. Additionally, he speculated that character formation in Japan accentuated an anaclitic orientation—reflecting the close interdependency during infancy, childhood, and later life, which concentrated potential anxiety into issues concerned with being left alone or abandoned. As a result of this, Caudill concluded that "individual autonomy and mastery are not so much valued in Japan as are the development of collateral relations in the sense of sharing." He went on to add the cross-cultural speculation that "genital primacy in all of its glory seems to be overstressed in the United States. There is a certain stridency in the urging of American girls to be women and boys to be men which makes something of a mockery out of genital behavior" (Caudill 1962a, 412).

In commenting on this same period of development, Wagatsuma (1973) composed a psychoanalytic literary criticism of some post-war novels by Shintaro Ishihara in their preoedipal and oedipal implications. Although emphatically denying the generalization that all Japanese men are inclined toward phallic adaptations, he speculates that the strong dependency on the preoedipal mother and a difficulty in negotiating hostility with father may complicate late juvenile development. In the phallic-narcissistic scenarios illustrated by Ishihara's protagonists, themes of aggression toward men and fears of showing tenderness toward women are prominent. In his interpretation of these novels, Wagatsuma describes a conflict where the passivity of close preoedipal connection to mother is disguised and denied by an active phallic narcissism, both in the physical competitiveness toward men, and in the pursuit of women as dispensable sexual objects. As in Caudill (1962b), this is depicted as a splitting of sexuality away from the dependent, preoedipal satisfactions toward phallic-aggressive attachments to accessible but devalued women of the "water trades" (bar girls, hostesses, prostitutes). It also is accompanied by both wanting to destroy father and being terrified about the possible consequences of this desire.

In a sensitive case study of a recollected oedipal period, Taketomo (1989b) has discussed the resolution of maternal and paternal transferences encountered during a training analysis. The memories of an early exclusive attachment to mother as oldest son were punctuated by changes accompanying the successive birth of siblings amid an atmosphere of general mystification concerning sexuality. A sense of oedipal rivalry with the father is recalled; however, this remained vague because of the distant relationship with what the analysand perceived as a passive although affectionate figure. Resolution of the father transference focused on identifying the warm, nurturant, and tutorial aspects of the psychoanalytic relationship, which recreated the nostalgic relationship with the now-deceased father. In the same publication, Taketomo (1989b) also reflected on the significantly smaller number of themes and images devoted to castration and genital mutilation in Japan, speculating that this may be related to a lowered cultural consciousness concerning genital vulnerability per se, in a society that historically did not use castration as a form of corporal punishment, and did not practice circumcision. (Wagatsuma [1980] also speculated about this same issue.) However, despite the relative lack of genital castration themes in Japanese literature, the concentration on decapitation and evisceration as ritualistic means for dealing with failure or severe shame putatively pick up unconscious superego referents for potential punishment—in the form of self-inflicted "castrations."

Both the real life of the author Yukio Mishima (Nathan 1974) and his numerous literary works (Mishima 1949, 1951, 1965, 1970) testify to his preoccupation with phallic-narcissistic characters and plots. His own early life—partly fictionalized in Confessions of a Mask—pivots on the effects of early separation from mother, gender confusion, and a "weak constitution." These infirmities are accompanied by a spectacular fantasy life concerning masochistic experiences of pain, suffering, and sacrificial death. The complicated and tormented lives of both Ishihara and Mishima underscore Wagatsuma's injunction that extraordinary depictions of phallic narcissism are as exceptional to average Japanese as they are to other national groups.[10]

In regard to phallic fixations, Anne Parsons's (1969) formulations concerning the universality of the oedipal complex are relevant here. She argued that while evidence for juvenile sexual awareness and some form of incest taboo were observed worldwide, the patterning and significance of such relationships varied according to kinship patterns and the qualitative features of mother-son and father-daughter relationships in specific cultures. She discussed the nature of triadic relationships in a southern Italian society that was intermediate between the extended lineage system found in Japan and the discontinuous nuclear family structure upon which the turn-of-the-century Freudian oedipal hypotheses were based. She also speculated that a close mother-son relationship was associated with the splitting of the preoedipal and oedipal female figure into a classic (Western) Madonna/prostitute configuration. However, unlike in Japanese society, her Italian sample fostered an openly hostile and competitive relationship between the father and son. Moreover, the family communication was characterized by periodic expressions of overt aggression and conflict, along with a high degree of directly expressed emotionality. As in Japan, the continuity observed in the mother-son relationship was characterized as the basis for the connectedness within both the nuclear and the extended family.

Parsons concluded that the question of whether the Oedipus complex is universal is not meaningfully addressed through reference to any one ethnocentric version. Rather, the question should be about "what is the possible range within which culture can utilize and elaborate the instinctually given human potentialities, and what are the psychologically-given limits of this range?" (Parsons 1969, 398).

In finishing this section, one further comment regarding Japanese culture should be considered:

During the post-oedipal period, for both boys and girls, latency would seem to be prolonged in Japan, and one of the main tasks of latency—the psychological separation from the parent and the establishment of a personal identity—is made more difficult . . . because of the strong interdependency among people. (Caudill and Doi 1963, 414)

Implications of Japanese Childrearing for
Ego-Ideal and Superego Development

Despite qualitative differences between ego ideal and superego, some psychoanalytic theoreticians connect these two structures through a parallelism and overlap in some of their functioning, and a similarity in manifest content, although not in development. Ego ideal, as depicted by Freud (1914), was seen as a residue of primary narcissism that becomes diverted into conscious projections of power and strength imputed to the immediate, caregiving family members. These ego-ideal contents are predominantly positive, but are connected to negative apprehensions of escaping the pangs of shame, ridicule, or loss of regard by an inspiring love object. As Freud (1914) noted, the perfectionistic standards of ego ideal are formed in specialized (cultural) contexts reflecting the values of the parents, and are judged according to the prevailing rules for performance. Therefore, ego ideal—although connected to unconscious identifications —is consciously associated with its contemporaneous referents, which are readily interpersonalized. Characteristically, ego ideal is connected to activating shame or embarrassment set off by the public exposure to failure, error, or miscalculation in both prosaic or extraordinary performances (Piers and Singer 1953).

Early identifications with the parents undergo modification and extension to other exemplars in the social environment, fixing on role models such as older siblings, teachers, coaches, political figures, talented friends, sports heroes, and famous persons. Ego ideal also attaches to abstract moral and ethical categories that inspire exemplary performance and achievement. Positively, comparisons made between real and idealized performance are normatively related to mastery in the progression toward adulthood, and the acquisition of culturally defined, functional competence. Negatively, the absence of such competence is experienced as potential embarrassment and shame.

In contrast, superego development, which also begins early in infancy, is prototypically associated with negative affects of discomfort, displeasure, and fear. Even during a prerepresentational period, these emotions progressively become associated with restraint and accommodation to the interpersonal environment. Later these become associated with a succession of semiconscious prohibitory contents dealing with dread of punishment, parental displeasure, and loss of love. The power and strength of these prohibitions are related in psychoanalytic theories to fantasies concerning possible annihilation, castration, and the projected fantasied destruction of loved objects. At first manifestly unconscious, the precursors of superego acquire the quality of severe, automatically engaged avoidance mechanisms that directly counteract or prohibit threatening drives and impulses.

Development is influenced by mediating factors, including innate temperament and the degree of maturity that the ego has reached at the time of the most critical consolidation of superego (Hartmann and Loewenstein 1968). Traditionally, the earliest development of the superego is seen as clustering around the ego-id conflicts, mediated through the developing unconscious mechanisms of defense. Development is influenced next by what are regarded as anal countercathexes concerned generically with the curtailment of aggression. However, according to Hartmann and Loewenstein (1968), the major consolidation of the superego awaits the initial resolution of the oedipal transition, ordinarily between the ages of four and six.

Similar to ego ideal, conscious superego contents following latency undergo progressive modification in response to the extrapsychic stresses encountered during adolescence and young adulthood. The strong resurgence of genitalized sexual drives during puberty is generally regarded as disturbing the stability of the initial oedipal resolution, and may provoke guilt in the form of a reawakened punitive superego. Regressions in the face of early adolescent superego/ego conflicts may include attempts to avert punishment through the use of compulsive fixations or psychosocial regression that forestalls the consequences of heterosexual awareness.

In summary, superego is traditionally understood as an intrapsychic structure opposing both libidinal and aggressive drive pressures through equally powerful countercathexes reflecting negative sanctioning imposed both by the intrapsychic and cultural environments. Sanctioning is present at an unconscious, signal level, established during prereflective childhood and solidified during the oedipal transition. The superego's content and intensity reflect the particular nature of childrearing, as well as the cultural values present in the social environment. Such development is normatively associated with the mastery of expectations for internally regulated behavior in connection with feeding, grooming, tending for oneself, and controlling impulses—particularly those involving aggression, sexuality, and unwarranted narcissistic demands. Such constraints are also associated with the gradually diminishing limitation of biological and, to a certain extent, emotional dependency in terms of expectations for being held, rocked, cleansed, soothed, comforted, and protected.

The question, here, is how to generalize characteristics of Japanese culture and childrearing and their possible effects on ego-ideal and superego development?

Japanese Cultural Themes and Ego Ideal. In terms of ego-ideal formation, one of the distinctive aspects of Japanese childrearing is that there is a high correspondence between behaviors extolled within the family and those that are consistently reinforced in the general society (Kiefer 1970; Lebra 1976). Moreover, the normative prescriptions and proscriptions in Japan are relatively standardized when compared to those in pluralistic and heterogeneous societies. Also, there is a high degree of awareness concerning the public presentation of self, and an anticipation about the predictable dispositions and potential reactions of other persons. Social performance is more consciously formalized and regulated than in most comparable Western life situations. Consequently, expectations for courteous or ritualized forms of behavior are quite explicit and apply to a broad range of public and private encounters. Because of this, ego-ideal formation is more overt and standardized than in Western countries. Another difference that reflects Japanese childrearing focuses on the early acquisition of behaviors that relate to ego-idealized performance inculcated at both a conscious (i.e., representational/verbal) and nonverbal (semiotic/signal) level. Such behavior includes sitting up straight with legs folded neatly under the torso, learning to bow, and learning to use proper forms of address. These behaviors are reinforced through repetition, reward, and the ever-present example of the parents and other role models.

An interesting feature about the socialization of ego-ideal content in Japan is that the renunciation of personal narcissism is established as an important goal irrespective of high or low social status. Paradoxically, receiving esteem from others is fulfilled by seeming, or even pretending, to have a low esteem for oneself. This socialization toward exemplary behavior and maintenance of self-esteem occurs in conjunction with the continuation of direct pregenital satisfaction of needs for physical closeness to others, and a permissiveness toward continued prerogatives for indulgent dependency from mother and maternal surrogates.

Japanese Cultural Themes, Guilt, and Superego. Theoretical attempts to dichotomize shame and guilt have been ably criticized by Lebra (1969, 1983). In the past, a number of theories posited that these two reactions to perceived failure occurred within a bilinear polarity of internal sanctions associated with *guilt,* and external sanctions attributed to real persons and associated with *shame.*[11] Because Japanese culture contains conspicuous social sanctions regarding competent performance, it has been susceptible to being portrayed as a "shame-oriented culture" (as in Benedict 1946). Piers and Singer (1953), in a theoretically oriented discussion of shame and guilt, also hypothesized these polar distinctions. However, Hartmann and Loewenstein (1968) criticized their position:

> There is no reason to object to a descriptive distinction between "guilt" and "shame," but it is very difficult to account for this difference in terms of analytic psychology. One may well see a difference between acting contrary to an imperative and not reaching an ideal aim one has set for himself [sic]. . . . It seems unlikely to us that one can, as these authors assume, distinguish between shame and guilt in terms of outer and inner sanction. . . . Such a link seems to us to present primarily a distinction in terms of developmental level. Shame as well as guilt are reactions to the danger of loss of love, to ridicule, or to anger. (Hartmann and Loewenstein 1968, 66)

Ausubel (1955), in an earlier discussion of the relation between shame and guilt, takes the same position, seeing guilt and shame as coincidently activated but separate reactions manifesting in various combined expressions, according to different circumstances and contingencies. Ausubel assumes that most experiences of failure include referents that arouse internalized sanctions, as well as those that are connected to potential social condemnation. In his classification, guilt and shame coexist amid a spectrum of possible reactions involving combined levels of awareness. He comments that "an emotion is adjudged to be guilt or shame on the basis of its behavioral characteristics, its situational excitant, and its subjective properties, and not because it fails to meet certain arbitrary, ethnocentric criteria that apply to a single culture or phase of development" (Ausubel 1955, 385).

DeVos (1960) has offered an illuminating formulation for the structuring of guilt in Japanese personality in the context of the unusually strong developmental attachment to mother aroused in the contexts of achievement, and activated by courtship and the anticipation of marriage. Also, while rejecting Piers and Singer's (1953) distinctions, DeVos concedes that shame

is a more conscious phenomenon among the Japanese, hence more readily perceived as influencing behavior. But guilt in many instances seems to be a stronger basic determinant. Although the ego ideal is involved in Japanese strivings toward success, day-by-day hard work and purposeful activities leading to long-range goals are directly related to guilt feelings toward parents. Transgression in the form of "laziness" or other non-productive behavior is felt to "injure the parents," and thus leads to feelings of guilt. There is a psychological analogy between this Japanese sense of responsibility to parents for social conformity and achievement, and the traditional association sometimes found in the Protestant West between work activity and a personal relationship with a deity. (DeVos 1960, 289)

As DeVos suggests, there is a highly articulated, normative structure for ego ideal in Japanese life. This may mislead observers from outside Japan in their tendency to regard strivings for achievement as predominantly connected to external and, hence, superficial social determinants influencing success and failure. DeVos deflates this by showing the internalized determinants of such achievement based on his Thematic Apperception Test (TAT) research. In his survey of test results, he methodically analyzed recurrent themes of guilt in stories where fantasized parental death occurs following a child's disobedience.

As summarized earlier, cultural prohibitions and rules are explicitly articulated in Japanese childrearing regarding externalized superego referents. These deal with themes regarding the ritual need for apology, personal modesty, and requests for forgiveness. They also are manifest in attempting to stave off ridicule, embarrassment, or punishment. Prominent among these are attitudes connected to the early socialization of self-control directed toward posture, emotional display, physical poise, and use of honorific status language. Control also includes toilet training, and the filtering of observable emotion. Since the consciousness of emotion is not extinguished by such control, awareness of feeling is retained, and in fact may be potentially increased, since it is displayed through comparatively subtle nonverbal cues, which demand careful monitoring.

Conscious recognition of superego and ego-ideal contents are also connected to the principles of honor and dignity. Honor is accorded individuals who display internal strength, impassivity, perseverance, kindness, patience, obedience, and other virtues that exemplify the maintenance of culturally desirable ego ideals. Conversely, from a superego standpoint, the subjective perception of failure to meet these objectives may release strong feelings of mortification and self-contempt. An added motive for avoiding dishonor is that publicly witnessed disgrace constitutes a stain of impropriety that spreads to include family, school, company, political party—and even nation.

As mentioned previously, socialization practices that encourage the acquisition of exemplary behavior include teasing, pinching, and ridicule, along with mild admonitions. Stronger prohibitory measures may employ threats of spanking or slapping, although these are rarely carried out. Banishment is used to control behavior; temporary expulsion from the home or seclusion in a closet is not uncommon. At the same time, there is more indulgence for continuing pregenital dependency and closeness, including cosleeping, delayed weaning, nonmoralistic toilet training, and low degrees of embarrassment concerning nudity per se. Accompanying the culturally determined superego relaxation toward pregenital satisfactions is the lifelong expectancy of prerogatives for infantile acceptance and cherishment. These privileges may be expected not only from parents or spouse but also from other selected individuals. In contrast to this indulgence, however, superego prohibitions against the expression of aggression are quite severe, and are earliest socialized through persuasion, distraction, and tacit example. Other techniques involve the indirect restraint of aggression through concentration on the control of behavioral and linguistic modes of deference (bowing, using honorifics, remaining silent in the presence of status superiors).

. As discussed earlier, erotization through kissing, nuzzling, and tickling is avoided. Thus, the superego controls in Western children —necessary to restrain adultomorphic sensual stimulation—are not ordinarily activated. One might speculate that the relative lack of conscious guilt about sexuality may be connected to childrearing practices that avoid both adultomorphic sexual stimulation and confrontations provoking aggression. Instead, superego contents converge on the areas of bodily posture and control of emotion generally, rather than in the context of overt aggressive or adultomorphic sexual activities.

Another prominent diversion uses superego referents to counteract aggression through the control of emotion in social relationships. This involves the attention devoted to conspicuous courtesy, deference, and obedience, as exemplified in *enryo* behaviors. These ritualistically deny self-importance and utilize ceremonialized modes of appeasement and feigned abasement. In superego terms, *enryo* operates as a kind of "insurance" against punishment through ritualized denial and self-abnegation established *before the fact*. Also, the injunctions against envy of other persons' privileges or property is another aspect of neutralizing and denying selfish entitlement. A corollary protection against superego punishment is an almost institutionalized pessimism conspicuous among Japanese. This reflects a fatalistic acceptance of lowered expectations, and a preparation for things not turning out well. It also constitutes a recognition of the powerfulness of nature and outside forces, which control the destinies of relatively puny individuals. However, such statements of fatalism are not posed in the Western portrayal of the environment as an antagonist against the individual (i.e., something to be subdued) but merely as an abstract superior force. Finally, ego ideal connected to perseverance and reliance on internal strength is reinforced preventively by the superego prohibitions against crying, complaining, or demanding.

There is another way of looking at manifestations of Japanese ego ideal and superego. This is to see their intrapsychic contents as being more socially externalized. Conflicts between positive, exemplary standards (ego ideal) and the awareness of prohibitory punishments (superego) tend to be publicly and visibly transacted in Japan. This ritualistically exhibits what otherwise might remain intrapsychic defenses against either discrepancies in ego ideal or feared superego prohibitions. Such ceremonial behavior defensively denies instinctual, narcissistic, or self-aggrandizing impulses through ceremonial attributions of gratitude, humility, and deference. Thus, these mechanisms mask internal conflict, and instead seek relief through extrapsychic projections of the ego defenses. Moreover, these conflicts are manifested publicly through the indirect, implicitly understood perception of underlying sensitivities and mood states among other participants. These perceptions can be verified through close observation and the use of empathy and intuition concerning the sensitivities of others in a way not so conspicuously cultivated in Western situations.

In psychoanalytic terms, it is as if the internal conflict is projected into a public, formal ritual. This tends to deny the submerged conflict and disarmingly exhibit these defenses through a public transaction. Similarly, such an exhibition allows the underlying drive to be sensed or felt by both individuals, albeit in the form of its denial. These defenses are demonstrated more publicly and consciously than in other societies where they may tend to remain internalized, private, or concealed. Such behavior can facilitate the neutralization of conflict, in that it permits a publicly enacted version of an internal conflict. Hence, this serves as a partial resolution—in the same manner that other social rituals (confession, apology, or spontaneous catharsis) may relieve the sense of guilt in Western situations. Also, the ritual is restorative, in that the individual is enacting propitiatory behavior in a real social frame of reference from which these normative rules derive. That is to say that he or she is apologizing to a collective third party system through the vehicle of actual, living representatives of that system. Hence, the penitent will be able to relieve some of the primordial fear of punishment connected to the power and strength of the original prohibitory determinants. However, in situations where obligation is experienced as unlimited (as in certain asymmetric status relations), the real or imagined enormity of any injury may not be placated by prescriptive apologies or *enryo*. In the face of such major transgressions, ritual propitiation is not satisfactory. In these instances relief may not be possible through the use of ceremonials, third parties, or the exhibition of severe mortification. If these mechanisms fail, the consciousness of destructive consequences of one's behavior (toward parents, coworkers, the nation, or the emperor in prewar times) makes the combined experience of guilt and shame unbearable. When propitiation or resolution is perceived to be impossible, the ultimate mortification and self-punishment of suicide may result.

Summary of Consequences of Japanese Socialization

Earlier in this chapter it was suggested that cross-cultural differences in childrearing, socialization, and adult modal personality might be analyzed according to factors of *timing*, *depth*, and *significance*. Factors of depth and significance both are affected by degrees of intensity regarding cross-cultural variation, which differ according to the prominence of certain behavioral manifestations as they are emphasized or obscured in different societies. Since these all are components of a complex, unitary phenomenology of childhood development, considerable overlap in the effects of these factors should be expected.

It is easiest and briefest to discuss differences in timing. Numerous ethnographies and socialization data make clear that Japanese culture consistently supports and extends dependent and interdependent connections between selected persons. These are most dramatically evident during juvenile and latency periods, when the close connections and prerogatives for indulgent dependency are continued, notably in the relationship to mother but also with other special surrogates. Doi and others regard these conspicuous behaviors as evidence of the need for affiliation and dependency as a basic psychological drive, which separately or in conjunction with other drives remains prominent throughout the life cycle in the establishment and persistence of certain distinctive relationships. Looked at reversely, Western societies can be seen as supporting cultural procedures aimed at the reduction of allowable dependency through obscuring the interdependent characteristics of adolescent and adult relationships. This tendency is fostered by the intense ideological support for independency, individualism, and the conceptual bias of emphasizing *individual personality* as the primary heuristic focus for the explanation of personal functioning.

Examined against conventional psychoanalytic developmental theories, these extensions in timing observed among Japanese can be conceptualized as promoting nonsexual explanations for personal affiliation during infantile, juvenile, and later periods. Because of the protraction of the close intersubjective connection between mother and child, psychological individuation occurs in a more gradual and less specific way during the prerepresentational period. This earlier deemphasis on individuation is followed by a developing awareness of self in terms of relationships with others. This sociocentric focus inculcates a system of personal awareness that accentuates status indicators and defines the individual person in positional terms of relativity to others, both in the immediate family and elsewhere.

The oral phase is psychoanalytically regarded as the high-water mark of overt dependency. In these terms, Japanese continue to enjoy lifelong opportunities for selective dependent relationships involving close physical attachments, shared bathing and sleeping, and unashamed expression of desires for pregenital physical comforts. However, the continuation of these privileges is accompanied by more phobic concerns about not touching other people and refraining from any exhibition of heterosexual tenderness in public situations. Those are both suppressed and repressed except in frivolous, nonfamily contexts—possibly as a reaction formation against their expression.

This qualitative extension of nonsexual, pregenital gratifications not only alters the timing of what is conventionally considered the oral stage, but also affects the timing and quality of subsequent periods of development. For example, the onset of the anal stage is modified by the continuation of allowable indulgence of the previous period, and the extended close coalition with the maternal object. This presumably softens some of the socialization effects designed to promote control of aggression and willfulness normatively encountered between ages one and a half and three in all cultures.

Similarly, the protraction of indulgent dependency in the form of abundant pregenital gratifications blunts the dawning genital awareness evident during both the phallic and oedipal stages. It has been repeatedly suggested in the literature that the lack of overt romantic union between Japanese parents tends to modify the triadic, competitive tension of the oedipal transition. The father's instrumental needs are taken care of in a way that does not detract from the provision of resources for the child. The father's emotional needs are inconspicuous and do not arouse jealousy.

In looking at cross-cultural differences, questions regarding *significance*, rather than timing, present an even broader field of contrasts. Such differences are routinely noted in studies investigating societies where both the normative standards for behavior and the behaviors themselves are relatively distinctive to the culture and clearly differ cross-culturally—particularly between Japan and the United States. Such differences have been described throughout this book and consist of norms and interaction rules that in Japan enforce strong control over the exhibition of emotion, and are designed to thwart both the awareness and behaviors that might suggest undue narcissism or selfishness. The interconnection between the need to display personal humility *(enryo)* and certain superego prohibitions concerning the control of aggression have been frequently noted and are prominent in early Japanese socialization. Along with these, the high degree of self-consciousness and awareness about personal performance have been contrasted to the ordinary subjective awareness among Westerners or North Americans. In Japan, the highest superego dread seems to have referents that extend to unconscious and conscious fears of hurting others, being humiliated, failing in a conspicuous manner, or bringing disgrace to oneself, family, or others. In contrast, superego referents concerning sexuality per se do not appear to be as influential or as prominent in Japan as in Western societies.

At a number of points in prior chapters, the effects of the more standardized normative structure within the nonpluralistic society in Japan have suggested that ego ideal is more uniform, consciously socialized, and uniformly reacted to than in Western communities. Although both shame and guilt are felt to characterize Japanese reactions to failure, shame is unquestionably more conspicuous insofar as individual Japanese tend to conceptualize their behaviors in specific interpersonal terms rather than in abstractions of cosmic transgression and ambiguous mortification. This does not make Japanese less susceptible to guilt, but rather makes the manifestations of failure more publicly observable, and hence attributable to shame.

Qualitative issues regarding anality have been related to the distinctive way in which the restraint of motor activity, emotionality, and verbal behavior are carefully inculcated in children during early childhood. This tends to focus the superego dreads of rule breaking into the areas of kinesic (muscular) control and the necessity for status observances rather than centering on issues of soiling.

More difficult to analyze are questions regarding *depth*. As noted before, the use of the term itself is ambiguous. "Depth" refers to the putative existence of certain structural programs and patterns that underlie manifest behavior. These operate at an unconscious level and account for the initial direction of the action process (i.e., as a motivation, drive, or "desire"). The question of what constitutes deep underlying permanent structures versus the superficial variations manifested between cultures will be discussed in the concluding chapter. Before this, however, other evidence for extended periods of dependency in childrearing will be offered to conclude this presentation of ethnographic information. Such information summarizes the work of a number of anthropologists, psychologists, and psychoanalysts who have looked at some of the qualities of affiliation and dependency emphasized in childrearing practices from other societies. These are included here by way of substantiating some of the differences already comprehensively reported in terms of Japanese society.

Other Evidence for Extended Dependency in Childrearing

Dependency and Interdependency in India

Some of the comprehensive summaries of (Hindu) Indian culture have presented detailed descriptions, interpretations, and comparisons to Western European and American cultures. Specialists from anthropology, sociology, psychology, and psychoanalysis have described childrearing in the context of Indian spirituality, world views, notion of lifespan, and patterns of observed behavior within and outside the family. With the exception of Hsu's (1963) comparative work on Chinese and Asian societies, very little literature has been concerned with contrasts *between* various Asian societies until the recent publication of Roland (1988). Also, in the main, such descriptions have concentrated on Hindu/Indian experience, although these have implications for similar cultural practices in Pakistan, as well as among Muslim families residing in India (Sinha 1981; Zaidi 1969).

Lannoy (1971), Kakar (1979, 1982, 1990), and Roland (1980, 1982, 1988) have described aspects of Indian infancy, childhood, and adolescence from a psychoanalytic perspective. All of these comment on factors relating to conspicuous childhood dependency and the overt and highly acceptable interdependency within and outside the family. All have documented the prominence of protracted dependency, which extends in various forms throughout the life course.

There are a number of parallels as well as differences between Japanese and Indian childrearing. In India, the extended family forms the primary conceptual and symbolical matrix within which individuals are socially identified. Kinship articulates circles of intimate relationship governed by degrees of closeness that qualitatively affect the nature of these associations. Although not connected to Confucian values, there is a hierarchy of strict male supremacy that forms one of the important determinants of status designation. Also, as in Japan, a close attention to age hierarchy regulates dominance and subordination among siblings, kin, and friends according to relatively small degrees of age differential. In both societies, a strong and close relationship between mothers and their young children is standard, although in India this is prominent primarily during the first five years of life. Nonetheless, the exclusiveness of this intimate connection nostalgically leaves its traces throughout life. Similar to Japan, fathers are relatively aloof and inattentive to their juvenile children, and have an ambiguous role in the everyday discipline and governance within the matriarchical household. Unlike Japanese, however, Indian fathers become prominent in the socialization of male children after age five, at which time mothers progressively recede from direct intervention.

There is a strong emphasis on the continuity of the family lineage in India and Japan, focusing on the extensions of patriarchal kin. As individuals grow up, they locate their developing sense of self within the collective identity of the family. In India, however, this ontological continuity not only relates to family identification (including ancestors), but is complicated by the dogmatic Hindu belief in reincarnation. Theologically, this holds that current existence is merely one in a series of stages that individuals traverse in their quest toward spiritual perfection.

In both Japanese and Indian societies, there is strong and explicit demand for filial loyalty, obedience, and respect, although this is more openly and strenuously enforced in India. The extent of education, choice of occupation, place of residence, and marital selection continue to be superintended largely by parents. In both societies there is a high awareness of empathic, nonverbal communication, and a strong desire to avoid ridicule, criticism, or shame. Also in both Japan and India, children are looked on as intrinsically innocent and good, even though their behaviors may contradict this.

In terms of actual practices, both societies foster close physical contact between infants/children and their mothers. Indian children are held and virtually never left alone. Close cooperative sleeping is the rule—dictated partly by the architecture of homes, but also by the desire to seek physical and emotional security through cosleeping. As a consequence of this, witnessing or overhearing primal scene in both societies may be common. According to Kakar (1979, 1982, 1990), this does not produce much psychic trauma among Indian children. Mothers nurse their children for periods that would seem protracted by Western standards. As in Japan, Indian toilet training is relaxed and accomplished in a nonmoralistic manner. The mother's devotion to young children includes spoon feeding until they are about five years old.

A number of differences between Japanese and Indian childrearing are apparent. For one thing, babies and children are bathed separately from adults, since the use of a common tub *(furo)* is not part of Indian cultural practice. Also, women and young children are physically segregated in the multigenerational home in a way that is not observable in Japan.

Another difference is that the recognition of social hierarchies in Indian life is accompanied by both verbal and physical aggression from status superiors in a way that is not tolerated in Japan except on the playground or later in the military. As noted previously, Indian children are provided indulgence and accessibility to mother until they are five, when this is suddenly reversed—rather than continued as in Japan. This approximately coincides with the timing of the Western oedipal crisis, but also is coincident with the Indian tradition about being "twice born." "Twice born" refers to the traditional belief that for the first five years of life the child is "born into the family," but at age five is "reborn" as a social creature—becoming a member of society at large.

Also, the effects of the caste system in India offer an additional dimension of stratification among individuals and families according to traditional values, occupational status, and eligibility for marriage. The intricacy of the Hindu caste system adds to other factors affecting hierarchic stratification according to region of the country, level of education, degree of affluence, occupational role, skin color, and family background. In contrast, in a broad, public context, Japanese society tends to downplay the consequences of social stratification except in regard to "outcasts," regional ethnic populations, or "strangers." However, this apparent diffidence is accompanied by a highly sensitive awareness of class-related differences among in-groups. Also, social discrimination based purely on religious affiliation is uncommon in Japan, but highly volatile and politicized in India and Pakistan.

Additionally, there is a distinct difference in regard to how aggression is handled in the two cultures. In India, aggression (and assertiveness) are condoned on the basis of status superiority, while aggression from subordinates toward superiors is strongly sanctioned and punishable. Also, considerably more physical punishment is used as a normal part of juvenile behavioral training and later socialization. Moreover, the strong familial loyalty in India is generalized to a sense of fraternal solidarity involving conspicuous emotional bonds between brothers, sisters, cousins, and other kin. The emotionality and attachment of sibling solidarity is higher and more conscious in India than in Japan.

Another difference between Indian and Japanese childrearing is the prerogative for the father to have increasing influence with his sons after age five. There is a frequently quoted Indian proverb that instructs the father to treat his son like a *raja* (prince) for the first five years, like a slave for the next ten, and like a friend thereafter (Lannoy 1971). This proverb underscores the influence of the father over the son in Indian childrearing in a manner that is uncharacteristic in Japan. In the opinion of some specialists (Kakar, Lannoy, Roland) the Indian male child is exposed to an identification with both parents established during early childhood but consciously continued later in life. Because of the intense closeness to the mother (and other women) during the first five years, boys tend to take on more of an overt but partial feminine identification, including nurturant and affectionate behaviors that are not part of the more strict "masculine" identity in Japan. Along with this is an ambivalence toward females, which is expressed overtly. Indian women are seen as powerful and dangerous "goddesses" as well as nurturant, caring, and self-sacrificing creatures. In mythic dimensions of Indian life, females are depicted both as nurturing, nonsexual mothers, and as lascivious voluptuaries whose sexuality is stronger than that of average males. Such a characterization of female potentiality is inconsistent with Japanese cultural conceptions of idealized femininity.

Although status designations abound, nothing approximating the lavish Japanese use of honorifics occurs in Hindi. Differential titles and words are employed, as well as kinesic forms of subordination. However, status markers are not embedded in the language to the degree that they are in Japanese.

Aspects of Indian social hierarchy have received attention from Dumont (1970), Marriott (1976), Roland (1982), and Kakar (1971, 1979). These testify to the exquisite attention paid to small degrees of status difference, and the tendency to form dominance/submission dyadic relations that lend themselves to reciprocal interdependent relations throughout life. Similar to the asymmetric relations characterized by *on* in Japan, this devotion is calculated to induce a benevolent and indulgent disposition from the superior partner toward subordinates. In the other direction, it imposes a kind of chronic helplessness, indecisiveness, and need for direction on the part of the inferior partner. This helplessness is more overtly demonstrated in Indian relationships than in Japan.

Neki (1976a, 1976b, 1977) has confronted the issue of dependency and interdependency in Indian life comparing both etymological and behavioral features when compared with other societies. He summarized linguistic and sociohistorical features of Western life that tend to derogate the appearance of dependency in adult human relationships—and in psychotherapeutic transactions. Kanungo (1986) has discussed the influences of Indian socialization in producing a behavioral disposition and work ethic that accentuates a personal style of passive-aggressive helplessness, an organizational ethic of highly personalized dominant/subordinate relationships, and an idealized family productively modeled on a joint work ethic. Sinha (1981), in discussing Hindu identity, sees interdependence flourishing on the basis of physical proximity, low social mobility, scarce resources, and the extensive occurrence of poverty. He feels that these factors contribute to a deemphasis of individual autonomy and individuality in favor of collective and mutually dependent relations.

A number of authors (Kakar 1982; Sinha 1981; Neki 1976a) have emphasized that the acquisition of self-reliance, autonomy, and a high sense of individuality are actually avoided in Indian life. Such states are looked on as potentially pathological and may constitute indications for psychotherapeutic treatment or rehabilitation (Kakar 1985). Surya (1969), in discussing ego structure in the Indian family, accentuates the fact that personal property within an extended family is not always clearly demarcated. Many material possessions are regarded as collectively owned, which blurs a "mine/not-mine" differentiation. He cites the fact that maturity is signified by the capacity to sustain satisfying interdependent relationships with various family members as well as in school or work situations.

As Neki (1976a) has pointed out, Hindi words that approximate the meaning of "dependency" actually translate as "bond" or "kinship," and do not allude to dependency per se. In fact, Neki substitutes the word "dependability" for adult dependency in Indian life, suggesting that individuals crave states of reliable, reciprocal interrelationship with dependable superiors throughout life. However, this is not looked on in the same way that dependency might be seen in the West. Neki (1976a) also drew a comparison between Eastern and Western mentalities through what he calls "two psychic systems": a differentiating, analytic (Western) mentality, which is associated with self-reliance and individuality, contrasted to an affiliating (Asian) mentality emphasizing dependability, interdependence, orientation to other people, and an actual *fear* of independence.

A number of commentators have looked at dependency in Indian psychoanalytic situations, all concluding that the therapeutic relationship explicitly contains an overt dominance/submission paralleling the status hierarchies observed in the general society. Pande (1968) examined what he called the "mystique of Western psychotherapy" as a culturally congruent system of rehabilitation emphasizing premises that are distinctive to Western life, but conflictual with Eastern experience. He saw these as including an emphasis on work rather than family relationships, and a focus on self-direction and independence fostered over interdependency. This is accompanied by a directional and linear attitude toward the use of time, and an encapsulated sense of individual rather than social or cosmic consciousness. Consonant with these assumptive propositions, Western psychotherapies are concerned with problem solving through a logical, deductive approach leading to insight and conflict resolution. Neki (1976b) contrasted the guru-student relationship in psychotherapeutic transactions in India, and speculated that one of the factors differentiating Indian from Western psychotherapy related to the amount and quality of dependency socialized during childhood and expected in later life. He commented that "the amount of dependency that is permitted in India during adulthood is comparatively enormous" (Neki 1976b, 15).

Although not commenting directly on psychotherapy, Erikson (1969) discussed the emotional ambience in Indian society, wherein

one moves in a space-time so filled with visual and auditory occurrences that it is very difficult to lift an episode out of the flux of events, a fact out of the stream of feelings, a circumscribed relationship out of the fusion of multiple encounters. If, in all this, I should endow one word with a meaning which captures it all, the word is *fusion.* (Erikson 1969, 40; italics original)

As reported in Lannoy (1971), Erikson sees this fusion as related to joint family living, which induces a deep need and nostalgia for affiliating with others in an exclusive and lasting fashion. This is related by Erikson to the child's frustrated wish for exclusive possession of his mother (Kakar 1990).

Zaidi (1969), in commenting on sociocultural changes in Pakistan, made a number of similar observations regarding both the authority structure and childrearing practices among Muslim families. He makes direct comparisons to both Mexican and Hindu Indian family structures, which stress the fundamental values of supremacy of the father and conspicuous self-sacrifice of the mother.

In the past, such practices have led to the inculcation of both submission and obedience in children and adolescents. Even following Partition, childrearing practices have remained the same, especially in small towns and villages where the child is the total responsibility of the mother until age six or seven, and where traditional maternal roles have not changed. As in India, children are given the unconditional love of both parents until about age five or six, when pressure for conformity to social rules are instituted.

Dependency and Interdependency in Other Asian and African Societies

Slote (1972) has discussed childrearing practices among Vietnamese. Somewhat parallel to the Japanese experience, Vietnamese children are subjected to a push/pull socialization combining an apparent permissiveness with a stringent supervisory control over personal interaction in a manner that is largely inconspicuous to the child. Extreme indulgence, ostensible permissiveness, and casual toilet training are accompanied by what Slote calls "rigorous absolutes in interpersonal behavior, essential modes of conduct, and a basic value system" (Slote 1972, 124). Another parallel to Japanese culture is that the child's ability to create a sense of legitimate, conscious personhood is dependent upon its capacity to elicit nurturant and caring behavior from the parents. This operates in a manner parallel to *amae*. The sense of permissiveness is based upon the child's capacity to promote authentication of a developing self based on the closeness of dependency with mother. However, this intimacy is connected to a feeling of relative powerlessness in making determinations concerning significant events in the absence of mother. This places Vietnamese children in a position of helplessness that is accompanied by a heavy sense of dependency in requiring approval from adults to whom they are instrumentally and emotionally connected. As in Japanese and most other Asian cultures, identity formation is consolidated at the interface of relationships to self and others. Since persons are more decentered in these cultures, the connections (identifications) with others remain more conscious and substantiated. Failure to make and continue these connections puts Asian children (and, eventually, adults) at more risk in terms of identity crisis than their Western counterparts.

In an early publication, Muensterberger (1951) discussed aspects of childrearing among relocated southern Chinese immigrants residing in New York and San Francisco. Although disavowing generalization to all Chinese societies or classes, the author noted the presence of cosleeping, protracted breast feeding, and the inculcation of Confucian status values, which designated males as superior to females and reinforced a respect for a closely calibrated age hierarchy. The preference for male children among Chinese was noted to be even more insistent than in Japan, and was manifested by allowing considerably more privileges and favoritism to boys than girls.

In a later publication, Muensterberger (1969a, 1969b) surveyed a number of ethnographic reports in his cross-cultural examination of variation in separation/individuation. He cited Freud's reflections (in *Female Sexuality*, 1931) contrasting mothers in so-called primitive societies, who were devoted to longer breast feeding compared to individuals raised in less nurturant Western settings.[12] Muensterberger also commented that psychoanalysis had not dealt distributively with the issues of childrearing as they appeared in other cultures. He cited Whiting and Child's (1953) findings, which reported that nearly thirty-three out of fifty-two societies in their survey indicated that weaning occurred between twenty-four and thirty-six months, whereas the American middle-class sample at that time typically began weaning after only six months. His own studies and surveys in Southeast Asia and Africa showed the same relative extension of breast feeding, along with closer physical contact and the tendency to take the child into work or social areas where the mother was occupied both during day and nighttime. Muensterberger also emphasized the significance of synesthetic-cutaneous contact between mother and infant, along with cosleeping and a pattern of closely shared activities. He saw these as deepening the dependency relationship with the mother.

Dependency and Interdependency among Some Eskimo Societies

Muensterberger (1969b) also cited reports of extended breast feeding among several Eskimo societies based on the observations and summarizations of Freuchen (1965). Freuchen had observed that lactation and the ability to nurse signified youth, competence, and social usefulness for adult women. Because of this, some Eskimo mothers refrained from weaning their last child until a subsequent pregnancy. If this did not occur, a mother might continue to nurse the child up to quite advanced ages—at least occasionally. Freuchen (1965) goes on to say,

I thus saw several times, both among Hudson Bay and the Polar Eskimos, and even in southern Greenland, mothers giving the breast to fourteen-year-old boys who were already sporting in Kayaks and taking part in the hunt. (Freuchen 1965, 82; as in Muensterberger 1969a)

Briggs (1970) composed a sensitive ethnography of an Eskimo group called the Utku. At the end of her fine-grained description of this fishing and hunting society, she organized a list of emotion concepts based upon diverse informants' commentary concerning semantic, behavioral, and attitudinal dimensions of words used to define moods, feelings, and emotional states. She organized some of these emotion terms into conceptual categories, based both upon her informants' testimony as well as her own intuitions developed during her intimate participation within the culture.[13]

In a category comprising *affection,* she found that the Utku differentiate three aspects within what would ordinarily be collectively characterized as "affection" in North American culture:

1. the desire to be with a loved person;
2. demonstrativeness: a desire to kiss, touch, or express tenderness verbally;
3. protectiveness: the desire to take care of the physical and emotional needs of another. (Briggs 1970, 314)

The six terms that she translates to define affectionate feelings or behaviors are glossed by her as follows:

unga: to wish or to arouse the wish to be with another person;
niviuq: to wish or to arouse the wish to kiss or touch another affectionately;
aqaq: to communicate tenderly with another by speech or by gesture (other than touch);
iva: to lie next to someone in bed, with connotations of affectionate cuddling;
huqu: in certain contexts, to heed; to respond, with nurturant connotations;
naklik: to feel or to arouse concern for another's physical or emotional welfare; to wish or to arouse the wish to be with another. (Briggs 1970, 315)

The first, fourth, and last of these expressions *(unga, iva,* and *naklik)* are clearly parallel to the Japanese term *amae* and to some of its derivative behaviors. These Utku terms have to do with words that focus on the desire to be with another person, to arouse concern for others, or to express the wish to be with another, and overlap with the connotation of "passive love" in *amaeru*.

The second term, *niviuq*, is more actively concerned with touching and kissing—something that in Japanese is interdicted, but is common as a strong and exuberant affectional gesture, particularly toward Eskimo children. The term *aqaq* is another aspect of *amaeru* insofar as it connotes a desire to communicate tenderly and intimately either by speech or gesture—although, as she notes, this gesture does not include direct touching.

Finally, *huqu* is more specifically related to the cognates in Japanese that define the reciprocal of *amaeru* (*amaesaseru*), described in chapters 6 and 7.

Summary

This chapter has summarized some of the historical background of cross-cultural ethnographic studies in regard to evidence concerning socialization of infants and children in a number of societies—particularly Japan. Cultural issues and factors associated with fostering continued dependency were reviewed in a number of other ethnographic contexts. The favoring of collective versus "individual" identity and the high acceptability of overt interdependency were reviewed, particularly in regard to Japanese and Indian societies.

As in chapter 8, some of the possible psychoanalytic aspects of the effects of normative Japanese childrearing for personality structure have been discussed according to theories concerning the unconscious, instincts and drives, separation-individuation, psychosexual stages of development, and superego/ego ideal formation.

Some issues concerning "universalism" and "relativism" were reviewed in anticipation of a concluding chapter that will address these in terms of their application to the fields of anthropology and psychoanalysis.

Some parallels in childrearing among Hindu/Indian, Pakistani, Asian, Eskimo, and selected African societies have been presented. As in Muensterberger (1969a) these reveal the experience of a relatively long and close connection between mothers and children, comparatively protracted breast feeding, higher exposure to primal scene, and more prominent connection to a less individualized development of self.

Notes

1. The division between metapsychological theory and clinical treatment is erased by the practical necessity of formulating explanations during real clinical encounters. Such formulations routinely examine and interpret clinical events in terms of metapsychological theories regarding putative structural, topographic, and dynamic explanations. A critical discussion of factors concerning the epistemological basis of patients' free-associative productions have recently been summarized by Spence (1982) in terms of "historical versus narrative truth." Taking a somewhat more conservative position, Edwin Wallace (1989) has argued for a more phenomenologically based metapsychology that would close the distance between "theory" and "practice." A more nihilistic philosophical challenge to both metapsychological theory and explanations of clinical practice has been expounded by Grünbaum (1984). His critique raises fundamental questions about the validity of psychoanalytic theory in general.

2. Issues concerning cross-cultural differences in developmental timing are easiest to investigate. Issues concerning differential significance and meaning are more elusive and harder to pin down in research contrasting two or more societies (LeVine 1982, 215). Researchable questions regarding putative *depth* of structure are even more forbidding. Deep structures imply the presence of a biologically based, genotypic organization through which the experiences of bodily sensations, perceptions, and thought are organized according to the innate (biological) capacity of the individual human organism. Such patterns for organization are seen as relatively permanent, but progressively modified by maturational factors and the impact of learning and experience—including, of course, the specialized cultural forms in which such learning and experience occur.

The problem is that the term "deep structure" is itself metaphorical. Its stratigraphic connotations imply that certain patterns of internal organization are prior to and more basic (or profound) in influencing thought, feeling, *and* manifest behavior—hence "deep." However, as LeVine (1982, 219) states, the potential range of meanings and transsituational circumstantiality of human behaviors are considerably more complex and inclusive than are the variations in deep structures associated with speech and written language. To some extent, deep structures concerned with behavior coincide with those regulating language and communication, but also include the activation of motility, emotion, and strategic planning.

3. It should again be stated that *norms* refer to unwritten, informally codified, and socially reinforced *standards of behavior* and not to behavior

itself. Always complex and sometimes contradictory, these standards constitute a body of cultural information that provides general indications for the direction and evaluation of performance. In contrast, *interaction rules* (Goffman 1959; Johnson and Johnson 1975; Hochschild 1979) reflect the prevailing norms, but are less generalistic. They consist of the moment-to-moment application of various normative propositions to the fluctuating circumstances of real-life situations. Both norms and interaction rules are concerned with a kind of specialized explanation—even casuistry—used not only to control but also to justify specific actions. It should be recalled that norms and interaction rules reflect idealized standards and heavily rationalized descriptions pertaining to behavior. They are not prophetic or directly indicative of what actually takes place in ordinary interaction.

4. The confusion perpetrated by the English translation of *Treib* ("drive") into "instinct" has been well publicized but perhaps unduly criticized. At the time these translations were done, the English-language meanings of "instinct" and "drive" were considerably closer than during the past forty years. During that interval, the term "instinct" has become disparaged, while "drive" has maintained a neutral ambiguity. Practically, the two terms seem to be used in a roughly equivalent manner by clinicians in the colloquial conversations about clinical or theoretical matters.

5. Despite the cultural emphasis on protracted dependency, Japanese mothers promote and reward functional independence and self-reliance *(jiritsu-teki)*. Behaviors regarding the care of belongings, cleanliness, and assuming age-appropriate autonomy for minor tasks and responsibilities are carefully taught and gratefully rewarded. Also, although mothers remain in close, indulgent association to their children at home, they make every effort to have the children adapt to the social contexts of playing with selected other children and to the preschool and elementary school environment.

6. The author recalls seeing a grandfather traveling from Kamakura with his three-and-a-half-year-old granddaughter on a suburban train. The granddaughter became fussy and began to clutch and then painfully twist her grandfather's hair. Throughout this, her facial expression was neutral, while he showed alternating pain and feigned "amusement." Because she was so young, the grandfather did not detach her from his lap to stand on the floor or sit next to him. He made half-hearted attempts to disentangle her fingers by moving his head, instead of directly detaching her hands. However, most remarkable was the length of time that elapsed before she finally tired of hurting him. Most passengers studiously ignored the scene, except myself (who couldn't help staring) and a thirtyish woman with two young children who showed strong disapproval through her facial expression. When the train arrived in Tokyo, the little girl romped ahead of her grandfather and began to tap people and objects on the station platform with a balloon that she was carrying on a long stick—again without her

grandfather's restraint. The young mother who had been staring at her in the train walked briskly ahead of the little girl but took a swipe at the balloon as she and her well-behaved children accelerated down the platform.

7. However, Fisher and Greenberg (1977) point out, Freud himself regarded the basic description of the oedipal resolution as an oversimplification, covering the multiple variations in form and intensity experienced by children in the development of gender identification, consolidation of sexual object choice, and beginning development of a mature superego. Traditional theories about male heterosexual development appear to be more satisfactory and substantiated by clinical and research findings than are theories about heterosexual resolution among females (Fisher and Greenberg 1977, 224).

8. Garrick (1989, personal communication) points out that girls are thrust into experiencing more separation and individuation than are boys. Partly, this may be explained psychologically, insofar as the girl sublimates her dependency through identifying with her mother, and thereafter becomes more similar to her in altruistically assuming caretaking, nurturant, and supportive functions associated with feminine roles. Also, sociologically, this separation is related to the patrilineal basis of Japanese families where females eventually "marry out" and leave the family of origin to join the husband's family. Awareness of this eventual departure may generate a sense of disconnection with the natal family different from that experienced by boys.

9. Interestingly, mother-son incest in Japan appears to be more common than sexual contact between father and daughter. Mother-son incest reflects the combination of both maternal closeness and permissiveness, added to the son's prerogatives for dominating the mother, or at least making vehement claims on her for indulgent gratification. However, as Wagatsuma and DeVos (1983) mention, ordinarily the close relation between mothers and sons is manifestly nonflirtatious and nonsexual.

10. Such aggressive, hypermasculine scenarios are in no sense distinctive to the Japanese. In many national versions, "tough guy" protagonists are portrayed as loners, devoid of tenderness, who relate aggressively to other men and abusively toward women. Sometimes cast as spies, detectives, or adventurers, they are characteristically cynical and indifferent toward customary social values. Frequently they are cast in roles involving dangerous and clandestine work, pursued in a way that defies convention and reduces emotional attachments to other persons.

11. Illustrating the variety of opinion about the separateness or overlap of ego ideal and superego, some authors consistently point to the differences in the conscious element of *shame* connected to ego ideal, versus *guilt* as connected to superego (Piers and Singer 1953; Lampl-DeGroot 1962). Hartmann and Loewenstein (1968), however, see this differentiation

as artificial, and most reactions to failure as containing blendings of both superego and ego ideal. Thus, failures in performance evoke both conscious and unconscious, interpersonalized and internalized reactions combining the loss of esteem plus the fear of potential punishment. These theoreticians, therefore, see the "oughts" and the "ought-nots" as being closely associated as coordinating parts of both structures.

12. As cited in Muensterberger (1969a), Freud's (1931) reflections on the effects of differential childrearing are especially poignant:

It would seem rather that this accusation gives expression to the general dissatisfaction of children who, in our monogamous civilization, are weaned from the breast after six or nine months, whereas the primitive mother devotes herself exclusively to her child for two to three years. It is as though our children had remained forever unsated, as though they had never sucked long enough at their mother's breasts. (Freud 1910, 234)

13. The author is indebted to Regina Garrick for pointing out the similarities to *amae* in some aspects of interdependency among the Utku Eskimos in northern Canada.

CHAPTER 10

Current Issues in Anthropology and Psychoanalysis: Some Concluding Observations

Earlier chapters have presented information about aspects of dependency theory, psychocultural observations of Japanese behavior, and methodological issues concerned with research in both cross-cultural and developmental contexts. This concluding chapter represents a synthesis, and will cover three conceptual areas: the first concerning dependency manifestations and theory; the second regarding epistemology and method in the human sciences; and the third involving the juxtaposition of theory and practical considerations in psychoanalysis and anthropology.

Conclusions Concerning Dependency as a Social-Scientific and Psychological Construct

The utility of "dependency" as a constructional term in social and psychological research has been seriously questioned in the last twenty years. As reviewed in chapter 1, the concept is seen as having accumulated increasingly complicated and diffuse meanings. First regarded as a trait description of an essential need system in the infant/mother partnership, the term expanded to define requirements for physical attachment, nutrition, warmth, security, and emotional satisfaction. The acknowledgment of alternate drives, and the multivariate nature of dependency situations, have seriously reduced the capacity of this term to be operationalized in studies of later infantile and juvenile behaviors. Introduced in 1960, the term "attachment" has gradually replaced "dependency" as a constructional expression. "Attachment" more concisely refers to the emotional and instrumental factors present in specific intimate partnerships. In developmental psychology, "dependency" has been demoted to a qualitative term defining the expression of needs involving nonexclusive affiliation constituted during various periods of the lifespan. Another extension of dependency theory has involved the introduction of the term "interdependency," which takes into account the reciprocal exchanges in dyadic or multiple-partner sharing of need solicitation and need gratification. In these situations, a variety of interdependent connections may be examined, dealing with both emotional and instrumental factors pertaining to the continuity of relationship, reciprocity of need fulfillment, and negotiation of fluctuating states of obligation, trust, and mutuality.

Distinctions concerning the differences in attachment, dependency, and interdependency have clarified some of the conceptual problems inherent in typifying characteristics of close, affiliative partnerships. However, other problems remain. One of these involves distinguishing between the strong bonds of partnership present in asymmetrical relationships based upon *status* (or power) versus those primarily based on emotional ties modeled on an infant/mother paradigm. This has been addressed analytically by Lebra (1976), in her apt distinctions concerning "dependency of obligation" and "dependency of indulgence." Since status recognition based on age, gender, social role, and economic power is ubiquitous, a strong argument may be made for a structural basis separately accounting for the dependency connected to obligation or deference (as in *on*), distinguished from dependency connected to indulgence and nonsexualized love (as in *amae*). However, as Lebra has suggested, these and other modes of dependent interconnection may overlap. Thus, persons may be involved in interdependent relationships characterized by security and love, coexisting with the intimidation and fear generated by subordination to a status superior.

Psychoanalytic theories of dependency raise yet other problems concerning putative structures ("drives," "defenses") that dynamically activate and channel personal behaviors involving close affiliation. As Parens and Saul (1971) observe, psychoanalytic theory posits a fundamental libidinous drive underlying the infant/mother attachment, which also accounts for intense, positive affiliations developed later in life. Nonsexualized affiliations such as the dependency of indulgence, obligation, or pity (Lebra 1976) are seen as secondary drives, energized through a redirected or sublimated sexual drive (libido). Previous chapters have summarized other positions within and outside psychoanalysis that argue for a separate and freestanding structural basis accounting for nonsexualized affiliation and operating as an ego instinct. A possible resolution of this conflict in psychoanalytic theory might be to consider that there are at least *three* separate drives that are potentially activated in intense, interpersonal affiliations: *sexual, indulgent,* and *status oriented.* Partnerships characterized by strongly held emotional bonds might then be examined as reflecting one, two, or all three of these drives, singly or in combination.

Problems that involve the differential cultural framing of dependency experience have also been reviewed. The ideological disparagement of dependency in Western life has been emphasized in terms of pathologizing helplessness, and promoting idealized versions of individualism, independency, and self-sufficiency. Also, the structural egocentricity of Western descriptions of self have been contrasted to sociocentric explanations of self (or personality) in more collective definitions of interactional personhood. Although conspicuous in Japanese psychocultural depictions of self, such sociocentric versions are also routine in Indian, Korean, and other Asian societies.

Partly based on this cultural evidence, an argument for a freestanding structural drive for affiliation centering on "indulgent dependency" has been made using Doi's comprehensive depiction of *amae* in Japanese culture, folk psychology, and social organization. This cultural commentary complements the deductive conclusions of a number of Western psychoanalytic theorists (e.g., Fairbairn, Winnicott) who have depicted nonsexualized dependency as a central, panhuman ego drive.

From a structural standpoint, Hsu's (1971b) taxonomy of human social relations constitutes another systematic psychosocial model depicting various forms of affiliation, and employing a sociocentric mode of explaining the "psychology" of relationships (see chapter 7). Taken together, the speculations of these theorists seriously challenge Western psychological and psychoanalytic formulations stressing egocentricity and personal autonomy.

Shweder and Bourne (1984) also have addressed the ethnocentricity of Western psychologizing in a chapter concerning cultural variation and the conceptualization of personhood:

> The ego's view of its "self" is the product of the collective imagination. In the West, the messages implicit in many of our child handling *practices* may well socialize deep *intuitions* about the "indecency" of outside (external) intrusions, regulations, or invasions of our imagined inviolatable self. Practices cultivate intuitions . . . which then support such Western notions as "free to choose" . . . , "autonomy in decision-making," "sanctuary" and "my own business." (Shweder and Bourne 1984, 194; italics original)

Some Current Issues in Anthropology

Epistemic and Methodological Considerations

Many of the materials presented in earlier chapters are directly abstracted from anthropological descriptions concerning dependency theory and experience in various cultures—particularly Japan. Although Doi's formulations about dependency emphasize psychological and psychoanalytic aspects of *amae*, these are contextualized in the cultural matrix of Japan, and involve an intricate use of emic terminologies and indigenously based explanations.

Some of the earlier connections between anthropology and psychoanalysis have been sketched in various forms of collaboration that reached a peak in field studies attempting to relate "culture and personality" during the 1950s.[1] Following that, the focus on culture and personality has yielded to a series of changes in theory and field methods. In a parallel but entirely independent manner, some of the basic tenets of psychoanalytic theory and method have also been challenged and rethought. Although institutionally disconnected, theorizations in both of these fields contain interesting similarities that will be examined in these concluding sections.

Hymes (1972) confronted controversial historical issues in anthropology against the backdrop of experience accumulated during a century of investigation, reporting, and theorizing. A series of essays examined the occult ethnocentrism embedded in the neocolonial origins of the discipline, and documented the earlier inattention to biases implicit in Western political and scientific propositions. The advent of ethnomethodological insights and procedures during the 1970s introduced an antidote to trends that made invidious comparisons to Western societies, and implicitly supported a view of evolutionary progression in a hierarchical view of cultural development.

In a later publication, Salzman (1988) summarized changes in anthropology beginning in the 1960s, evolving from a normatively dominated and descriptive structural functionalism, through a period that emphasized *symbolical* aspects of human behavior (as in Turner, Firth, Barthes). Here the encoding of symbolization underlying cultural appearances began to achieve equal if not ascendant importance over the earlier Boasian emphasis on "pure description." Salzman (1988) then described a later wave of interest in *structural anthropology* epitomized by the work of Levi-Strauss. This emphasis pursued even deeper significance and meanings implicit in the symbols of individual subjects and cultures. These explanations involved the weaving together of prevailing myths, rituals, and symbols into a systematic fabric displaying deep structural components held to best epitomize specific cultures.

At this point Salzman reflected,

I was beginning to see, through my increasing weariness, a pattern in our disciplinary progression, a demidecadal molting as the old theoretical/ methodological/epistemological skin is shed and a bright new, totally different, much better anthropology emerges. (Salzman 1988, 32)

He then described the prominence of a combination of *semiotic* and *interpretive* approaches during the 1980s. These approaches have emphasized the examination of ethnographic records as "texts," and take meaning as the primary focus of inquiry—"replacing natural science with literary criticism as its model" (1988, 32).

As Levi-Strauss is emblematic of anthropological structuralism, Clifford Geertz exemplifies the interpretist position. In a series of articulate writings, Geertz has promoted the interpretation of culture through meaning, based upon a method employing "thick," emic description. He has composed a series of eloquent ethnographies documenting his research in Morocco, Bali, and Indonesia, including some reports on diachronic contrasts. His second and most important contribution has been a series of deductive writings advocating a method for ethnographic study based on the interpretation of detailed, naturalistic observations relatively devoid of reference to etic generalities, "universals," or comparisons to other cultures.

In an early publication, Geertz (1973) undertook to establish an interpretive theory of culture based upon a close, hovering attention to the actual phenomenology of symbolic interactions observed in the field. Removing himself from the more functionally oriented, comprehensive study of small societies, Geertz saw the ethnographer's task as sorting out particular "structures of signification" naturalistically encountered in the field, and employing an interpretation of specific events in and of themselves. He illustrated this by incorporating Gilbert Ryle's (1957) term "thick description," which Ryle had used to examine the multiple possible meanings connected to the ostensibly simple act of *winking*. In his hands, "thick description" involved making a series of cautious inferences and implications based on culturally contextualized events (Shankman 1984).

Geertz characterizes the ethnographer as operating partly as a literary critic, and argues that the culture is tantamount to a *text* that is "read," rendered, and interpreted by the ethnographer. While advocating phenomenologically based explanatory descriptions of what is actually happening, he carefully dissociates himself both from the more intense ethnoscientific methods and those associated with cognitive anthropology. For example, he does not see culture being reduced to the cognitive processes of particular culture bearers, nor to collective extrapolations of these. In the opposite direction, he does not endorse trying to integrate diverse symbolical interpretations in a search for transcendental abstractions that might reveal an inherent, supraorganic culture—as in the structuralist position of Levi-Strauss. Instead, he sees the ethnographer as inscribing social discourse in a manner similar to the literary author, who (in the case of creating a *fictional* text) may suggest some plausible implications and explanations of what in the instance of fiction is a narration of an imaginary action process. The interpretive method seeks to comprehend and portray metalinguistic, discourse-bound meanings that are connected to various events. However, as Geertz points out, his method is concerned with presenting a fine microscopy of social activities involving both ordinary and distinctive cultural events—for example, in his interpretation of the meaning of a Balinese cockfight.

His interests are not in looking at culture as content, but rather as *context* through which various kinds of content are shaped, formed, and framed. Thus he is devoted to tracing the circumstantiality of everyday existence, and not especially concerned about how such events might generalize or compare with those of other societies. Theories, therefore, are insinuated rather than boldly stated, and moreover stay close to the grounded substance of "thick," phenomenal description. Somewhat like Boas, he avoids generalizing across cases, and confines explanations to what Shweder (1984) calls "culture frames."[2] Even with meticulous attention to detail, Geertz acknowledges that his own ethnographies are forever incomplete and unfinished. Moreover, they are fully capable of different and alternate formulations. This variability is similar to the manner in which both literary works as well as real-life experiences can be subject to multiple interpretive explanations, based on the varying perspectives of the observers, and subject to the imputation of different meanings at different times by different interpreters.

Geertz concedes that sticking close to the phenomenological scene tends to ignore generalization and deter theory construction. However, he envisions a potential growth in general knowledge about culture through the cumulative accretion of various thick descriptions of monocultural situations. As another inherent weakness in descriptions that stress circumstantial and contextual factors, such ethnographies are only weakly predictive. Variations in time, actors, and modes of representation are bound to change even over short periods of time; these variations render prediction hazardous.

One of the problems with Geertz's view of the interpretive process is the difficulty in substantiating what constitutes a "real," "authentic," or "true" interpretation. His explanation is that "a good interpretation of anything . . . takes us into the heart of that of which it is the interpretation" (Geertz 1973, 18). In addition to being tautological, such instruction is not very practical. As Geertz himself points out, even the ethnographer's most sensitive interpretations of festivals, conversations, or ordinary life events may not meet the standards of explanation of the culture bearers themselves. The problem, however, is that numerous alternate speculations might be "authentically" and "truly" made about these same phenomena.

As Keesing (1987) states in a critical article concerning thick description, the problem is that "cultures as texts" may be differently read and construed by various ethnographers, potentially creating a *Rashōmon* effect. Such a situation undercuts the opportunity for verification and validity in the human sciences.[3] Keesing also comments about the ambiguity concerning cultural phenomena that are layered in terms of their differential visibility and understanding even *within* the culture. For example, how many Balinese participate in or even care about cockfights; and among these, how do their explanations of significance vary? This introduces the question of representativeness *and* significance of behaviors witnessed and described by ethnographers, which may lead to a form of selection bias. As Keesing says,

I will suggest that we anthropologists have been overinterpreting, misinterpreting the talk of other peoples on the basis of our professional preconceptions and even our vested interests in the academic division of labor. And I will suggest that paradoxes and ambiguities in cultural translation lie at the very heart of symbolic anthropology's project, the deep reading of culture as texts. (Keesing 1987, 167)

In commenting on revisions in field study and the emphasis on interpretative process, Sass (1986) has summarized the positions of some traditional and contemporary anthropologists. Similar to Sass, Shweder (1986) has characterized ethnography as "storytelling," and likens anthropological writings to casuistry. Often regarded as intellectually suspect, casuistry may more neutrally be viewed as a systematic application of explanations and rationalizations to justify or exonerate controversial positions, behaviors, or persons.

Shweder says,

Just as it takes a while to figure out what actually happened to you in the field, it takes a while to figure out which point of view will have the greatest impact on your audience. That may sound like casuistry, and it is, for it's casuists who write the best enthnographies. (Shweder 1986, 38)[4]

In a series of publications, Shweder has confronted many of the complex issues regarding the application of anthropological theory and method to monocultural and cross-cultural studies of diverse societies. Broadly, two opposing schools of thought have addressed the issue of how to study and interpret behaviors observed in exotic societies. One school, typified by Shewder as "Enlightenment," has attempted to derive broad generalizations, universal laws, and the substantiation of deep structures, partly through using positivist, empirical methods modeled after the natural sciences. The other school—characterized as "Romantic"—has consistently taken the position that the extraordinary range of human variability vitiates the capacity to arrive at anything but trivial, universal generalizations.

From that romanticist tenet flows the concept of arbitrariness and culture, subordination of deep structure to surface content, the celebration of local context, the idea of paradigm, cultural frames, and constitutive presuppositions, the view that action is expressive, symbolic, or semiotic, and a strong anti-normative, anti-developmental presumption culminating in the view that the primitive and modern are coequal and that the history of ideas is a history of a sequence of entrenched ideational fashions. (Shweder 1984, 28)

Shweder describes both collective and individual consciousness as distributing across rational, irrational, and *non*rational categories, within the broad range of reality testing in all cultures. Rational aspects of culture and individual subjectivity stress the application of reasoning, which emphasizes attention to empirical evidence, application of actuarial probabilities, and a belief in the existence of abstract, universal forms and lawfully regular processes. Irrational ingredients of culture are expressed in animistic or magical propositions based on unprovable ideologies that explain and justify the guidance of personal and collective behaviors. *Non*rational aspects of culture apply to a quantitatively predominant number of propositions that are neither rational nor irrational. These constitute a large body of representational schemes based upon the complicated, indigenous assumptions germane to particular cultural frames of reference. They are embedded in a large body of aphorisms, customary explanations, and suppositions that simply cannot be pinned down through appeals to logic and science, truth and falsity, error and validity, practicality and efficiency (Shweder 1984, 39).[5]

Shweder's stratified system of rationality constitutes a refinement of earlier anthropological theorists who saw the homology between the so-called primitive mind and the fluctuations of consciousness present in members of all human societies. This view of human consciousness also evokes Freud's observations concerning the natural aberrations and ellipses manifested in the "psychopathology of everyday life," and Goffman's commentaries concerning the vagaries of logic and reason governing moment-to-moment awareness accompanying prosaic human interaction. However, what is so ingenious in Shweder's classification is his assertion of the quantitatively disproportionate amount of *non*rational beliefs and practices that "explain" culturally framed behavior, and provide the normative background through which actions are evaluated and judged on a moment-to-moment basis.

An important corollary to the presence of nonrational cultural beliefs is the fact that once posited, these assumptions are there-

after subject to explanations and defenses of such beliefs and practices, which do, in fact, follow syllogistic and logical (i.e., "rational") rules, albeit within a nonrational culture frame. His argument
emphasizes that taking a purely Enlightenment, positivist-empiri-
cal approach to the study of culture runs the risk of packaging social
information in a manner that represents more of the ethnographer's
bias than the actual context and circumstances in which such behaviors are experienced. While conceding that some socialization
in all societies involves acquiring apparently universal principles
concerning deductive inferences, Shweder nevertheless feels that
most of what is incorporated during childhood has to do with learning the tacitly revealed, nonrational propositions that constitute
emic explanations of interpersonal behaviors, and that superintend
the direction of the action process.

Although Shweder's arguments posit a strong, even radical cultural relativism, he concedes the presence of some universals in
terms of markers for *descriptions of personality* (as in White 1980),
connotative meanings (Osgood, May, and Myron 1975), *emotional
indicators* of facial expression (Ekman, Sorenson, and Friesen 1969),
capacity for *color discrimination* (Berlin and Kay 1969), and *influence of group size on responsible behavior* (Barker 1968). However,
he does not deal with the significance of many other putative deep
structures, such as those that conceivably underlie the superficial
variations in recognition and greeting behaviors, styles of eating,
ornamentation and dress codes, socialization practices, discourse
sequencing, and so forth—presumably because the superficial variation in these behavioral areas is so extraordinarily diverse.

Some Problems with Universalism
versus Relativism

In the preceding chapter, a number of traditional schemes suggesting both behavioral and cognitive universalism were examined.
Other commentators have deductively organized lists of universal
human conceptions and propensities. For example, Andrew Lock
(1981) posits an innate self/nonself categorization underlying the
differentiation of object relations, involving both the physical environment and other persons. This self/nonself differentiation can be
seen as fundamental to the capacity for *motivational orientation*—
where self or other is implicated as causal instigator of action. It
also may be seen as a *normative orientation*—through which the

actions of self and others are compared, judged, and evaluated predicated on a motivational actor being a responsible moral agent. Further dimensions of the nature and locus of control have been also posited as universal tendencies, including the ubiquitous dimensions of dividing experiences into "extrinsic versus intrinsic," "active versus passive," and "being-in-control versus being-under-control."

Also, the presence of universal *positional and spatial* concepts has been explored by Lock (additionally by R. Horton 1982) in regard to the indexical qualities of up/down, near/far, right/left, and the temporal frames of reference dividing experience into "past," "present," "future," and "timeless." In a parallel manner, the uniform appearance of indexical, demonstrative pronouns has been noted by Yoshida (1980) in a study of 479 languages and dialects. This uniformity would suggest an innate propensity to stipulate spatial dimensions through pronouns that localize ("index") experience.

In a psychoanalytic approach, Fried (1970) has examined both developmental and clinical aspects of self/nonself discrimination related in terms of *activity* and *passivity*. In a parallel manner, F. Johnson (1988c) has discussed putatively universal ontological awareness of self/nonself against the background of alienation theory. Illustrating the universal properties of multiple dimensions of *intelligence*, Gardner (1983) has delineated a series of "frames of mind" that apply to human intelligence transculturally. Unlike instruments designed for classifying abilities in monocultural contexts, Gardner's list includes a series of inborn capacities for intrapersonal knowledge, interpersonal knowledge, spatial processing, temporal awareness, deductive reasoning, and category formation. Such "frames of mind" not only take into account sensory and cognitive processing, but also are critically concerned with the acquisition of performance skills. Although universal, these capacities for intelligence are channeled by specific cultural conditioning, individual differences, and socialization variables. Socialization experience includes *protolearning* based on private observations and independent deductions, *tacit learning* based on observations about others, and *formal learning* grounded in explicit procedures that equip the culture bearer with specialized information concerning prevailing ideologies, explanations of physical reality, sociolinguistic conventions, and causal-motivational descriptions of competent social performance.

Other evidence suggestive of universal patterning has been investigated in the extensive, multicultural expressions of *complementary opposites* involved in systems of "dual symbolical classification" (hot/cold, dark/light, night/day). Some of these paired opposites are related to extreme points of objective dichotomies inherent in the properties of the real world. Others are partly embedded in anatomical or kinetic aspects of the body image and bodily experience (right/left, front/back, skin/orifice). However, despite the broad transcultural capacity for such dichotomizations, the specific encoding, labeling, and meaning for these classifications vary considerably. Moreover, as with color terms, *multiple* meanings may be associated with these antonymic expressions, which vary according to numerous contexual variables. Needham (1973) concludes that both ethnographic and analytical investigations strongly suggest certain "constant tendencies of the human mind" that recurrently emerge in different cultures.

This wide comparison creates the strong impression that human beings all over the world tend to order themselves and their environments in remarkably similar ways, and by implicit recourse to classificatory principles so general and adaptive as to appear natural proclivities of the human mind. (Needham 1973, xxxiii)

However, as Spiro (1986) has suggested, Needham cautions that the "proof" for universals is basically an empirical matter, and not merely answered by the deductive methods of analytical philosophy. Lakoff (1987) thoroughly documents this caution by reviewing some of the history of philosophical and psychological attempts to generalize about what systems of category formation actually mean. Writing in the area of what he calls "cognitive semantics," he capably demonstrates that the bedrock beliefs in pure objectivist science have been seriously eroded by empirical studies that argue for a more *relativistic realism*. As Shweder (1984) has discussed, there has been an abiding, postenlightenment conviction that a true and fixed reality existed "someplace out there," which could be comprehended and codified through careful objectivist experimentation. While such techniques have in fact led to considerable illumination, particularly about physical objects (e.g., planetary bodies) or physiological processes (e.g., the Krebs cycle), strict application to social, psychological, and communicative processes has been limited by the complex contextual and situational variables—particularly evident in multicultural contrasts.

Lakoff (1987) challenges a series of tenets of objectivist science: that the mind is an abstract machine that manipulates certain fixed symbols; that internal, symbolic representations faithfully correspond to a precise external reality; that thought is disembodied and abstract; that thought is basically logical and channeled by inexorable processes; and, finally, that correct reasoning ineluctably mirrors the intrinsic logic and order of the external world. He does not suggest that categorization is illusory, but rather that cognitive, emotional, and behavioral states vary in ways that use *multiple categorizations* in an atmosphere of what he calls "experiential realism." Citing the works of a series of psycholinguists, anthropologists, and cognitive scientists, he sees categories of both "things" and "processes" clustering around "prototypes" (rather than around fixed polarities), with loose, extendable boundaries (rather than fixed extremes), graded relativistic sets (rather than absolute standards), and multiple rather than unitary imposition of possible symbolical meanings. Adding to the resume of other contributors' work, he adds his own extensive scholarship in the semiotic and semantic significance of metaphor to emphasize the contributions of bodily experiences to the formation of conceptual categories and classifications. Milton Singer (1984) has also developed this same insight into the relationships between embodiment and symbolization in a text concerning semiotic anthropology.

In a direct response to Shweder's (1984) essay on "Anthropology's Romantic Rebellion," Spiro (1984) has reflected on conflicts between universalism and relativism using arguments that reinstate the significance of transcultural patterns of human behavior. Spiro clearly applauds Shweder's observations about the profusion of nonrational explanations in "culture frames" that differentiate, contextualize, and normatize human practices. However, he advances a series of arguments that qualify the alleged arbitrariness of these specific "assumptive worlds." First, he reflects that cultural determinants of behavior are not the only factors influencing social structure, social organization, or social interaction. He cites additional factors that impinge on the action process and are readily encountered transculturally: including situational variables, ecological givens, political processes, biological substrates (e.g., "needs"), and emotional patterns. He sees these operating as deep structures that direct and channel human experience in a universal manner despite the profuse superficial variations attributable to culture.

In several publications (1979, 1984, 1986), Spiro suggests that the presence of deep, organized patterns of behavior are not the residue of Western, postenlightenment science, but in fact attest to structures underlying the display of emotion, distinctions between rationality and irrationality, and the cues that influence ordinary discourse and interaction. These include panhuman (and certainly *nontrivial*) aspects of status designation, gender distinction, and hierarchies concerned with moral sensitivity, reward and punishment, "good" and "bad."

Spiro (1986) also mobilizes criticisms against extreme positions in both normative and epistemological relativism. In regard to normative relativism, it is evident that all cultures have discriminations concerning "good and bad," "true and false," "beautiful and ugly," although such distinctions pivot on non–rationally established evaluative criteria pertinent to each culture. However, Spiro believes that both the "arbitrariness" and the nonrationality of cultural frames have been overstated. Superficial variability within the emic range of possibilities still is subject to deeper patterning and dynamisms influencing human performance. Some of these involve what Spiro refers to as unconscious and antecedent *needs*, which operate beneath the superficial, emic variability of specific cultures. This commonality also pertains to the object-seeking behaviors expressing basic needs in the form of purposeful actions—again, despite the presence of outstanding cultural variation.

Beyond this, it can be argued that supposedly noncommensurable features of different cultures may be normatively compared when particular questions are asked. For example, it is hard to resist positing a hierarchy of moral consequence regarding head hunting as a periodic expressive ritual, versus sublimated forms of aggression featuring regulated, semiviolent activities—as in monitored sporting events. Also, the allegation that all sciences, including ethnosciences, are somehow equivalent rings hollow when operational questions are asked about explanations of physical reality in regard to particular purposes—for example, the development of sophisticated metallurgy, the treatment of infections, the creation of multiple-story buildings, and so forth.

Spiro's most incisive critiques also point toward the existence of deep structures through the biological bases of emotion. This does not contradict the observed variability in emotion rules, or the suppression and augmentation of certain feelings in certain cultures. However, it does assert that relativistic accounts often ignore evidence for a universal spectrum of emotions that accompany behavior, and are connected to proactive strategies guiding both the immanent action process and subsequent feedback regarding the evaluation of behavior. Evidence for a universal substrate for emotions posits a highly sophisticated central nervous organization involving panhuman characteristics—particularly evident in emotions but also in other fundamental functional activities.[6]

Some of the criticism of exaggerated relativistic interpretation parallels the critiques of literary criticism associated with postmodernism and more specifically with *deconstruction*. As noted in Spiro (1986, 275), the metaphor of "culture as text" suggests that behavioral phenomena are submissible to multiple readings and interpretations. This tenuously leads to the conclusion that there may be as many interpretations as there are interpreters, and "the question of validating any particular reading does not have to be confronted; either because that question is irrelevant, or because it is impossible of resolution" (as critically reported by Spiro 1986, 275).

In regard to the information in earlier chapters summarizing dependency experience in Japan, it might be said that both relativistic and universal dimensions have been presented. Peter Dale's (1986) arguments (see chapters 6 and 7) assert that both indigenous and outside ethnographers have invented a chauvinistic glamorization of Japanese culture, and given an undue signification to commonly used words and terms, including *amae*. His position constitutes a strongly universalist perspective—one that denies even a mild, let alone moderate, form of descriptive cultural relativism. Certainly in Doi's presentation of dependency phenomena, it is explicitly stated that these emic Japanese versions of *amae* are expressions of a universal drive involving psychological, social-interactional, and even ideological manifestations of dependency, which are in no sense exclusively Japanese.

Experimental Trends in Ethnographic Reporting

Marcus and Fischer (1986) have depicted some developments in interpretive anthropology as part of a general "crisis of representation" in the human sciences. This crisis is related to a series of challenges in sociology and anthropology towards "establishment positivism" (reported earlier in Giddens 1976), and a growing conviction that the implications of contextuality and indeterminacy generate a profound uncertainty concerning an adequate method for describing and capturing social reality.

As they observe,

because all perspectives and interpretations are subject to critical review, they must finally be left as multiple and open-ended alternatives. The only way to an accurate view and confident knowledge of the world is through sophisticated epistemology that takes full account of intractable contradiction, paradox, irony and uncertainty in the explanation of human activities. (Marcus and Fischer 1986, 15)

The influence of postmodernism has promoted the use of more reportorial styles in the presentation of ethnography. This has caused some anthropologists to move from a field experience synthesized into an internally coherent report and analyzed as a *text*, to a more microscopic focus on ethnography presented as an untainted, and only scantly edited, *discourse*. In these innovative procedures, the ethnographic method itself, along with the ethnographer's foundation of knowledge, become coequivalent foci of interest. As Rabinow (1986) comments, such reports attempt to subvert the conventional epistemological explanation of the process of observation by suggesting that this epistemology itself is merely an artifact of Western, postenlightenment philosophy, which equates knowledge with internal mental representations. Employing more emically based epistemologies, some newer experimental ethnographies (S. Tyler 1986; Crapanzano 1980, 1986) attempt to reproduce the phenomenological givens of the field situation, and move away from reporting as a monographic series of reflections toward a more dialogical, conversational documentary of the actual transactions. In attempting to bracket out what are considered to be extraneous comparisons or characterizations, these reports are designed to place the reader of ethnography in the position of vicariously participating in the research. Hence the reader partly shares the task of making deductions based on exposure to the raw communicative data. As Marcus and Fischer (1986) comment, this highly self-conscious, microscopic presentation of data constitutes a *meta*ethnography, which is concerned with rendering an uncontaminated picture of exotic events at the same time that it examines assumptions of the ethnographer's own society and consciousness. The result of this newer methodology can be seen as creating a documentary concerning "an ethnography of ethnographies."

Ethnography and Contemporary Literary Theory

Recent experimental methods in ethnography have been explicitly related to *deconstruction* as a movement in literary criticism that has become prominent in the last several decades. As in anthropology, the deconstructive analysis of literature has brought about a radical and critical questioning regarding the description and interpretation of human behavior. It emphasizes the kaleidoscopic variability and unpredictability of interaction, and the fragility of achieving consensus concerning observations, descriptions, and synthetic reports. As McConnell (1990) describes it,

Desconstruction is a critical theory, deeply French at least in its origins, that finds the real significance of literary and philosophical texts not in their explicit meanings, nor even in their implied meanings, but in the unintentional meanings—in the slips, evasions, and false analogies that betray the text's "ideology." It is a way of reading *against* the text, and its aim is to achieve an unprejudiced, value-free vision of the societal and political power structures underlying the classical "canon" of great works of Western literature. (McConnell 1990, 100)

Deconstruction in the United States has been strongly identified with Jacques Derrida and a group of literary critics at Yale. Its popularity as an experimental, epistemologically self-conscious mode of interpretation has significantly infiltrated the field of literature and criticism in the United States. As Alter (1983) described it, Derrida (1977, 1978) has given a particular twist to the relationship between the "signifier" and the "signified" at both a semantic and a psycholinguistic level. Ordinarily, the relationships between words and their referents are basically regarded as both conventional and arbitrary. Deconstruction, however, contrives to examine meaning by emphasizing the inherent slipperiness of representation, and through exaggerating the arbitrariness of meaning. Derrida thus generates a deconstructive method that allows the imposition of an extraordinary range of meanings onto specific words and texts and, by extrapolation, on accounts of human behavior.

From this primordial disjuncture, Derrida causes a whole world of chasms to open up. The *presence* of objects, persons and experience that literature repeatedly pretends to offer us turns out to be ... ineluctable *absence*; what appears to be literal is necessarily metaphorical; what is proffered as reality is in fact fiction; all literary manifestations of voice and assertions of its primacy merely mask the awareness that writing ... always underlies the illusion of voice. (Alter 1983, 27; italics original)

Similar to postmodern ethnographic reporting, the gist of any text is ultimately seen as embedded in the negotiated intersubjectivity of author and reader. Thus, meaning becomes a product of a series of mediated transactions suspended somewhere amid the original events, the composition of the text, the text itself, and the reader's gloss or interpreted sense of what is read. The distinction between the composer of the synthesis and the reader's creative reading of the synthesis is heuristically blurred.

Deconstruction concentrates on the fluctuating cognitive processes that establish meaning, and focuses intensely on the process of representation between the signifier and signified. Beyond merely tolerating multiple interpretations of whole narratives, deconstruction advocates the imposition of variable meanings through the microscopic examination of specific words and phrases. A common manipulation of the relation of sign and signifier is to look at the implied antonymic meanings—quite simply to suggest that the words may well stand for their opposites. Also, in a way that seems contrived and playful, words are omitted or excised as a way of throwing new light onto the interpretation of the text. As another alternative, the most elliptical and eccentric connotative meanings for words may be advocated in place of their conventional, denotative significations. Interpretation of text (or of observed human interaction) then becomes a *meta*interpretation of fragmentary portions of dialogue, narrative, or behavior. In the hands of the deconstructive critic, this metalevel interpretation continuously calls attention to the shifting intersubjectivity between partners: actors and observers, writers and readers, speakers and listeners. This atomization and diffusion of meaning severely challenges Western epistemological principles concerning the use of conventional sign/signifier representations to look for standard denotative meanings, reliable generalizations, "laws," and regularities. However, for the deconstructionist, looking for stability and unity either within or outside the text is regarded as illusory. As McConnell laments, "literature is no longer the test of universal civilization; instead it constitutes personal civilization" (McConnell 1990, 105).

Epistemic and Methodological Considerations in Psychoanalysis

The issues discussed about anthropological theory, method, and reporting have some parallels in the field of psychoanalysis. Paralleling the empirical/theoretical, objective/subjective dialectic common to most human sciences, a heuristic division is maintained in psychoanalytic thinking between the epistemological basis of actual clinical situations and the hypothetical basis of metapsychological speculations.[7]

In regard to the treatment of empirical information, there are a number of epistemological and methodological similarities between the ethnographer/informant and analyst/analysand relationships (F. Johnson 1988b). Both anthropological field work and clinical psychoanalysis impose explicitly asymmetric statuses among the participants, and are governed by communication rules that center attention on the patient's and informant's narrations—rather than those of the psychotherapist or ethnographer. However, ethnography characteristically uses multiple informants and primarily concentrates on conscious aspects of conversational content, although dreams, myths, and rituals may be explored. In contrast, clinical psychoanalysis uses free association, dream analysis, and a close attention to the anachronistic aspects of the transference, all focusing on a single "informant"—the patient. Psychoanalysis also inherently posits a belief in the sequentially patterned, epigenetic nature of human experience, and supports theories concerning innate drives and a biologically based, deep structuralization.

Both clinical psychoanalysis and anthropological field work pivot on an intersubjective, communicative process in constructing a conceptual understanding of personal and cultural patterns through the process of observation, description, and interpretation. Both disciplines are internally divided on the dialectic between universalism and particularism, but there is considerably more consensus among American anthropologists for what Spiro (1986) calls "strong normative relativism." In both psychiatry and psychoanalysis relativism takes the form of maintaining an ethical neutrality concerning what might conventionally be regarded as "abnormality" (Offer and Sabshin 1966, 1984). Both fields avoid taking moral positions in regard to the evaluation and understanding of individual and group behavior.

As in anthropology, psychoanalysis supports an epistemological relativism that posits a developmental tabula rasa, onto which the sequential effects of individual experience and socialization are inscribed in a way that promotes a highly specified sense of personal history. However, psychoanalytic metapsychology has formulated detailed, universalistic structural models of personality involving complicated internalized schemata reflecting the putative presence of innate patterning. Thus, psychoanalysis takes an eclectic stance toward relativism and universalism.

Another comparison between psychoanalysis and anthropology resides in the treatment of historical information and the establishment of historicity. Discounting history per se, anthropology has generally emphasized the detailed, *synchronic* account of observed events. Some investigators, however, have made observations of different time periods either to substantiate prior work or to indicate culture change. Nonetheless, these interests in history pale in comparison to the central significance of historical sequencing in clinical and theoretical psychoanalysis.

Within the literate societies inhabited by psychoanalytic theoreticians, an immense repository of historical literature is available to generate hypothetical statements concerning causal-motivational propositions about the structuralization and patterning of human behavior. Also, in the immediate clinical situation, the historiographic significance of a particular patient's recollection of the past is central to the therapeutic work. Because of this, the epistemic status of the patient's recollections is more crucial than the testimonies of anthropological informants concerning the historical veracity of information.

The question of the validity of personal, historical reminiscence has been a long-standing but smoldering issue in psychoanalysis, recently brought to the surface by Spence's (1982) distinctions between "narrative" and "historical" truth. As mentioned previously, Spence defines narrative truth as a consensual agreement concerning the recent and remote past as these become established during the intensive psychoanalytic procedure occurring over time between the analyst and analysand. Historical truth refers to the kind of critically established, factual representation of remote events as documented through a long and painstaking examination of the past—customarily using multiple reports and verified primary sources. In taking the position that psychoanalytic transactions involve an intersubjective consensus concerning *re*construction of prior events, Spence supports a hermeneutic, interpretist position following in the tradition of Ricoeur (1970, 1981), Wachtel (1979), and Langes (1973).[8]

Spence (1982) also examines two contexts in which the determination of "truth" concerning the patient's history have an application: first in the actual, ongoing treatment situation, and second in the examination of retrospective case reports, summaries, and scholarly reporting generated *after the fact*—the latter more like "ethnographies" in relation to the "field work" of clinical encounter. Spence offers a work-a-day description of the analyst's capacity to arrive at a plausible account of the patient's past history. This parallels the emic/etic distinction in anthropology (see Harris 1968) and applies to two different kinds of competence: "normative" and "privileged." "Normative competence" is Spence's term for the *etic*, cumulative knowledge concerning clinical events learned and assimilated by the psychoanalyst as a result of life experience, specialized training, and exposure to an extensive literature regarding both clinical and metapsychological theory. Adding to this scientific competence are formal courses, training analysis, supervised clinical treatment, and, finally, the experiences and introspections associated with clinical practice throughout the analyst's professional career. In anthropology, such "normative competence" consists of the ethnographer's prior life experience, the content of his or her graduate education, and access to an extensive anthropological literature containing both practical and theoretical information. This background and field study culminates in composing an ethnography that involves a synthesis of all of these elements— including the specific details of field study, which are subsequently described and interpreted.

The psychoanalyst's "privileged competence" is emically established through the close intersubjectivity fostered in the therapeutic relationships with specific, individual patients intensively seen over protracted periods of time. This privileged competence is paralleled by the anthropologist's authentic understanding of the "field," which develops following repeated contacts with multiple informants during immersion in the foreign society.

Since the 1970s, the ethnographer/informant relationship has come under increased scrutiny. Because ethnographers, like psychoanalysts, are actively involved in interpreting the narrations of their informants, there is a concern about the "countertransference" effects of their own past history and world view, which may seriously bias their observations. Attempts to achieve fidelity of observation have been explicitly promoted since Boas, but have become more of a self-conscious and overt issue since the advent of ethnomethodological awareness in the 1970s. Some investigators, such as LeVine (1973b, 1982, 1987) and Devereux (1969), have explicitly emphasized *countertransference* considerations in the same sense as used in psychoanalytic techniques. Recently, such precautions have also been applied to the retrospective recording of field notes, and to the synthetic activity of composing an ethnography applying to unconscious as well as overt factors involved in observing and writing (Crapanzano 1981).

Concerns about the process and nature of communication have always been prominent in psychoanalysis. Freud initially took the pseudoempiricist position that the analyst was behaviorally outside of the situation, and that the psychic events of the patient were scientifically examined almost as if they were material products— like a "chemical analysis" (Nelson 1958). As discussed in chapter 2, this structural/objectivist position was directly contradicted by Freud's emphasis on the nonobjectivist use of *interpretation*. This required the analyst to understand, intuit, decode, and transform the raw data of "psychic material" revealed through free associations and dreams. The additional complication of relating "psychic reality" to "external reality" was unfortunately postponed and neglected through making a more or less complete dichotomization between the two categories. In a series of publications, Wallerstein has written about how psychoanalytic theory has addressed this problematic distinction. In an important synthetic statement, Wallerstein and Smelser (1969) charted some of the conceptual territory between psychoanalysis and sociology searching for possible "complementary articulations" and applications from the knowledge bases of both fields. In a later article, Wallerstein (1983) carefully traced the evolution of the concept of reality, building on Freud's early distinction concerning reality testing as both a theoretical and pragmatic consideration. Hartmann's contributions to the expansion of ego functioning were accompanied by specifically addressing the problem of reality, and the dynamic interplay between intra- and extrapsychic worlds (Hartmann 1956). The contributions of Arlow (1969) and Frosh (1966) were also listed as progressively refining the formerly ambiguous domain of the "reality principle" into a detailed and dynamic interplay among various ego functions and the complex world of external objects.

Wallerstein (1973) earlier had extended the growing significance of the concept of reality by summarizing its more comprehensive articulations with internal representations.

Implicit in all this is that there is not ... one large and encompassing reality (or world of reality) that we deal with psychologically, the same and uniform for all, but rather many smaller, varyingly overlapping and varyingly congruent partial realities, man-constructed realities, to which different men in turn declare varying and differentiated allegiances. (Wallerstein 1973, 17–19)

This clarification is remarkably parallel to the microsociological explanations of "the social construction of reality" as introduced by Berger and Luckmann (1967). It also is virtually identical to the anthropological propositions concerning the "native's point of view" and "culture frames" cited elsewhere in this volume. However, Wallerstein's statement is *broader* than these, since he simultaneously suggests the possibility of an idiosyncratic reality both for individual persons and collective (cultural) groups.

Looked at from these perspectives, what *social reality* really phenomenologically consists of is a series of multichanneled, communicative signals that indicate the orientations of self/other relationships involved in some kind of prior, incipient, or imminent action process. Looked at internally, these action possibilities include recollections of the past as well as rehearsals for future performance. Although allowing for the presence of fantasy, these activities are synthesized within the background of what the individual "knows" and "believes" to be the limits of true experience.

Despite some of these newer views of reality, there has been a continuing tension between structural and interpretive modes of explanation. Newer modes of explanation have attempted to cut through this impasse by way of more phenomenologically based modeling (as advocated by Edwin Wallace 1989). For example, there has been increasing attention paid to the dialogical and communicative aspects of the psychoanalytic situation, and to the factors of empathy and intuition that are essential in the treatment process —as discussed by Schafer (1976), Havens (1976), Schlesinger (1981), Lichtenberg (1981), and Brothers (1989). This position is remarkably close to the emphasis on intersubjectivity and microscopic attention to communicative variables advocated by recent experimental trends in ethnography and in postmodern literary criticism.

Observations Concerning Method in History, Psychoanalysis, and Natural Science

Edwin Wallace (1985) has examined some comparisons and contrasts in the fields of psychoanalysis and history regarding historiography. Both fields are centrally concerned with attempts to reconstruct and interpret the past. Each uses a hermeneutic process to organize and explain events retrospectively. As Wallace points out, historians and psychoanalysts both study symbolically mediated behaviors and impose explanations of these through "interpretations" that implicate intentional factors in prior actions. Psychoanalysis and history also share a concern with the diachronic sequencing of actions, with searching for a consecutive ordering of events, and with making comparisons between different time periods. Quoting Florovsky (1969), Wallace appears to agree that "the knowledge of the past is necessarily indirect and inferential. It is always an interpretation. The past can only be reconstructed" (Florovsky 1969, 351).

Both historians and psychoanalysts face the problem of how recounted stories change over time, even when rendered by the same informant or patient. In contrast to workers in natural and physical sciences, historians and psychoanalysts have to deal with chroniclers and patients who may consciously and unconsciously delete, disguise, or distort their recollections. Anthropologists face this same dilemma in the capriciousness of individual informants' recollections. Additionally, they must come to grips with the composite and sometimes conflicting explanations picked up from multiple testimonials.

As already mentioned, Spence (1982) has examined epistemic and historiographic issues in psychoanalysis using the constast between "narrative" and "historical" truth. Apparently favoring a more moderate position, Edwin Wallace (1985) finds Spence's statements regarding the difficulty of establishing historical truth to be overly relativistic. As an historian, he feels that Collingwood (1965) also maintains an overly relativistic position in regard to interpreting the past. For example, Collingwood has stated that "the past is simply nonexistent, and until the historian fully realizes this, his technique is precarious" (1965, 101). However, similar to Collingwood, Spence's arguments about the nonveridical recollection of the past are stated in a precautionary spirit, and apply to the psychoanalyst's sensitivity about the *re*constructive nature of what is being recounted in the patient's narratives. These warnings ontologically state that the past "does not exist," but do not suggest that the past *did not exist*. The problem is that recovering the past is subject to potential slippage and distortion.

Issues connected with causation (or more narrowly with "motivation") are conspicuous in both psychoanalysis and history, but less problematic in anthropology. However, all three fields deal with the problem of identifying and integrating multiple "stories" and explanations, which then may be used to speculate about and interpret causation and meaning. One of the most important insights from psychoanalysis about causation is the concept of "overdetermination." This holds that ongoing consciousness and behavior are the resultants of multiple and complex factors—including the effects of prior experience in combination with innate drives and structural organization. Some of these factors may be more "fundamental" than others, but the principle that multiple ingredients are involved is standard in Freudian psychic determinism. Historians and anthropologists similarly see human behavior as determined by a confluence of forces and factors operating at particular times and in particular situations. Edwin Wallace (1985, 1989) has introduced the felicitous word "intersectional" to apply to this explanation of behavioral events. This term goes beyond overdetermination, and explains behavioral events according to a blending of the *multidetermined* purposes and intentions of more than one person. Observed behavior is thus regarded as reflecting the conjunctions, collisions, and conflicts between various individuals examined within a dynamic, interactional system involving more than one person. Using this perspective, the interpretation of behavior seeks to identify and implicate plausible motives through the use of interpretist, hermeneutic explanations involving both participants.[9]

Interpretation in the Natural Sciences

In looking at the natural sciences, the potential distortions, casuistry, and "story telling" in the human sciences are largely unobtrusive because of the use of precise, replicable measurements, the objectivity of observation, and the application of statistical procedures. Leaps between practical experimentation and conclusions are achieved with more sureness, follow actuarial principles, and employ deductive logic. The relationship among the processes of observation, description, and explanation has recently been summarized illustrating the uses of experiment in the natural sciences (Gooding, Pinch, and Schaeffer 1989). However, as these authors point out, the production of validatable and verifiable results in the "hard sciences" has been inflated. Although enjoying a clear advantage in temporal precision, quantifiability, and opportunity for replication, the *interpretation* of experimental results and the transmission of this information to others raises issues that are identical to those encountered in the human sciences and psychoanalysis. As Gingras

(1990) comments, "it is one thing to do an experiment and another to talk about it to convince people" (1990). Problems accompanying the synthetic acts of reporting and interpretation are inherent in all literary work, and influence the meaning and significance of experimental results in the natural sciences. Gooding (1986) emphasizes that any experiment undergoes a conceptual transformation through the synthesis of the experimenter. Also, in all sciences, constraints on reporting are shaped by the social processes that channel scientific reports into forms dictated by both tradition and the canons of particular disciplines. In commenting on this transformational process, Nickles (1989) makes the point that although experimental work in the natural sciences deals in objectivist facts concerning the real world, its significance is invested with contextual implications concerning meaning, social significance, and ethics. This bears a remarkable similarity to the problems addressed in the process of reporting in psychoanalysis and the social sciences.

Pickering (1989) has cautioned about the need to pay more attention to the relation between actual experimentation and articulated knowledge. This concern parallels Geertz's conviction that the study of how anthropologists work is a phenomenological issue, requiring the use of close observation and "thick description." Similarly, in psychoanalysis the study of actual psychoanalytic processes through transcripts and audiovisual recordings has suggested that the understanding of what "really happens" must be closely grounded in the phenomenological substance of the actual situation.

Pickering also identified three overlapping stages in the establishment of experimental fact in the natural sciences: first, the material procedure itself; second, the instrumental model used for understanding the procedure: and third, the phenomenal model used to interpret and explain the significance of the results. He uses the term "coherence" as an essential measure of plausibility and integrity that ties together these three stages. By "coherence" he means that observation, synthesis, and interpretation must demonstrate internal integrity and sequential logic in presenting meaningful information about natural phenomena. This definition of "coherence" is parallel to Sherwood's (1969) use of this same term for the understanding of the psychoanalytic situation. The attainment of plausibility in any science requires a coherence, correspondence, and integration between observational data, conceptual modeling, and "story telling."[10]

Hermeneutics and the Limits
of Interpretation

Doi's Interpretation of Dependency
and Interdependency

Within this book, Doi's comprehensive work on *amae* has functioned as a centerpiece for summarizing a number of observations
about dependency and interdependency—primarily but not exclusively in regard to Japan. His own observations are based on clinical
encounters, comparisons with various hypothetical models of personality, information from anthropological writings, and his existential experience of alternately being a participant-observer in the
cultures of North America and Asia.

Doi's conclusions about dependency have been crystallized from
a series of observations in clinical, research, and naturalistic situations in both the United States and Japan distributed over a number
of years. His cultural observations have used the informal study of
persons in natural encounters within the workplace, private homes,
institutional settings, training contacts, and public places. These
have been sharpened and refined by a process of curiosity, reflection, and cross-cultural comparison concerning the possible meanings and significance of various behaviors in both countries. (Any-
one who has lived in a foreign culture is aware of the amount of
reflection spent in processing public and private behaviors witnessed in the "exotic setting.")

Beginning from a direct experimental level, Doi's observations
have been progressively organized through what Pickering (1989)
calls "instrumental models," where these behaviors are categorized
into a number of functional and expressive systems. Because of
Doi's breadth of background, knowledge of several cultures, interest
in literature (Japanese, English, German), and skills in communication, he has been able to utilize and select from a number of explanatory systems, including metapsychological theory, Western and
Eastern personality models, plus culturological information pertaining to both societies in which he has lived. Building on these
instrumental models, Doi has imposed a process of *interpretation*,
particularly in regard to a series of hypotheses relating to the significance of *amae*like, primary attachments (Doi 1973a) and configurations concerning the "anatomy of Japanese self" (Doi 1986). These

have been extensively reviewed in earlier chapters. The question now might be raised of how valid are Doi's interpretations concerning the significance of indulgent dependency?

Doi's work pivots on an inductive method involving his own clinical and naturalistic observations, as well as the investigations of other clinicians and social scientists. His deductions are based on interpretations made concerning the nature of nurturant affiliations, paradigmatically between infant and mother but also in intimate, dependent connections throughout the lifespan. As such, these observations and conclusions are posited using an epistemology and logic conventionally associated with anthropological field work. Such methods also apply to clinical investigation in psychoanalysis and the process of information gathering in other behavioral sciences that address formulations concerning object relations. As mentioned repeatedly, Doi's convictions about the centrality of dependency (as a putative ego drive) conflicts with the more indirect conceptualizations of dependency in traditional psychoanalytic metapsychology.

Although not exclusively conceptualized in terms of interaction, the concept of *amae* rests on a paradigm of the relationship between the infant and mother. While asymmetrical, such a relationship is based on mutual interchange and a rudimentary reciprocity. Looked at overall, his formulations reflect both universal and relative dimensions of human dependency, analogically similar to Chomsky's (1972) formulations about a stratified, structural basis underlying language acquisition, competence, and usage. Other scholars have speculated that, similar to language, behavioral repertories utilize a biologically structuralized, "deep" basis upon which superficial patterning is solidified. In this sense Doi operates as a structuralist whose interpretations point toward the presence of deep, underlying patterns and motives that are universal, but subject to diverse manifestations when channeled through the regulating features of specific cultural frames and individual variability. His work supports the structuralist position that surface events are underlaid by structural components beneath the ebb and flow of the overt action process.[11]

In these explanations, human behavior is depicted as involving deep intentional (that is, purposeful) structures. Speculatively, these structures are associated with the neurophysiological processes involving memory, attention, cognition, and emotion. In psychoanalysis, motivational structures are represented as being underlying psychological forces ("drives"), seen as channeled and influenced by other systems that modify their admission to consciousness, or alter their effects on manifest behavior. Thereafter, these drives are filtered through systems of interaction rules, selectively associated with particular "culture frames." As in Shweder's explanations, such culture-specific rules contain mixtures of rational, irrational, and nonrational ingredients, and furthermore vary according to particular situations, contexts, and anticipated performances.

In this connection Doi's work contributes to a "depth psychology" (Wyss 1959) through suggesting the manner in which indulgent dependency constitutes a fundamental affectional and motivational system activating nonsexualized, intimate relations among individuals. At the same time, Doi (1973a) has composed a list of social-psychological formulations describing how interdependent transactions are navigated in Japan, illustrated in various kinds of partnerships and in a number of circumstances and situations. The consequences of these interactions are also examined in regard to a range of basic or blended emotions (anger, joy, sadness, etc.) experienced in the midst of satisfaction, frustration, or displacement of the desire to receive (or give) indulgent dependency.

Beyond this, Doi's descriptions center on both the consciousness and behavioral manifestations of *amae* (and *amaeru*). Taken together, these constitute a psychocultural documentary of the "native's point of view" in Japan regarding the nature of approved and permissible expression of dependent affiliations. Doi's observations about the Japanese are filtered through the explanatory models of psychocultural studies of the Japanese connected to a structural, metapsychological theory of drive and human development that in his view establishes *amae* as a basic, panhuman drive.[12]

Restraints on the Process of Interpretation

In psychoanalysis, interpretation is central in both treatment and metapsychological theory. Beginning with Freud's earliest writings, the manifest content of dreams and the symbolisms of patients' symptoms were regarded as representational rather than concrete. The decoding of dreams, symptoms, free associations, and symbolical actions required the psychoanalyst to grasp the underlying meaning of these productions, and to interpret them to the patient. Interpretations were formulated as creating otherwise inapparent connections between psychic events and certain putative causes, motives, or activating systems. Interpretations involved the use of *analogy* (for manifestly comparable associations), *metaphor* (in establishing more remote comparisons), and *metonymy* (where "parts" were alleged to stand for both real and symbolical totalities). Therapeutically designed interpretations were seen as making comparisons between representations from the present to past experience, mobilized in a search for anachronistic and maladaptive remnants in contemporary behavior. For example, a patient's tendency to be intimidated by older men might be related ("interpreted") to juvenile experiences with a frightening, authoritarian father. In this explanation the "signifier" of current emotional experience would be historically connected to prior experiences. In a similar manner, transference interpretations would employ this same comparison between past and present but use the contemporaneous feelings and fantasies generated by the patient toward the analyst to illustrate the projections of past experience onto the therapeutic relationship.

The accuracy and substantiation of such interpretations are established in two ways. First, at the level of direct experience, the "validity" of interpretations is tested according to the practical effect produced on the patient through both emotional and intellectual acceptance of a new insight. Second, at a more hypothetical level, the plausibility of particular interpretations may be judged according to Sherwood's (1969) criteria of coherence, correspondence, and integrity. However, even using these criteria does not offer exact guidelines of how to constrain a deductively based interpretative process that makes assertions concerning the relationship between signs and signifiers. This is especially critical when such symbolical connections are used to substantiate *processes* (e.g., "cathecting"), *structures* (e.g., "superego"), or *dynamisms* (e.g., "reaction formation"). Dealing with the narrative information from subjective events—themselves removed from the objective inspection—involves the establishment of meaning, which is *inferred* about motives and feelings based on the communicative process. It also includes making inferences and interpretations concerning meaning based upon thematic content and other qualities of the "narrative" generated by analysands.

Unlike interpretations of experimental findings in natural science, interpretations applied to behavioral situations are organized according to rules and conventions that apply to decoding and explaining human communication and interaction. Some of these investigate more universal, fundamental, and basic patterns, and may use explanations that are governed and constrained according to the canons of traditional science. These may examine representations on the basis of *similarities* (identity), *contiguity in space,* and *continuity in time.* Syllogistically tight explanations are expressed in the form of actuarial, statistical probabilities. These interpretations may also use accepted principles of deductive logic. However, such nomothetically oriented, objectivist procedures often succeed at the expense of bracketing off variables regarding specific contexts, situations, and other fluctuating ingredients that would render such methodology impossible.

In contrast, canons regarding the limits of interpretations in the human sciences more frequently involve explanations of naturalistic events imposed on personal reports of individual consciousness, the recitation of discourse, description of rituals, or the retrospective examination of literary works, dreams, or free association. These involve the use of interpretations in ways that are not uniform. Interpretations vary according to the *phenomenological givens* (dreams versus descriptions of cockfights), *method* (clinical psychoanalysis versus field observation), and the *interpreter* (literary critic versus ethnologist). Such interpretations also are influenced by traditional canons regarding explanation according to accepted models of human development, compendia of conventional wisdom, and a reference to various metaphorical and analogical systems on which such interpretations are pinned.

Some of these limitations parallel the principles associated with *rhetoric* and deal with persuasive argumentation using metonomy, metaphor, simile, and analogy to embroider basic, phenomenal narrations or descriptions. Within these attempts to persuade and explain, the "authorial presence" of the writer is a crucial element lending plausibility to descriptions and explanations. Often this presence is effaced in the apparent impersonality of the reportorial description of events and may be difficult to distinguish from the writer's inferential and hypothesis-generating *interpretation* of events. As Geertz (1988) has commented, the authorial, explanatory power is often based on the ontological fact that *"I was there,"* in answer to the hypothetical question, "Vas you dere, Charlie?" (Geertz 1988, 5).

The application of interpretation in the behavioral sciences and psychoanalysis in itself is a tenuous enterprise, open to challenge and debate (see Grünbaum 1984). Ricoeur (1970, 1981) is frequently cited as providing solid philosophical arguments for the scientific acceptability of the interpretative method in psychoanalysis. Other disciplines dealing with discourse, narrative, and semiotics also try to validate a scientific approach to the study of spoken and written communication using methods that incorporate law-abiding procedures.

Other general caveats concerning the limits of interpretation follow the pattern of Geertz's precautions, which state that thick descriptions should involve a minimum of theorization and employ interpretation that hovers close to the observational and behavioral givens. In a different direction, other authors such as Crapanzano (1981) have looked at hermeneutic explanations as inevitably relativistic. In an article concerning transference interpretation, he states that the limits of interpretation are strained by Western philosophical and cultural preoccupations about looking for the *deepest* (and hence "truest") explanations that may lurk beneath the manifest content of human situations. This raises the potential for "overanalyzing" and creating an interpretative regression leading to reductionism and reification (see F. Johnson 1988a).

Future Directions in Anthropology and Psychoanalysis

Research Trends in Psychoanalysis

This entire volume has looked at dependency and interdependency, particularly emphasizing the work of Takeo Doi. Part of the power of Doi's scholarship derives from his simultaneous use of psychological, psychoanalytic, literary, and ethnographic perspectives to illuminate the nature of these crucial affiliations. Future work will conceivably be carried out in anthropology and psychiatry to advance the understanding of dependency and attachment.

Currently, psychoanalysis is regarded as a pluralistic rather than a monolithic discipline (Wallerstein 1987). Its complex metapsychology contains a layering of id-psychological, ego-psychological, and object-relations theories, which may be compatible at the edges, but just as often engender serious conflicts. Within recent trends (reviewed by Settlage and Brockbank 1985), a number of directions can be noted influencing contemporary research, theory, and practice. In general, the interest in object relations has tended to pull the field in a gravitational way toward more phenomenologically based descriptions regarding both practice and theory. Research concerning clinical practice increasingly uses videotape recordings, transcripts, and multiple-person codings designed to abstract nomothetic qualities from the givens of the situation examined microscopically over time. Accompanying this close attention to real events, abstract metaphenomenal explanations are avoided in favor of more objective commentary. Similarly, in research on child development there is a decline in conceptualizing childhood according to retrospective accounts of adult analysands, in favor of observational research that prospectively examines ongoing infantile, juvenile, and adolescent behavior (Horowitz 1985). Yet another emphasis is derived from object relations, namely a focus on the *interactional* dimensions of experience. While not dismissing intrapsychic structuralization, interactional formulations take into account more complex variables in behaviors heuristically conceptualized as *shared* between individuals.

In terms of developmental theory, Shane and Shane (1985) have discussed the discrediting of hallucinatory wish fulfillment in early infantile experience in favor of more multichannel reactivity in the infant present from birth, (as in Daniel Stern 1985). They also mention the growing acknowledgment of interdependency between the child and its mother, and the presence of shared intersubjectivity (as in Lichtenberg 1981). They also cite the questioning of development formulated according to a lock-step progression of erogenous zones centered on the migration of libido. While not denying stage-specific concentrations, many contemporary theorists stress broader-based adaptations (as in Basch 1980, 1983). Shane and Shane also note what they believe to be a diminished concentration on "autonomy" as a psychological principle, in favor of "integration," which is a more interactive and socially oriented concept. In support of traditional observations concerning the oedipal period, Shane and Shane feel that these are standing up to observational research, but that the preoedipal period is undergoing revision in the face of psychoanalytic and other developmental evidence. This tends to support Doi's work, which has contributed cross-cultural observations about the fundamental and independent significance of nonlibidinal affiliations involving *amae*.

As mentioned before, there has been an increasing interest in phenomenologically based research, regarding both treatment and theory. This research is concerned concerned with looking at behavior through the description of spontaneous communication examined in terms of varying situational and contextual elements, instead of regarding free association as a "pure" indicator of unconscious forces, internal objects, or other deep structures. Perhaps one of the most influential phenomenological shifts has been to designate the *self* (or person) as a central component analyzed in the complex of introspective, communicative, and interactive behaviors. A strong trend toward focusing on the self as both a phenomenal and unconscious entity has been particularly prominent in psychoanalytic circles during the past fifteen years.

Kohut's work (1966, 1971, 1977) is especially well publicized and has turned away from conventional drive/structure models common in traditional metapsychology. Although his methods, terminologies, and descriptions have achieved a high degree of popularity, his theoretical suppositions have raised a good deal of criticism and backlash. Despite retaining an acknowledgment of intrapsychic topography and structure, his formulations are distinctly phenomenological and center on development based at an ego-level exposition of the self system ("selfobject"). His clinical and theoretical formulations concentrate on the phenomenology of *narcissism* as a central issue both in normal development and in various states of disability. Although undeniably responsible for redirecting a focus on the self in psychoanalysis, Kohut's work is curiously devoid of acknowledgments of a long tradition of scholarship concerning the "self" in philosophy and sociology. For example, his popularization of "mirroring" between the infant and his mother is a pale repetition of work done by Mead, Cooley, Baldwin, and James early in the century. Also, there is virtually no attribution made to the significant trends in academic psychology that have recentered interest in interactional, situational, and naturalistic aspects of human experience—typified by the work of Mischel (1977) and summarized in Frank Johnson (1985). Popper and Eccles (1981) have also composed a creative and comprehensive approach to self theory.[13]

Phenomenological, Interactional, and Linguistic Emphases

George Klein (1967) presented a new focus for the analysis of spontaneous chains of association by introducing the concept of *peremptory ideation*. This term described the surge of irrepressible chains of thoughts and recollections observable during the process of clinical psychoanalysis. These consisted of ideas that combined aspects of perception and imagery connected to the symbolical construction of speech, gesture, and action. In creating this shift, Klein was moving from a tradition that utilized a more reductionistic attribution of "drives" to account for observed behavior, thoughts, feelings, or fantasies. This switched from a consideration of putative drives to a more phenomenological emphasis on specific memories, ideas, affects, or incipient actions that spontaneously and irrepressibly (peremptorily) leap into consciousness.

In a more general manner, Horowitz (1979, 1988) has concentrated his research into the process of psychotherapy away from traditional structural constraints, toward an analysis of recurrent patterns identified as "states of minds," "themes," operational "styles," and qualities of role relationships. These constitute phenomenally based constructs that are operationalized in direct terms (for example, "role relationship with therapist" instead of "transference"). Such methods trace thematic frequency, communicative styles, and changes over time, and include a study of the content and form of the psychotherapist's interventions in accounting for the possible effects of psychotherapeutic change. (See also Wallerstein 1985a.)

As another shift toward a more phenomenological basis of study, Schafer (1976, 1978a) has steered away from metapsychological generalities and concentrated on semantic and sociolinguistic properties revealed through the psychotherapeutic dialogue. Schafer's concentration on what he calls "action language" constitutes an *emic* emphasis that looks for motives, intentions, and goal directions in the actual semantic and connotative meanings of the patient's particular verbal productions. As he states, "action language is more metatheoretical than clinical-theoretical: it has to do with how to formulate theoretical, psychoanalytic propositions non-mechanistically far more than it has to do with the content of specific propositions" (Schafer 1978b, 84). Again, the phenomenal focus is on the *person* or "self" as the instigator of thought, feeling, and action rather than on various aspects of the intrapsychic mental apparatus.

As Schafer has concentrated on the phraseology of "action language," Dahl has focused on a more microscopical study of "emotion words" themselves. Dahl (1977, 1978) has based his analysis of emotion words on de Rivera's (1977) "structural theory of emotions." As footnoted earlier, de Rivera examines emotions as *interactional phenomena* displaying ranges of possible feeling according to situational, semantic, semiotic, and positional variables within the "feeling partnership." He examines emotions in their social-communicative significance created during interactions between two or more participants. These are channeled according to their dimensional properties regarding activity/passivity, subject/object, and toward/away-from. In a series of publications (Teller and Dahl 1989; Dahl 1978; Dahl and Stengel 1978) emotion words are examined as "appetites" and "messages" indicating significant themes and properties of the analysand's flow of consciousness. Interpreted in this way, such "emotion words" provide an economical method for examining transcripted psychotherapeutic texts. As Dahl states it, his purpose is to show novel ways to condense the flow of free association through a computerized analysis of large blocks of text extracted through transcripts from cassette recordings.

Of all revisionist trends involving the logocentric study of psychoanalytic process, Lacan (1970) emerges as the most radical. Again, focusing on the phenomenology of actual words, terms, expressions, and circumstances of discourse, Lacan has brought a postmodern, deconstructive method to examine the psychotherapeutic communicative process. As Sass (1988) has noted, Lacan's own intellectual development was connected to an early interest in surrealism as a postmodern form of aesthetic creativity. Exhibiting some of these surrealistic elements, Lacan has composed an imaginative psycholinguistic approach to the analysis of clinical narrations and "text." He examines manifest content by concentrating on the occult, implied, and eccentric possibilities of meaning lurking within free association and reported happenings. As in deconstructive literary criticism, this involves "reading against the grain," looking for opposite meanings, and imposing omissions and eccentric connotations. His approach to the analysis of psychic events also centers on the issue of ontological closeness between conversational partners or readers of various texts.

Taken together, these various innovations (and others not listed here) are parallel to some of the theoretical positions in the newer, experimental ethnographies cited earlier. These are increasingly concerned with concentrating on naturalistic events, and observing the contextualizations and situational variations affecting communication and action. They also have the potential for concentrating on certain latent, deconstructive properties inherent in the contexts of public and private communication.

Problems in Universalism and Relativism

As outlined by Spiro (1984, 1986), there is a chronic and inevitable tension between universalism and relativism regarding scientific credibility in anthropology, psychoanalysis, and other human sciences. Basically, this problem pivots on the differing epistemological statuses of procedures that emphasize hermeneutic (semiotic and interpretive) methods compared to explanations that focus on observations looking for law-abiding patterns based upon directly measurable properties reflecting fixed, structural organization and predictable end points. However, an attempt to blend these two approaches is possible: namely, the obvious conclusion that deep structural patterns exist concurrently with superficial structures. Deep structures are concerned with elementary forms influencing the patterning of impulses, thought, feeling, and motivation—all of which are regulated and channeled in a manner that reflects the patterning conforming to particular culture frames and adapting to the immediate contextual and situational features of direct experience.

Here again Doi's work seems happily to traverse both of these dimensions. He clearly asserts that the impulse, desire, or motive for affiliation is an emergent (ego) structure evident at birth and enduring in various forms throughout the life cycle as a nonlibidinized activation for intense association with other creatures (and their representations). He has comprehensively documented the manner in which these forms of dependency and interdependency flourish in Japan in a variety of interactions and linguistic expressions implicating culturally distinctive behavior. He has gone further by describing a number of interpersonal situations where either the frustration, accentuation, or diversion of indulgent dependency (amae) underlies certain kinds of readily observable behaviors in social-psychological interchanges (see chapters 6 and 7).

Future work by himself and others will still rely on the act of interpretation to give meaning to the definition of dependent relationships examined in psychological, social-scientific, and psychoanalytic situations. Unfortunately, none of the modes listed earlier concerning the constraints of the "hermeneutic circle" can (or should) impose the control that is constituted in observations, measurements, and deductions concerning objective physical events. However, as Harris (1968) suggests, science, in all its forms, is distinguished by a systematic collection of facts that are carefully cross-checked for accuracy. But, even the most fastidious adherence to inductive methods and careful observation does not in itself necessarily lead to discovery of regularities and "laws."

The trouble is that a random sampling of any field of observation will prove beyond the shadow of a doubt that nature is chaotic. One has merely to observe birds flying, smoke rising, clouds drifting, feathers floating and stones plummeting, to realize that Galileo's formulation of the laws of motion could not possibly have resulted from the mere collection of facts. (Harris 1968, 281)

Amae as Universal Trait and Culture Frame

Throughout this book, patterns of intimate affiliation and indulgent dependency have been reviewed as universal (panhuman) phenomena, prominently represented in Japanese and Asian cultures. Some of the history of Western developmental approaches to dependency were summarized, followed by an examination of the largely indirect manner in which dependency has been formulated in psychoanalytic theory—basically as a derivative of a monolithic sexual drive. In response to Pelzel's (1977) criticism, the particular Japanese cultural framing of amae has been articulated in relation to the literature on Japanese history, early socialization, and education. Amae was also examined in its interrelationships with other clusters of Japanese norms regarding obligation (on), social relations (giri), emotional reactivity (ninjō), and ritualized modesty (enryo). One of the major purposes of the book has been concerned with a comprehensive and critical exposition of Takeo Doi's published work in English and Japanese, involving the multilevel manifestations and implications of indulgent dependency (amae). These were first examined as a putative drive accompanying the imperative need to activate a strong infant/mother connectedness, essential for the provision of security, nutrition, warmth, and emotional responsiveness. The more complex behavioral representations of various interdependent relationships were also reviewed, illustrating the reciprocal effects of both frustration and overindulgence of amae. Other manifestations involving the channeling of dependency were then described. These hypothesized the filtering and conversion of this basic drive for intimate affiliation into forms of sullenness (suneru), mild paranoia (higami), feigned indifference (wadakamari), overt hostility (futekusareru), mortification (kuyashii), or egocentric demandingness *(wagamama)*, as summarized in chapter 6.

At a social-philosophic level, Doi's reflections on postwar changes in Japan were also reviewed in terms of their possible influence on national ethos, or on trends affecting styles of recent childrearing and family life. An impressionistic portrayal of the psychocultural characteristics of the "Japanese self" (chapter 8) has referred to Doi's work (1986) as well as other published commentary regarding Japanese personality style formulated by various psychologists, psychiatrists, and behavioral scientists.

Throughout this, the quality of indulgent dependency *(amae)* has been highlighted along with other conspicuous elements affecting both subjective life and presentation of self. This was portrayed, first, as a subjective trait, temperament, and motivational orientation focusing on the interior self, and, second, as an interactional performance involving a consciousness centering on the relationship between self and others. In both private self-awareness and ongoing presentation of self, consciousness concerning the emotional navigation of closeness and reciprocal interdependency has been presented as particularly conspicuous among Japanese persons. A subsequent chapter has reviewed the history of cross-cultural studies, seeking comparisons and contrasts between Japanese and other societies in regard to childrearing practices, conceptions of self and other, and the qualitative nature of dependency and interdependency. Some of these involved looking at attempts to identify "universal" dimensions of family and personal organization through resumes and schedules devised by various psychologists and anthropologists. Other developmental studies regarding dependency were noted that reported on dependency experience in a number of different cultures (Indian, African, Vietnamese, Eskimo, etc.).

This concluding chapter has examined some of the epistemological bases for both social-scientific and psychoanalytic methods of inquiry and reporting. Since both anthropology and psychoanalysis have been involved in Doi's interpretations of *amae*, future work in these disciplines will conceivably contribute to the elucidation of both monocultural and universal dimensions of *amae*. In that regard, current trends in psychoanalysis that emphasize phenomenological procedures and take into account both social and intrapsychic variables might help to extend the validity of *amae* through providing evidence for a freestanding, nonsexualized primary drive fostering intimate, interdependent affiliation. Also, the increasing concentration on psychoanalytic concepts of *self* basically reinforces the combination of psychological and social approaches in formulations regarding object relations. Other recent research trends involving studies of transcripts containing specific themes, "states of mind," and role relationships (again at a *phenomenal* level) would lend support to the exposition of shared need systems, and the complex ways in which these are manifested in particular contexts and situations—notably within differing "culture frames."

In a parallel manner, the current "interpretist" emphasis within mainline anthropology endorses a phenomenological concentration on the "close and thick description" of monocultural behavioral events. Although this anthropological endorsement, as noted previously, is strongly relativistic, some "patches" of universalism are conceded—tentatively by such commentators as Shweder (1984), but unequivocally by Spiro (1978, 1984, 1986). Within an "interpretist" method, both the ethnographic study of specific societies and the clinical psychoanalysis of particular individuals contain an inevitable trade-off between "thick description" and "thin generalization." However, as in the metalevel summarizations of case studies of individual patients, certain universal trends may be inferred that suggest unmistakable evidence for generalization.

In contrast to these phenomenologically based, interpretive studies of individuals and cultures, the more radical, deconstructive methods would seem less promising—except as reminders that all observation of social and clinical phenomena involve a tender intersubjective process, readily influenced by the conscious and unconscious bias of observers. Also, it can be conceded that examining behavioral or communicative situations "against the grain" or from eccentric perspectives has the possibility of contributing significant new information about whatever is being studied. However, these deconstructive methods—whether in psychoanalysis (Lacan 1970) or in anthropology (S. Tyler 1986) would seem hazardous if not accompanied by more sober, distributive, and comprehensive description of behavioral phenomena. Instances of deconstructive analysis go beyond the clever transposition of parts, antonymic reversals of meaning, or selective omissions of content, and actually border on *de*struction rather than deconstruction.[14] Some of this problem may relate to imposing eccentric and surrealistic interpretations onto aspects of social reality that are themselves already ambiguous and uncertain—as contrasted to applying surrealistic insights to phenomena or objects that are readily recognizable and understood in their more basic concrete properties (like pocket watches in Dali's famous painting).

While dismissing deconstructionist methods, progress in the human sciences would appear to be favored by the separate but simultaneous application of methods from both positivist and semiotic perspectives. The phenomenology of human experience is obviously larger than the capacities of selected methodologies to contain and compress "reality" into formulated, precise renditions. Thus, attempts to designate universal structures, processes, or properties may be pursued at the same time that knowledge concerning the particulars of "framed" cultural experience are examined through thick description and closely hovering, nongeneralistic interpretations.

Among a number of promising possibilities, both mono- and cross-cultural studies of "inner psychological states" (Needham 1973, 1981) and "indigenous markers of personality" (G. M. White 1980) might be used to look for the existence of conceptual universals. Such studies, in a cumulative manner, might help distinguish classifications (categories) according to regularly appearing common features (called *monothetic*) from those based upon more sporadic or accidental resemblances (called *polythetic*).

After qualifying the premise for comparative analysis of "social facts," Needham addresses this issue:

> If quasi-constants among inner states can be discerned, even if only a polythetic definition, then they will at least serve as relatively steady points of reference in comparative researches. They may not be so independent or so certain as ideally we should like, but they will be more reliable bench-marks in the topography of human nature than our common presuppositions have proved to be. The very postulation of their existence conduces, moreover, to the formulation of interesting questions. (Needham 1981, 76)

It is sincerely hoped that such researches will be applied to the interdisciplinary study of indulgent dependency *(amae)* to illuminate this underlying ego drive for primary affiliation.

Notes

1. As Harris (1968, 393–463) has suggested, virtually all ethnographies are implicitly psychological, and include statements that allude to the

"native's point of view" concerning indigenous explanations of motives, emotions, traits, and dispositions. Thus, most field reports deal either explicitly or indirectly with the relationship between culture and modal personality. However, the "culture and personality school" in American anthropology combined a strong, post-Boasian relativism with a neo-Freudian psychoanalysis concentrating on developmental and presentational aspects of personhood witnessed in various societies. Using these methods, a number of large-scale, comparative studies were conducted in an attempt to relate early socialization practices to adult personality traits.

2. Shweder's (1984) use of the term "frame" pertains to the culture-specific contextualizations that simultaneously channel and "explain" personal and group interactions within any bounded society. Such normative and ideological frames, although generally understood and supported in any particular culture, are elusive and cannot easily be subjected to strict empirical confirmation or logical proof. Culture frames are therefore largely nonrational, and as Spiro (1984, 326) points out, may be subliminally acknowledged by typical culture bearers, but with varying levels of emotional investment. Shweder's meaning of "frame" is broader than Goffman's (1974) use of the term for communicatively contextualized performances in discursive monocultural situations.

3. Rashōmon (Akutagawa 1952 [1915]) is an artful Japanese novelette about the abduction of a young bride, related from the standpoints of three interpreters who were the principal participants. All three interpreters seriously conflict in their descriptions of the actual happenings, and in their speculations about the intentions of the participants. The charm and eeriness of the book lie in its portrayal of the chimerical nature of subjective reporting, and the potentially fragile process involved in substantiating social reality.

4. The use of casuistry (Jonsen and Toulmin 1988) has periodically been regarded as tarnished and morally suspect. Its methods include bringing ingenious and eccentric explanations to bear on reasoning and rule following in legal, ethical, and canonical arguments. The purpose of the casuist is to outflank traditional and conventional explanations through argumentation and persuasion, often involving exaggeration or even duplicity. The application of casuistry to "storytelling" in anthropology addresses the need of the ethnographer to interest and inform readers about what they are prepared to resist as incredible, odd, immoral, or even disgusting.

5. To illustrate Shweder's classification, the measurement of sidereal time constitutes a rational aspect of culture, involving the methodical division of elapsed experience into units that coordinate with the daily rotation of the earth and its annual elliptical course around the sun. Contrastingly, irrational cultural beliefs are maintained about the relationships between time, individual persons, planets, and stellar constellations, involving complex astrological speculations about the zodiac. Finally, the

arbitrarily named calendars used in various societies are an example of *nonrational* cultural systems. These involve the division of time according to certain historical dates of reference, along with the selection of names to stand for seasons, times of the year, and designations for "days," "weeks," and "months." Thus the expressions "Thursday," "August," or "1492" are neither rational *nor* irrational, but simply arbitrary, consensually accepted designations.

6. In an article titled "Whatever Happened to the Id?" Spiro (1979) has confronted some of the nearly phobic avoidance of biological explanations of human behavior in both structural and symbolic anthropology. At times, behaviors manifestly involving sexuality or aggression are primarily "interpreted" through metaphors stressing social transactions, communication, ritual, or myths as primary explanatory elements, while ignoring more straightforward explanations based on biological needs or motives. Spiro's criticism may also be applied to hermeneutic methods that suppress or simply ignore the possibility of deeper motives or of the coexistence of drives underlying manifest behavior.

7. As mentioned in chapters 2 and 9, the heuristic division between the phenomenology of actual clinical practice and the abstractions of metapsychological theory are overdrawn. Partly this is because the psychoanalytic situation itself is not ordinarily studied in terms of precisely measurable, directly empirical methods—although there are interesting and important exceptions to this. Also, it is evident that metapsychological theory has always used clinical practice (or "field experience") as one of the most important "laboratories" from which theories are generated in regard to internal structuralization, stages of development, abnormality, and (curative) change. In the reverse direction, the realities of clinical practice require the application of metapsychological principles to organize the nature of the patient's free associations, dreams, feelings, and patterns of behavior. Thus, there exists a kind of circularity—even tautology—between explanations of theory and practice.

8. In both psychoanalysis and anthropology, the issue of absolute veracity has been secondary to accepting the patients' and/or informants' *points of view* as "best recollections" of personal history—however deviant or idiosyncratic these may appear to be. In psychoanalysis, sequential changes and differences in the analysand's recounting of the past are routine. These are "interpreted" in order to understand the complex of early (or later) life events in terms of various defensive patterns.

In his 1982 book, Spence uses the word "construction" rather than "*reconstruction*" to indicate attempts to recapture the past through a narrative recollection of events in clinical psychoanalysis. However, the term *reconstruction* would seem to be more in keeping with current neuropsychological theories regarding memory. These posit that the accessing of prior information is an *active* process involving a number of factors (including aspects of the immediate communicative encounter), which makes recollection a synthetic and creative activity—in other words, a *recon*struction.

9. In a parallel manner, de Rivera (1977) has composed a structural theory of emotion that looks at the vectors existing *interactionally* between and among specific participants in particular situations. Although not contradicting biological or individual/psychological explanations of emotions, his work is a refined model of interactional study, where structural characteristics are established as units of study based on the coalitions of *two* or more participants.

10. Another version of what constitutes "truth in storytelling" involves the relationship between real-life experience and imaginative creativity in fictional literary work. This raises the question of how much of the novelist's own life and actual observations are consciously or unconsciously transmitted in his or her writing of what is purportedly *fiction*. Huddle (1990) has discussed this in speculating on his own and other novelists' writing, and addresses the issue of the interplay between the real experiences of the author versus the aesthetically transformed accounts of imaginary characters portrayed in supposedly fictional transactions within the novel. Atlas (1991) has also summarized some of the difficulties in establishing "truth" in both historical and journalistic reporting. He concludes that in the end the reader is left to accept or question the information largely on the basis of the credibility of an "authorial presence."

11. Another recent substantiation of Chomsky's deep-structural formulations of language has been reported by Petitto and Marentette (1991) in their observations of nonphonic (i.e., manual) "babbling" among deaf children who were exposed to *signed language* (ASL) since birth. Their observations suggest that babbling—whether vocal, or through ASL hand signals —is a product of a generic, structural language capacity in which phonetic and syllabic particles are produced by the infant in its progression toward constructing a mature communicative system.

12. DeGeorge and DeGeorge (1972) trace the connections between earlier and present-day structuralists in their common devotion to "deep interpretations":

The attempt to uncover deep structures, unconscious motivations, and underlying causes which account for human actions at a more basic and profound level than do individual conscious decisions, and which shape, influence, and structure these decisions, is an enterprise which unites Marx, Freud, Saussure, and modern structuralists. (DeGeorge and DeGeorge 1972, xii)

13. In a dialogical format, Popper and Eccles (1981) address the relationships between self and the brain, combining approaches from the philosophy of mind and contemporary knowledge in neuropsychology and neurophysiology. They divide *reality* into three separate but overlapping "worlds"— each with its own internal consistency. One of these is objectivist and

constitutes the universe of physical entities ("World 1"). This world conforms to historically established, Western philosophic traditions that address the law-abiding structuralization of the physical characteristics of real objects—animate and inanimate. "World 2" consists of mental states—conscious and unconscious—along with psychological intuitions, dispositions, and explanations. "World 3" consists of the particular contents and organization of thought, including a vast array of cultural and linguistic phenomena constituting products of the human mind. This latter world is similar to the domain of Shweder's "culture frames" that surround the naming, categorization, and explanations of objects, persons, processes, actions, and ideas in particular societies.

14. Grayson (1992, private communication) points out that most literary criticism is *constructionist* and works toward assembling evidence to sustain a particular interpretation. She also concludes that deconstructive methods examining literature are more radical than those used in the "new ethnographies" since they go beyond "intersubjectivity" to a pure "intertextuality."

Glossary of Japanese Terms

Regina J. Garrick

This glossary provides operational definitions of Japanese terms, expressions, and words that appear in the text. A few words and expressions from other languages are also included. Conventional definitions of Japanese words have been obtained from Kenkyusha's *New Japanese-English Dictionary* and Iwanami Shoten's *Kōjien*. Additional contributions from outside arbiters have been included to enhance the colloquial or technical extensions of these definitions.

The modified Hepburn system of romanization has been followed throughout this work. The following is not meant to be an exhaustive description of Japanese pronunciation, but merely a brief guide.

Unlike English, the pronunciation of Japanese words is uniform, with relatively few orthographic changes in standard, colloquial speech. Vowels are pronounced as in Italian or Spanish: "a" is pronounced "ah" as in "dot"; "e" is pronounced "eh" as in "met"; "i" is pronounced "ee" as in "peek"; "o" is pronounced "oh"; and "u" is pronounced "oo" as in "coop." When vowel clusters occur in a word, the vowel sounds are not merged (dipthongized). Instead, each vowel sound retains its original value in both pronunciation and duration ("beat"). When two identical vowels occur consecutively, the sound is simply extended in duration, and is indicated by a macron above the vowel (as in *shūchū* meaning "concentration"; *dōjō* meaning "sympathy"). The extended duration of a vowel (or of a glottal

Dr. Garrick acquired her experience with colloquial Japanese during an eight-year residence in several regions of Japan. She completed graduate programs at the University of Illinois (Asian Studies) and the University of California, Berkeley (Anthropology) before receiving a Ph.D. in Public Health/Mental Health at the University of Tokyo. She is a former student of Professors Takeo Doi and Takemitsu Hemmi.

stop between two consonants) also affects meaning. For example, *kiite* (pronounced "kee-eet-eh") means "listen," *kite* ("kee-teh") means "come," while *kitte* ("keet-teh") means "stamp," *O-ba-san* ("oh-bah-sahn") means "aunt," and *o-baa-san* ("oh-baah-sahn") means "grandmother."

Most consonants are pronounced like their counterparts in English, with a few exceptions. Consonant clusters are treated as a single phoneme, such as "shi," "chi," "tsu."

The cadence of spoken Japanese is distinctly different than pronunciation in Romance languages. As Lange (1988) indicates, the Japanese phonic equivalent of "syllable" in English is called a *mora*, which is not merely a unit of sound (phoneme) but also a unit of *timing* (or metering), more like a "beat" in musical composition.

People may speak quickly or slowly, but within a given stream of speech each mora will occupy the same length of time. This is true regardless of the type or number of sounds which make up each mora. (Roland Lange 1988, vii)

In standard Japanese (or Tokyo dialect), words are pronounced with a pitch accent, rather than with a stress accent as in English. The proper name "Yamashita" is divided into four equal syllables ("Yah-mah-shee-tah"), each of which receives the same amount of stress accent, but different relative pitch. Mastering this metered equalization may be difficult for English-speaking students, who are inclined to place emphasis on one (or two) syllables in standard pronunciation (e.g., the tendency to say "Ya-mah'-shee-ta" or "Ya-mah-shee'-ta").

Glossary

aijō: Love, of the general and platonic sort rather than the sexual or romantic kind; affection, devotion

Ainu: Name of a small, indigenous Caucasoid population, now largely intermingled with Japanese and located in Hokkaido

aizuchi: Literally, to alternate strikes with a hammer or mallet; the ryhthmic, vocal interjections of a listener indicating accord and understanding of a speaker's conversation

alus: Javanese word (See Geertz 1976) collectively meaning "pure," refined, exquisite, civilized—describing ideal adaptation within the culture

amae: The need to be responded to, taken care of, and cherished; the mutually interactive attitude or behavior whereby one seeks and (ideally) receives the indulgence of another

amaekko: (*amaenbō,* colloquial) A child who clings to its mother seeking her nurturant response; a child whose behavior may be perceived as "cuddly," demanding, or "spoiled"; a "big baby"; a child or person who actively seeks the indulgence (attention, care, protection, support, and/ or services) of another

amaeru: To seek the indulgence of another; to presume and rely upon the cherishment and security provided by another

amaesaseru: To gratify the dependency needs for nurturance and cherishment of another; to confer care or succor upon another (See *amayakasu*)

amai: Sweet, sugary, sweet-flavored; indulgent, fond, not-strict; too optimistic, naive, guileless, or even puerile

amakudari: Literally, a descent from heaven or, more figuratively, an appointment due to influence from on high; specifically, the reemployment of influential retirees from government or public corporations into senior positions in private business

amanzuru: To appear to be resigned to, to put up with, a situation that is below one's deserved station in life

Amaterasu ōmikami: The mythical Sun Goddess; the ancestress of Japan's imperial family

amayakasu: To indulge another's expectations for dependency, nurturance, or cherishment; to dote upon actively; to pamper, to coddle, to spoil (See *amaesaseru*)

atama: Head; mind, brains, intellect

boku: First-person singular, masculine, informal pronoun; "I"

Buddhism: A belief system originated by Gautama (ca. 563–483 b.c.), the historical Buddha, in north India; transported to Japan via the Chinese mainland and ultimately from Korea (Paekche) in the mid–sixth century a.d.

buraku: A village, hamlet, community; a shortened form of *tokushu buraku* used historically, and now pejoratively, to refer to "special communities" of people of pariah status

Burakumin: A term, now outdated and pejorative, meaning Japanese persons of pariah or "outcast" status (The self-descriptive term recently preferred by the political representatives of this group is *Dōwa no hito.*) (See also *Eta* and *hinin*)

Bushidō: A code of ethics associated with the "way of the warrior" in feudal Japan; now a nostalgic reference to idealized virtues, including self-control, honor, loyalty, and fortitude (See *samurai*)

butsudan: A household Buddhist altar where a family's ancestors are memorialized

chi: Mind, in the sense of rational, logical, mental functioning; intellect

chūi: Attention, heed, cognitive alertness; caution

Confucian training: Ethical precepts developed in China by Confucius (ca. 551–479 b.c.); standardization of interpersonal relationships based on filial dyads emphasizing a hierarchy of gender superiority (men over women) and correlative roles of duty and obedience; strong dedication to filial piety

daimyō: A lord controlling and overseeing a feudal fief during the Tokugawa era (See *shōgun*)

enryo: Positively valued social behavior characterized by modest reticence, hesitation, restraint, reserve; deference

Eta: A term, now archaic and pejorative, meaning "polluted person," referring to Japanese persons of pariah, outcast status (See also *Burakumin* and *hinin*)

furo: A deep bathtub in which people soak after first washing with soap and rinsing outside the bath

fusuma: Sliding doors covered with thick, opaque paper, used to separate rooms in the Japanese house (See *shōji*)

futekusareru: To act sullen or sulky; to become spiteful and act irresponsibly

futon: Japanese bedding that is spread onto *tatami* floor at night, folded and put away during the day

ga ga tsuyoi: (Ga means "ego," the self) Selfishness, self-centeredness; self-assertion (at the expense of others) (See *sunao*)

gaijin: Foreigner, alien; now refers especially to Caucasians; used generically as a term that emphasizes the non-Japanese status of a person

gaikan: External appearance

gaman: Fortitude, endurance, capacity to survive; also, may suggest a suppression of one's own (selfish) wishes or desires

geisha: A professional female entertainer, trained in the performance of traditional music, songs, and dance; certified through many years of apprenticeship

gimu: Duty, responsibility, obligation

giri: A deep sense of duty or social obligation toward (an)other person(s), as dictated by relationship of relative closeness or distance (See *ninjō*)

gurūpu: Loan word from English "group," as a study group or small division at work (See *han,* kumi)

habatsu: Clique or faction (in politics, business, or academics)

hai: "Yes," in the sense of positive affirmation. Also used as a common vocal interjection (See *aizuchi*)

haji: Shame, disgrace, dishonor, humiliation (See *hazukashii*)

han: Squad or group, as a study or work group (See *gurūpu, kumi*)

hara: Literally "belly"; source of "heart," mind, feeling, intention, or courage

haragei: The art of communicating nonverbally with another person through concentrating on, creating, and interpreting omissions, pauses, and ellipses in the verbal exchange

hazukashii: Shy, bashful; disgraceful, shameful (See *haji, tereru*)

higaisha-ishiki: Awareness or feeling of having been victimized, of being the injured party (due to realistic circumstances, rather than paranoia)

higamu: To feel unfairly treated (due to an insubstantial complaint); to be prejudiced against, biased; warped, twisted; to regard with (unreasonable) suspicion

himitsu: Secret

hinekureru: To act perverse, negative, unduly suspicious; to have a distorted perception of others' intentions

hinin: Literally "nonhuman"; contemptible, inferior persons not worthy of recognition as humans, such as outcasts, beggars, criminals (See also *Burakumin* and *Eta*)

hiragana: The cursive, phonetic syllabary of written Japanese, now consisting of forty-six different symbols (See *kanji, katakana*)

Hirohito: The given name of the recently deceased Japanese Shōwa emperor (1925–1989). The given name of the reigning sovereign is not used by Japanese people as either a term of address or reference; *Tennō heika* (His Majesty the Emperor) is used; appropriate reference in English is *Shōwa tennō* (the *Shōwa* emperor)

hito de nashi: An unfeeling, inhuman wretch; a brute

hoikuen: Day-care centers or nursery schools, some of which are licensed by the Ministry of Welfare to provide educational and custodial care for preschool children (See *yōchien*)

honne: Inner feelings; "true motives" or sincere opinions that are concealed from others (See *tatemae*)

hosutesu: Loan word from English "hostess," meaning a bar waitress

ie: Patrilineal stem family household denoting primary kinship affiliation

iemoto: The founder of a lineage or headmaster of a school of art

ii-ko: A "good child," an idealized child

ijimeru: To torment, persecute; to bully or haze by an individual or group

ikigai: One's purpose in life

ito: Intention, purpose

jen: Chinese word for man, person, or personage

jibun: The self, both representationally and internally

jiritsu-teki: Independent, self-reliant; able to stand on one's own two feet

jishin: Self; oneself; emphasizes a pronoun as in *watakushi-jishin* or *jibun-jishin*, meaning "I myself"

juku: Private extracurricular "cram" schools, commercially and privately operated to promote better scores on entrance examinations through tutoring, drills, and the administration of practice exams (See yobikō)

Kabuki: A popular form of theater entertainment that attained its florescence in the seventeenth century, featuring an all-male cast who sing and dance

kamikaze: Literally, "divine wind"; Japanese suicide pilots in World War II

kan: Perception, intuition; knack, instinct

kanji: Ideographs derived from Chinese writing system in the fourth century a.d. Standard written Japanese employs more than two thousand authorized Chinese characters, each of which will have one, and often several different, pronunciations. (See *hiragana, katakana*)

kanjō: Emotion, affect

kao: Face; expression; honor, prestige; persona

karma: (Indian) Hindi term for fatalistic view of life course

katakana: The square, phonetic syllabary of written Japanese, now consisting of forty-six different symbols; primarily used to transliterate foreign words into Japanese (See *hiragana, kanji*)

keigo: Honorific Japanese; a spoken and written language dependent upon a system of relative status that is reflected in word choice, special verbs, prefixes, and suffixes

keiretsu: Corporations that are linked by interlocking directorates, and sometimes the same stockholders (See *zaibatsu*)

kejime o tsukeru: To evaluate, discriminate, distinguish; to select, recognize or decide (with an awareness of one's social responsibilities)

ki: Spirit, mind, heart; senses

kidate: Disposition, temperament

kisha-kurabu: Press club

kōban: Police boxes; small buildings where police officers work in a visible and integrative way in Japanese neighborhoods

kobiru: To be obsequious, to ingratiate oneself, to curry favor with; to fawn, to flatter, to cringe; to humor (a patron) (See *nedaru*)

kodawaru: To be overly finicky; too concerned with details; to be difficult; obsessed

kōhai: Younger, junior, inexperienced, or new member(s) of a group or organization (See *senpai*)

koi: Love in the sense of physical, sexual attraction and passion; romantic love

kokoro: Literally, "the heart," but representing various aspects of mind, feeling, spirit, sentiment, intention, and mood

kokusui: National ethos; the characteristics, virtues, or genius of a nation

kokutai: National polity; fundamental character of the state; the unique essence and moral virtues of Japanese society. A term used from the Meiji era, but especially during the 1930s and 1940s, *kokutai* referred to a pattern of national unity, articulated through state-sponsored *Shintō*, which revered the emperor as preeminent while extolling the Japanese as a pure, ascendant race. (See *Shintō*)

kōsai: Relationships of association, acquaintance; the company one keeps; fraternization (See *tsukiai*)

kotodama: The spirit or mystique of the Japanese language

kumi: A fixed-membership work or school group (See *gurūpu* and *han*)

kuyashii: Mortified, frustrated, vexed; chagrined

kyōiku-mama: "Education mommies," i.e., mothers who are heavily involved in their children's adaptations to school and homework

magokoro: Sincerity; true hearted; purity of intent or motive

Meiji: Name of a period in Japanese history from 1868 to 1912 that brought great social and political change, often called the "Meiji Restoration"

miai: The formal introduction of potential marriage candidates to each other and each other's families through a third party (See *nakōdo*)

miai kekkon: Arranged marriage; negotiated through a supervised system of introduction, investigation of backgrounds, and formality of meetings (See *ren'ai kekkon*)

MITI: Abbreviation for Ministry of International Trade and Industry, the powerful central organization partly responsible for Japan's spectacular postwar economic recovery and development. MITI coordinates national assets, capital, and market.

mitsugo no tamashii: The spirit of a three-year-old; the "terrible threes"

miuchi: Kin, relatives (See *nakama,* also *tanin*)

mizushōbai: Literally, "the water trades," meaning a variety of drinking, eating, and entertainment establishments, many of which cater almost solely to men

Morita ryōhō: Japanese psychotherapeutic method involving hospitalization accompanied by a careful regimen of rest, focused contemplation, and gradual reintroduction of regular activities

moxa: (mogusa) Punk-like herbal substance (mugwort or Artemisia vulgaris) burned on the skin as a folk treatment for various medical and behavioral problems

mushi: A literal and/or figurative worm, thought to infest the body, causing illness and/or behavioral disturbances; temper

Naikan ryōhō: Japanese therapeutic method involving concentrated, supervised reminiscence in semi-isolated seven-day schedule with the purpose of rehabilitating dependent and obligatory relationships

nakama: Colleagues, fellow workers; companions, circle of friends (See *tanin*)

nakōdo: Matchmaker or professional go-between; marriage broker (See *miai kekkon*)

nedaru: To clamor for, beg for, importune, demand (See *kobiru*)

nemawashi: The process through which group consensus is achieved, usually by advance individual "politicking"

Nihon: Japan (The same *kanji* also may be pronounced *Nippon,* which renders a nationalistic nuance. *Yamato,* written with different *kanji,* is an older term also meaning Japan.)

nihonjinron: "Theory of being Japanese"; a chauvinistic belief system that insists upon and extols Japanese superiority and uniqueness

ninjō: Human feelings, sympathy, kind-heartedness (See *giri*)

Nisei: A second-generation person of Japanese extraction born and residing outside Japan

Noh: A symbolic, highly stylized drama, patronized by *shōguns* in the fourteenth century, based on Buddhist tenets, performed by male actors, sometimes masked and accompanied by a narrative chorus playing instruments

obi: Belt or sash worn with traditional Japanese *kimono*

omoiyari: Sensitivity to the intentions, meanings, and feelings of others

omote: The exterior, face, or front; a facade, superficial or public appearance (See *ura,* also *tatemae*)

on: A sense of ongoing, undischargeable obligation within a relationship; a concept of permanent indebtedness to another

onbu suru: (Colloquial form of *obuu*) To carry a person, usually an infant or small child, on the back

o-temba: Tomboy

oyabun-kobun: Patron-client relationship based upon the model of the parent-child relationship

ōyake: Public; open; official

oya-ko shinjū: Joint suicide of parent(s) and little children in response to severe distress

ren'ai kekkon: Love marriage based on romantic sentiment (See *miai kekkon*)

risei: Reason

Romaji: Roman alphabet and script

sake: Rice wine, about 18 percent alcohol, used for ritual ceremonies and convivial pleasure

samurai: Warrior; member of Tokugawa era military class serving the aristocracy and nobility (See *Bushidō*)

seishin: Mind, spirit; intention, motive; mentality

seken: The world, society, people, the public view; the watchful presence of individuals in one's circle of social acquaintances, the neighborhood, and the society at large

senpai: A person who is senior in age, status, or experience in a group or organization (See *kōhai*)

sensei: Teacher; often used as an honorary term of address or reference for an esteemed person, such as a doctor, professor, mentor, or master

shibui: Astringent; somber, subdued

shibumi: Aesthetic astringence; tastefully subdued understatement associated with elegance, simplicity, and beauty; an ineffable and sought-after artistic restraint

shiken jigoku: Examination hell; the preparation and taking of academic entrance examinations that determine academic, occupational, and social futures

shinkeishitsu: Nervousness, neurosis, nervosity (This term was introduced in the early twentieth century to indicate a cluster of psychiatric conditions parallel to some Western versions of psychoneurosis.)

Shintō: Indigenous, animistic Japanese religion. During the 1930s and 1940s a form of state-sponsored *Shintō* encouraged reverence of the emperor and belief in the virtuous ascendancy of the Japanese race. (See *kokutai*)

Shōgun: Commander in chief, general; powerful rulers whose title was bestowed for life and who, during the feudal era, exercised unlimited power

Shōgunate: Central government headed by a general or *shōgun* during the Tokugawa era (See *daimyō, Tokugawa*)

shōji: Sliding lattice-work door(s) that are covered with translucent, white paper, used to separate rooms within the Japanese house (See *fusuma*)

shōki: Consciousness, awareness, senses

shūshin: Moral training, ethics; especially moral indoctrination authorized in educational curricula from the Meiji era (ca. 1890) until after the end of World War II, emphasizing values of Confucianism and state-sponsored *Shintō* (See Confucianism, *Shintō*)

soto: Literally, outside, external; also refers to individuals not connected by personal relationship (See *uchi*, also *omote*)

sumanai: To feel guilty, obligated, or in need of apologizing

sunao: Agreeable, affable, pleasant; composite personality traits characterizing a nonegoistic demeanor (See *ga ga tsuyoi*)

suneru: To pout, sulk, demonstrate overt petulance; to be in a stew following the direct frustration of *amae* (See *amae, futekusareru, yakekuso ni naru*)

sushi: Boiled rice flavored with rice vinegar and eaten in combination with seaweed, fish, vegetables, or egg

taijin-kyōfushō: A psychiatric condition characterized by avoidance of other people, fears of interaction, concern about eye contact, and fears of generating odors

Taishō: An era in Japanese history corresponding to the reign of the Taishō emperor (1912–1926)

taishō-kankei: "Object relations" in the psychoanalytic sense

tanin: Other people, strangers, outsiders; people unrelated or unconnected with the self (See *miuchi*, also *nakama*)

tanjōbi: Birthday

tanomoshikō: Mutual financing associations that pool resources to help each other

tanomu: To ask, or make requests on others; to turn to for assistance; to rely, to depend on

tatami: Thick, heavy floor mats made of woven rush in 3' x 6' dimensions

tatemae: Overt aspect; the public version; the ostensible story (See *honne*)

tereru: To be excessively shy, unusually bashful (See *hazukashii*)

Tokugawa: A Japanese historical era (ca. 1615–1868) named for the Japanese military family that controlled the government for 250 years (See *Shōgun, Shogunate*)

torawareru: (toraware, noun) To be caught up; bound; constrained; seized; and preoccupied; enslaved

toriiru: To seek strategic advantage; to manipulate favor for oneself; to ingratiate oneself, to curry favor with, to get in favor with another

tsukiai: Association, acquaintanceship, friendship with; keep company with; social network (See *kōsai*)

uchi: Inside, interior; domestic; an "in-group" related by close association (See *soto*)

ura: Back, the reverse; behind the facade, beneath the surface; concealed, hidden (See *omote*)

uramu: To resent; to harbor a grudge; to feel rancor, bitterness (against someone)

wa: Social harmony, tranquility, peace; cooperation

wadakamaru: (wadakamari, noun) To feign indifference in order to disguise resentment; to harbor a negative emotion secretly

wagamama: Self-centered, egocentric, willful; self-indulgent, spoiled, selfish

wakaraseru: To make (someone, especially a child) understand or comprehend

watakushi: First-person singular formal pronoun; I (See *boku*)

yakekuso ni naru: To give oneself up to extreme action; to become desperate; to display a loss of control (following frustration or disappointment)

yakuza: Gangster; person involved in organized crime

Yamato damashii: Literally, the soul or spirit of Japan; a rhetorical patriotic ethos idealizing Japanese virtue(s)

yobikō: Preparatory schools at the secondary level; cram schools (See *juku*)

yōchien: Kindergartens licensed and operated under the auspices of the Japanese Ministry of Education (See *hoikuen*)

yutori: Leeway; ample (space, time, or money); leisure, relaxation, absence of stress; peace of mind

zaibatsu: Pre–World War II conglomerates or monopolies that controlled capital and market resources, disbanded by the Occupation government, but effectively reconstituted in present Japan (See *keiretsu*)

Zen Buddhism: A sect of Buddhism emphasizing contemplation, meditation, development of inner control, and abnegation of the self

zōri: Japanese sandals worn with a thong between the first and second toes

References

Aaronfreed, Jason (1968) *Conduct and Conscience: The Socialization of Internalized Control over Behavior.* New York: Academic.

Abe, Kobo (1966) *The Face of Another.* Translated by E. Dale Saunders. New York: Perigee.

Abraham, Karl (1927) *Selected Works.* London: Hogarth.

Ainsworth, Mary S. (1976) Attachment and Dependency: A Comparison. In J. L. Gewirtz (Ed.), *Attachment and Dependency.* Washington, DC: Winston.

—— (1982) Attachment: Retrospect and Prospect. In C. M. Parkes and J. Stevenson-Hinde (Eds.), *The Place of Attachment in Human Behavior.* New York: Basic.

Ainsworth, Mary S., and Wittig, B. A. (1969) Attachment and Exploratory Behavior of One-Year-Olds in a Strange Situation. In B. M. Foss (Ed.), *Determinants of Infant Behavior.* Vol. 4. New York: Methuen.

Akutagawa, Ryunosuke (1952 [1915]) *Rashōmon and Other Stories.* Translated by T. Kojima. New York: Grove.

Alter, R. (1983) Deconstruction in America. *New Republic,* April 25, 1983.

American Psychiatric Association (1968) *Diagnostic and Statistical Manual of Mental Disorders, II.* (DSM-II) Washington, DC: American Psychiatric Association.

—— (1987) *Diagnostic and Statistical Manual of Mental Disorders.* Rev. 3d. ed. (DSM III-R) Washington, DC: American Psychiatric Association.

Ames, Walter L. (1981) *Police and Community in Japan.* Berkeley: University of California Press.

Angrosino, Michael V. (1976) The Evolution of the New Applied Anthropology. In M. V. Angrosino (Ed.), *Do Applied Anthropologists Apply Anthropology?* Athens, GA: University of Georgia Press.

Ansbacher, Heinz L., and Ansbacher, Rowena R. (1969) *The Individual Psychology of Alfred Adler.* New York: Basic.

383

Aoki, Tamotsu (1988) Culture in the Age of Antirelativism. *Japan Echo* 15:44–51.

Arkoff, Abe (1957) Need Patterns in Two Generations of Japanese Americans in Hawaii. *Social Psychology* 50:75–79.

Arkoff, Abe; Meridith, G.; Iwahara, S. (1964) Male-Dominant Equalitarian Attitudes in Japanese-Americans and Caucasian-American Students. *Journal of Social Psychology* 64:225–29.

Arlow, Jacob A. (1969) Fantasy, Memory, and Reality-Testing. *Psychoanalytic Quarterly* 38:28–51.

Asayama, Shin'ichi (1974) Adolescent Sex Development and Adult Sex Behavior in Japan. *Association for Sex Education Series.* Tokyo: JASE.

Atlas, James (1991) Stranger Than Fiction: Writers of Nonfiction Can Get All the Facts Straight—and Still Be Wrong. *New York Times Magazine,* May 22, 22.

Ausubel, David P. (1955) Relationships between Shame and Guilt in the Socializing Process. *Psychological Review* 62:378–90.

Baldwin, James M. (1974 [1911]) *The Individual and Society: Psychology and Sociology.* Salem, NH: Ayer.

Balint, Alice (1965) Love for the Mother and Mother Love. In M. Balint, *Primary Love and Psychoanalytic Technique.* London: Hogarth.

Balint, Michael (1952) *Primary Love and Psychoanalytic Technique.* London: Hogarth.

Bandura, Albert, and Walters, Richard H. (1963) Aggression. In. H. W. Stevenson (Ed.), *Child Psychology.* Chicago: University of Chicago Press.

Barker, Roger G. (1968) *Ecological Psychology.* Stanford: Stanford University Press.

Barnlund, Dean (1975) *Public and Private Self in Japan and the U.S.* Tokyo: Simul.

Basch, Michael F. (1980) *Doing Therapy.* New York: Basic.

——— (1983) The Concept of Self: An Operational Definition. In B. Lee and G. G. Noam (Eds.), *Developmental Approaches to the Self.* New York: Plenum.

Baumbacher, Gordon (1983) The Transitional Object and Transitional Phenomena in Development. *Contemporary Psychiatry* 2:36–41.

Bayley, David H. (1976) *Forces of Order: Police Behavior in Japan and the U.S.* Berkeley: University of California Press.

Beardsley, Richard K.; Hall, John W.; Ward, Robert E. (1959) *Village Japan.* Chicago: University of Chicago Press.

Beattie, Walter (1975) Discussion: Aging and the Future. *Gerontologist* 13:39–40.

Beck, Aaron (1976) *Cognitive Therapy and the Emotional Disorders.* New York: Meridian.

Becker, Ernest (1962) *The Birth and Death of Meaning.* New York: Free Press.

——— (1963) Adler and the Modern World. *Journal of Individual Psychology* 19:83–89.

———— (1964) *The Revolution in Psychiatry.* New York: Free Press.

Befu, Harumi (1968) Gift-Giving in a Modernizing Japan. *Monumenta Nipponica* 23:445–56.

———— (1970) *Japan: An Anthropological Introduction.* New York: Harper & Row.

———— (1986) The Social and Cultural Background of Child Development in Japan and the U.S. In H. Stevenson, H. Azuma, and K. Hakuta (Eds.), *Child Development and Education in Japan.* New York: Freeman.

———— (1988) *Nihonrinjin.* In *Kodansha Encyclopedia of Japan.* Tokyo: Kodansha.

———— (1989) Private Communication.

Behrends, Rebecca S., and Blatt, Sidney J. (1985) Internalization and Psychological Development throughout the Life Cycle. *Psychoanalytic Study of the Child* 40:11–39.

Bellah, Robert (1957) *Tokugawa Religion.* Glencoe, IL: Free Press.

Benedict, Ruth (1946) *The Chrysanthemum and the Sword: Patterns of Japanese Culture.* Boston: Houghton Mifflin.

Bennett, John W.; Passin, Herbert; McKnight, Robert (1958) *In Search of Identity.* Minneapolis: University of Minnesota Press.

Berger, Peter, and Luckmann, Thomas (1967) *The Social Construction of Reality.* Garden City, NY: Doubleday.

Berlin, B., and Kay, P. (1969) *Basic Color Terms: Their Universality and Evolution.* Berkeley: University of California Press.

Berne, Erik (1978) *Games People Play.* New York: Ballantine.

Bernstein, Richard (1988) Anthropologist Retracing Steps after three Decades. *New York Times,* May 11, B9.

Bidney, David (1967) *Theoretical Anthropology.* New York: Schocken.

Binswanger, Ludwig (1963) *Being in the World.* Translated by Jacob Needleman. New York: Basic.

Birchnell, John (1984) Dependence and Its Relationship to Depression. *British Journal of Medical Psychology* 57:215–25.

Bleuler, Eugen (1924) *Textbook of Psychiatry.* Translated by A. A. Brill. New York: Macmillan.

Blood, Robert O. (1967) *Love Match and Arranged Marriage.* New York: Free Press.

Boas, Franz (1938 [1896]) *The Mind of Primitive Man.* New York: Macmillan.

Bonaparte, E. Marie (1967) Some Psychoanalytic and Anthropological Insights Applied to Sociology. In G. B. Wilbur and W. Muensterberger (Eds.), *Psychoanalysis and Culture.* New York: Wiley.

Bonner, Hubert (1964) Dependency. In J. Gould and W. L. Kolb (Eds.), *A Dictionary of the Social Sciences.* Glencoe, IL: Free Press.

Boocock, Sarane (1989) Controlled Diversity: An Overview of the Japanese Pre-School System. *Journal of Japanese Studies* 15:41–65.

Booth, Wayne C. (1961) *The Rhetoric of Fiction.* Chicago: University of Chicago Press.

Booth, Wayne C., and Gregory, Marshall W. (1987) *The Harper and Row Rhetoric.* New York: Harper & Row.

Boszormenyi-Nagy, Ivan, and Spark, Geraldine (1973) *Invisible Loyalties: Reciprocity in Intergenerational Family Therapy.* New York: Harper & Row.

Bourguignon, E. (1979) *Psychological Anthropology: An Introduction to Human Nature and Cultural Differences.* New York: Holt, Rinehart, & Winston.

Bowlby, John (1958) The Nature of the Child's Tie to His Mother. *International Journal of Psycho-Analysis* 39:350–57.

——— (1960) Symposium on Psychoanalysis and Ethology, II: The Development of Object Relations. *International Journal of Psycho-Analysis* 41:313–17.

——— (1969) Attachment: *Attachment and Loss.* Vol. 1. New York: Basic.

——— (1972) *Attachment and Loss.* Vol. 2. *Separation, Anxiety, and Anger.* New York: Basic.

——— (1979) *The Making and Breaking of Affectional Bonds.* London: Tavistock.

——— (1980) *Attachment and Loss.* Vol. 3, *Loss, Sadness, and Depression.* New York: Basic.

——— (1988) Developmental Psychiatry Comes of Age. *American Journal of Psychiatry* 145:1–10.

Boyer, L. B. (1984) On Aspects of the Mutual Influences of Anthropology and Psychoanalysis. *Journal of Psychological Anthropology* 7:265–95.

Briggs, Jean L. (1970) *Never in Anger: Portrait of an Eskimo Girl.* Cambridge, MA: Harvard University Press.

Brothers, Leslie (1989) A Biological Perspective on Empathy. *American Journal of Psychiatry* 146:10–19.

Buckley, Peter (Ed.) (1986) *Essential Papers on Object Relations.* New York: New York University Press.

Burgner, M., and Edgcumbe, R. (1972) Some Problems in the Conceptualization of Early Object Relationships: The Concept of Object Constancy. *Psychoanalytic Study of the Child* 27:315–33.

Buruma, Ian (1984) *Behind the Mask.* New York: Pantheon.

Cairns, Robert B. (1976a). Attachment and Dependency: A Psychobiological and Social Learning Synthesis. In J. R. Gewirtz (Ed.), *Attachment and Dependency.* Washington, DC: Winston.

——— (1976b). Summary of Issues in the Attachment-Dependency Area. In J. L. Gewirtz (Ed.), *Attachment and Dependency.* Washington, DC: Winston.

Caron, Francesco, and Shouten, Joost (1935 [1636]) *A True Description of the Mighty Kingdoms of Japan and Siam.* London: Boxer.

Carter, Rose, and Dilatush, Lois (1976) Office Ladies. In J. Lebra, J. Paulson, and E. Powers (Eds.), *Women in Changing Japan.* Stanford, CA: Stanford University Press.

Caudill, William (1962a) Patterns of Emotion in Modern Japan. In R. J.

Smith and R. K. Beardsley (Eds.), *Japanese Culture: Its Development and Characteristics*. Chicago: Aldine.

——— (1962b) Anthropology and Psychoanalysis: Some Theoretical Issues. In T. Gladwin and W. C. Sturdevant (Eds.), *Anthropology and Human Behavior*. Washington, DC: Anthropological Society.

——— (1972) Tiny Dramas: Vocal Communication between Mother and Infant in Japanese and American Families. In W. P. Lebra (Ed.), *Transcultural Research in Mental Health*. Honolulu: University of Hawaii Press.

——— (1973) The Influence of Social Structure and Culture on Behavior in Japan. *Ethos* 1:349–54.

Caudill, William, and Doi, Takeo (1963) Interrelations of Psychiatry, Culture, and Emotion in Japan. In I. Galston (Ed.), *Man's Image in Medicine and Anthropology*. New York: International Universities Press.

Caudill, William, and Plath, David W. (1966) Who Sleeps by Whom? Parent-Child Involvement in Urban Japanese Families. *Psychiatry* 29:344–66.

Caudill, William, and Scarr, Harry A. (1962) Japanese Value Orientations and Culture Change. *Ethnology* 1:53–91.

Caudill, William, and Schooler, Carmi (1973) Child Behavior and Child-rearing in Japan and the United States: An Interim Report. *Journal of Nervous and Mental Disease* 157:323–38.

Caudill, William, and Weinstein, Helen (1969) Maternal Care and Infant Behavior in Japan and America. *Psychiatry* 32:12–43.

Chamberlain, Basil Hall (1971 [1904]) *Japanese Things*. Rutland, VT: Tuttle.

Chang, Suk C. (1965) The Cultural Context of Japanese Psychiatry. *American Journal of Psychotherapy* 19:593–606.

Chen, Shing-Jen, and Miyake, Kazuko (1986) Japanese Studies and Infant Development. In H. Stevenson, H. Azuma, and K. Hakuta (Eds.), *Child Development and Education in Japan*. New York: Freeman.

Chess, Sella, and Thomas, Alexander (1982) Infant Bonding: Mystique and Reality. *American Journal of Orthopsychiatry* 52:213–22.

Child, Irwin L. (1968) Personality in Culture. In E. Borgatta and W. Lambert (Eds.), *Handbook of Personality Theory and Research*. Chicago: Rand.

Choate, Pat (1990) *Agents of Influence*. New York: Knopf.

Chomsky, Noam (1965) *Aspects of the Theory of Syntax*. Cambridge, MA: MIT Press.

——— (1972) *Language and Mind*. New York: Harcourt, Brace, & World.

Christopher, Robert E. (1983) *The Japanese Mind: The Goliath Explained*. New York: Simon & Schuster.

Clark, Margaret (1966) Cultural Values and Dependency in Later Life. In R. A. Kalish (Ed.), *The Dependencies of Old People*. Ann Arbor: Institute of Gerontology.

Clark, Margaret, and Anderson, Barbara G. (1967) *Culture and Aging*. Springfield, IL: Thomas.

Clifford, James, and Marcus George E. (Eds.) (1986) *Writing Culture: The*

Poetics and Politics of Ethnography. Berkeley: University of California Press.

Cohler, Bertram J., and Geyer, Scott (1970) Psychological Autonomy and Interdependence within the Family. In F. Walsh (Ed.), *Normal Family Processes*. New York: Guilford.

Coleman, Samuel (1982) *Japanese Family Planning: Traditional Birth Control in an Urban Culture*. Princeton, NJ: Princeton University Press.

Collingwood, R. (1965). *Essays in the History of Philosophy*. Austin: University of Texas Press.

Cooper, Michael (Ed.) (1981) *They Came to Japan*. Berkeley: University of California Press.

Craig, Albert M. (1970) Introduction: Perspectives on Personality in Japanese History. In A. M. Craig and D. H. Shiveley (Eds.), *Personality in Japanese History*. Berkeley: University of California Press.

Crapanzano, Vincent (1980) *Tuhami: Portrait of a Moroccan*. Chicago: University of Chicago Press.

—— (1981) Text, Transference, and Indexicality. *Ethos* 9:122–48.

—— (1986) Hermes' Dilemma: The Masking of Subversion in Ethnographic Description. In J. Clifford and G. E. Marcus (Eds.), *Writing Culture: The Poetics and Politics of Ethnography*. Berkeley: University of California Press.

Dahl, Hartwig (1977) Foreword: Considerations for a Theory of Emotions. In J. de Rivera, *A Structural Theory of Emotions. (Psychological Issues*, no. 40) New York: International Universities Press.

—— (1978) A New Psychoanalytic Model of Emotion: Emotions as Appetites and Messages. *Psychoanalysis and Contemporary Thought* 1:373–407.

Dahl, Hartwig, and Stengel, Barry (1978) A Classification of Emotion Words: Modification and Partial Test of de Rivera's Decision Theory of Emotions. *Psychoanalysis and Contemporary Thought* 1:269–322.

Dale, Peter (1986) *The Myth of Japanese Uniqueness*. New York: St. Martin's.

Dale, Philip S. (1972) *Language Development: Structure and Function*. Hinsdale, IL: Dryden.

D'Andrade, Roy (1986) Three Scientific World Views and the Covering Law Model. In D. W. Fiske and R. A. Shweder (Eds.), *Metatheory in Social Science: Pluralisms and Subjectivities*. Chicago: University of Chicago Press.

Dazai, Osamu (1958) *No Longer Human*. New York: New Directions.

DeGeorge, Richard, and DeGeorge, Fernand (1972) *The Structuralists: From Marx to Levi-Strauss*. Garden City, NY: Anchor.

de Rivera, Joseph (1977) *A Structural Theory of Emotions. (Psychological Issues*, Monograph 40) New York: International Universities Press.

Derrida, Jacques (1977) *Of Grammatology*. Translated by G. C. Spivak. Baltimore, MD: Johns Hopkins University Press.

—— (1978) *Writing and Difference.* Translated by Alan Bass. London: Routledge & Kegan Paul.

Devereux, George (1969) *From Anxiety to Method in the Social Sciences.* New York: Humanities.

DeVos, George A. (1960) The Relation of Guilt toward Parents to Achievement and Arranged Marriage among the Japanese. *Psychiatry* 23:287–301.

—— (1973) *Socialization for Achievement: Essays on the Cultural Psychology of the Japanese.* Berkeley: University of California Press.

—— (1975) The Dangers of Pure Theory in Social Anthropology. *Ethos* 3:77–91.

—— (1978) The Japanese Adapt to Change. In D. Spindler (Ed.), *The Making of Psychological Anthropology.* Berkeley: University of California Press.

—— (1979) Alienation and Suicide: A Japanese Case. Conference Presentation, San Francisco Psychoanalytic Institute (February 5).

—— (1980) Afterword. In D. Reynolds, *The Quiet Therapies.* Honolulu: University of Hawaii Press.

—— (1981) The Self as Interpersonal: The Perception of Self in the Context of Others. In C. Lee and G. A. DeVos, *Koreans in Japan: Ethnic Conflict and Accommodation.* Berkeley: University of California Press.

—— (1985) Dimensions of the Self in Japanese Culture. In A. Marsella, G. DeVos, and F. Hsu (Eds.), *Culture and Self.* New York: Tavistock.

—— (1988) Private Communication.

—— (1989) Private Communication.

DeVos, George A., and Hippler, Arthur A. (1969) Cultural Psychology: Comparative Studies of Human Behavior. In G. Lindzey and E. Aronson (Eds.), *The Handbook of Social Psychology.* Vol. 4. Reading, MA: Addison-Wesley.

DeVos, George A., and Romanucci-Ross, Lola (1975) *Ethnic Identity: Cultural Continuities in Change.* Palo Alto, CA: Mayfield.

DeVos, George A., and Wagatsuma, Hiroshi (1967) *Japan's Invisible Race: Caste in Culture and Personality.* Berkeley: University of California Press.

—— (1973) Socialization, Self-Perception, and Burakumin Status. In George A. DeVos, *Socialization for Achievement.* Berkeley: University of California Press.

Doi, Takeo (1956) Japanese Language as an Expression of Japanese Psychology. *Western Speech* 20:90–96.

—— (1962a) *Amae:* A Key Concept for Understanding Japanese Personality Structure. In R. J. Smith and R. K. Beardsley (Eds.), *Japanese Culture: Its Development and Characteristics.* Chicago: Aldine.

—— (1962b) An Attempt at Reformulation of the Concept of Narcissism. Presentation, Fall Meeting, American Psychoanalytic Association, New York.

——— (1964) Psychoanalytic Therapy and "Western Man": A Japanese View. *International Journal of Social Psychiatry* 1:13–18.

——— (1967) *Giri-Ninjō:* An Interpretation. In R. P. Dore (Ed.), *Aspects of Social Change in Modern Japan.* Princeton, NJ: Princeton University Press.

——— (1969) Japanese Psychology: Dependency Need and Mental Health. In W. Caudill and T. Lin (Eds.), *Mental Health Research in Asia and the Pacific.* Honolulu: East-West Center Press.

——— (1970) A Psychiatrist's View on *Zeitgeist.* Presentation, American Foreign Service Corps, Tokyo.

——— (1971) *Amae no kozo* (The Anatomy of Dependence). Tokyo: Kobundo (in Japanese).

——— (1972) A Japanese Interpretation of Erich Segal's *Love Story. Psychiatry* 35:385–91.

——— (1973a) *The Anatomy of Dependence.* Translated by John Bester. Tokyo: Kodansha.

——— (1973b) *Omote* and *Ura:* Concepts Derived from the Japanese Two-Fold Structure of Consciousness. *Journal of Nervous and Mental Disease* 157:258–61.

——— (1973c) Student Problems in Japan. *World Medical Journal* 20:50–51.

——— (1973d) The Japanese Patterns of Communication and the Concept of *Amae. Quarterly Journal of Speech* 59:180–85.

——— (1973e) Psychotherapy as "Hide-and-Seek." *Bulletin of the Menninger Clinic* 37:174–77.

——— (1974) *Higaisha-Ishiki:* The Psychology of Revolting Youth in Japan. In W. P. Lebra (Ed.), *Youth, Socialization, and Mental Health.* Honolulu: University of Hawaii Press.

——— (1976a) Madness, Dependence, and Illness. Presentation, International Congress of Psychoanalysis on Madness, Milan, Italy.

——— (1976b) *The Psychological World of Natsume Soseki.* Translated by William J. Tyler. Cambridge, MA: Harvard University Press.

——— (1977) Folie, Dépendence et Maladie. In A. Verdiglione (Ed.), *La Folie dans la Psychanalyse.* Paris: Payot.

——— (1983a) *Yutori,* or the Leisurely State of Mind. Presentation, Conference on Human Values, Tsukuba University, Tsukuba, Japan.

——— (1983b) *In Search for the Japanese Identity of Modern Age.* Unpublished ms. Tokyo.

——— (1984) *Psychotherapy: A Cross-Cultural Perspective from Japan.* In C. B. Pederson, N. Sartorius, and A. J. Marsella (Eds.), *Mental Health Services: The Cross-Cultural Context.* San Francisco: Sage.

——— (1986) *The Anatomy of Self: The Individual versus Society.* Translated by Mark A. Harbison. Tokyo: Kodansha.

——— (1987) Personal Communication.

——— (1987a) The Concept of *Amae* and Its Psychoanalytic Implications.

Presentation, International Psychoanalytic Association Meeting, Toronto, Canada.

—— (1987b) The Cultural Assumptions of Psychoanalysis. Presentation, Chicago Symposium on Culture and Human Development, University of Chicago, Chicago, IL.

—— (1988a) Rethinking the *Amae* Theory: Rebuttal to Yasuhiko Taketomo's Criticism. *Shisa* 9:5, 99–118 (in Japanese).

—— (1988b) Private Communication.

—— (1989a) The Concept of *Amae* and Its Psychoanalytic Implications. *International Review of Psycho-Analysis* 16:349–54.

—— (1989b) Personal Communication.

—— (1990a) The Cultural Assumptions of Psychoanalysis. In J. W. Stigler, R. A. Shweder, and G. Herdt (Eds.), *Cultural Psychology: Essays on Comparative Human Development.* Cambridge: Cambridge University Press.

—— (1990b) Introducing the Concept of *Amae. Papua New Guinea Medical Journal* 33:147–50.

Doi, Takeo, and Wagatsuma, Hiroshi (1984) Radio Interview: *Amae* and Personality. Transcript translated by R. J. Garrick. NHK, Tokyo.

Dore, Ronald (1958) *City Life in Japan: A Study of a Tokyo Ward.* Berkeley: University of California Press.

—— (1967) Mobility, Equality, and Individuation in Modern Japan. In R. P. Dore (Ed.), *Aspects of Change in Modern Japan.* Princeton, NJ: Princeton University Press.

Douglas, Mary (1966) *Purity and Danger.* New York: Praeger.

Duke, Benjamin (1986) *The Japanese School: Lessons for Industrial America.* New York: Praeger.

Dumont, Louis (1970) *Homo Hierarchicus.* Chicago: University of Chicago Press.

—— (1986) *Essays on Individualism: Modern Ideology in Anthropological Perspectives.* Chicago: University of Chicago Press.

Durkheim, Emile (1951) *Suicide.* Glencoe, IL: Free Press.

Eagle, Morris N. (Ed.) (1987) *Recent Developments in Psychoanalysis: A Critical Evaluation.* Cambridge, MA: Harvard University Press.

Eagleton, Terry (1983) *Literary Theory: An Introduction.* Minneapolis: University of Minnesota Press.

Edgcumbe, R., and Burgner, M. (1972) Some Problems in the Conceptualization of Early Object Relationships: The Concepts of Need Satisfaction and Need Satisfying Relationships. *Psychoanalytic Study of the Child* 27:283–315.

Ekman, Paul (1984) Expression and the Nature of Emotion. In K. R. Scherer and P. F. Ekman (Eds.), *Approaches to Emotion.* Hillsdale, NJ: Erlbaum.

Ekman, Paul; Levinson, Robert W.; Friesen, Wallace V. (1983) Autonomic Nervous System Activity Distinguishes between Emotions. *Science* 221:1208–10.

Ekman, Paul; Sorenson, E. R.; Friesen, Wallace V. (1969) Pan-Cultural Elements in Facial Displays of Emotion. *Science* 164:86–88.

Emde, Robert N. (1980) Levels of Meaning for Infant Emotions: A Biosocial View. In W. A. Collins (Ed.), *Development of Cognition, Emotion, and Social Relations*. Hillsdale, NJ: Erlbaum.

―――― (1983) The Prerepresentational Self. *Psychoanalytic Study of the Child* 38:165–92.

Emde, Robert N., and Robinson, John (1979) The First Two Months. In J. D. Noshpitz (Ed.), *Basic Handbook of Child Psychiatry*. New York: Basic.

Emerson, Richard M. (1962) Power-Dependence Relation. *American Sociological Review* 22:31–41.

Enchi, Fumiko (1983) *Masks*. Translated by Juliet Winters Carpenter. New York: Vintage.

Erikson, Erik H. (1950) *Childhood and Society*. New York: Norton.

―――― (1959) *Identity and the Life Cycle. (Psychological Issues*, no. 1). New York: International Universities Press.

―――― (1969) *Ghandi's Truth*. New York: Norton.

Evans-Pritchard, E. E. (1973) Forward. In R. Needham (Ed.), *Right and Left: Essays on Dual Symbolic Classification*. Chicago: University of Chicago Press.

Ewing, Katherine P. (1991) Can Psychoanalytic Theories Explain the Pakistani Woman? Intrapsychic Autonomy and Interpersonal Engagement in the Extended Family. *Ethos* 19:131–60.

Fairbairn, Ronald M. (1954) *An Object Relations Theory of Personality*. New York: Basic.

Fallows, James (1989a) The Far East: A Few Pointers. *Atlantic* 264:24–32.

―――― (1989b) Containing Japan. *Atlantic* 263:40–54.

Fenichel, Otto (1945) *The Psychoanalytic Theory of Neurosis*. New York: Norton.

Ferenczi, Sandor (1950 [1913]) Stages in the Development of a Sense of Reality. In *Sex in Psychoanalysis*. New York: Basic.

Fisher, John L. (1964a) Linguistic Socialization: Japan and the United States. In D. Hymes (Ed.), *Language and Culture in Society*. New York: Harper & Row.

―――― (1964b) Words for Self and Others in Some Japanese Families. *American Anthropologist* 66:15–126.

Fisher, Seymour, and Greenberg, Roger P. (1977) *The Scientific Credibility of Freud's Theories and Therapy*. New York: Basic.

Florovsky, G. (1969) The Study of the Past. In M. McDonald (Ed.), *Philosophy and Analysis*. New York: Philosophical Library.

Ford, Charles V.; King, Bryan H.; Hollender, Marc H. (1988) Lies and Liars: Psychiatric Aspects of Prevarication. *American Journal of Psychiatry* 145:554–62.

Frager, Robert (1971) Jewish Mothering in Japan. *Sociological Inquiry* 42:11–17.

Freedman, Daniel G. (1968) Personality Development in Infancy: A Biological Approach. In S. L. Washburn and P. Dohlinon (Eds.), *Perspectives on Human Evolution*. New York: Holt, Rinehart, & Winston.

—— (1970) *Human Sociobiology: A Holistic Approach*. New York: Free Press.

Freuchen, Peter (1965) *Book of The Eskimos*. New York: Fawcett World Library.

Freud, Anna (1946 [1936]) *The Ego and the Mechanisms of Defense*. New York: International Universities Press.

Freud, Sigmund (1895) Project for a Scientific Psychology. Standard Edition. Vol. 1. London: Hogarth, 1966.

—— (1905) *Three Essays on Sexuality*. Standard Edition. Vol. 7. London: Hogarth, 1953.

—— (1910) *Five Lectures on Psychoanalysis*. Standard Edition. Vol. 11. London: Hogarth, 1957.

—— (1912) *Totem and Taboo*. Standard Edition. Vol. 13. London: Hogarth, 1953.

—— (1914) *On Narcissism: An Introduction*. Standard Edition. Vol. 14. London: Hogarth, 1950.

—— (1915) *Instincts and Their Vicissitudes*. Standard Edition. Vol. 14. London: Hogarth, 1950.

—— (1920) *Beyond the Pleasure Principle*. Standard Edition. Vol. 18. London: Hogarth, 1955.

—— (1921) *Group Psychology and the Analysis of the Ego*. Standard Edition. Vol. 18. London: Hogarth, 1955.

—— (1923) *The Ego and the Id*. Standard Edition. Vol. 19. London: Hogarth, 1961.

—— (1926) *Inhibitions, Symptoms, and Anxiety*. Standard Edition. Vol. 20. London: Hogarth, 1959.

—— (1927) *The Future of an Illusion*. Standard Edition. Vol. 21. London: Hogarth, 1961.

—— (1930) *Civilization and Its Discontents*. Standard Edition. Vol. 21. London: Hogarth, 1961.

—— (1931) *Female Sexuality*. Standard Edition. Vol. 21. London: Hogarth, 1961.

Fried, Edrida (1970) *Active/Passive: The Crucial Psychological Dimension*. New York: Grune & Stratton.

Friedman, Michael (1985) Toward a Reconceptualization of Guilt. *Contemporary Psychoanalysis* 21:501–47.

Fromm, Erich (1944) Individual and Social Origins of Neurosis. *American Sociological Review* 9:382–94.

Frosh, John (1966) Psychoanalytic Considerations of the Psychotic Character. *Journal of the American Psychoanalytic Association* 18:25–50.

Gaddini, Renata, and Gaddini, Eugenio (1975) Transitional Objects and the Process of Individuation: A Study in Three Different Social Groups. *Journal of the American Academy of Child Psychiatry* 9:347–85.

Gardner, Howard (1983) *Frames of Mind: The Theory of Multiple Intelligences*. New York: Basic.

Garrick, Regina J. (1986) Private Communication.

———— (1987) Private Communication.

———— (1988) Private Communication.

———— (1989) Private Communication.

———— (1990) Private Communication.

———— (1991) Private Communication.

Gedo, John, E. (1979) *Beyond Interpretation: Toward a Revised Theory for Psychoanalysis*. New York: International Universities Press.

———— (1980) Reflections on Some Current Controversies in Psychoanalysis. *Journal of the American Psychoanalytic Association* 28:363–83.

Geertz, Clifford (1973) *The Interpretation of Cultures*. New York: Basic.

———— (1976) From the Native's Point of View: On the Nature of Anthropological Understanding." In K. H. Basso and H. A. Selby (Eds.). Albuquerque, NM: University of New Mexico Press.

———— (1988) *Works as Lives: The Anthropologist as Author*. Stanford, CA: Stanford University Press.

———— (1990) After the Fact: Indonesia, Morocco, and the Recurrent Anthropologist. Hitchcock Foundation Lecture, University of California, San Francisco, April 11, 1990.

Gehrie, Marc (1978) The Psychoanalytic Study of Social Phenomena: A Review Essay. *The Annual of Psychoanalysis* 6:143–64.

Gewirtz, J. W. and Cairns, Robert B. (1976) Summary of Issues in the Attachment-Dependency Area. In J. L. Gewirtz (Ed.), *Attachment and Dependency*. Washington, DC: Winston.

Gibney, Frank (1979) *Japan: The Fragile Superpower*. Rev. Ed. Tokyo: Tuttle.

Giddens, Anthony (1976) *New Rules of Sociological Method: A Positive Critique of Interpretive Sociologies*. New York: Basic.

Gill, Merton M. (1983) The Point of View of Psychoanalysis: Energy Discharge or Person? *Psychoanalysis and Contemporary Thought* 6:523–51.

Gill, Merton M., and Goldberger, Leo (1976) Editors' Preface. In Klein, G. S., *Psychoanalytic Theory: An Exploration of Essentials*. New York: International Universities Press.

Gingras, Yves (1990) Review of *The Uses of Experiment: Studies in the Natural Sciences*. In D. Gooding, T. Pinch, and S. Schaeffer (Eds.), *Science* 247:1592–93.

Glover, Edward (1956) *The Technique of Psychoanalysis*. New York: International Universities Press.

Goffman, Erving (1959) *The Presentation of Self in Everyday Life:* Garden City, NY: Doubleday.

———— (1967) *Interaction Ritual*. Garden City, NY: Doubleday.

———— (1969) *Strategic Interaction*. Philadelphia: University of Pennsylvania Press.

———— (1974) *Frame Analysis.* New York: Harper.

Goldfarb, Alvin I. (1965). Psychodynamics and the Three-Generation Family. In E. Shanas and G. Streib (Eds.), *Social Structure and the Family.* Englewood Cliffs, NJ: Prentice-Hall.

Gomberg, Edith L. (1989) On Terms Used and Abused: The Concept of Codependency. *Drugs and Society* 3:113–32.

Gooding, David (1986) How Do Scientists Reach Agreement about Novel Observations? *Studies in the History and Philosophy of Science* 17:205–30.

Gooding, David; Pinch, Trevor; Schaeffer, Simon (1989) *The Uses of Experiment: Studies in the Natural Sciences.* New York: Cambridge University Press.

Goodman, Stanley (Reporter) (1969) Current Status of the Theory of the Superego. *Journal of the American Psychoanalytic Association* 14:172–80.

Gorer, Geoffrey (1943) Themes in Japanese Culture. *Transactions of the New York Academy of Sciences* 5:105–24.

Gould, Julius, and Kolb, William B. (1964) *A Dictionary of the Social Sciences.* New York: Free Press of Glencoe.

Gould, Thomas (1963) *Platonic Love.* New York: Free Press of Glencoe.

Gouldner, Alvin (1960) The Norm of Reciprocity: A Preliminary Statement. *American Sociological Review* 25:161–79.

Gove, Philip (Ed.) (1966) *Websters New Third International Dictionary of the English Language.* Springfield, MA: Merriam.

Grayson, Sandra (1992) Private Communication.

Greenacre, Phyllis (1963) On the Gratifications of the Analyst in the Analytic Situation. *International Journal of Psycho-Analysis* 44:444–452.

Greenberg, Jay R., and Mitchell, Stephen A. (1983) *Object Relations in Psychoanalytic Theory.* Cambridge, MA: Harvard University Press.

Greene, Marshall (1984) The Self Psychology of Heinz Kohut: A Synopsis and Critique. *Bulletin of the Menninger Clinic* 48:37–53.

Greenson, Ralph (1965) The Working Alliance and the Transference Neurosis. *Psychoanalytic Quarterly* 34:155–81.

Grünbaum, Arnold (1984) *The Foundations of Psychoanalysis.* Berkeley: University of California Press.

Gumperz, John (1982) *Discourse Strategies.* Cambridge: Cambridge University Press.

Guntrip, Harry (1961) *Personality Structure and Human Integration.* New York: International Universities Press.

Gurian, Jay P. (1984) Dependency. In J. Gould and W. B. Kolb (Eds.), *A Dictionary of the Social Sciences.* New York: Free Press.

Gurian, Jay P., and Gurian, Julia M. (1983) *The Dependency Tendency.* Lanham, MD: University Press of America.

Guttman, S. A. (1984) *The Concordance to the Standard Edition of the Complete Psychological Works of Sigmund Freud.* New York: International Universities Press.

Haley, Jay (1958) The Art of Psychoanalysis. *Etc.* 15:190–200.

Hall, Judith A. (1984) *Nonverbal Sex Differences: Communication and Accuracy and Expressive Style.* Baltimore, MD: Johns Hopkins University Press.

Hamaguchi, E. (1985) A Contextual Model of the Japanese: Toward a Methodological Innovation in Japan Studies. *Journal of Japanese Studies* 11:289–321.

Hammerman, Steven (1965) Conceptions of Superego Development. *Journal of the American Psychoanalytic Association* 14:320–55.

Hane, Mikiso (1982) *Peasants, Rebels, and Outcasts: The Underside of Modern Japan.* New York: Pantheon.

Harlow, Harry F. (1966) The Primate Socialization Motives. *Transactions and Studies of College Physicians of Philadelphia* 33:224–37.

Harlow, Harry F., and Harlow, Margaret K. (1962) The Effect of Rearing Conditions on Behavior. *Bulletin of the Menninger Clinic* 26:213–24.

Harris, Marvin (1968) *The Rise of Anthropological Theory.* New York: Crowell.

Hartmann, Heinz (1956) Notes on the Reality Principle. In *Essays on Ego Psychology: Selected Problems in Psychoanalytic Theory.* New York: International Universities Press.

——— (1958 [1939]) *Ego Psychology and the Problems of Adaptation.* New York: International Universities Press.

Hartmann, Heinz; Kris, Ernst; Loewenstein, Rudolph M. (1951) Some Psychoanalytic Comments on "Culture and Personality." In G. B. Wilbur and W. Muensterberger (Eds.), *Psychoanalysis and Culture.* New York: International Universities Press.

Hartmann, Heinz, and Loewenstein, Rudolph M. (1968) Notes on the Superego. *Journal of the American Psychoanalytic Association* 16:42–81.

Hasegawa, Nyozekan (1966) *The Japanese Character: A Cultural Profile.* Tokyo: Kodansha.

Havens, Leston (1976) *Participant Observation.* New York: Atherton.

Hearn, Lafcadio (1971 [1901]) *Japan: An Attempt at Interpretation.* Tokyo: Tuttle.

Heelas, P., and Lock, A. (1981) *Indigenous Psychologies: The Anthropology of the Self.* London: Academic.

Heidegger, Martin (1927) *Sein und Zeit.* Halle: Niemeyer.

Hendry, Joy (1981) *Marriage in Changing Japan: Community and Society.* Rutland, VT: Tuttle.

——— (1986) *Becoming Japanese: The World of the Pre-School Child.* Honolulu: University of Hawaii Press.

Hess, Robert, et al. (1986) Family Influences on School Readiness and Achievement in Japan and the United States: An Overview of a Longitudinal Study. In H. Stevenson, H. Azuma, and K. Hakuta (Eds.), *Child Development and Education in Japan.* New York: Freeman.

Hinde, Robert A. (1956). Ethological Models and the Concept of Drive. *British Journal for the Philosophy of Science* 6:321–31.

Hochschild, Arlie (1979) Emotion Work, Feeling Rules, and Social Structure. *American Journal of Sociology* 85:551–75.

Hong, R. Michael (1978) The Transitional Phenomena. *Psychoanalytic Study of the Child* 33:47–49.

Horney, Karen (1945) *Our Inner Conflicts*. New York: Norton.

Horowitz, Mardi J. (1979) *States of Mind: Analysis of Change in Psychotherapy*. New York: Aronson.

——— (1985) Research in Psychoanalysis. In C. Settlage and R. Brockbank (Eds.), *New Ideas in Psychoanalysis: The Process of Change in a Humanistic Science*. Hillsdale, NJ: Erlbaum.

——— (1987) Structure and Process of Change. In M. J. Horowitz (Ed.), *Hysterical Personality*. New York: Aronson.

——— (1988) *Introduction to Psychodynamics: A New Synthesis*. New York: Basic.

Horton, Paul C. (1981) *Solace: The Missing Dimension in Psychiatry*. Chicago: University of Chicago Press.

Horton, R. (1982) Tradition and Modernity Revisited. In M. Hollis and S. Lukes (Eds.), *Rationality and Relativism*. Cambridge: MIT Press.

Hsu, Francis L. K. (1961) *Psychological Anthropology: Approaches to Culture and Personality*. Homewood, IL: Dorsey.

——— (1963) *Clan, Caste, and Club*. Princeton, NJ: Van Nostrand.

——— (1971a) Eros, Affect, and *Pao*. In F. L. K. Hsu (Ed.), *Kinship and Culture*. Chicago: Aldine.

——— (1971b) Psychosocial Homeostasis and *Jen*: Conceptual Tools for Advancing Psychological Anthropology. *American Anthropologist* 73:23–44.

Huddle, David (1990) How Much of My Story Is True? That's A Terrific Question! *New York Times*, October 7, 1990, 31.

Husserl, Edmund (1952) *Ideas*. Translated by W. R. Boyce Gibson. London: Abernathy.

Hymes, Dell (1972) *Reinventing Anthropology*. New York: Pantheon.

Iga, Mamoru (1968) Japanese Adolescent Suicide and Social Structure. In E. S. Schneidman (Ed.), *Essays in Self-Destruction*. New York: Science House.

Inouye, Junichi (1985 [1910]) *Home Life in Tokyo*. London: KPI.

Ishida, Eiichiro (1974) *Japanese Culture: Study of Origins and Characteristics*. Honolulu: University of Hawaii Press.

Ishida, Takeshi (1984) Conflict and Its Accommodation: *Omote-Ura* and *Uchi-Soto* Relations. In E. Kriss, T. Rohlen, and P. Steinhoff (Eds.), *Conflict in Japan*. Honolulu: University of Hawaii Press.

Izard, Carroll (1971) *The Face of Emotion*. New York: Appelton-Century-Crofts.

——— (1977) *Human Emotions*. New York: Plenum.

James, William (1950 [1890]) *The Principles of Psychology*. New York: Holt.

Johnson, Chalmers (1982) *MITI and the Japanese Miracle*. Stanford, CA: Stanford University Press.

—— (1983) The Internationalization of the Japanese Economy. In H. Mannari and H. Befu (Eds.), *The Challenge of Japan's Internationalization*. Tokyo: Kodansha.

Johnson, Colleen L. (1974) Gift-Giving among Japanese Americans. *American Ethnologist* 1:295–308.

—— (1977) Interdependence, Reciprocity, and Indebtedness: An Analysis of Japanese American Kinship Relationships. *Journal of Marriage and the Family* 39:351–63.

Johnson, Colleen L., and Johnson, F. A. (1975) Interaction Rules and Ethnicity. *Social Forces* 54:452–66.

Johnson, Frank (Ed.) (1973) *Alienation: Concept, Term, and Meaning*. New York: Seminar.

—— (1984) A Multi-Level of Analysis of the Concept of *Amae:* Implications for Metapsychological Theory. Presentation, 73d Annual Meeting, American Psychoanalytic Association, San Diego, CA.

—— (1985) The Western Concept of Self. In A. J. Marsella, G. DeVos, and F. Hsu (Eds.), *Culture and Self*. New York: Tavistock.

—— (1988a) Transference Interpretation, Semiotics, and Psychotherapeutic Change. *Psychoanalysis and Contemporary Thought* 11:57–116.

—— (1988b) *Therapist/Patient and Ethnographer/Informant Relationships: A Critical Comparison*. Unpublished, working paper.

—— (1988c) On the Subjective Experience of Alienation: Separation of Self and Non/Self. In F. Geyer and D. Schweitzer (Eds.), *Alienation Theory and Social Change Strategies*. London: Science Reviews.

Jones, Ernest (1925) Mother-Right and the Sexual Ignorance of Savages. In *Psycho-myth, Psychohistory*. Vol. 2. New York: Stonehill.

Jonsen, Albert R., and Toulmin, Stephen (1988) *The Abuse of Casuistry*. Berkeley: University of California Press.

Jung, Carl G. (1956 [1912]) *Symbols of Transformation*. New York: Pantheon.

—— (1961 [1921]) The Theory of Psychoanalysis: The Concept of Libido. In R. F. C. Hull (Ed.), *The Collected Works of C. G. Jung*. New York: Pantheon.

Kahn, Herman (1970) *The Emerging Japanese Superstate: Challenge and Response*. Englewood Cliffs, NJ: Prentice-Hall.

Kakar, Sudhir (1971) The Theme of Authority in Social Relations in India. *Journal of Social Psychology* 84:93–101.

—— (1979) *Indian Childhood: Cultural Ideals and Social Reality*. Cambridge: Oxford University Press.

—— (1982) *The Inner World: A Psychoanalytic Study of Childhood and*

Society in India. 2d ed. Cambridge: Oxford University Press. (1st ed., 1978.)
——— (1985) Psychoanalysis and Non-Western Cultures. *International Review of Psycho-Analysis* 12:441–48.
——— (1990) Stories from Indian Psychoanalysis: Context and Text. In J. W. Stigler, R. A. Shweder, and G. Herdt (Eds.), *Cultural Psychology: Essays on Comparative Human Development.* Cambridge: Cambridge University Press.
Kanungo, Rabindra N. (1986) Understanding Working Alienation in Developing Nations. Presentation, 11th World Congress, International Sociological Association, New Delhi, India, August 1986.
Kaplan, Bert (1961) *Studying Personality Cross-Culturally.* New York: Harper & Row.
Kasahara, Y., and Sakamoto, K. (1971) Erythrophobia and Allied Conditions. In S. Arieti (Ed.), *World Biennial of Psychiatry and Pyschotherapy.* Vol. 1. New York: Basic.
Keene, Donald (1956) *Modern Japanese Literature.* New York: Grove.
Keesing, Roger M. (1987) Anthropology as Interpretative Quest. *Current Anthropology* 28:161–76.
Kelly, William (1988) Review Article: Japanology Bashing. *American Ethnologist* 15:365–68.
Kernberg, Otto (1972) Early Ego Integration and Object Relations. *Annals of the New York Academy of Sciences* 193:233–47.
——— (1974) Barriers to Being in Love. *Journal of the American Psychoanalytic Association* 22:486–511.
——— (1975) *Borderline Conditions and Pathological Narcissism.* New York: Aronson.
——— (1976) *Object Relations Theory and Clinical Psychoanalysis.* New York: Aronson.
——— (1980) *Internal World and External Reality: Object Relations Theory Applied.* New York: Aronson.
——— (1982) Self, Ego, Affects, and Drives. *Journal of the American Psychoanalytic Association* 30:893–917.
Kiefer, Christie W. (1970) The Psychological Interdependence of Family, School, and Bureaucracy in Japan. *American Anthropologist* 72:66–75, 346.
——— (1980) Loneliness and Japanese Social Structure. In J. Hartog, J. R. Audy, and Y. A. Cohen (Eds.), *The Anatomy of Loneliness.* New York: International Universities Press.
——— (1988) *The Mantle of Maturity.* Albany, NY: State University of New York Press.
Kinoshita, Yasuhito (1985) Private Communication.
Kitaoji, Hironobu (1971) The Structure of the Japanese Family. *American Anthropolgist* 73:1036–57.
Klein, George S. (1967) Peremptory Ideation: Structure and Force in Motivated Ideas. In R. R. Holt (Ed.), *Motives and Thought: Psychoanalytic*

Essays in Honor of David Rappaport. (Psychological Issues, nos. 18, 19) New York: International Universities Press.

Klein, Melanie (1946) Notes on Some Schizoid Mechanisms. In *Contributions to Psychoanalysis, 1921–1945.* London: Hogarth.

Kleinman, Arthur (1980) *Patients and Healers in the Context of Culture.* Berkeley: University of California Press.

—— (1988). *Rethinking Psychiatry: From Cultural Category to Personal Experience.* New York: Free Press.

Kline, Milton (1981) On Mahler's Autistic and Symbiotic Phases. *Psychoanalysis and Contemporary Thought* 4:69–105

Kluckhohn, Florence (1950) Dominant and Substitute Profiles of Cultural Orientations: Their Significance for the Analysis of Social Stratification. *Social Forces* 28:376–93.

Knudson, Frances W. (1976) Life-Span Attachment: Complexities, Questions, Considerations. *Human Development* 19:182–96.

Kohut, Heinz (1966) Forms and Transformations of Narcissism. *Journal of American Psychoanalytic Association* 14:243–72.

—— (1971) *The Analysis of the Self.* New York: International Universities Press.

—— (1977) *The Restoration of the Self.* New York: International Universities Press.

Kojima, Hideo (1979) Lectures on Psychology of Parent-Child Relations. *Child Study* 33:938–55.

—— (1984) A Significant Stride toward the Comparative Study of Control. *American Psychologist* 39:972–73.

Kondo, A. (1953) Morita Therapy: A Japanese Therapy for Neurosis. *American Journal of Psycho-analysis* 13:31–37.

Kondo, Dorinne K. (1987) Creating an Ideal Self: Theories of Selfhood and Pedagogy at a Japanese Ethics Retreat. *Ethos* 15:241–72.

Kopp, Clair B. (1982) Antecedents of Self-Regulation: A Developmental Perspective. *Developmental Psychology* 18:199–214.

Krauss, Ellis S.; Rohlen, Thomas P.; Steinhoff, Patricia G. (1984) *Conflict in Japan.* Honolulu: University of Hawaii Press.

Kroeber, Alfred L. (1920) Totem and Taboo: An Ethnologic Psychoanalysis. *American Anthropologist* 22:48–55.

—— (1939) Totem and Taboo in Retrospect. In B. Mazlish (Ed.), *Psychoanalysis and History.* New York: Grosset & Dunlap.

Kumagai, Fumie (1984) The Life Cycle of the Japanese Family. *Journal of Marriage and the Family* 84:191–204.

Kumagai, Hisa (1981) A Dissection of Intimacy: A Study of "Bipolar Posturing" in Japanese Social Interaction. *Culture, Medicine, and Psychiatry* 5:249–72.

—— (1988) *Ki:* "The Fervor of Vitality" and the Subjective Self. *Symbolic Interaction* 11:175–90.

Kumagai, Hisa, and Kumagai, Arno (1986) The Hidden "I" in *Amae:* "Passive Love" and Japanese Social Perception. *Ethos* 14:305–20.

Kumakura, Nabuhiro (1984) Private Communication.

Kumakura, Nabuhiro, and Ito, Masahira (1984) *Amae Riron No Kenkyu* (Research on the Theory of *Amae*). Tokyo: Seiwa Shoten (in Japanese).

LaBarre, Weston (1945) Some Observations on Character Structure in the Orient. *Psychiatry* 8:319–42.

Lacan, Jacques (1970) *Écrits: A Selection.* Translated by Alan Sheridan. New York: Norton.

Lakoff, George (1987) *Women, Fire, and Dangerous Things.* Chicago: University of Chicago Press.

Lakoff, George, and Johnson, Mark (1980) *Metaphors We Live By.* Chicago: University of Chicago Press.

Lamb, Michael E., et al. (1984) Security of Infantile Attachment as Assessed in the "Strange Situation": Its Study and Biological Interpretation. *Behavioral and Brain Sciences* 7:127–71.

Lampl-DeGroot, J. (1962) Ego Ideal and Superego. *The Psychoanalytic Study of the Child* 17:94–106.

Lange, Roland (1988) *501 Japanese Verbs.* New York: Barron's Education Series.

Langes, Robert (1973) The Patient's View of the Therapist: Reality or Fantasy? *International Journal of Psychoanalytic Therapy* 2:411–31.

Lanham, Betty (1956) Aspects of Childcaring in Japan: Preliminary Report. In D. G. Haring (Ed.), *Personal Character and Cultural Milieu.* Syracuse, NY: Syracuse University Press.

——— (1962) Aspects of Child Care in Japan. In B. S. Silberman (Ed.), *Japanese Character and Culture.* Tucson: University of Arizona Press.

Lannoy, Richard (1971) *The Speaking Tree: A Study of Indian Culture and Society.* London: Oxford University Press.

Lasch, Christopher (1977) *Haven in a Heartless World: The Family Besieged.* New York: Basic.

——— (1979) *The Culture of Narcissism.* New York: Warner.

——— (1984) *The Minimal Self: Psychic Survival in Troubled Times.* New York: Norton.

Leach, Edmund (1972) The Influence of Cultural Context on Non-Verbal Communication in Man. In R. A. Hinde (Ed.), *Non-Verbal Communication.* Cambridge: Cambridge University Press.

Lebra, Takie S. (1969) Reciprocity and the Asymmetric Principle: An Analytic Appraisal of the Japanese Concept of *On. Psychologia* 12:129–38.

——— (1971) The Social Mechanism of Guilt and Shame: The Japanese Case. *Anthropological Quarterly* 44:241–55.

——— (1976) *Japanese Patterns of Behavior.* Honolulu: University of Hawaii Press.

——— (1983) Shame and Guilt: A Psychocultural View of the Japanese Self. *Ethos* 11:192–209.

——— (1984a) *Japanese Women: Constraint and Fulfillment.* Honolulu: University of Hawaii Press.

——— (1984b) Nonconfrontational Strategies for Management of Interpersonal Conflicts. In E. Krauss, T. Rohlen, and P. Steinhoff (Eds.), *Conflict in Japan*. Honolulu: University of Hawaii Press.

Lee, Benjamin, and Noam, Gil G. (Eds.) (1983) *Developmental Approaches to the Self*. New York: Plenum.

Lenneberg, Eric H. (1967) *Biological Foundations of Language*. New York: Wiley.

LeVine, Robert A. (1970) Crosscultural Study in Child Psychology. In P. Mussen (Ed.), *Carmichael's Manual of Child Psychology*. 3d ed. New York: Wiley.

—— (1973a) *Culture, Behavior, and Personality*. 1st ed. Chicago: Aldine.

—— (1973b) Ego Function and Socio-cultural Evolution. Presentation to the American Psychoanalytic Association, May 7, 1973, Honolulu.

—— (1977) Child Rearing as Cultural Adaptation. In P. H. Leiderman, S. R. Tulkin, and A. Rosenfeld (Eds.), *Culture and Infancy: Variations in the Human Experience*. New York: Academic.

—— (1982) Universal Categories and the Translation Problem. In R. A. LeVine, *Culture, Behavior, and Personality*. 2d ed. Chicago: Aldine.

—— (1987) Beyond the Average Expectable Environment of Psychoanalysis: Crosscultural Evidence on Mother-Child Interaction. Presentation, Chicago Symposium on Culture and Human Development, University of Chicago.

Levi-Strauss, Claude (1969) *The Elementary Structures of Kinship*. Boston: Beacon.

Levy, Howard S. (1971) *Sex, Love, and the Japanese*. Washington, DC: Warm-Soft.

Levy, Robert I. (1973) *Tahitians: Mind and Experiences in the Society Islands*. Chicago: University of Chicago Press.

—— (1984) The Emotions in Comparative Perspective. In K. R. Scherer and P. Ekman (Eds.), *Approaches to Emotion*. Hillsdale, NJ: Erlbaum.

Lewis, Catherine C. (1984) Cooperation and Control in Japanese Nursery Schools. *Comparative Education Review* 28:69–84.

—— (1987) Observations of First-Grade Classrooms: Implications for U.S. Theory and Research. *Comparative Education Review* 32:159–72.

—— (1989) From Indulgence to Internalization: Social Control in the Early School Years. *Journal of Japanese Studies* 15:139–57.

—— (1990) Early Childhood in Japan. In S. Feeney (Ed.), *Early Childhood Education in Asia and the Pacific*. New York: Garland.

Lewis, G. C. (1891 [1841]) *An Essay on the Government of Dependencies*. Oxford: Clarendon.

Lichtenberg, Joseph D. (1981) The Empathic Mode of Perception. *Psychoanalytic Inquiry* 3:329–55.

Livingston, John; Moore, Joe; Oldfather, Felicia (Eds.) (1973) *Postwar Japan: 1945 to Present*. New York, Pantheon.

Lock, Andrew (1981) Universals in Human Conception. In P. Heelas and A. Lock (Eds.), *Indigenous Psychologies: The Anthropology of the Self*. London: Academic.

Lock, Margaret (1980) *East Asian Medicine in Urban Japan: Varieties of Medical Experience*. Berkeley: University of California Press.

Long, Susan Orpett (1987) *Family Change and the Life Course in Japan*. Ithaca, NY: Cornell East Asia Papers.

Lonner, Walter J. (1981) The Search for Psychological Universals. In H. Triandis and A. Heron (Eds.), *Handbook of Cross-Cultural Psychology*. Vol. 4. Boston: Allyn & Bacon.

Lynd, Helen M. (1958) *On Shame and the Search for Identity*. New York: Harcourt Brace.

Maccoby, Eleanor B., and Masters, John C. (1970) Attachment and Dependency. In J. Mussen (Ed.), *Carmichael's Manual of Developmental Psychology*. 3d ed. New York: Wiley.

McClelland, David C., et al. (1953) *The Achievement Motive*. New York: Appleton.

McConnell, Frank D. (1990) Will Deconstruction Be the Death of Literature? *Wilson Quarterly* (Winter): 99–109.

Mahler, Margaret S. (1965) On the Significance of the Normal Separation-Individuation Phase. In M. Schur (Ed.), *Drives, Affects, and Behavior*. Vol. 2. New York: International Universities Press.

———— (1972) On the First Three Subphases of the Separation-Individuation Process. *American Journal of Psychoanalysis* 53:333–38.

Mahler, Margaret S., and Gosliner, B. J. (1955) On Symbiotic Child Psychosis: Genetic, Dynamic, and Restitutive Aspects. *Psychoanalytic Study of the Child* 10:332–36.

Malinowski, Bronislaw (1927) *Sex and Repression in Savage Society*. London: Routledge & Kegan Paul.

———— (1944) *A Scientific Theory of Culture*. Chapel Hill: University of North Carolina Press.

———— (1967) *A Diary in the Strict Sense of the Term*. New York: Harcourt, Brace, & World.

Maloney, James C. (1953) Understanding the Paradox of Japanese Psychoanalysis. *International Journal of Psycho-Analysis* 34:291–303.

———— (1968 [1954]) *Understanding the Japanese Mind*. New York: Greenwood.

Mandler, G. (1963) Parent and Child in the Development of the Oedipus Complex. *Journal Nervous and Mental Disease* 136:227–35.

Marcus, George E., and Fischer, Michael M. (1986) *Anthropology as Cultural Critique: An Experimental Moment in the Human Sciences*. Chicago: University of Chicago Press.

Markus, Rose H., and Kitayama, Shinobu (1991) Culture and Self: Implications for Cognition, Emotion, and Motivation. *Psychological Review* 98:224–53.

Marriott, McKim (1976) Interpreting Indian Society: A Monistic Alternative to Dumont's Dualism. *Journal of Asian Studies* 36:189–95.

Marshall, Robert C. (1989) Review of The Myth of Japanese Uniqueness. *Journal of Japan Studies* 15:266–72.

Masterson, James F. (1985) *The Real Self: A Developmental and Object Relations Approach.* New York: Brunner/Maezel.

Masuda, M. (1959) *Kenkyusha's New Pocket Japanese-English Dictionary.* Tokyo: Kenkyusha.

Matsuda, Kokichi (1981) *Fufu kankei* (Conjugal Relations). In T. Kamiko and K. Mastuda (Eds.), *Nihonjin no Kazoku Kankei.* Tokyo: Yuhikaku (in Japanese).

Matsuda, Michio (1967) *Ikuji No Hyakka.* Tokyo: Iwanami Shoten (in Japanese).

———— (1973) *Nihonshiki Iky-jiho.* Tokyo: Kodensha (in Japanese).

Matsumoto, Michihiro (1984). *Haragei.* Tokyo: Kodansha.

May, Rollo (1950) *Existence.* New York: Basic.

Mead, George Herbert (1934) *Mind, Self, and Society.* Chicago: University of Chicago Press.

Miller, Roy A. (1967) *The Japanese Language.* Chicago: University of Chicago Press.

———— (1982) *Japan's Modern Myth: The Language and Beyond.* New York: Weatherhill.

———— (1986) *Nihongo: In Defense of Japanese.* London: Athlone.

Minami, Hiroko (1982) The Construction and Validation of *Amae* Network. Ph.D. diss., School of Nursing, University of California, San Francisco.

Minami, Hiroshi (1971) *Psychology of Japanese People.* Toronto: University of Toronto Press.

Miner, Horace (1956) Body Ritual among the Nacirema. *American Anthropologist* 55:520–26

Mischel, Theodore (1977) Conceptual Issues in the Psychology of the Self: An Introduction. In T. Mischel, *The Self: Psychological and Philosophical Issues.* Oxford: Blackwell.

Mishima, Yukio (1949) *Confessions of a Mask.* Translated by Meredith Wetherby. New York: New Directions.

———— (1951) *Forbidden Colors.* Translated by Alfred H. Marks. New York: Knopf.

———— (1964) [Interview] A Famous Japanese Judges the U.S. Giant. *Life,* Sept. 11, 84.

———— (1965) *The Sailor Who Fell from Grace with the Sea.* Translated by John Nathan. New York: Borzoi.

———— (1970) *Sun and Steel.* Translated by John Bester. New York: Grove.

———— (1972) *Spring Snow.* Translated by E. Dale Sanders. New York: Knopf.

———— (1973) *The Temple of Dawn.* Translated by E. Dale Sanders and Cecilia Segava Seigle. New York: Knopf.

Mitchell, Douglas O. (1976) *Amaeru: The Expression of Reciprocal Dependency in Japanese Politics and Law.* Boulder, CO: Westview.

Miyamoto, Tadao (1973) The Japanese and Psychoanalysis. *The Japan Interpreter* 8:387–89.

Miyoshi, Masao (1974) *Accomplices of Silence: The Modern Japanese Novel.* Berkeley: University of California Press.

Moore, Charles A. (Ed.) (1967) *The Japanese Mind: Essentials of Japanese Philosophy and Culture.* Honolulu: East-West Center Press.

Morita, Shoma (1922) *The Nature of Shinkeishitsu and Its Treatment.* Tokyo: Hakuyosha (in Japanese).

Morris, Ivan (1962) *Modern Japanese Stories.* Rutland, VT: Tuttle.

Morsbach, Helmut (1973) Aspects of Nonverbal Communication in Japan. *Journal of Nervous and Mental Disease* 157:262–78.

Mouer, Ross, and Sugimoto, Yoshio (Eds.) (1981) *Japanese Society: Reappraisals and New Directions.* Bedford Park: University of Adelaide.

Muensterberger, Warner (1951) Orality and Dependence: Characteristics of Southern Chinese. In G. Roheim (Ed.), *Psychoanalysis and Social Sciences.* Vol. 3. New York: International Universities Press.

—— (1969a) Psyche and Environment: Sociocultural Variations in Separation and Individuation. *Psychoanalytic Quarterly* 38:191–216.

—— (1969b) On the Cultural Determination of Individual Development. In W. Muensterberger (Ed.), *Man and His Culture: Psychoanalytic Anthropology after Totem and Taboo.* London: Rapp & Whiting.

Munnichs, Joep (1976) Dependency, Interdependency, and Autonomy: An Introduction. In J. Munnichs and W. J. A. Van Den Heuvel (Eds.), *Dependency or Independency in Old Age.* The Hague: Martinus-Nijhoff.

Munroe, Robert L., and Munroe, Ruth H. (1975) *Cross-Cultural Human Development.* Monterey, CA: Brooks/Cole.

Munroe, R. H.; Munroe, R. L.; Whiting, John W. M. (1979) *The Handbook of Cross-Cultural Human Development.* New York: Garland.

Murakami, Hyoe (1982) *Japan: The Years of Trial, 1919–52.* Tokyo: Japan Culture Institute.

Muramatsu, Tsuneo (1949) Japan: Some Psychological Perspectives. *Background Report.* Washington, DC: U.S. Occupation Proceedings.

Murase, Takeo (1982) *Sunao:* A Central Value in Japanese Psychotherapy. In A. J. Marsella and G. M. White (Eds.), *Cultural Conceptions of Mental Health and Therapy.* Dordrecht: Reidell.

Murase, Takeo, and Johnson, Frank (1974) Naikan, Morita, and Western Psychotherapy. *Archives of General Psychiatry* 31:121–28.

Murdoch, George P. (1945) The Common Denominator of Cultures. In R. Linton (Ed.), *The Science of Man in the World Crisis.* New York: Columbia University Press.

—— (1949) *Social Structure.* New York: Macmillan.

Murdoch, George P., et al. (1962) *The Ethnographic Atlas.* New York: Macmillan.

Murray, Henry, et al. (1938) *Explorations in Personality: A Clinical and Experimental Study of Fifty Men of College Age.* New York: Oxford.

Nagano, Miho (1985) How to Say I'm Sorry: Use of Apology in Japan and the United States. Masters thesis, Dept. of Communication, San Francisco State University.

Nagera, Humberto, et al. (1970) *Basic Psychoanalytic Conceptions.* Vol. 3, *The Theory of Instincts.* New York: Basic.

Nakakuki, Masafumi (1984) Two Major Characteristics of Japanese Culture: Amae and Shibumi—A Psychoanalytic Interpretation. Presentation, 73d Annual Meeting of the American Psychoanalytic Association, San Diego, CA.

Nakamura, Hajime (1964) *Ways of Thinking of Eastern Peoples: India, China, Tibet, Japan.* Honolulu: East-West Center Press.

——— (1967) Consciousness of the Individual and the Universal among the Japanese. In C. A. Moore (Ed.), *The Japanese Mind: Essentials of Japanese Philosophy and Culture.* Honolulu: East-West Center Press.

Nakane, Chie (1970) *Japanese Society.* Berkeley: University of California Press.

Namahira, Emiko (1987) Pollution in the Folk Belief-System. *Current Anthropology* 28:65–74.

Nathan, John (1974) *Mishima: A Biography.* Boston: Little, Brown.

Needham, Rodney (1973) Introduction. In R. Needham (Ed.), *Right and Left: Essays on Dual Symbolic Classification.* Chicago: University of Chicago Press.

——— (1981) Inner States as Universals. In P. Heelas and A. Lock, *Indigenous Psychologies: The Anthropology of Self.* London: Academic.

——— (Ed.) (1973) *Right and Left: Essays on Dual Symbolic Classification.* Chicago: University of Chicago Press.

Neki, J. S. (1976a) An Examination of the Cultural Relativism of Dependence as a Dynamic of Social and Therapeutic Relationships: I Basic Considerations. *British Journal of Medical Psychology* 49:1–10.

——— (1976b). An Examination of the Cultural Relativism of Dependence as a Dynamic of Social and Therapeutic Relationships: II Therapeutic Implications. *British Journal of Medical Psychology* 49:11–22.

——— (1977) Dependence: Cross-Cultural Consideration of Dynamics. In S. Arieti and G. Chrzanowski (Eds.), *New Dimensions in Psychiatry: A World View.* New York: Wiley.

Nelson, Benjamin (1958) Social Science, Utopian Myths, and the Oedipus Complex. *Psychoanalytic Review* 45:120–26.

Neugarten, Bernice (1979) Time, Age, and the Life-Cycle. *American Journal of Psychiatry* 136:887–94.

Nickles, Thomas (1989) Justification and Experiment. In D. Gooding, T. Pinch, and S. Schaeffer (Eds.), *The Uses of Experiment: Studies in the Natural Sciences.* New York: Cambridge University Press.

Nitobe, Inazo (1969) *Bushidō, The Soul of Japan.* Tokyo: Tuttle.

Norbeck, Edward (1978) *Country to City: The Urbanization of a Japanese Hamlet.* Salt Lake City: University of Utah Press.

Norris, Christopher (1982) *Deconstruction: Theory and Practice.* London: Methuen.

Offer, Daniel, and Sabshin, Melvin (1966) *Normality: Theoretical and Clinical Concepts of Mental Health.* New York: Basic.

———— (1984) *Normality and the Life Cycle: A Critical Integration.* New York: Basic.

Ohnuki-Tierney, Emiko (1984) *Illness and Culture in Contemporary Japan: An Anthropological View.* Cambridge: Cambridge University Press.

Olnick, Stanley L. (1959) The Analytic Paradox. *Psychiatry* 22:333–39.

O'Meara, Tim (1989) Anthropology as Empirical Science. *American Anthropologist* 91:354–69.

Orr, Douglas W. (1954) Transference and Countertransference: A Historical Survey. *Journal American Psychoanalytic Association* 2:621–70.

Osgood, Charles E. (1964) Semantic Differential Technique in the Comparative Study of Cultures. *American Anthropologist* 66:171–200.

Osgood, Charles E.; May, W. H.; and Myron, M. S. (1975) *Cross-Cultural Universals of Affective Meaning.* Urbana: University of Illinois Press.

Osgood, Charles E.; Suci, G. J.; Tannenbaum, P. H. (1957) *The Measurement of Meaning.* Urbana: University of Illinois Press.

Pande, Shashi K. (1968) The Mystique of "Western" Psychotherapy: An Eastern Interpretation. *Journal of Nervous and Mental Disease* 146:425–32.

Panel (1984) On Psychoanalysis and Japanese Cultural Characteristics. Annual Meeting, American Psychoanalytic Association, San Diego, CA, May 5.

Parens, Henri (1970) Inner Sustainment: Methodological Considerations. *Psychoanalytic Quarterly* 34:223–39.

Parens, Henri, and Saul, L. J. (1971) *Dependence in Man: A Psychoanalytic Study.* New York: International Universities Press.

Parsons, Anne (1969) *Belief, Magic, and Anomie: Essays in Psychosocial Anthropology.* New York: Free Press.

Parsons, Talcott (1951) *The Social System.* New York: Free Press.

Passin, Herbert (1982) *Encounter with Japan.* Tokyo: Kodansha.

Pavenstedt, Eleanor (1965) Observations in Five Japanese Homes. *Journal of the American Academy of Child Psychiatry* 4:413–25.

Peak, Lois (1987) Learning to Go to School in Japan: The Transition from Home to Pre-School Life. Ph.D. diss., Harvard Graduate School of Education.

———— (1988) Formal Pre-Elementary Education in Japan. In R. Leestma and H. Walberg (Eds.), *Japanese Education Today.* Vol. 2. Washington, DC: U.S. Department of Education.

———— (1989) Learning to Become Part of the Group: The Japanese Child's Transition to Preschool Life. *Journal of Japanese Studies* 15:93–123.

Pelzel, John (1970) Human Nature in Japanese Myths. In A. M. Craig and D. H. Shively (Eds.), *Personality in Japanese History.* Berkeley: University of California Press.

———— (1977) Book Review: Japanese Personality in Culture. *Culture, Medicine, and Psychiatry* 1:299–315.

Peterfreund, Emmanuel (1978) Some Critical Comments on the Psychoanalytic Conception of Infancy. *International Journal of Psycho-Analysis* 59:427–41.

Peterfreund, Emmanuel, and Schwartz, Jacob T. (1971) *Information Systems and Psychoanalysis. (Psychological Issues,* nos. 25, 26) New York: International Universities Press.

Peterson, P. C., Peterson, J. L., and Seeto, D. (1983) Developmental Changes in Ideas about Lying. *Child Development* 54:1529–35.

Petitto, Laura Ann, and Marentette, Paula F. (1991) Babbling in the Manual Mode: Evidence for the Ontogeny of Language. *Science* 251:1493–96.

Piaget, Jean (1970) Piaget's Theory. In J. Mussen (Ed.), *Carmichael's Manual of Developmental Psychology.* 3d ed. New York: Wiley.

——— (1971) *Structuralism.* Translated by Chaninah Maschler. London: Routledge & Kegan Paul.

Pickering, Andy (1989) *Living in the Material World.* In D. Gooding, T. Pinch, and S. Schaeffer (Eds.), *The Uses of Experiment: Studies in the Natural Sciences.* New York: Cambridge University Press.

Piers, Gerhardt, and Singer, Milton B. (1953) *Shame and Guilt.* Springfield, IL: Thomas.

Pike, Kenneth (1954) *Language in Relation to a Unified Theory of Structure of Human Behavior.* Vol. 1. Glendale, CA: Summer Institute of Linguistics.

Plath, David (1964) *The After Hours: Modern Japan and the Search for Enjoyment.* Berkeley: University of California Press.

——— (1987) Private Communication in Kondo (1987).

Popper, Karl R., and Eccles, John C. (1981) *The Self and Its Brain.* New York: Springer-Verlag.

Potter, Steven (1978) *The Complete Upmanship.* New York: Norton.

Prestowitz, Clyde V. (1988) *Trading Places.* New York: Basic.

Rabinow, Paul (1986) Representations and Social Facts: Modernity and Post-Modernity in Anthropology. In J. Clifford and G. F. Marcus (Eds.), *Writing Culture: The Poetics and Politics of Ethnography.* Berkeley: University of California Press.

Rappaport, David (1960) *The Structure of Psychoanalytic Theory: A Systematizing Attempt (Psychological Issues,* no. 6) New York: International Universities Press.

Reich, Wilhelm (1949 [1933]) *Character Analysis.* New York: Noonday.

Reischauer, Edwin (1964) *Japan, Past and Present.* New York: Knopf.

Reynolds, David K. (1976) *Morita Psychotherapy.* Berkeley: University of California Press.

——— (1980) *The Quiet Therapies.* Honolulu: University of Hawaii Press.

Reynolds, David, and Kiefer, Christie (1977) Cultural Adaptability as an Attribute of Therapies: The Case of Morita Psychotherapy. *Culture, Medicine, and Psychiatry* 1:395–412.

Rheingold, Harriet L. (1961) The Effect of Environmental Stimulation upon

Social and Exploratory Behavior in the Human Infant. In B. M. Foss (Ed.), *Determinants of Infant Behavior.* New York: Wiley.

Rheingold, Harriet L., and Eckermann, Christine D. (1970) The Infant Separates Himself from His Mother. *Science* 168:78–83.

Ricoeur, Paul (1970) *Freud and Philosophy.* New Haven, CT: Yale University Press.

―――― (1981) *Hermeneutics and the Human Science.* New York: Cambridge University Press.

Rohlen, Thomas P. (1974a) *For Harmony and Strength.* Berkeley: University of California Press.

―――― (1974b) *Ki and Kokoro:* Japanese Perspectives on the Nature of the Person. Presentation, Center for Japanese and Korean Studies, Berkeley, California, May 24.

―――― (1983) *Japan's High Schools.* Berkeley: University of California Press.

―――― (1989) Order in Japanese Society: Attachment, Authority, and Routine. *Journal of Japanese Studies* 15:5–40.

Roland, Alan (1980) Psychoanalytic Perspectives on Personality Development in India. *International Review of Psycho-Analysis* 7:73–80.

―――― (1982) Toward a Psychoanalytical Psychology of Hierarchical Relationships in Hindu India. *Ethos* 10:232–53.

―――― (1988) *In Search of Self in India and Japan: Toward a Cross-Cultural Psychology.* Princeton, NJ: Princeton University Press.

Rosenberg, Morris (1979) *Conceiving the Self.* New York: Basic.

Ryle, Gilbert (1957) The Theory of Meaning. In C. A. Mace (Ed.), *British Philosophy in the Mid-Century.* London: Hutchinson's University Library.

Salzman, Philip C. (1988) Fads and Fashions in Anthropology. *Anthropology Newsletter* 29:31–33.

Sandler, Joseph (1960) On the Concept of Superego. *Psychoanalytic Study of the Child* 15:128–62.

Sass, Louis A. (1986) Anthropology's Native Problems: Revisionism in the Field. *Harper's,* May 1986, 48–57.

―――― (1988) The Self and Its Vicissitudes: An "Archeological" Study of the Psychoanalytic Avant-Garde. *Social Research* 55:551–607.

Saul, Leon J. (1970) Inner Sustainment: The Concept. *Psychoanalytic Quarterly* 34:215–22.

Saville-Troike, Muriel (1985) The Place of Silence in an Integrated Period of Communication. In D. Tannen and M. Saville-Troike (Eds.), *Perspectives on Silence.* Norwood, NJ: Ablex.

Schachter, Stanley (1959) *The Psychology of Affiliation: Experimental Studies of the Sources of Gregariousness.* Stanford, CA: Stanford University Press.

Schafer, Roy (1976) *A New Language for Psychoanalysis.* New Haven, CT: Yale University Press.

—— (1978a) *Language and Thought*. New Haven, CT: Yale University Press.

—— (1978b) Action Language and the Psychology of Self. *Annual of Psychoanalysis* 6:83–92.

Schlesinger, Herbert (1981) The Process of Empathetic Response. *Psychoanalytic Inquiry* 3:393–416.

Schodt, Frederik (1986) *Inside the Robot Kingdom*. Tokyo: Kodansha.

Segal, Erich (1970) *Love Story*. New York: Signet.

Settlage, Calvin (1980). Psychoanalytic Developmental Theory in Current and Historical Perspectives. *Psychoanalysis and Contemporary Thought* 3:139–71.

Settlage, Calvin F., and Brockbank, Reed (Eds.) (1985) *New Ideas in Psychoanalysis: The Process of Change in a Humanistic Science*. Hillsdale, NJ: Erlbaum.

Shand, Nancy, and Kosawa, Yorio (1985) Culture Transmission: Caudill's Model and Alternate Hypotheses. *American Anthropologist* 87:862–71.

Shane, Morton, and Shane, Estelle (1985) Change and Integration in Psychoanalytic Development Theory. In C. F. Settlage and R. Brockbank (Eds.), *New Ideas in Psychoanalysis: The Process of Change in a Humanistic Science*. Hillsdale NJ: Erlbaum.

Shankman, Paul (1984) The Thick and the Thin: On the Interpretive Theoretical Program of Clifford Geertz. *Current Anthropology* 25:261–79.

Shaw, George B. (1983[1887]) *Pygmalion*. Middlesex: Penguin.

Sherwood, Michael (1969) *The Logic of Understanding in Psychoanalysis*. New York: Academic.

Shibamoto, Janet (1985) *Japanese Women's Language*. Orlando, FL: Academic.

Shields, Robert W. (1964) The Too-Good Mother. *International Journal of Psycho-Analysis* 45:85–88.

Shinozaki, N. (1957) Report on Sexual Life of Japanese. Research Data C. No. 11, mimeograph. Tokyo: Institute of Population Studies.

Shishido, Toshio (1980) Japanese Industrial Development and Policies for Science and Technology. *Science* 219:259–64.

Shweder, Richard A. (1984) Anthropology's Romantic Rebellion against the Enlightenment; or, There's More to Thinking Than Reason and Evidence. In R. A. Shweder and R. A. LeVine (Eds.), *Culture Theory: Essays on Mind, Self, and Emotion*. Cambridge: Cambridge University Press.

—— (1986) Storytelling among the Anthropologists. *New York Times Book Review*, September 21, 38–39.

Shweder, Richard, and Bourne, Edmund J. (1984) Does the Concept of Person Vary Crossculturally? In R. A. Shweder and R. A. LeVine (Eds.), *Culture Theory: Essays on Mind, Self, and Emotion*. Cambridge: Cambridge University Press.

Siegler, Robert S. (1983) Five Generalizations about Cognitive Development. *American Psychologist* 38:263–77.

Sikkema, Mildred (1947) Observations on Japanese Early Training. *Psychiatry* 10:423–32.

Singer, Jerome L. (1973) *The Child's World of Make-Believe: Experimental Studies of Imagination and Play*. New York: Academic.

Singer, Milton (1961) A Survey of Culture and Personality Theory and Research. In B. Kaplan (Ed.), *Studying Personality Cross-Culturally*. Evanston, IL: Peterson.

——— (1984) *Man's Glassy Essence: Explanations in Semiotic Anthropology*. Bloomington: Indiana University Press.

Sinha, Jai B. P. (1981) The Hindu (Indian) Identity. Presentation, 13th International Symposium of the German Academy of Psychoanalysis, München, Germany.

Slote, Walter H. (1972) Psychodynamic Structures in Vietnamese Personality. In W. Lebra (Ed.), *Transcultural Research in Mental Health*. Honolulu: East-West Center Press.

Smith, Karen, and Schooler, Carmi (1978) Women as Mothers in Japan: The Effects of Social Structure and Culture on Values and Behavior. *Journal of Marriage and the Family* 40:613–19.

Smith, Robert J. (1978) *Kurusu: The Price of Progress in a Japanese Village*. Stanford, CA: Stanford University Press.

——— (1983) *Japanese Society: Tradition, Self, and the Social Order*. Cambridge: Cambridge University Press.

Snyder, William U. (1963) *Dependency in Psychotherapy: A Casebook*. New York: Macmillan.

Soseki, Natsume (1957 [1914]) *Kokoro*. Translated by Edwin McClelland. Chicago: University of Chicago Press.

Spence, Donald (1982) *Narrative Truth and Historical Truth*. New York: Norton.

Spiro, Melford E. (1978) Culture and Human Nature. In G. Spindler (Ed.), *The Making of Psychological Anthropology*. Berkeley: University of California Press.

——— (1979) Whatever Happened to the Id? *American Anthropologist* 81:5–13.

——— (1984) Reflections on Cultural Determinism and Relativism. In R. A. Shweder and R. A. LeVine (Eds.), *Culture Theory: Essays on Mind, Self, and Emotion*. Cambridge: Cambridge University Press.

——— (1986) Cultural Relativism and the Future of Anthropology. *Cultural Anthropology* 1:259–86.

Spitz, Rene A. (1958) On the Genesis of Superego Component. *Psychoanalytic Study of the Child* 13:375–404.

——— (1965) *The First Year of Life*. New York: International Universities Press.

Stern, Daniel N. (1983) The Early Development of Schemas of Self, Other, and Self-with-Other. In J. D. Lichtenberg and S. Kaplan (Eds.), *Reflections on Self-Psychology*. Hillsdale, NJ: Analytic.

——— (1985) *The Interpersonal World of the Infant*. New York: Basic.

Stierlin, H. (1958) The Adaptation to the Stronger Person's Reality. *Psychiatry* 21:142–52.

Sugimoto, Etsu I. (1934) *Daughter of the Samurai*. Garden City, NY: Doubleday, Doran.

Sullivan, Harry S. (1962) *Schizophrenia as a Human Process*. New York: Norton.

——— (1964) *The Fusion of Psychiatry and Social Science*. New York: Norton.

Surya, N. C. (1969) Ego Structure in the Hindu Joint Family: Some Considerations. In W. Caudill and T. Lin (Eds.), *Mental Health Research in Asia and the Pacific*. Honolulu: East-West Center Press.

Suzuki, Takao (1978) *Japanese and the Japanese*. Tokyo: Kodansha.

——— (1986) Language and Behavior in Japan: The Conceptualization of Personal Relations. In T. S. Lebra and W. P. Lebra (Eds.), *Japanese Culture and Behavior*. Honolulu: University of Hawaii Press.

Svejda, Marilyn J; Compos, Joseph J.; Emde, Robert N. (1980) Mother-Infant "Bonding": Failure to Generalize. *Child Development* 51:775–79.

Szalay, Lorand B., and Maday, Bela C. (1973) Verbal Associations in the Analysis of Subjective Culture. *Current Anthropology* 14:33–50.

Szasz, Thomas S. (1961) *The Myth of Mental Illness*. New York: Hoeber-Harper.

——— (1963) The Concept of Transference. *International Journal of Psycho-Analysis* 44:432–43.

Takahashi, Tetsuro (1980) Adolescent Symbiotic Psychopathology: A Cultural Comparison of Japanese and American Patterns and Resolutions. *Bulletin of the Menninger Clinic* 44:272–88.

——— (1983) Cultural Conflicts and Related Illnesses (English translation of chapter). In N. Iwamami (Ed.), *Culture and Treatment*. Tokyo: Seishimno Kagaku.

——— (1984) A Comparative Study of Japanese and American Group Dynamics. Presentation, 73d Annual Meeting of the American Psychoanalytic Association, San Diego, CA.

Taketomo, Yasuhiko (1984) A Critique of Doi's Theory of *Amae*. Presentation, 73d Annual Meeting, American Psychoanalytic Association, San Diego, CA.

——— (1986) *Amae* as Metalanguage: A Critique of Doi's Theory of *Amae*. *Journal of American Academy of Psychoanalysis* 14:525–44.

——— (1988) *Amae* as Meta-Language. *Shiso* 758:6–25 (in Japanese).

——— (1989a) A Debate over *Amae* and Its Metalinguistic Considerations. *Shiso* 5:100–124 (in Japanese).

——— (1989b) An American-Japanese Psychoanalysis and the Issue of Teacher Transference. *Journal of the American Academy of Psychoanalysis* 17:427–50.

——— (1990) Private Communication.

Tanaka-Matsumi, Junko (1979) *Taijin Kyōfushō:* Diagnostic and Cultural Issues in Japanese Psychiatry. *Culture, Medicine, and Psychiatry* 3:231–45.

Tanazaki, Junichiro (1957) *The Makioka Sisters.* New York: Knopf.

Tapp, June L. (1981) Studying Personality Development. In H. Triandis and A. Heron (Eds.), *Handbook of Cross-Cultural Psychology.* Vol. 4. Boston: Allyn & Bacon.

Tatara, Mikihachiro (1974) Problem of Separation and Dependence: Some Personality Characteristics Met in Psychotherapy in Japan. *Journal of American Academy of Psychoanalysis* 2:231–41.

Teller, Virginia, and Dahl, Hartvig (1989) The Microstructure of Free Association. *Psychoanalysis and Contemporary Thought* 8:793–99.

Tobin, Joseph (1982) Strange Foreigners: American Reactions to Living in Japan. Ph.D. diss., Committee on Human Development, University of Chicago.

Tobin, Joseph; Wu, David; Davidson, Dana H. (1989) *Preschool Education in Three Countries.* New Haven, CT: Yale University Press.

Townsend, John M. (1979) Personal Communication.

Triandis, Harry C. (1972) An Approach to the Analysis of Subjective Culture. New York: Wiley.

———— (1989) The Self and Social Behavior in Differing Cultural Contexts. *Psychological Review* 96:506–20.

Triandis, Harry C., and Heron, Alastair (Eds.) (1981) *Handbook of Cross-Cultural Psychology, Developmental Psychology.* Vol. 4. Boston: Allyn & Bacon.

Trilling, Lionel C. (1962) *Sincerity and Authenticity.* Cambridge, MA: Harvard University Press.

Troll, Lillian, and Smith, Jean (1976) Attachment through the Life Span: Some Questions about Dyadic Bonds among Adults. *Human Development* 19:156–70.

Tyler, Stephen (1986) Post-Modern Ethnography: From Document of the Occult to Occult Document. In J. Clifford and G. E. Marcus (Eds.), *Writing Culture: The Poetics and Politics of Ethnography.* Berkeley: University of California Press.

Tyler, William (1983) *Amae.* In *Kodansha Encyclopedia of Japan.* Tokyo: Kodansha.

Uchinuma, Y. (1971) The Structure of Anthrophobia. *Psychiatrica et Neurologica Japonica* 73:359–96 (in Japanese).

Unger, J. Marshall (1987) *Why Japan Is Betting Its Future on Artificial Intelligence.* Oxford: Oxford University Press.

Valignano, Alessandro (1954 [1583]) *Sumario de las Cosas de Japan.* J. L. Alvarez-Taladriz (Ed.). Tokyo: Monumenta Nipponica Monographs.

Van den Heuvel, Wim (1979) The Meaning of Dependency. In J. Munnichs and W. Van den Heuvel (Eds.), *Dependency or Interdependency in Old Age.* The Hague: Martinus-Nijhoff.

van Wolferen, Karel (1989) *The Enigma of Japanese Power*. New York: Knopf.

Veith, Ilse (1974) Psychiatric Foundations in the Far East. In J. G. Howells (Ed.), *World History of Psychiatry*. New York: Brunner-Maezel.

Vogel, Ezra (1962) Entrance Examinations and Emotional Disturbance. In R. J. Smith and R. K. Beardsley (Eds.), *Japanese Culture: Its Development and Characteristics*. Chicago: Aldine.

—— (1967) Kinship Structure, Migration to the City, and Modernization. In R. P. Pore (Ed.), *Aspects of Social Change in Modern Japan*. Princeton, NJ: Princeton University Press.

—— (1979) *Japan as Number One*. New York: Harper & Row.

Vogel, Ezra F., and Vogel, Suzanne H. (1961) Family Security, Personal Immaturity, and Emotional Health in a Japanese Sample. *Marriage and Family Living* 23:161–66, 233, 247.

von Durckheim, Karlfried (1962) *Hara: The Vital Center of Man*. London: Allen & Unwin.

von Siebold, Phillip F. (1973 [1841]) *Manners and Customs of the Japanese in the Nineteenth Century*. Rutland, VT: Tuttle.

Wachtel, Paul L. (1979) Transference, Schema, and Assimilation. *Annual of Psychoanalysis* 7:59–76.

Wagatsuma, Hiroshi (1970) The Study of Personality and Behavior in Japanese Society and Culture. In E. Norbeck and S. Parman (Eds.), *The Study of Japan in the Behavioral Sciences*. Austin, TX: Rice University Studies.

—— (1973) Ishiwara Shintaro's Early Novels and Japanese Male Psychology. *Journal of Nervous and Mental Disease* 157:358–69.

—— (1977) Some Aspects of the Changing Family in Contemporary Japan: Once Confucian, Now Fatherless. *Daedelus* 106:181–210.

—— (1980) Child Abandonment and Infanticide: A Japanese Case. In J. Karbin (Ed.), *Child Abuse: A Cross-Cultural Perspective*. Berkeley: University of California Press.

—— (1983a) Childhood and Childrearing. In *Kodansha Encyclopedia of Japan*. Tokyo: Kodansha.

—— (1983b) Ki. In *Kodansha Encyclopedia of Japan*. Tokyo: Kodansha.

—— (1984) Some Cultural Assumptions among the Japanese. *Japan Quarterly* 32:371–79.

—— (1985) *Nihonjin to Amerikajin: Kokoga Ochigai* (Japanese and Americans: The Big Difference). Tokyo: Nesco (in Japanese).

Wagatsuma, Hiroshi, and DeVos, George A. (1962) Recent Attitudes toward Arranged Marriage in Rural Japanese. *Human Organization* 21:187–200.

—— (1983). *The Heritage of Endurance*. Berkeley: University of California Press.

Wagatsuma, Hiroshi, and Lanham, Betty (1983) Childhood and Childrearing. In *Kodansha Encyclopedia of Japan*. Tokyo: Kodansha.

Wagatsuma, Hiroshi, and Rosett, Arthur (1983) Cultural Attitudes toward

Contract Law: Japan and the United States Compared. *Pacific Basin Law Journal* 2:76–97.

Waley, Arthur (Tr.) (1935) *The Tale of Genji*. London: West.

Wallace, Anthony F. C. (1961) The Psychic Unity of Human Groups. In B. Kaplan (Ed.), *Studying Personality Cross-Culturally*. New York: Harper & Row.

Wallace, Edwin R. (1983) *Freud and Anthropology: A History and Reappraisal. (Psychological Issues,* Monograph no. 55) New York: International Universities Press.

——— (1985) *Historiography and Causation in Psychoanalysis*. Hillsdale, NJ: Analytic.

——— (1989) Toward a Phenomenological and Minimally Theoretical Psychoanalysis. *Annual of Psychoanalysis* 17:17–69.

Wallerstein, Robert S. (1973) Psychoanalytic Perspectives on the Problem of Reality. *Journal of the American Psychoanalytic Association* 21:5–33.

——— (1983) Reality and Its Attributes as Psychoanalytic Concepts: An Historical Overview. *International Review of Psycho-Analysis* 10:125–43.

——— (1983) Self Psychology and "Classical" Psychoanalytic Psychology: The Nature of Their Relationships. *Psychoanalysis and Contemporary Thought* 6:553–95.

——— (1985a) Change and Integration in Psychoanalysis as a Profession. In C. F. Settlage and R. Brockbend (Eds.), *New Ideas in Psychoanalysis: The Process of Change in a Humanistic Science*. Hillsdale, NJ: Analytic.

——— (1985b) The Concept of Psychic Reality: Its Meaning and Value. *Journal of the American Psychoanalytic Association* 33:555–69.

——— (1987) One Psychoanalysis or Many. *International Journal of Psycho-Analysis* 69:5–21.

Wallerstein, Robert S., and Smelser, Neil J. (1969) Psychoanalysis and Sociology: Articulations and Applications. *International Journal of Psycho-Analysis* 50:693–710.

Walsh, R. (1984) Asian Psychologies. In R. J. Corsini (Ed.), *Encyclopedia of Psychology* 1:90–94. New York: Wiley.

Watson, John B. (1928) *Psychological Care of the Infant and Child*. Salem, NH: Ayer.

Way, Lewis (1962) *Adler's Place in Psychology*. New York: Collier.

Weber, Max (1964) *The Theory of Social and Economic Organization*. New York: Free Press.

Weintraub, Marsha; Brooks, Jeanne; Lewis, Michael (1977) Social Network: A Reconsideration of the Concept of Attachment. *Human Development* 20:31–47.

Weiss, Joseph; Samson, Harold; Caston, Joseph (Eds.) (1977) *Research on the Psychoanalytic Process, I: A Comparison of Two Theories about Analytic Neutrality*. Bulletin 3, Mount Zion Hospital, San Francisco.

Weiss, Robert S. (1982) Attachment in Adult Life. In C. M. Parkes and J. Stevenson-Hinde (Eds.), *The Place of Attachment in Human Behavior.* New York: Basic.

Wetherall, William, and DeVos George A. (1975) Ethnic Minorities in Japan. In K. Veenhoven, et al. (Eds.), *Case Studies on Human Rights and Fundamental Freedoms.* The Hague: Martinus-Nijhoff.

White, Geoffrey M. (1980) Conceptual Universals in Interpersonal Language. *American Anthropologist* 82:759–81.

White, Merry I. (1987) *The Japanese Educational Challenge.* New York: Free Press.

White, Merry, and LeVine, Robert (1986) What Is an *Ii Ko* (Good Child)? In H. Stevenson, H. Azuma, and K. Hakuta (Eds.), *Child Development and Education in Japan.* New York: Freeman.

Whiting, John W. (1964) The Effects of Climate on Certain Cultural Practices. In W. H. Goodenough (Ed.), *Explorations in Anthropology: Essays in Honor of George Peter Murdock.* New York: McGraw Hill.

—— (1971) Causes and Consequences of the Amount of Body Contact Between Mother and Infant. Presentation, Annual Meeting, American Anthropological Association, New York.

Whiting, John W., and Child, W. M. (1953) *Child Training and Personality.* New Haven, CT: Yale University Press.

Whiting, John W., and Whiting, Beatrice B. (1975) *Children of Six Cultures: A Psychocultural Analysis.* Cambridge, MA: Harvard University Press.

Williams, David (1988) Japan and Voltaire's Children. *Nichi Bei Times* (Tokyo) October 21, 2–3.

Winestein, Muriel (1973) Panel: The Experience of Separation-Individuation in Infancy and Its Reverberations through the Course of Life, I: Infancy and Childhood. *Journal of the American Psychoanalytic Association* 21:135–54.

Winnicott, Donald W. (1953) Transitional Objects and Transitional Phenomena: A Study of the First Not-Me Possession. *International Journal of Psycho-Analysis* 34:89–97.

—— (1965a) From Dependence to Independence in the Development of the Individual. In *Maturational Processes and the Facilitating Environment.* New York: International Universities Press.

—— (1965b) Ego Distortion in Terms of True and False Self. In *Maturational Processes and the Facilitating Environment.* New York: International Universities Press.

Wisdom, J. O. (1987a) The Concept of *Amae. International Review of Psycho-Analysis* 14:263–64.

—— (1987b) Review of *The Anatomy of Self. International Review of Psycho-Analysis.* 14:278–79.

World Health Organization (1979) *International Classification of Diseases.* 9th ed. Geneva: WHO.

Wynne, Lyman C.; Rykoff, Irving M.; Day, Juliana; Hirsch, Stanley I. (1958)

Pseudo-Mutuality in the Family Relations of Schizophrenics. *Psychiatry* 21: 205–20.

Wysocki, Bernard (1989) The Buck Keeps Circulating. *Wall Street Journal,* April 21, 2–3.

Wyss, Dieter (1959) *Depth Psychology: A Critical History.* Translated by Gerald Orn. New York: Norton.

Yamamoto, Tatsuro (1964) Recent Studies on the Japanese National Character. In E. S. C. Northrup and H. Livingston (Eds.), *Cross-Cultural Understandings: Epistemology in Anthropology.* New York: Harper & Row.

Yap, P. M. (1969) The Culture-Bound Reactive Syndromes. In W. Caudill and T. Lin (Eds.), *Mental Health Research in Asia and the Pacific.* Honolulu: East-West Center Press.

Yarrow, Leon J. (1976) Attachment and Dependency: A Development Perspective. In J. L. Gewirtz (Ed.), *Attachment and Dependency.* Washington, DC: Winston.

Yokoyama, Minoru (1984) The Problem of the Physically Handicapped in Japan. *Social Science Questions* 1:26–46.

Yoshida, Shuji (1980) Typology and Universality of the Cognition of Space Division through the Analysis of Demonstratives. *Bulletin of the National Museum of Ethnology* (Osaka) 12:833–34.

Yuzawa, Yasukiko (1977) Senzo Kazoku Hendori Tokeiteki Kumsatsu (Statistical Consideration of Postwar Family Change). In M. Fukishima (Ed.), Kazoku: Seisaku, To Ho 2, Senzo Nihon Kazoko no Doko. Tokyo: University of Tokyo Press (in Japanese).

Zaidi, S. M. Hafeez (1969) Sociocultural Change and Value Conflict in Developing Countries: A Case Study of Pakistan. In W. Caudill and T. Lin (Eds.), *Mental Health Research in Asia and the Pacific.* Honolulu: East-West Center Press.

Zetzel, Elizabeth R. (1956) Current Concepts of Transference. *International Journal of Psycho-Analysis* 37:369–76.

Name Index

Subject Index

Abasement, 48, 242, 309
Abnormal (the), 57–59, 346
Above/below dichotomy, 91
Absence of boundaries, 55
Academic psychology, 7, 18, 361
Acceptance, 224
Accommodation, 270
Achievement, 100–101, 129, 226, 306, 307; evaluation of, 248–49; group, 146, 299; motivation toward, 247, 249–50; orientation, 249; in school, 137, 144, 147
Acquired immune deficiency syndrome (AIDS), 190 n.3
Action, theories of, 43
Action anthropology, 6
Action language, 362
Active dependency, 42
Activity (factor), 278
Activity/passivity, 338
Adaptation, anachronistic, 58
Adaptive ego, 230
Adjustment disorders, 32
Adjustment reactions, 175, 256
Adolescence, 93, 111, 120, 152 n.2, 290; superego development in, 304; *wagamama* in, 169
Adolescent socialization, 147–51, 299
Adversarial actions, 179
Affect, 20, 22; negative, 303–4

Affection, 28, 108, 130; in Utku, 322–23
Affilliation, 12, 14, 29, 34, 177, 249, 313; *amae* in, 84; in Doi, 160; drive toward, 101, 158, 211, 330, 368; motives for, 211–12, 364; nurturant, 355; primary, 190 n.7; prolonged states of, 250; as secondary drive, 45, 151; universality of, 198–99, 365
Affiliation needs, 159–60, 161, 280, 311
Affirmation cues, 264 n.7
African societies, 12, 190 n.7, 320–21, 323, 366
Age, 162, 260; norms, 100, 156
Age hierarchy, 314, 321
Aged (the). *See* Elderly (the)
Aggression, 44, 45, 95, 182, 242, 304; and anal stage, 293–95; in boys, 141–42; in children, 119, 128; control of, 84, 261, 308, 312; early socialization regarding, 87, 117–21, 283, 293; handling, in India, 316; handling, in schools, 141–42, 146; introjective displacement of, 248; norms regarding, 86–88; reaction formations against, 100; toward self, 48; in status hierarchies, 316; strategies to diminish, 131–33; sublimation of, 101; suppressed, 285; universals in, 341

427

Subordination, 255, 260; kinesic forms of, 317
Suffering, 89–90, 101, 245
Sufism, 257
Suicide, 77, 241, 249–50, 310; joint parent-child, 127–28
Sulking, 163, 166, 365
Sumanai, 167
Sunao/sunaosa, 172–73, 236–37
Suneru, 163, 181, 365
Superego, 49, 50, 61 n.3, 132, 198, 247, 270, 279, 298, 357; dependency and development of, 47–49; enryo and, 84; Japanese cultural themes and, 306–10; in Japan's history/culture, 100; in phallic-oedipal stage, 298, 299; "third person" as, 123
Superego development, 10, 12, 43; implications of Japanese childrearing for, 303–10
Superego prohibitions, 293, 296, 298, 308–9, 312; against aggression, 308
Superiority, 11, 96, 100, 101, 188, 195, 197, 260. See also Uniqueness
Superstition, 188
Suppression: of aggression, 283; of conflict, 132–33
Survival, 189 n.2, 280; drives and, 279
Suspiciousness, 170
Symbiosis, 25, 52, 55, 159, 290
Symbolic anthropology, 7
Symbolic interactions, 333
Symbolization, 332
Synesthetic-cutaneous contact, 321

Tacit learning, 338
Taijin-kyōfushō, 256–57
Taishō kankei, 192–93
Tantrums, 119, 127, 294; in adults, 169; response to, 134 n.7
Taoism, 257
Tatemae, 99, 160, 218–20, 223, 231, 241, 248
Tatemae/honne balance, 257. See also Inside/outside dichotomy
Teachers, 128, 140–41, 144, 145, 147, 148; handling aggression, 141–42; high school, 150; maternal role of, 146; as role models, 250

Teaching by example, 117, 127, 294, 305
Technology, 68, 69, 72, 74
Temperament, 77, 236
Tereru, 171–72
"Terrible threes," 289
Text(s), 332, 333, 343, 363; culture as, 334–35, 342; interpretation of, 345
Thematic Apperception Test (TAT), 128, 248, 307
Themes, 362, 367
Theory: and practice, 370 n.7; in psychoanalysis and anthropology, 329
Therapeutic alliance, 57
Therapeutic relationship, 37 n.6; privileged competence in, 348
Therapeutic resistance, 251
Therapeutic situation, 186
"Thick" description, 332, 333, 334, 353, 359, 367, 368; criticism of, 334–35
Third party(ies): collective, 310; in conflict management, 87; in discipline, 123, 127
Threat: father as, 297; markers in, 277; in punishment, 123, 127, 133, 294, 308
Three Essays on Sexuality (Freud), 45–46
Thrift, 90, 91
Timing, questions of, 271, 272, 273, 310, 311
Toilet training, 91, 124–29, 132, 292, 293, 307, 308, 320; in India, 315
Tokugawa Shogunate, 65–66, 138
Toraware, 168
Toriiru, 171, 174
Touching, 108, 116–17, 284, 311–12, 323
Traits, 162, 242–43
Transcendence, 258
Transference, 10, 37 n.6, 43, 251, 346; dependency/"independency" in, 33, 56–57; Japan-Western differences in, 176; maternal/paternal, 301; unresolved, 190 n.4
Transference neurosis, 56, 175
Transitional objects, 25, 54, 115, 291
Treatment: clinical method in, 271
True self, 231, 233, 236